Othello
William Shakespeare

FULL TEXT & STUDY NOTES

BILLY RAMSELL & BRIAN FORRISTAL

ADDITIONAL WRITING BY BRENDA COLLINS AND JOVITA FINNEGAN

FORUM PUBLICATIONS LTD.

Published by Forum Publications
Unit 2 Hillview Campus
Eurobusiness Park
Littleisland
Cork
021-4232268
info@forum-publications.com
www.forum-publications.com

Design and layout by Faye Keegan
www.fayekeegandesign.com

Film stills courtesy of Warner Bros. Entertainment

ISBN: 978-1-906565-22-0

WHO WAS **WILLIAM SHAKESPEARE?**

For all his fame and celebration, we know almost nothing about William Shakespeare. His father, John, was a glover and leather merchant. He married Mary Arden, the daughter of the wealthy Robert Arden of Wilmcote, who owned a 60 acre farm.

The precise date of Shakespeare's brith is not known, but, rationally, 23 April – St George's Day – has been accepted as his birthday.

Shakespeare probably began his education at the age of six or seven at the Stratford grammar school. As was the case in all Elizabethan grammar schools, the focus would have been very much on Latin, history, poetry and drama.

There are other fragmented and dubious details about Shakespeare's life growing up in Stratford. Many believe that after leaving school he worked as a butcher and in his father's glove business.

When Shakespeare was 18 he married Anne Hathaway, who was 26 and already several months pregnant.

William's first child, Susanna, was baptised in Stratford sometime in May 1583. Baptism records reveal that twins – Hamnet and Judith – were born in February 1592. Hamnet, William's only son, died in 1596, just eleven years old.

No one knows for certain how Shakespeare first started his career in the theatre, but by 1592 he had become an established actor.

By late 1594, Shakespeare was an actor, writer and part-owner of a playing company, known as the Lord Chamberlain's Men. He wrote many great plays, achieving great fame, fortune and the praise of the king and queen. He died on 23 April 1616 at the age of 52.

THE THEATRE IN SHAKESPEARE'S TIME

Going to the theatre in Shakespeare's day was a very different experience from what it is now. Whereas going to a play today is a bit like going to Mass, with the audience expected to sit silent and respectful while the play is going on, in Shakespeare's time a visit to the theatre was more like going to a boxing match.

The audience was noisy and expressed its approval or disapproval of what they were watching with no

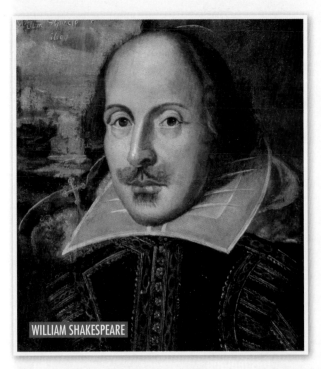

WILLIAM SHAKESPEARE

reservations whatsoever. Individual characters were booed or cheered and bad performances had the audience hissing and shouting their disapproval. The most common way for this to happen was for the crowd to shout 'Mew', which is where we get our expression 'cat call' from.

Eating and drinking during plays was very popular, and sellers of oranges, apples and nuts circulated amongst the audience during performances. The throwing of fruit at the stage was another way for the audience to express its disapproval of what they were watching. You could also buy beer and tobacco pipes.

The opening of the theatre was signalled by the blowing of a trumpet and the flying of a flag on the roof to let the people know the doors were open. A small orchestra would play three flourishes to signal the beginning of the play itself. Then a man dressed in a long black cloak with a false beard and a wreath of leaves would appear to introduce the play and ask for the audience to quieten down.

Plays started at two o'clock in the winter and three o'clock in the summer. A play typically lasted around two hours. When we read a play by Shakespeare, we see the work divided into different scenes ands acts, but this is an invention by editors. The plays were originally acted straight through without any obvious scene breaks, and with no intervals between acts.

At the end of each play the next upcoming drama would be announced and then prayers would be said for the king or queen, with all the actors kneeling on the stage. After this, there came a comic jig performed by the players that lasted around 20 minutes. This was one of the most popular parts of the theatre experience, with certain actors gaining reputations for being great dancers. It was also a way for both the audience and the actors to unwind and blow off steam, especially if they had been performing a tragedy.

One of the biggest differences between theatre in Shakespeare's time and now is that back then there were no female actors. All the parts were played by men and boys. As you can imagine, this must have created an air of comedy in the plays that doesn't come across when we read them today, especially in big romantic scenes.

THE GLOBE

The majority of Shakespeare's most famous plays were performed in the Globe Theatre, built on the south bank of the Thames around 1598. This was made of timber with a thatched roof, in the shape of a polygon. It was roughly 100 feet wide and could hold up to nearly 3,500 people.

The stage in the Globe was only a metre or so off the ground, and was surrounded on three sides by the audience. There was a trapdoor in the middle of the stage that led down to the 'underworld', a space where ghosts and other supernatural characters could make a dramatic appearance during a play. Above the stage was the musician's gallery, which was also used to represent walls and balconies.

On either side of the gallery were the Lord's Rooms, which were used viewing points reserved exclusively for noblemen and women. Above all of this was what was called 'The Heavens', an overhanging canopy, from which more friendly supernatural characters such as angles and gods could be lowered to the stage.

Compared to the theatrical performances of today, props and special effects in Shakespeare's time were pretty minimal. The audience had to be willing to suspend disbelief and use their imagination to create the play's setting in their mind's eye. If a scene was set at night, for example, or in a desert or a forest, only the actors' words could convey this.

Although the stage always looked the same, a great deal of importance was placed in elaborate costumes and make-up. Gory special effects were also available. The organs of sheep and pigs were used as human hearts in murder scenes, and sheep's blood was used for human blood on swords, axes and spears.

In 1613, the Globe was completely destroyed by fire when a canon shot during a performance of Henry VIII set fire to the thatched roof. ◆

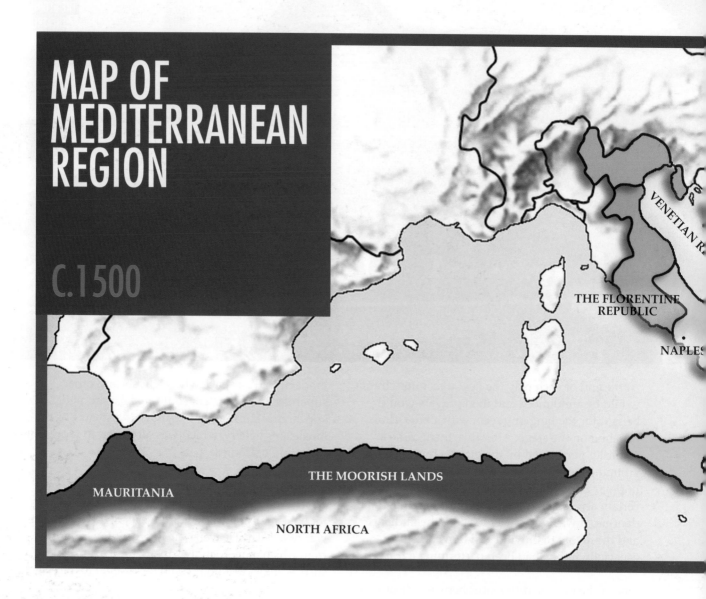

MAP OF MEDITERRANEAN REGION

C.1500

VENETIAN R

THE FLORENTINE REPUBLIC

NAPLES

THE MOORISH LANDS

MAURITANIA

NORTH AFRICA

THE VENETIAN REPUBLIC:

Venice was the centre of military and economic power, controlling territories throughout the Mediterranean.

THE OTTOMAN EMPIRE:

The vast empire of the Turks, which was ruled by the Sultan from Istanbul. This was a Muslim stronghold and in Shakespeare's time was hated and feared by the Christian poplulation of Western Europe.

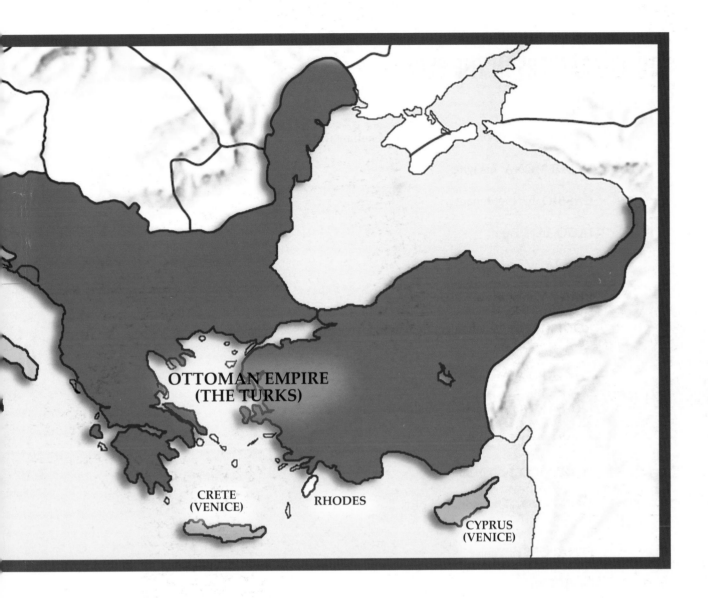

OTTOMAN EMPIRE
(THE TURKS)

CRETE
(VENICE)

RHODES

CYPRUS
(VENICE)

THE FLORENTINE REPUBLIC:

A military and economic power centred on the city of Florence. It was sometimes an ally to Venice and sometimes a rival. Cassio is a Florentine serving in the Venetian army.

THE MOORISH LANDS:

The Moors were the Muslim inhabitants of North Africa. The Moorish kingdoms spanned what is now Morocco, Algeria, Mauritania and parts of the Sahara. Othello is a Moor who has converted to Christianity and serves as a general in the army of Venice.

THE CHARACTERS IN THE PLAY

OTHELLO, A Moor, General in the Venetian army

DESDEMONA, his wife

CASSIO, his Lieutenant

IAGO, his Ensign

EMILIA, wife of Iago

BIANCA, mistress of Cassio

RODERIGO, a Venetian gentleman in love with Desdemona

THE DUKE of Venice

BRABANTIO, a Venetian Senator, Desdemona's father

GRATIANO, his brother

LODOVICO, his kinsman

MONTANO, Governor of Cyprus

SENATORS of Venice

OFFICERS

SAILOR

MESSANGER

GENTLEMEN of Cyprus

HERALD

A CLOWN in Othell's household

MUSICIANS

Soldiers, attendants, and servants

ACT 1

SCENE 1

Venice. A street.

Enter RODERIGO and IAGO

RODERIGO	Tush! never tell me; I take it much unkindly
	That thou, Iago, who hast had my purse
	As if the strings were thine, shouldst know of this.
IAGO	'Sblood, but you will not hear me: If ever I
	Did dream of such a matter, abhor me.
RODERIGO	Thou told'st me thou didst hold him in thy hate.
IAGO	Despise me, if I do not. Three great ones of the city,
	In personal suit to make me his lieutenant,
	Off-capped to him: and, by the faith of man,
	I know my price, I am worth no worse a place:
	But he – as loving his own pride and purposes –
	Evades them, with a bombast circumstance
	Horribly stuffed with epithets of war;
	And, in conclusion,
	Non-suits my mediators. For 'Certes,' says he,
	'I have already chose my officer.'
	And what was he?
	Forsooth, a great arithmetician,
	One Michael Cassio, a Florentine,
	A fellow almost damned in a fair wife;
	That never set a squadron in the field,
	Nor the division of a battle knows
	More than a spinster – unless the bookish theoric,
	Wherein the toga'd consuls can propose
	As masterly as he! Mere prattle without practise
	Is all his soldiership. But he, sir, had the election:
	And I – of whom his eyes had seen the proof
	At Rhodes, at Cyprus, and on other grounds,
	Christian and heathen – must be beleed and calmed
	By debitor and creditor. This counter-caster,
	He, in good time, must his lieutenant be,
	And I – God bless the mark! – his Moorship's ensign.
RODERIGO	By heaven, I rather would have been his hangman!
IAGO	Why, there's no remedy, 'tis the curse of service,
	Preferment goes by letter and affection,
	And not by old gradation, where each second
	Stood heir to th' first. Now sir, be judge yourself
	Whether I in any just term am assigned
	To love the Moor.
RODERIGO	I would not follow him then.
IAGO	O sir, content you.
	I follow him to serve my turn upon him.
	We cannot all be masters, nor all masters
	Cannot be truly followed. You shall mark

Line numbers: 5, 10, 15, 20, 25, 30, 35, 40

1   *Tush:* Mild expletive expressing impatience

2   *thou:* you

3   *thine:* something belonging to you

5   *abhor:* hate, regard with contempt or disgust

9   *Off-capped:* removed their hats

12   *Evades:* avoids giving a direct answer
12   *bombast circumstance:* Bombastic beating about the bush
13   *stuffed:* Bombast was originally cotton used for stuffing clothes and quilts
13   *epithets of war:* specialised military terminology

15   *Non-suits:* Rejects the suit of
15   *'Certes':* Certainly

18   *Forsooth:* Indeed
18   *arithmetician:* Iago means that Cassio's knowledge of war is theoretical

21   *squadron:* body of troops drawn up in a defensive square

23   *bookish:* studious, fond of reading
23   *theoric:* theory
24   *propose:* put forward a scheme

26   *had the election:* was chosen

29   *beleed:* cut off from the wind

30   *counter-caster:* accountant

32   *ensign:* standard-bearer

36   *letter and affection:* Influence and nepotism.

38   *just:* fair and reasonable

39   *the Moor:* Othello

41   *to serve my turn upon him:* exploit him in my own best interests

43   *shall mark:* cannot help noticing

Many a duteous and knee-crooking knave

That, doting on his own obsequious bondage,

Wears out his time, much like his master's ass, — 45

For nought but provender, and when he's old – cashiered:

Whip me such honest knaves! Others there are

Who, trimmed in forms and visages of duty,

Keep yet their hearts attending on themselves, — 50

And, throwing but shows of service on their lords,

Do well thrive by them, and when they have lined their coats

Do themselves homage. These fellows have some soul,

And such a one do I profess myself – for, sir,

It is as sure as you are Roderigo, — 55

Were I the Moor, I would not be Iago:

In following him, I follow but myself –

Heaven is my judge, not I for love and duty,

But seeming so, for my peculiar end;

For when my outward action doth demonstrate — 60

The native act and figure of my heart

In compliment extern, 'tis not long after

But I will wear my heart upon my sleeve

For daws to peck at: I am not what I am. *derogatory ref to Othello.*

RODERIGO What a full fortune does the thick-lips owe — 65

If he can carry't thus!

IAGO   Call up her father,

Rouse him, make after him, poison his delight,

Proclaim him in the streets. Incense her kinsmen,

And, though he in a fertile climate dwell,

Plague him with flies: though that his joy be joy, — 70

Yet throw such changes of vexation on't,

As it may lose some colour.

RODERIGO Here is her father's house, I'll call aloud.

IAGO Do, with like timorous accent and dire yell

As when, by night and negligence, the fire — 75

Is spied in populous cities.

RODERIGO What ho! Brabantio, Signior Brabantio, ho!

IAGO Awake! What ho, Brabantio! Thieves! thieves! thieves!

Look to your house, your daughter and your bags!

Thieves! thieves! — 80

BRABANTIO appears above, at a window

BRABANTIO What is the reason of this terrible summons?

What is the matter there?

RODERIGO Signior, is all your family within?

IAGO Are your doors locked?

BRABANTIO   Why, wherefore ask you this?

IAGO 'Zounds, sir, you're robbed; for shame, put on — 85

    your gown!

Your heart is burst, you have lost half your soul:

Even now, now, very now, an old black ram *clear Black and white imagery*

Is tupping your white ewe. Arise, arise!

Awake the snorting citizens with the bell, — 90

Or else the devil will make a grandsire of you:

Arise, I say!

Line	Gloss
44	*knave:* servant, rogue, one of low degree
45	*obsequious:* compliant, obedient or attentive
47	*provender:* food
49	*trimmed in forms and visages:* dressed in the appropriate attire
51	*shows:* appearances
53	*Do themselves homage:* become their own masters
56	*Were I the Moor, I would not be Iago:* If I were the General, I would not wish to be a subordinate
59	*peculiar:* personal
60	*doth:* a third person singular present tense of 'do'
61	*native:* natural, innate
63	*But I will wear my heart upon my sleeve:* expose my feelings to everyone
64	*daws:* jack-daws, bird
65	*thick-lips:* reference to Othello's lips, first indication that Othello is black
66	*If he can carry't thus!:* If he can get away with it
68	*Proclaim:* denounce as a traitor
68	*Incense:* infuriate
69-70	*though he in a fertile climate dwell,/ Plague him with flies:* though he is in a state of apparent good fortune and happiness, torment him with miseries
74	*timorous:* fearful, terrifying
85	*'Zounds:* God's wounds (a strong oath)
89	*tupping:* copulating with
90	*snorting:* snoring
91	*grandsire:* grandfather, a male ancestor

BRABANTIO	What, have you lost your wits?
RODERIGO	Most reverend signior, do you know my voice?
BRABANTIO	Not I; what are you?
RODERIGO	My name is Roderigo.
BRABANTIO	The worser welcome:
	I have charged thee not to haunt about my doors:
	In honest plainness thou hast heard me say
	My daughter is not for thee; and now in madness,
	Being full of supper and distempering draughts,
	Upon malicious bravery, dost thou come
	To start my quiet.
RODERIGO	Sir, sir, sir –
BRABANTIO	But thou must needs be sure
	My spirit and my place have in them power
	To make this bitter to thee.
RODERIGO	Patience, good sir!
BRABANTIO	What tell'st thou me of robbing? This is Venice:
	My house is not a grange.
RODERIGO	Most grave Brabantio,
	In simple and pure soul, I come to you.
IAGO	'Zounds, sir, you are one of those that will not serve God, if the devil bid you. Because we come to do you service and you think we are ruffians, you'll have your daughter covered with a Barbary horse; you'll have your nephews neigh to you; you'll have coursers for cousins and gennets for germans.
BRABANTIO	What profane wretch art thou?
IAGO	I am one, sir, that comes to tell you your daughter and the Moor are now making the beast with two backs.
BRABANTIO	Thou art a villain.
IAGO	You are a senator.
BRABANTIO	This thou shalt answer. I know thee, Roderigo.
RODERIGO	Sir, I will answer anything. But, I beseech you,
	If't be your pleasure and most wise consent,
	As partly I find it is, that your fair daughter,
	At this odd-even and dull watch o' the night,
	Transported, with no worse nor better guard
	But with a knave of common hire, a gondolier,
	To the gross clasps of a lascivious Moor –
	If this be known to you and your allowance,
	We then have done you bold and saucy wrongs.
	But if you know not this, my manners tell me
	We have your wrong rebuke. Do not believe
	That, from the sense of all civility,
	I thus would play and trifle with your reverence.
	Your daughter, if you have not given her leave,
	I say again, hath made a gross revolt,
	Tying her duty, beauty, wit and fortunes
	In an extravagant and wheeling stranger
	Of here and every where. Straight satisfy yourself:
	If she be in her chamber or your house,
	Let loose on me the justice of the state
	For thus deluding you.

Handwritten margin note: Iago malice. (wicked intentions)

Line numbers and glossary (right margin):

95

100

105

110

115

120

125

130

135

140

94 *reverend:* worthy of respect

100 *distempering draughts:* intoxicating drinks

102 *start my quiet:* disturb my peace

107 *grange:* country house (somewhere isolated and vulnerable)
108 *simple:* honest

112 *Barbary horse:* an arab stallion, referring to Othello, i.e. the Moor

114 *coursers:* war-horses
114 *jennets:* small Spanish horses
115 *profane:* foul mouthed

117-8 *making the beast with two backs:* engaging in sexual intercourse

121 *beseech:* beg

127 *lascivious:* sexually aroused

132 *from the sense of all civility:* contrary to good manners

137 *extravagant and wheeling:* vagrant

141 *tinder:* wood for the fire

11

BRABANTIO   Strike on the tinder, ho!
Give me a taper! Call up all my people!
This accident is not unlike my dream:
Belief of it oppresses me already.
Light, I say, light!   145

Exit above
IAGO   Farewell, for I must leave you:
It seems not meet, nor wholesome to my place,
To be produced – as, if I stay, I shall –
Against the Moor: for, I do know, the state,
However this may gall him with some check,
Cannot with safety cast him. For he's embarked   150
With such loud reason to the Cyprus wars
(Which even now stand in act) that, for their souls,
Another of his fathom they have none,
To lead their business; in which regard,
Though I do hate him as I do hell pains,   155
Yet, for necessity of present life,
I must show out a flag and sign of love –
Which is indeed but sign. That you shall surely find him,
Lead to the Sagittary the raised search,
And there will I be with him. So farewell.   160

Exit
Enter, below, BRABANTIO, and Servants with torches
BRABANTIO   It is too true an evil. Gone she is;
And what's to come of my despised time
Is nought but bitterness. Now Roderigo,
Where didst thou see her? O unhappy girl!
With the Moor, say'st thou? Who would be a father?   165
How didst thou know 'twas she? O she deceives me
Past thought! What said she to you? Get more tapers:
Raise all my kindred. Are they married, think you?
RODERIGO   Truly, I think they are.
BRABANTIO   O heaven, how got she out? O treason of the blood!   170
Fathers, from hence trust not your daughters' minds
By what you see them act. Is there not charms
By which the property of youth and maidhood
May be abused? Have you not read, Roderigo,
Of some such thing?   175
RODERIGO   Yes, sir, I have indeed.
BRABANTIO   Call up my brother. O, would you had had her!
Some one way, some another. Do you know
Where we may apprehend her and the Moor?
RODERIGO   I think I can discover him, if you please,
To get good guard and go along with me.   180
BRABANTIO   Pray you, lead on. At every house I'll call –
I may command at most. Get weapons, ho!
And raise some special officers of night.
On, good Roderigo; I'll deserve your pains.   184

Exeunt

142 *taper:* wax candle

146 *meet:* fitting

149 *gall him with some check:* discipline him

150 *embarked:* engaged

153 *fathom:* understanding, grasp

159 *Sagittary:* name of the inn or house where Othello and Desdemona are lodging

162 *And what's to come of my despised time:* the rest of my despicable life

172 *charms:* Enchantments (the first of many references to witchcraft)

174 *abused:* deceived or taken advantage of

184 *deserve your pains:* compensate you for your troubles

RODERIGO AND IAGO
AT BRABANTIO'S

Iago has just told Roderigo of the marriage between Othello and Desdemona. Roderigo is very upset at hearing this – he had hoped to marry Desdemona himself. Iago, Othello's ensign, tells Roderigo that he hates Othello because the General overlooked him when recently appointing a new lieutenant. He encourages Roderigo to wake Brabantio, Desdemona's father, with the news of her marriage. The senator is shocked and angered to hear that his daughter has married Othello. He decides to gather his people and go find Othello.

ACTION

LINE BY LINE

▶ LINES 1-40: RODERIGO AND IAGO SPEAK

It is late at night. Roderigo, a wealthy nobleman, and Iago, a solider, are walking along a street in Venice. Iago has just told Roderigo of a marriage between Desdemona, a rich young Venetian lady, and Othello, a general in the Venetian army. The news greatly upsets Roderigo. He had been attempting to woo Desdemona and had hoped to marry her himself. He has also been employing Iago, it seems, to assist him in his efforts. He fears now that Iago might have been party to Othello's courtship of Desdemona and that his money has been squandered: 'I take it much unkindly / That thou, Iago, who hast had my purse / As if the strings were thine, shouldst know of this' (1-3). Iago desperately tries to convince Roderigo that the news of the wedding is as much a surprise to him: ''Sblood, but you will not hear me! If ever I / Did dream of such a matter, / abhor me' (4-5).

Iago tells Roderigo that he hates Othello because the General recently overlooked him when appointing a new Lieutenant. Iago claims that he had three very very influential people visit Othello on his behalf to recommend him for the position: 'Three great ones of the city, / In personal suit to make me his lieutenant' (7-8). He says that Othello refused to give them a straight answer, preferring instead to talk boastfully in lofty and complicated terms of military matters: 'Evades them with a bombast circumstance, / Horribly stuffed with epithets of war' (12-3). He then told them that he had already chosen another, Michael Cassio, to be his Lieutenant.

Iago feels that he deserved the promotion: 'I know my price, I am worth no worse a place' (10). He has much experience of battle and Othello has seen him prove himself on many different occasions: 'his eyes had seen the proof / At Rhodes, at Cyprus, and on other grounds, / Christian and heathen' (27-9). Cassio, on the other hand, has 'never set a squadron in the field' and does not know how to prepare an army for war: 'Nor the division of a battle knows' (22). All he knows of war is what he has read in books. He is a theorist, a 'great arithmetician' (18), something more akin to an accountant ('counter-caster') than a lieutenant (30). Promotion, Iago bitterly observes, is now decided by letters of recommendation and favouritism rather than the old way of seniority: 'Preferment goes by letter and affection, / And not by old gradation, where each second / Stood heir to th'first' (35-7). Despite his many years of service Iago remains Othello's 'ensign', a position he despises.

RODERIGO

RODERIGO

A GULLIBLE DUPE

Roderigo is what we might term a dupe – someone who is easily manipulated and deceived. He has plenty of money and has been paying Iago handsomely, possibly to bring gifts to Desdemona in the hope that she will marry him. We might suppose that Iago has been pocketing this money for himself and never spent anything on the cause for which it was intended. Though Iago tells him quite plainly that he is dishonest and that he uses people for his own gain, Roderigo never for a moment thinks that Iago is deceiving or using him.

► LINES 41-66: IAGO DESCRIBES HIMSELF

When Roderigo suggests that he stops serving Othello, Iago says that he only continues to do so for selfish reasons. There are some, he tells Roderigo, who serve all their lives in a meek and readily compliant manner for little more than the food they are fed, only to find that their services are no longer required when old. Iago finds such loyal and devoted servants despicable and calls for them to be whipped for their foolishness: 'Whip me such honest knaves' (48). There are others, however, who serve out of self-interest. Such people dress and act in the appropriate servile manner in order to profit from their actions: 'throwing but shows of service on their lords, / Do well thrive by them' (51-2).

It is to this latter category of servant that Iago says he belongs: 'such a one do I profess myself' (54). He follows Othello because it serves his own interests to do so: 'In following him, I follow but myself' (57). It is not out of any sense of love or duty that he serves, merely self-interest. He pretends to be dutiful and caring for his own end: 'not I for love and duty, / But seeming so for my peculiar end' (58-9). What he does outwardly masks his true inner feelings and motivations. In short, he tells Roderigo, he is not who he seems to be: 'I am not what I am' (64).

CHARACTER DEVELOPMENT

HOPELESS ROMANTIC

Roderigo is hopelessly in love with Desdemona and has been desperately trying to secure her hand in marriage. We learn from Brabantio that he has been turning up at the senator's house in the hope of winning his daughter's hand but that the old man has told him to stay away: 'In honest plainness thou hast heard me say / My daughter is not for thee' (98-9). He has also been allowing Iago to spend vast amounts of his money, very likely on gifts that he believes the ensign has been bringing to Desdemona on his behalf. He is, therefore, devastated when he hears that Desdemona has married Othello. However, when he informs Brabantio of his daughter's marriage to the Moor, Roderigo's hopes of winning her are suddenly given new life. Brabantio tells him that he now wishes it were Roderigo she had married.

IAGO

BACKGROUND AND SOCIAL CLASS

Iago is a career soldier, someone who has attained the rank of ensign or standard-bearer, a junior officer in the Venetian army whose duty it is to carry the flag of his general into battle. It is not a position he takes any pride in – if he were the General, he tells Roderigo, he would certainly not trade places with the person he is now: 'Were I the Moor, I would not be Iago' (56). Iago seems also to be a member of the lower classes in Venice and there is a sense in which he feels that his social status prevented him from being promoted. Cassio is an educated man, someone who seems to have powerful friends and these earned him the position that Iago felt ought to have been his.

A MASTER PLOTTER

The first thing we learn about Iago is that he has convinced a wealthy Venetian nobleman to allow him seemingly unlimited access to his funds: 'thou, Iago, who hast had my purse/ As if the strings were thine' (2-3). That Iago should have such free and easy access to Roderigo's money gives us an early indication of his ability to manipulate people to his own ends.

Iago is also an exceptionally persuasive character. The play begins with him desperately needing to convince Roderigo that he hates Othello. Roderigo, it seems, has been emplying Iago to help him win Desdemona's hand in marriage. If he thought that Iago knew all along of Othello's courtship of Desdemona it would mean the end of their relationship. Iago is successful, persuading Roderigo that he knew nothing of Othello's courship: 'If ever I/ Did dream of such a matter, abhor me' (4-5). He clearly explains his reasons for hating Othello and by the time he is finished Roderigo is sympathetic towards Iago and any frustration and anger he feels has been directed toward Othello.

MALICIOUS, CALLOUS AND DESTRUCTIVE

Iago hates Othello and wishes to see the general suffer. He maliciously encourages the heartbroken Roderigo to wake Desdemona's father with the news of her marriage, knowing that the senator will be incensed by the news: 'Call up her father,/ Rouse him, make after him, poison his delight' (66-7). Brabantio is a powerful man in Venice and Iago knows that he is capable of making life very difficult for Othello.

SHIFTING MOTIVATIONS

Iago acts in this callous manner against Othello because the general recently overlooked him when appointing a new lieutenant. Iago feels that he well deserved the position: 'I know my price, I am worth no worse a place' (10). He even had some powerful people approach Othello on his behalf to recommend him for the post. But Othello chose to appoint a man from Florence named Michael Cassio, someone with no experience of battle. This has greatly upset Iago and made him very bitter towards Othello.

But it seems that Iago hated Othello even before this happened, and that being passed over for promotion is just another reason to despise the general. Roderigo reminds him Iago how he once told him he hated Othello: 'Thou told'st me thou didst hold him in thy hate' (6). As we will discover when we read the play, Iago's motivations seem to shift and change and it is often hard to fathom exactly why he behaves the way he does.

SELF-BELIEF

Iago believes that he deserves to be more than he is. He considers his position as ensign or standard-bearer to be beneath him and is outraged at having been passed over for lieutenant: 'I know my price, I am worth no worse a place' (10). He tells Roderigo that he holds no pride in his current position. He might envy Othello's position but is quite sure that Othello does not envy his: 'Were I the Moor, I would not be Iago' (56).

Rather than just feel hard done by and dejected, Iago believes that he will find a way to rise above the position he currently holds. He is not like 'Many a duteous and knee-crooking knave' who humbly and meekly accepts his lot and serves another all his life (44). Iago will continue to serve Othello as long as it suits his interests to do so but seems sure that it is only a matter of time before he achieves greater things.

NO RESPECT FOR MORALS OR VALUES

Iago is someone who has no time or respect for the morals and values that govern most people's behaviour. He tells Roderigo that he despises servants who remain loyal and faithful to their masters: 'Whip me such honest knaves!' (48). Iago makes it clear that he does not hold the virtues of love and duty in any regard, but is happy to pretend to be loving and dutiful if helps him achieve his own ends: 'Not I for love and duty,/ But seeming so for my peculiar end' (58-9).

▶ LINES 67-160: A VISIT TO BRABANTIO'S

Iago's speech seems to do the trick and Roderigo's anger and bitterness is directed toward Othello. He refers to Othello unpleasantly as 'the thick-lips' and says that he is a lucky guy to have what he has if he can get away with it: 'What a full fortune does the thick-lips owe/ If he can carry't thus!' (65-6). Iago urges him to act on his feelings and to do something to spoil Othello's happiness: 'make after him, poison his delight' (67). Seeing that they are close to Desdemona's father's house, Iago tells him wake Brabantio with the news that his daughter has just eloped with Othello.

Both men call out to Brabantio, telling him that his daughter has been stolen away from him. The old man comes to a window and asks why he has been roused from his sleep in this manner. The idea that his house has been robbed strikes him as preposterous and he asks the two men to explain themselves. When Roderigo reveals his identity Brabantio reminds him that he is not welcome at the house – he has been told before to stay away and that Desdemona is not for him: 'I have charged thee not to haunt about my doors./ In honest plainness thou hast heard me say/ My daughter is not for thee' (97-9). Roderigo attempts to break the news to Brabantio but the old man does not give him the chance to speak. Remaining anonymous, Iago crudely brings the message home to Brabantio that at this very moment his daughter is making love to Othello:

- He tells him that 'an old black ram' is having sex with his 'white ewe': 'Even now, now, very now, an old black ram/ Is tupping your white ewe' (88-9).
- He says that if he does not act swiftly his daughter will be mating with a North African horse: 'you'll have your daughter covered with a Barbary horse' (111-2).
- Whilst still not referring to Othello by name he tells Brabantio that his 'daughter and the Moor' are now having sex: 'now making the beast with two backs' (117-8).

Brabantio is disgusted with by these words but when Roderigo insists he search his house for his daughter, saying that she has left home this very night to be with the Moor, he discovers that there is truth to what the two men have been saying.

Iago chooses this moment to slip away, telling Roderigo that it would not be wise for him to be found speaking against Othello considering his position as the general's ensign. He knows that

BRABANTIO

OTHELLO

EXOTIC ORIGINS

Othello does not appear in this scene but we are introduced to him through the descriptions the other characters offer. We learn that he is a Moor, someone of African descent. He is an outsider in Venice, marked by the fact that he is not from the city and often referred to simply as 'the Moor'. Roderigo, hinting at Othello's travels, describes him as a wandering vagrant of no fixed abode: 'an extravagant and wheeling stranger/ Of here and everywhere' (137-8).

Roderigo's unpleasant description of Othello as 'the thick-lips' gives us the first indication that Othello is black. Iago seems to confirm this when he describes Othello as a 'black ram'. Both characters try to depict him as barbaric – more animal than man. Iago describes him as a 'ram' and a 'horse'(112) and Roderigo speaks of 'the gross clasps of the lascivious Moor (127)'. Brabantio also hints at the possibility that Othello might have used magical devices or spells to steal his daughter away: 'Is there not charms/ By which the property of youth and maidhood/ May be abused' (172-4).

SOLIDER AND LEADER

According to Iago, Othello is a vain and boastful man who uses his military experience to confuse and manipulate the politicians he serves: 'But he as loving his own pride and purposes –/ Evades them, with a bombast circumstance/ Horribly stuffed with epithets of war' (11-3). But even Iago has to acknowledge that Othello is a great solider, telling Roderigo that the Venetian government do not have another to compare with the general: 'Another of his fathom they have none,/ To lead their business' (153-4).

Othello will probably be reprimanded by the state for his behaviour but he will not be dismissed – he is too important a solider for this to happen and will soon set sail for Cyprus where a war is unfolding: 'I do know the state – / However this may gall him with some check, / Cannot with safety cast him, for he's embarked / With such loud reason to the Cyprus wars' (148-51).

Othello is irreplaceable and Iago knows that for the moment he must continue to act as though he is loyal to him. He reassures Roderigo, however, that it is merely a show of loyalty and not the real thing: 'I must show out a flag and sign of love –/ Which is indeed but sign' (157-8). He tells Roderigo to lead Brabantio to the inn where Desdemona and Othello are lodging: 'Lead to the Sagittary the raised search; / And there will I be with him' (159-60).

▶ LINES 161-184:
   BRABANTIO LAMENTS HIS DAUGHTER'S MARRIAGE
Brabantio cannot believe that his daughter would deceive him in this manner: 'O, she deceives me, / Past thought' (166-7). He suspects that Othello must have used some magical devices or spells to steal Desdemona away: 'Is there not charms / By

which the property of youth and maidhood / May be abused?' (172-4). Suddenly Roderigo, the very man he dismissed earlier as a nuisance, is seen as the ideal suitor: 'O would you had had her!' (176). He calls for weapons to be gathered and for officers of the law to accompany them in their search for Othello. Roderigo says that he knows where Othello is to be found and offers to lead Brabantio there. ◆

CASSIO

Cassio is the man that Othello chose to be his Lieutenant. We learn in this scene that he is not from Venice – he is 'a Florentine', someone from Florence (19). We also learn that Casssio does not have any battle experience. He has 'never set a squadron in the field, / Not the division of a battle knows' (21-2). He is an educated man, a 'great arithmetician', something more akin to an accountant ('counter-caster') than a lieutenant (31). As Iago bitterly remarks, 'Mere prattle without practice / Is all his soldiership' (25-6).

IAGO AND BRABANTIO

ACT 1

SCENE 2

Another street

Enter OTHELLO, IAGO, and Attendants with torches

IAGO   Though in the trade of war I have slain men,
Yet do I hold it very stuff o' the conscience
To do no contrived murder: I lack iniquity
Sometimes to do me service: nine or ten times
I had thought to have yerk'd him here under the ribs.   5

[handwritten: during I have slane But to kill somebody outside Battle Im not wicked enough.]

OTHELLO   'Tis better as it is.

IAGO   Nay, but he prated,
And spoke such scurvy and provoking terms
Against your honour
That, with the little godliness I have,
I did full hard forbear him. But, I pray you, sir,   10
Are you fast married? Be assured of this,
That the magnifico is much beloved,
And hath in his effect a voice potential
As double as the Duke's: he will divorce you;
Or put upon you what restraint and grievance   15
The law, with all his might to enforce it on,
Will give him cable.

[handwritten: have mee slept togetner]

OTHELLO   Let him do his spite:
My services which I have done the signiory
Shall out-tongue his complaints. 'Tis yet to know –
Which, when I know that boasting is an honour,   20
I shall promulgate – I fetch my life and being
From men of royal siege, and my demerits
May speak unbonneted to as proud a fortune
As this that I have reach'd: for know, Iago,
But that I love the gentle Desdemona,   25
I would not my unhoused free condition
Put into circumscription and confine
For the sea's worth. But, look! what lights come yond?

[handwritten: Two faced]

IAGO   Those are the raised father and his friends:
You were best go in.   29

OTHELLO   Not I – I must be found: 30
My parts, my title and my perfect soul
Shall manifest me rightly. Is it they?

IAGO   By Janus, I think no. *[handwritten: Roman god.]*

Enter CASSIO, and certain Officers with torches

OTHELLO   The servants of the Duke, and my lieutenant.
The goodness of the night upon you, friends!   35
What is the news?

CASSIO   The Duke does greet you, general,
And he requires your haste-post-haste appearance,
Even on the instant.

OTHELLO   What is the matter, think you?

---

3   *contrived:* premeditated

3   *iniquity:* sin, evil (crime)

5   *yerk'd:* struck

6   *prated:* babbled

7   *scurvy:* insulting, contemptible

11   *fast:* firmly

12   *magnifico:* Brabantio's title

13-4   *hath in his effect a voice potential | As double as the Duke's:* has a voice potentially as influential as the Duke's, which is worth twice that of any other senator.

17   *give him cable:* give him rope (scope)

18   *Signory:* Venetian government

19   *out-tongue:* speak louder than

21   *promulgate:* to make known, a public declaration

22   *siege:* rank

23   *unbonneted:* without my hat on, with all due modesty

27   *circumscription and confine:* restriction and restraint

29   *raised:* roused from sleep

31   *parts:* talents

33   *Janus:* Roman god. Traditionally represented as two-faced, he is an appropriate deity for the shifty Iago to invoke.

CASSIO	Something from Cyprus as I may divine:	
	It is a business of some heat: the galleys	40
	Have sent a dozen sequent messengers	
	This very night at one another's heels,	
	And many of the consuls, raised and met,	
	Are at the duke's already: you have been	
	hotly call'd for;	45
	When, being not at your lodging to be found,	
	The senate hath sent about three several guests	
	To search you out.	
OTHELLO	'Tis well I am found by you.	
	I will but spend a word here in the house,	
	And go with you.	

Exit

CASSIO	Ensign, what makes he here?	50
IAGO	'Faith, he tonight hath boarded a land carack:	
	If it prove lawful prize, he's made for ever.	
CASSIO	I do not understand.	
IAGO	He's married.	
CASSIO	To who?	
IAGO	Marry, to –	

Re-enter OTHELLO

	Come, captain, will you go?	
OTHELLO	Have with you.	
CASSIO	Here comes another troop to seek for you.	55
IAGO	It is Brabantio. General, be advised;	
	He comes to bad intent.	

Enter BRABANTIO, RODERIGO, and Officers with torches and weapons

OTHELLO	Holla! stand there!	
RODERIGO	Signior, it is the Moor.	
BRABANTIO	Down with him, thief!	

They draw on both sides

IAGO	You, Roderigo! come, sir, I am for you.	60
OTHELLO	Keep up your bright swords, for the dew will rust them.	
	Good signior, you shall more command with years	
	Than with your weapons.	
BRABANTIO	O thou foul thief, where hast thou stow'd my daughter?	64
	Damn'd as thou art, thou hast enchanted her;	65
	For I'll refer me to all things of sense,	
	If she in chains of magic were not bound,	
	Whether a maid so tender, fair and happy,	68
	So opposite to marriage that she shunned	69
	The wealthy curled darlings of our nation,	70
	Would ever have, to incur a general mock,	
	Run from her guardage to the sooty bosom	72
	Of such a thing as thou, to fear, not to delight.	
	Judge me the world, if 'tis not gross in sense	74
	That thou hast practised on her with foul charms,	75
	Abused her delicate youth with drugs or minerals	
	That weaken motion: I'll have't disputed on;	
	'Tis probable and palpable to thinking.	78
	I therefore apprehend and do attach thee	79
	For an abuser of the world, a practiser	80
	Of arts inhibited and out of warrant.	81

Glossary notes:
- 39 *divine:* guess
- 40 *heat:* urgency
- 41 *sequent:* successive
- 47 *several:* distinct; separate
- 51 *carack:* large ship
- 54 *Have with you:* Let's go together
- 55 *seek:* look
- 60 *come, sir, I am for you:* Iago pretends to fight Roderigo
- 64 *foul:* wicked, ugly, loathsome
- 68 *fair:* beautiful
- 69 *opposite:* opposed
- 72 *her guardage:* safety and guardianship of her father
- 74 *gross in sense:* obvious to any observer
- 78 *palpable:* clear, obvious
- 79 *attach:* arrest
- 81 *arts inhibited:* the black arts

Handwritten annotations:
- O very valuable soldier
- [Othello – confident self-assured. Civil.
- Racist (next to Brabantio)
- B doesn't need his sword to get O attention his age
- ← accusing him of black magic.
- ← A black chest (next to "sooty bosom")
- B: cannot fathom that Des has fallen in love with Othello
- He is sure Othello must have be-witched her. (CC)

Lay hold upon him: if he do resist,
Subdue him at his peril.

OTHELLO   Hold your hands,
Both you of my inclining, and the rest:
Were it my cue to fight, I should have known it   85
Without a prompter. Where will you that I go
To answer this your charge?

BRABANTIO   To prison, till fit time
Of law and course of direct session
Call thee to answer.

OTHELLO   What if I do obey?
How may the Duke be therewith satisfied,   90
Whose messengers are here about my side,
Upon some present business of the state
To bring me to him?

First Officer   'Tis true, most worthy signior;
The Duke's in council and your noble self,
I am sure, is sent for.

BRABANTIO   How! The Duke in council!   95
In this time of the night! Bring him away:
Mine's not an idle cause: the Duke himself,
Or any of my brothers of the state,
Cannot but feel this wrong as 'twere their own;
For if such actions may have passage free,   100
Bond-slaves and pagans shall our statesmen be.

Exeunt

---

84   *inclining:* party, faction

88   *course of direct session:* due process of an immediate
      court sitting

100   *may have passage free:* be freely allowed

101   *Bond-slaves and Pagans:* men who are both slaves
      and heathen

IAGO AND OTHELLO

Iago tells Othello that Roderigo has been saying unpleasant things about him and that Brabantio now knows of his marriage to Desdemona. Othello says that he has nothing to be ashamed of and that his good character will ensure that the senator cannot harm him. Cassio comes to tell Othello that he is urgently needed at the Duke's – a situation is brewing in Cyprus and a council has convened to decide what action is required. Brabantio and his men find Othello and seek to arrest him, accusing him of using witchcraft to lure Desdemona. Othello tells Brabantio that the Duke has called upon him to attend an urgent meeting and it is best they go there to address any grievance the senator might have.

ACTION

LINE BY LINE

▶ LINES 1-28: IAGO AND OTHELLO SPEAK

Iago is with Othello on a street in Venice. He tells Othello that Roderigo has been saying unpleasant things about him: 'he prated, / And spoke such scurvy and provoking terms / Against your honour' (6-8). Iago claims that when he heard these insulting comments he felt like stabbing Roderigo: 'I had thought to have yerk'd him here under the ribs' (5). However, though he has killed many times in battle, premeditated murder is not something he is capable of: 'I hold it very stuff o'th' conscience / To do no contrived murder' (2-3). He tells Othello that he lacks the necessary wickedness sometimes to do what is necessary: 'I lack iniquity Sometimes to do me service' (3-4).

Iago wonders if Othello has consummated his marriage with Desdemona: 'Are you fast married?' (11). He tells Othello that Brabantio will look to have the marriage annulled if he can. If this proves impossible he will use whatever legal means he can to make Othello's life as miserable as possible: 'put upon you what restraint and grievance / That law... Will give him cable' (15-7). Brabantio is a respected and powerful citizen of Venice and has even more influence, Iago says, than the Duke himself.

Othello is unshaken by all of this:
• He is sure that the services he has done the state in battle will outweigh any grievance that Brabantio might have about his marriage: 'My services, which I have done the signory, / Shall out-tongue his complaints' (18-19).

OTHELLO

- His merits make him more than worthy of marriage to Desdemona: 'my demerits/ May speak unbonneted to as proud a fortune/ As this' (22-4).
- He also loves Desdemona and would not have given up the freedom of being a bachelor for anyone less than she: 'I would not my unhoused free condition/ Put into circumscription and confine/ For the sea's worth' (26-8).

▶ LINES 29-54: TROUBLE IN CYPRUS

A party of men is seen approaching. Iago assumes that it is Brabantio and his men and urges Othello to leave but the general stands firm and says that he has nothing to feel guilty about: 'My parts, my title, and my perfect soul/ Shall manifest me rightly' (31-2). The approaching group turns out to be Cassio and servants of the Duke who have been sent to find Othello. A situation has arisen in Cyprus and Othello must attend an urgent meeting at the Duke's: 'Something from Cyprus, as I may divine:/ It is business of some heat' (39-40). Messengers have been arriving from Cyprus all night with reports of a grave situation and those in command in Venice are now gathering at the Duke's palace to plan whatever action might be required. Othello was not to be found at his lodgings and so a number of groups were sent to search for him.

Othello re-merges from the house just in time to see Brabantio and Roderigo arrive with some officers in tow. Brabantio immediately accuses Othello of being a 'thief' and calls on his men to attack (59). Swords are raised on both sides and Iago makes as if he will fight Roderigo: 'You, Roderigo! come, sir, I am for you' (56). Othello remains perfectly calm and respectful towards Brabantio, telling him that his

OTHELLO

DIGNITY AND SELF-POSSESSION

Despite being provoked, insulted and threatened in this scene, Othello remains calm and self-possessed at all times:

- When Iago tries to incense him with tales of Roderigo saying terrible things about him, Othello refuses to get wound up. It is best, he tells Iago, that the ensign didn't resort to violence on his behalf: ''Tis better as it is' (6).
- When he hears that Brabantio wishes to have him divorced or make him suffer for marrying his daughter, Othello tells Iago to let him do what he wishes: 'Let him do his spite' (17).
- When it seems that Brabantio and his men are approaching, Othello refuses to run and hide, though this is what Iago tells him to do: 'Not I – I must be found' (30).
- When Brabantio and his men do arrive and swords are raised, Othello tells everyone to lower their weapons and suggests to Brabantio that his age will command more respect than the weapons he brings: 'Good signor, you shall more command with years/ Than with your weapons' (62-3).
- Though Brabantio insults him and accuses him of practicing 'arts inhibited and out of warrent' Othello never loses his temper, calmly asking the senator where he would like him to go to answer these charges: 'Where will you that I go/ To answer this your charge?' (86-7).

We also get a sense of Othello's pride and dignity in this scene. He tells Iago that it is not well known that he is descended from royalty: ''Tis yet to know...I fetch my life and being/ From men of royal seige' (19-22). This, however, is not something he wishes to broadcast or boast about: 'when I know that boasting is an honour,/ I shall promulgate' (20-1).

Othello is proud of what he has achieved and is sure that his actions will speak against any accusations or threats the senator is likely to bring: 'My services, which I have done the signory,/ Shall out-tongue his complaints' (18-9). He is not someone who runs and hides when things look set to get difficult. When Iago tells him to hide from Brabantio, Othello says that he will stay and face the senator: 'My parts, my title, and my perfect soul/ Shall manifest me rightly' (31-2). His merits also make him more than worthy of marriage to Desdemona: 'my demerits/ May speak unbonneted to as proud a fortune/ As this that I have reach'd' (22-4).

age commands more respect than the weapons he brings: 'Good signor, you shall more command with years / Than with your weapons' (62-3).

▶ LINES 55-61: BRABANTIO CONFRONTS OTHELLO

Brabantio is in no mood to calm down:

- He calls Othello a 'foul thief' and accuses him of stealing his daughter away: 'where hast thou stow'd my daughter' (64).
- He says that Othello is someone who practices forbidden and illegal arts: 'a practiser / Of arts inhibited and out of warrant' (80-1). Othello used this black magic to take possession of Desdemona: 'thou hast enchanted her' (65).
- He accuses Othello of using medicines to weaken his daughter's will: 'Abused her delicate youth with drugs or minerals / That weaken motion' (76-7).
- Any reasonable person, he says, will see immediately that his daughter must be under some dark spell: 'For I'll refer me to all things of sense, / If she in chains of magic were not bound' (66-7).

Desdemona is a beautiful and fortunate girl, someone who enjoys the guardianship of a loving father. Why, Brabantio asks, would she leave the safety of her home, open herself to ridicule, to be with a man like Othello, someone inspires fear rather than delight? 'Whether a maid so tender, fair, and happy...Would ever have, to incur a general mock, / Run from her guardage to the sooty bosom / Of such a thing as thou – to fear, not to delight?' (68-73). After all, Desdemona was someone so opposed to marriage that she turned down offers from the wealthiest Venetian men: 'So opposite to marriage that she shunned / The wealthy curled darlings of our nation' (69-70).

Brabantio calls on his men to arrest Othello and bring him to jail. Othello tells the senator that it would not please the Duke if he was to be taken to prison this night – he has just been called upon to attend an urgent meeting of the state. Brabantio is surprised to hear that the Duke is holding council so late at night but is not willing to let the issue of his daughter's marriage rest. He says that the Duke and other senior members of government will sympathise with him when they hear of what Othello has done. If men such as Othello are free to behave in the manner he has just described then the future statesmen of the city will be 'Bond-slaves and pagans' (101). ◆

IAGO

A BRILLIANT ACTOR

In Act 1 Scene 1 Iago tells us that his loyalty and faithfulness to Othello is merely an act – he despises the general but knows that it serves his interests for the moment to seem the faithful servant. In this scene we get to see Iago play the part of devoted ensign:

- He tells Othello that Roderigo has been saying terrible things about him and that he was so angered by the nobleman's words that he thought to defend his master's honour with violence: 'I did full hard forebear him' (10).
- He claims that he wanted to strike Roderigo with his dagger: 'I had thought t'have yerk'd him here under the ribs' (5).
- He also acts as if he has Othello's best interests at heart when he tells him that Brabantio is looking for him and that the senator is a powerful man, capable of making Othello's life a misery: 'Be assured of this, That the magnifico is much beloved, / And hath in his effect a voice potential / As double as the Duke's' (11-4).

Little does Othello know that it was Iago who spoke ill of him and helped Roderigo rouse the sleeping senator with the news of the marriage.

NO RESPECT FOR MORALS AND VALUES

In this scene Iago presents himself as a moral person, someone with strong values.

- He claims to be outraged at Roderigo insulting Othello's honour (6-10).
- He says that premeditated murder is something he abhors and would never commit: 'I hold it very stuff o'th' conscience / To do no contrived murder' (2-3).
- He says that he is not wicked by nature: 'I lack iniquity / Sometimes to do me service' (3-4).
- He says that he wanted to stab Roderigo for bad-mouthing Othello but was incapable of acting in this manner (3-5).

But this is all just an act, a conscious effort to present himself in a certain way to Othello. As the play progresses we will see that Iago has little or no time for the morals and values he pretends here to uphold.

TALK ABOUT IT
Do you think that Brabantio's anger is justified and his speech reasonable given the way his daughter has just behaved?

ACT 1

SCENE 3

A council-chamber

The DUKE and Senators sitting at a table; Officers attending

DUKE OF VENICE	There is no composition in these news
	That gives them credit.
First Senator	Indeed, they are disproportion'd;
	My letters say a hundred and seven galleys.
DUKE OF VENICE	And mine, a hundred and forty.
Second Senator	And mine, two hundred:
	But though they jump not on a just account –
	As in these cases, where the aim reports,
	'Tis oft with difference – yet do they all confirm
	A Turkish fleet, and bearing up to Cyprus.
DUKE OF VENICE	Nay, it is possible enough to judgment:
	I do not so secure me in the error,
	But the main article I do approve
	In fearful sense.
Sailor	*[Within]* What, ho! what, ho! what, ho!
First Officer	A messenger from the galleys.

Enter a Sailor

DUKE OF VENICE	Now, what's the business?
Sailor	The Turkish preparation makes for Rhodes;
	So was I bid report here to the state
	By Signior Angelo.
DUKE OF VENICE	How say you by this change?
First Senator	This cannot be,
	By no assay of reason: 'tis a pageant,
	To keep us in false gaze. When we consider
	The importance of Cyprus to the Turk,
	And let ourselves again but understand,
	That as it more concerns the Turk than Rhodes,
	So may he with more facile question bear it,
	For that it stands not in such warlike brace,
	But altogether lacks the abilities
	That Rhodes is dress'd in: if we make thought of this,
	We must not think the Turk is so unskilful
	To leave that latest which concerns him first,
	Neglecting an attempt of ease and gain,
	To wake and wage a danger profitless.
DUKE OF VENICE	Nay, in all confidence, he's not for Rhodes.
First Officer	Here is more news.

Enter a Messenger

Messenger	The Ottomites, reverend and gracious,
	Steering with due course towards the isle of Rhodes,
	Have there injointed them with an after fleet.
First Senator	Ay, so I thought. How many, as you guess?
Messenger	Of thirty sail: and now they do restem

Cultural context turkish empior.

5

10

15

20

25

30

35

1 *composition:* consistency.

3 *disproportioned:* inconsistent. The numbers in the reports don't make sense.

5 *jump:* tally, agree.
5 *just account:* accurate estimate.
6-7 *Where the aim report... all confirm:* where there are differences between one report and another.

10-11 *I do not so secure... approve:* the errors in the various reports are not significant enough to stop him from believing their common conclusion (that the Turks are launching an attack on Cyprus).

19 *assay:* test.
19 *'tis a pageant,/To keep us in false gaze:* it's a distraction, a performance designed to fool us.

24 *with more facile question bear it:* capture it more easily.
25 *brace:* military readiness.

27 *dress'd in:* equipped with

31 *wage a danger profitless:* to face, manage, or grapple with perils that are not worth the risk.

34 *The Ottomites:* another word for Turks. At this time, Turkey was part of the Ottoman Empire, which stretched across parts of North Africa, the Middle East, and eastern Europe.
36 *injointed:* joined up, united.

38 *restem:* return, re-trace.

	Their backward course, bearing with frank appearance	39	*bearing... appearance:* **with obvious intention**
	Their purposes toward Cyprus. Signior Montano,	40	
	Your trusty and most valiant servitor,	41	*servitor:* **servant.**
	With his free duty recommends you thus,		
	And prays you to believe him.		
DUKE OF VENICE	'Tis certain, then, for Cyprus.		
	Marcus Luccicos, is not he in town?	45	
First Senator	He's now in Florence.		
DUKE OF VENICE	Write from us to him; post-post-haste dispatch.	47	*post-post-haste:* **very quickly.**
First Senator	Here comes Brabantio and the valiant Moor.		

Enter BRABANTIO, OTHELLO, IAGO, RODERIGO, and Officers

DUKE OF VENICE	BvousValiant Othello, we must straight employ you		
	Against the general enemy Ottoman.	50	
	[To BRABANTIO]		
	I did not see you; welcome, gentle signior;		
	We lack'd your counsel and your help tonight.		
BRABANTIO	So did I yours. Good your grace, pardon me;		
	Neither my place nor aught I heard of business		
	Hath raised me from my bed, nor doth the general care	55	
	Take hold on me, for my particular grief		
	Is of so flood-gate and o'erbearing nature		
	That it engluts and swallows other sorrows	57	*engluts:* **eat, gobble.**
	And it is still itself.		
DUKE OF VENICE	Why, what's the matter?		
BRABANTIO	My daughter! O, my daughter!		
Senators	Dead?		
BRABANTIO	Ay, to me;	60	
	She is abused, stol'n from me, and corrupted		
	By spells and medicines bought of mountebanks;	62	*mountebanks:* **quacks; con artists who sold questionable medicines.**
	For nature so preposterously to err,		
	Being not deficient, blind, or lame of sense,	64	*Sans:* **without.**
	Sans witchcraft could not.	65	
DUKE OF VENICE	Whoe'er he be that in this foul proceeding		
	Hath thus beguiled your daughter of herself		
	And you of her, the bloody book of law	68	*the bloody book... sense:* **the Duke insists that Brabantio is entitled to be judge, jury and executioner of whoever has committed this crime.**
	You shall yourself read in the bitter letter		
	After your own sense, yea, though our proper son	70	
	Stood in your action.		
BRABANTIO	Humbly I thank your grace.		
	Here is the man, this Moor, whom now, it seems,		
	Your special mandate for the state-affairs		
	Hath hither brought.		
All	We are very sorry for't.	75	
DUKE OF VENICE	*[To OTHELLO]*		
	What, in your own part, can you say to this?		
BRABANTIO	Nothing, but this is so.		
OTHELLO	Most potent, grave, and reverend signiors,		
	My very noble and approved good masters,		
	That I have ta'en away this old man's daughter,	80	
	It is most true; true, I have married her:		
	The very head and front of my offending	82	*head and front:* **height and breadth; extent.**
	Hath this extent, no more. Rude am I in my speech,	83	*Rude:* **unrefined.**
	And little bless'd with the soft phrase of peace:		
	For since these arms of mine had seven years' pith,	85	*seven years pith:* **since he was seven years old.**

Till now some nine moons wasted, they have used

Their dearest action in the tented field,

And little of this great world can I speak,

More than pertains to feats of broil and battle,

And therefore little shall I grace my cause   90

In speaking for myself. Yet, by your gracious patience,

I will a round unvarnish'd tale deliver

Of my whole course of love; what drugs, what charms,

What conjuration and what mighty magic,

For such proceeding I am charged withal,   95

I won his daughter.

BRABANTIO   A maiden never bold;

Of spirit so still and quiet, that her motion

Blush'd at herself; and she, in spite of nature,

Of years, of country, credit, every thing,

To fall in love with what she fear'd to look on!   100

It is a judgment maim'd and most imperfect

That will confess perfection so could err

Against all rules of nature, and must be driven

To find out practises of cunning hell,

Why this should be. I therefore vouch again   105

That with some mixtures powerful o'er the blood,

Or with some dram conjured to this effect,

He wrought upon her.

DUKE OF VENICE   To vouch this, is no proof,

Without more wider and more overt test

Than these thin habits and poor likelihoods   110

Of modern seeming do prefer against him.

First Senator   But, Othello, speak:

Did you by indirect and forced courses

Subdue and poison this young maid's affections?

Or came it by request and such fair question   115

As soul to soul affordeth?

OTHELLO   I do beseech you,

Send for the lady to the Sagittary,

And let her speak of me before her father:

If you do find me foul in her report,

The trust, the office I do hold of you,   120

Not only take away, but let your sentence

Even fall upon my life.

DUKE OF VENICE   Fetch Desdemona hither.

OTHELLO   Ensign, conduct them: you best know the place.

Exeunt IAGO and Attendants

And, till she come, as truly as to heaven

I do confess the vices of my blood,   125

So justly to your grave ears I'll present

How I did thrive in this fair lady's love,

And she in mine.

DUKE OF VENICE   Say it, Othello.

OTHELLO   Her father loved me; oft invited me;

Still question'd me the story of my life,

From year to year, the battles, sieges, fortunes,   130

That I have passed.

I ran it through, even from my boyish days,

To the very moment that he bade me tell it;

[Handwritten margin note:] This isn't like Des because she never did anything out of her way

86 *Till now some nine moons wasted:* until nine months ago.

94 *conjuration:* magic; trickery; incantation.

107 *dram... effect:* a potion made for just such a purpose.

109 *wider:* thorough.

110 *Than these thin habits... against him:* groundless and weak claims made against Othello based on Brabantio's superficial observations.

117 *Sagittary:* archer; possibly the name of the place where the characters are.

Wherein I spake of most disastrous chances,
Of moving accidents by flood and field   135
Of hair-breadth scapes i' the imminent deadly breach,
Of being taken by the insolent foe
And sold to slavery, of my redemption thence
And portance in my travels' history:

139   *portance:* behaviour.

Wherein of antres vast and deserts idle,   140

140   *antres:* cave

Rough quarries, rocks and hills whose heads touch heaven
It was my hint to speak, – such was the process;
And of the Cannibals that each other eat,
The Anthropophagi and men whose heads

144   *Anthropophagi:* man-eaters.

Do grow beneath their shoulders. This to hear   145
Would Desdemona seriously incline:
But still the house-affairs would draw her thence:
Which ever as she could with haste dispatch,
She'd come again, and with a greedy ear
Devour up my discourse: which I observing,   150
Took once a pliant hour, and found good means
To draw from her a prayer of earnest heart
That I would all my pilgrimage dilate,

153   *That I would... intentively:* that I would relate all of the detail of these stories and memories that Desdemona had only heard snatches of before.

Whereof by parcels she had something heard,
But not intentively: I did consent,   155
And often did beguile her of her tears,
When I did speak of some distressful stroke
That my youth suffer'd. My story being done,
She gave me for my pains a world of sighs:
She swore, in faith, 'twas strange, 'twas passing strange,   160
'Twas pitiful, 'twas wondrous pitiful:
She wish'd she had not heard it, yet she wish'd
That heaven had made her such a man: she thank'd me,
And bade me, if I had a friend that loved her,
I should but teach him how to tell my story   165
And that would woo her. Upon this hint I spake:
She loved me for the dangers I had pass'd,
And I loved her that she did pity them.
This only is the witchcraft I have used:
Here comes the lady; let her witness it.   170

Enter DESDEMONA, IAGO, and Attendants

DUKE OF VENICE   I think this tale would win my daughter too.
Good Brabantio,
Take up this mangled matter at the best:
Men do their broken weapons rather use
Than their bare hands.

173   *Take up this mangled matter at the best:* make the best of this situation.

BRABANTIO   I pray you, hear her speak: 175
If she confess that she was half the wooer,
Destruction on my head, if my bad blame
Light on the man! Come hither, gentle mistress:
Do you perceive in all this noble company
Where most you owe obedience?

DESDEMONA   My noble father,   180
I do perceive here a divided duty:
To you I am bound for life and education;
My life and education both do learn me
How to respect you; you are the lord of duty;

27

In respect I'm your daughter but her husband is more important.

I am hitherto your daughter: but here's my husband,   185
And so much duty as my mother show'd
To you, preferring you before her father,
So much I challenge that I may profess
Due to the Moor my lord.

BRABANTIO   Goodbye, I've done!
Please it your grace, on to the state-affairs: 190
I had rather to adopt a child than get it.
Come hither, Moor:
I here do give thee that with all my heart
Which, but thou hast already, with all my heart
I would keep from thee. For your sake, jewel,   195
I am glad at soul I have no other child:
For thy escape would teach me tyranny,
To hang clogs on them. I have done, my lord.   198 *clogs:* blocks of wood.

He'd be v strict

DUKE OF VENICE   Let me speak like yourself, and lay a sentence,
Which, as a grise or step, may help these lovers   200 200 *grise:* step
Into your favour.
When remedies are past, the griefs are ended
By seeing the worst, which late on hopes depended.
To mourn a mischief that is past and gone
Is the next way to draw new mischief on.   205
What cannot be preserved when fortune takes
Patience her injury a mockery makes.
The robb'd that smiles steals something from the thief;
He robs himself that spends a bootless grief.   209 *bootless:* vain.

BRABANTIO   So let the Turk of Cyprus us beguile;   210
We lose it not, so long as we can smile.
He bears the sentence well that nothing bears
But the free comfort which from thence he hears,
But he bears both the sentence and the sorrow
That, to pay grief, must of poor patience borrow.   215
These sentences, to sugar, or to gall,
Being strong on both sides, are equivocal:
But words are words; I never yet did hear   218-219
That the bruised heart was pierced through the ear.   *I never yet... the ear:* a broken heart was never
                                                                            mended by the consoling words of others.
I humbly beseech you, proceed to the affairs of state.   220

DUKE OF VENICE   The Turk with a most mighty preparation makes for
Cyprus. Othello, the fortitude of the place is best   222 *fortitude:* strength.
known to you; and though we have there a
substitute of most allowed sufficiency, yet opinion, a
sovereign mistress of effects, throws a more safer   225
voice on you: you must therefore be content to
slubber the gloss of your new fortunes with this   227 *slubber:* soil, stain, or darken.
more stubborn and boisterous expedition.

OTHELLO   The tyrant custom, most grave senators,
Hath made the flinty and steel couch of war   230
My thrice-driven bed of down: I do agnise   231 *Thrice-driven bed of down:* an extremely soft and
A natural and prompt alacrity   comfortable bed of down feathers
I find in hardness, and do undertake   231 *agnise:* acknowledge
These present wars against the Ottomites.   232 *alacrity:* eagerness, enthusiasm. Othello is hungry to
Most humbly therefore bending to your state,   235   embrace the hardship of battle.
I crave fit disposition for my wife.
Due reference of place and exhibition,   237 *exhibition:* financial provision.

28

	With such accommodation and besort	238 *besort:* a group of servants.
	As levels with her breeding.	
DUKE OF VENICE	If you please,	240
	Be't at her father's.	
BRABANTIO	I'll not have it so.	
OTHELLO	Nor I.	
DESDEMONA	Nor I; I would not there reside,	
	To put my father in impatient thoughts	
	By being in his eye. Most gracious Duke,	245
	To my unfolding lend your prosperous ear;	246 *unfolding:* proposal
	And let me find a charter in your voice,	
	To assist my simpleness.	
DUKE OF VENICE	What would you, Desdemona?	
DESDEMONA	That I did love the Moor to live with him,	
	My downright violence and storm of fortunes	250
	May trumpet to the world: my heart's subdued	
	Even to the very quality of my lord:	
	I saw Othello's visage in his mind,	
	And to his honour and his valiant parts	
	Did I my soul and fortunes consecrate.	255
	So that, dear lords, if I be left behind,	
	A moth of peace, and he go to the war,	
	The rites for which I love him are bereft me,	
	And I a heavy interim shall support	
	By his dear absence. Let me go with him.	260
OTHELLO	Let her have your voice.	
	Vouch with me, heaven, I therefore beg it not,	
	To please the palate of my appetite,	263-266
	Nor to comply with heat – the young affects	*To please the palate... mind:* Othello is saying that he is no longer a young man and that he wants Desdemona to accompany him to Cyprus not because he is driven by physical passion but because he desires her companionship.
	In me defunct – and proper satisfaction.	265
	But to be free and bounteous to her mind:	
	And heaven defend your good souls, that you think	
	I will your serious and great business scant	
	For she is with me: no, when light-wing'd toys	
	Of feather'd Cupid seal with wanton dullness	270
	My speculative and officed instruments,	
	That my disports corrupt and taint my business,	272 *disports:* sexual pleasures.
	Let housewives make a skillet of my helm,	273 *make a skillet of my helm:* a skillet is a small metal pot. Othello means that his skull should be used as a skillet in the event that his desire for his new wife interferes with his work as a soldier.
	And all indign and base adversities	
	Make head against my estimation!	275
DUKE OF VENICE	Be it as you shall privately determine,	
	Either for her stay or going: the affair cries haste,	
	And speed must answer it.	
First Senator	You must away tonight.	
DESDEMONA	Tonight, my lord?	
DUKE OF VENICE	This night.	
OTHELLO	With all my heart.	
DUKE OF VENICE	At nine i' the morning here we'll meet again.	280
	Othello, leave some officer behind,	
	And he shall our commission bring to you;	
	With such things else of quality and respect	
	As doth import you.	
OTHELLO	So please your grace, my ensign;	
	A man he is of honest and trust:	285

O- wants to see the good in people

	To his conveyance I assign my wife,	
	With what else needful your good grace shall think	
	To be sent after me.	
DUKE OF VENICE	Let it be so.	
	Good night to everyone.	
	To BRABANTIO And, noble signior,	
	If virtue no delighted beauty lack,	290
	Your son-in-law is far more fair than black.	
First Senator	Adieu, brave Moor, use Desdemona well.	
BRABANTIO	Look to her, Moor, if thou hast eyes to see:	
	She has deceived her father, and may thee.	

Exeunt DUKE OF VENICE, Senators, Officers, & attendants

[handwritten margin notes: — using her sexually / — shaken from what's going on.]

OTHELLO	My life upon her faith! Honest Iago,	295
	My Desdemona must I leave to thee:	
	I prithee, let thy wife attend on her:	
	And bring them after in the best advantage.	
	Come, Desdemona: I have but an hour	
	Of love, of worldly matters and direction,	300
	To spend with thee: we must obey the time.	

Exeunt OTHELLO and DESDEMONA

RODERIGO	Iago.	
IAGO	What say'st thou, noble heart?	
RODERIGO	What will I do, thinkest thou?	
IAGO	Why, go to bed, and sleep.	
RODERIGO	I will incontinently drown myself.	305
IAGO	If thou dost, I shall never love thee after.	
	Why, thou silly gentleman!	
RODERIGO	It is silliness to live when to live is torment; and	
	then have we a prescription to die when death is	
	our physician.	310
IAGO	O villainous! I have looked upon the world for four	
	times seven years; and since I could distinguish	
	betwixt a benefit and an injury, I never found man	
	that knew how to love himself. Ere I would say, I	
	would drown myself for the love of a guinea-hen, I	315
	would change my humanity with a baboon.	
RODERIGO	What should I do? I confess it is my shame to be so	
	fond; but it is not in my virtue to amend it.	
IAGO	Virtue! a fig! 'tis in ourselves that we are thus	
	or thus. Our bodies are our gardens, to the which	320
	our wills are gardeners: so that if we will plant	
	nettles, or sow lettuce, set hyssop and weed up	
	thyme, supply it with one gender of herbs, or	
	distract it with many, either to have it sterile	
	with idleness, or manured with industry, why, the	325
	power and corrigible authority of this lies in our	
	wills. If the balance of our lives had not one	
	scale of reason to poise another of sensuality, the	
	blood and baseness of our natures would conduct us	
	to most preposterous conclusions: but we have	330
	reason to cool our raging motions, our carnal	
	stings, our unbitted lusts, whereof I take this that	
	you call love to be a sect or scion.	
RODERIGO	It cannot be.	

[handwritten margin notes: metaphorical / if he plants good things good things will happen to him. / good advice. →]

315 *guinea-hen:* prostitute.
316 *baboon:* fool, buffoon.
322 *hyssop:* an aromatic herb.
326 *corrigible authority:* corrective power.
332 *unbitted:* unbridled.

IAGO

It is merely a lust of the blood and a permission of the will. Come, be a man. Drown thyself! drown cats and blind puppies. I have professed me thy friend and I confess me knit to thy deserving with cables of perdurable toughness; I could never better stead thee than now. Put money in thy purse; follow thou the wars; defeat thy favour with an usurped beard; I say, put money in thy purse. It cannot be that Desdemona should long continue her love to the Moor – put money in thy purse – nor he his to her: it was a violent commencement, and thou shalt see an answerable sequestration – put but money in thy purse. These Moors are changeable in their wills: fill thy purse with money – the food that to him now is as luscious as locusts, shall be to him shortly as bitter as coloquintida. She must change for youth: when she is sated with his body, she will find the error of her choice: she must have change, she must: therefore put money in thy purse. If thou wilt needs damn thyself, do it a more delicate way than drowning. Make all the money thou canst: if sanctimony and a frail vow betwixt an erring barbarian and a supersubtle Venetian not too hard for my wits and all the tribe of hell, thou shalt enjoy her; therefore make money. A pox of drowning thyself! it is clean out of the way: seek thou rather to be hanged in compassing thy joy than to be drowned and go without her.

Save money to go to cyprus.

335

340

345

350

355

Otrello

360

RODERIGO

Wilt thou be fast to my hopes, if I depend on the issue? *Can you make this happen?*

IAGO

Thou art sure of me – go, make money! – I have told thee often, and I re-tell thee again and again, I hate the Moor: my cause is hearted; thine hath no less reason. Let us be conjunctive in our revenge against him: if thou canst cuckold him, thou dost thyself a pleasure, me a sport. There are many events in the womb of time which will be delivered. Traverse! go, provide thy money. We will have more of this to-morrow. Adieu.

365

370

RODERIGO

Where shall we meet i' the morning?

IAGO

                          At my lodging.

RODERIGO

I'll be with thee betimes.

IAGO

                 Go to; farewell.

375

Do you hear, Roderigo?

RODERIGO

What say you?

IAGO

No more of drowning, do you hear?

RODERIGO

                   I am changed:

I'll go sell all my land.

IAGO

Go to, farewell, put money enough in your purse.

380

Exit Roderigo

Thus do I ever make my fool my purse:
For I mine own gain'd knowledge should profane,
If I would time expend with such a snipe. *Roderigo fool*
But for my sport and profit. I hate the Moor:

Margin notes

338   knit to thy deserving: Committed to achieving what you deserve
339   perdurable: long-lasting, durable.

345   *violent commencement:* a rushed start.

346   *answerable sequestration:* an equally violent separation or end.

350   *coloquintida:* plant that produces a bitter, yellow fruit that has a strong laxative effect.

Shakespears plays are a blend of all qualities & shows reality.

368   *conjunctive:* allied; united.

369   *cuckold:* a man with an unfaithful wife. This term is used frequently in the play. The cuckold is often the focus of social ridicule in Shakespearean dramas.

382   *profane:* abuse.

383   *snipe:* a fool.

And it is thought abroad, that 'twixt my sheets   385
He has done my office: I know not if't be true;
But I, for mere suspicion in that kind,
Will do as if for surety. He holds me well;
The better shall my purpose work on him.
Cassio's a proper man: let me see now: 390
To get his place and to plume up my will
In double knavery – How, how? Let's see –
After some time, to abuse Othello's ear
That he is too familiar with his wife.
He hath a person and a smooth dispose   395
To be suspected, framed to make women false. The
Moor is of a free and open nature,
That thinks men honest that but seem to be so,
And will as tenderly be led by the nose
As asses are.   400
I have't. It is engender'd. Hell and night
Must bring this monstrous birth to the world's light.

Exit

386   *He has done my office:* Iago has heard rumours that Othello slept with his wife (Emilia).

391   *Plume up my will:* put a feather in his (Iago's) cap.

392   *knavery:* Mischief; boyish; the behaviour of a knave.

395   *dispose:* disposition.

401   *engendered:* conceived; produced; brought into being; also, to copulate or reproduce.

The Duke and his senators have gathered in the council chamber to discuss the imminent Turkish invasion. Rumours swirl as to the Turks' intentions. Eventually it is determined that a vast Turkish fleet is sailing toward Cyprus.

Brabantio claims Othello has seduced Desdemona by means of witchcraft and demands justice for this grievous crime. Othello tells his side of the story, describing how Desdemona fell in love with him as she listened to the exotic, sad and colourful story of his life. Desdemona is sent for and confirms Othello's version of events.

The Duke declares that Othello will leave that very night to lead the defence of Cyprus against the Turks. Desdemona, as his bride, will also travel to Cyprus.

Othello entrusts her to Iago's care. They will follow Othello to Cyprus the following day. Roderigo, convinced that he has lost Desdemona, threatens to kill himself. Iago, however, is determined to use him as a pawn in his schemes. He convinces Roderigo to sell all his land and accompany him to Cyprus. In a soliloquy Iago conceives a scheme that will destroy both Cassio and Othello: he will convince Othello that Cassio is having an affair with Desdemona.

ACTION

LINE BY LINE

▶ LINES 1-48: A COUNCIL OF WAR

The Duke and his senators have gathered to discuss the Turkish threat. It is a time of crisis and immediate action is required. (We might be reminded here of war films that depict the US President surrounded by his generals in the 'situation room' of the White House or the Pentagon.)

We can imagine the atmosphere of tension and uncertainty that fills the council chamber as the Duke and his advisors contemplate the imminent invasion: the nervous tension of a late-night meeting, the leaders poring over maps, the bustle of aides, soldiers and sailors in the background. The reports received by the senate are 'disproportion'd' or inconsistent (2). According to the Duke the reports received to date lack the consistency, certainty and 'composition' to be fully believed: 'There is no composition in these news / That gives them credit' (1-2).

• One report says that the Turkish fleet consists of 107 galleys or warships, another 140, yet another 200 (3, 4).

OTHELLO

OTHELLO'S EXOTIC ORIGINS

This scene gives us a sense of Othello's exotic beginnings. This is a man whose origins lie far from the prosperous, European city of Venice. He comes from a land beyond the Mediterranean, a place his Venetian colleagues know only through rumour and legend.

Othello describes his country of origin as a bleak place, a country of enormous caves ('antres vast') and endless deserts (140). It is a rugged, mountainous land full of 'Rough quarries, rocks and hills whose heads touch heaven' (141). According to Othello this wilderness is peopled by bizarre and fantastic races. He mentions cannibals, headless men whose features appear on their torsos and the 'Anthropophagi' who were a cannibalistic race from Greek legend (143-5). Othello has had a very colourful and difficult life:

- From an early age, it seems, he was involved in 'battles, sieges, fortunes' (130).
- There were times when he barely escaped with his life, escaping death by only hair's breadth: 'hair-breadth scapes i the imminent deadly breach' (136).
- He suffered 'disastrous chances' and many a 'distressful stroke' of bad fortune, enduring 'accidents' caused by war and by natural disaster (134, 135, 157).
- He was captured by his enemies and sold into slavery only to eventually win or be granted his freedom (137-8).

Desdemona, it seems, was simply blown away by Othello's tale. She found his story both fascinating and moving: 'She swore, in faith, 'twas strange, 'twas passing strange, / 'Twas pitiful, 'twas wondrous pitiful' (160-1).

It is hardly surprising that Desdemona fell for this exotic foreigner with his incredible tale. To her he must have seemed different and attractive, sexy and exciting. The Duke suggests that Othello and his story might well prove irresistible to any woman. As he puts it: 'I think this tale would win my daughter too' (171).

OTHELLO AS SOLDIER

Othello is someone who has experienced war and bloodshed his whole life. Since he was seven years old he has known little but the 'tented field' of battle (84-6). Lines 130-139 detail the 'battles' and 'sieges', disasters and 'hair-breadth' escapes that have marked his lifelong military career. Warfare, then, is his only area of expertise: 'And little of this great world can I speak, / More than pertains to feats of broil and battle' (187-8).

Yet what an expert he is. We get the sense that Othello must be a man of great bravery and resourcefulness to have endured so much fighting and killing, not to mention being sold into slavery and other misfortunes. His courage is indicated when the Duke greets him as 'Valiant Othello' (49).

Othello is also an accomplished strategist and general. No sooner has Othello reached the counsel chamber than the Duke asks him to lead the expedition against the Turks (49-50). Cyprus already has a commander in place: 'a substitute / of most allowed sufficiency' (223-4). Yet the Duke believes Othello should replace him and lead the island's defense: 'opinion, a sovereign mistress of effects, throws a more safer voice on you' (234-6). Othello, we're told, knows Cyprus's fortifications better than anyone, an indication of his vast military experience (222-3).

OTHELLO'S DIGNITY AND SELF-POSSESSION

In this scene Othello displays great calmness, dignity and self-possession. He has been falsely accused of a terrible crime, of having his way with Desdemona by means of witchcraft and black magic. However, he does not respond angrily. He does not physically or verbally attack Brabantio, his racist accuser. Instead he calmly and persuasively tells his side of the story, asks that Desdemona be brought to testify, and promises to abide by whatever decision the counsel reaches on the matter – even if it be putting him to death (117-22).

OTHELLO'S TRUSTING NATURE

Iago makes much of Othello's open trusting nature, describing how he assumes people are honest and takes them at face value: 'The Moor is of a free and open nature, / That thinks men honest that but seem to be so' (396-8). This is perhaps evident in how he trusts Iago himself, referring to him as a man of 'honest and trust' and entrusting Desdemona to his care (285-8). Othello's openness, perhaps we could even call it his naivety, will be used against him as the play progresses.

OTHELLO'S ELOQUENCE

Othello describes himself as a warrior rather an orator, someone whose warlike life has left his mode of speaking fairly rough and ready. 'Rude am I in my speech, / And little bless'd with the soft phrase of peace' (83-4). Yet Othello is surely being too humble here.

For throughout the scene he speaks formally, elegantly and persuasively, in a style that surely matches that of Venice's most eloquent courtiers and politicians. Yet his speeches are also filled with great passion, deploying colourful and vivid language to describe his life-story and how he won the hand of Desdemona.

OTHELLO'S DECENCY

All in all, then, this scene stresses Othello's fundamentally moral and decent nature. Desdemona refers to his 'honour and his valiant parts' (254). The Duke, meanwhile, urges Brabantio to recognise his new son-in-law's virtuous nature: 'And, noble signior, / If virtue no delighted beauty lack, / Your son-in-law is far more fair than black' (289-91). We shall see, however, that as the play goes on Othello's eloquence and self-possession – even his fundamentally decency – are threatened by jealousy that begins to consume him.

- The second senator states that despite their inconsistencies the reports all agree that the enemy is 'bearing up to Cyprus' (7-8).
- A sailor arrives with news that the Turkish force or 'preparation' is bound instead for the island of Rhodes (14).
- The first senator dismisses this as a 'pageant' or diversion by the enemy: Cyprus is an easier target, lacking Rhodes's defences or 'warlike brace', and has always been of great 'importancy' to the Turks (19-31).

Another messenger arrives and brings some clarity to the situation: the main Turkish navy has joined forces with an 'after fleet' or secondary force of thirty ships near Rhodes (36-8). Now, however, the enemy is done with tricks and diversions. The entire Turkish armada is sailing with 'frank appearance' toward Cyprus, which has been revealed as its true target (39-40).

▶ LINES 49-128: BRABANTIO AIRS HIS GRIEVANCE

Othello and Brabantio arrive at the council chamber. Othello, we remember, has been summoned because he is Venice's leading general, while Brabantio has come to seek justice for what he sees as the bewitchment of his daughter.

The Duke claims to have missed Brabantio's 'counsel' at this time of national crisis (52). Brabantio, however, responds that he is too wrapped up in his 'particular grief' at Desdemona's behaviour to heed the 'general care' that is the Turkish threat (55-6). The personal tragedy of his daughter's marriage to Othello is a 'flood-gate' of woe that 'engluts and swallows' all other concerns (57-8).

Brabantio claims that only 'witchcraft' could have made his daughter fall in love with a Moor (65). Desdemona, he says, is a quiet and well-bred girl, a creature of 'perfection' (102). Yet she has erred 'preposterously' and has gone against 'all rules of nature' by falling in love with a black man (103). According to Brabantio only someone with 'maim'd and most imperfect judgment' could believe this occured naturally (101). Othello, he says, must have 'corrupted' her with potions or dark magic, by 'spells and medicines', with some 'mixtures powerful o'er the blood' (61-2, 106). The Duke promises Brabantio justice. Brabantio, the Duke says, will be able to take vengeance on whoever bewitched Desdemona according to the 'bitter letter' of the 'bloody book of law' (68-9). Yet the Duke requires more proof, 'wider and more overt test', before the matter can be resolved (109). At Othello's request he sends for Desdemona so she can testify as to what really occurred.

▶ LINES 128-170: OTHELLO TELLS HIS SIDE OF THE STORY

While they wait for Desdemona to arrive, Othello tells his side of the story. Brabantio, he says, held him in very high esteem. Othello, therefore, was often invited to stay in Brabantio's house: 'Her father loved me; oft invited me' (128).

As Brabantio's guest Othello told the story of his life. It is a most exotic and romantic tale, full of battles and crazy adventures, of daring escapes and terrible misfortunes (129-45).

Desdemona was very taken with Othello's tale: 'This to hear / Would Desdemona seriously incline' (145-6). She would rush to complete her household

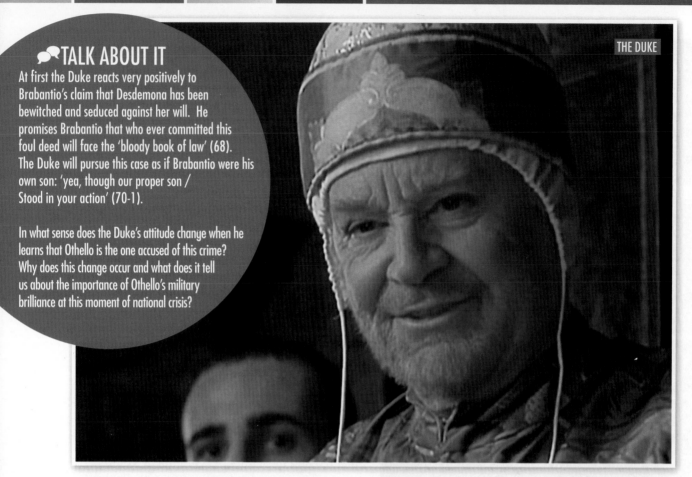

THE DUKE

💬 **TALK ABOUT IT**

At first the Duke reacts very positively to Brabantio's claim that Desdemona has been bewitched and seduced against her will. He promises Brabantio that who ever committed this foul deed will face the 'bloody book of law' (68). The Duke will pursue this case as if Brabantio were his own son: 'yea, though our proper son / Stood in your action' (70-1).

In what sense does the Duke's attitude change when he learns that Othello is the one accused of this crime? Why does this change occur and what does it tell us about the importance of Othello's military brilliance at this moment of national crisis?

chores in order to hear more of it: 'She'd come again, and with a greedy ear / Devour up my discourse' (149-50). She asked Othello to stretch the story out so it lasted as long as possible (151-3). She would often weep at some misfortune or 'distressful stroke' Othello had suffered during his youth (157).

Eventually Desdemona hinted to Othello that she had fallen in love with him (164-6). She had fallen for him due to his life of bravery, misfortune and resilience: 'She loved me for the dangers I had pass'd' (167). Othello, meanwhile, had fallen for her because of the sympathy with which she greeted his tales of woe: 'I loved her that she did pity them' (168). This, rather than through witchcraft, was how he won Desdemona's love (169).

▶ **LINES 171-219: DESDEMONA SETTLES THE MATTER**

Desdemona arrives and Brabantio asks her to whom she owes obedience (179). She responds that Brabantio is still her father, her 'lord of duty', to whom she owes her 'life and education' (182-4). Yet Othello is her husband. She must follow tradition and her own mother's example. Her first loyalty must be to her husband rather than to her father (185-9).

Brabantio has heard enough: 'I've done' (189). The testimony of Othello and Desdemona has made it obvious that their love is real, that no witchcraft was used to beguile or seduce his daughter. He very begrudgingly acknowledges Othello as his son-in-law, granting the Moor what he has already won and what 'with all my heart / I would keep from thee' (194-5). He asks the Duke to resume the discussion of the impending invasion: 'So let the Turk of Cyprus us beguile' (210).

▶ **LINES 220-291: A PLAN OF CAMPAIGN**

With this domestic dispute out of the way the assembled lords turn their attention once more to the Turkish menace. The Duke sends Othello to lead the defence of Cyprus from the approaching invaders (221-8). He apologises that Othello must 'slubber' or soil the joy of his new marriage with war and the affairs of state. Yet Othello knows Cyprus's fortifications better than anyone and will defend the island better than its present commander: 'the fortitude of the place is best known to you' (222-3).

Othello is happy to obey, asking only that during his absence accommodation be provided for Desdemona appropriate to her station in life:

IAGO

MALICIOUS, CALLOUS AND DESTRUCTIVE

Iago's malice, evident in the play's first scene, becomes even more pronounced here. We see it in the way he uses Roderigo for 'sport and profit' (384). We see it in the plan he conceives to destroy both Cassio and Othello. In his soliloquy he openly associates himself with evil, stressing how he wants to create 'knavery' or wickedness and aligning himself with the 'tribe of hell' and with the forces of 'hell and night' (392, 401).

A MASTER PLOTTER

In this scene we see Iago's plotting come into sharper focus. He keeps Roderigo onside in order to use him as a pawn in his schemes and also of course as a source of finance. Iago the master plotter is especially evident at the scene's conclusion when he conceives a plan that will effectively kill two birds with one stone: he will destroy both Cassio and Othello by convincing Othello that Cassio is sleeping with Desdemona (390-402).

However, it is important to note that Iago's plan is not detailed or complete. He is not yet sure how his ruse will take down its two targets. His plan has been conceived, fertilised, or 'engender'd' (401). But it has not yet fully developed or been born: 'Hell and night / Must bring this monstrous birth to the world's light' (402). Iago is more an improviser than a meticulous planner. He is content to draw the broad strokes of a plan and then work round events as they arise, using accident and circumstance to his advantage.

In this scene we get the sense that given enough time Iago could convince anyone of anything. His powers of persuasion are truly remarkable. It is obvious to any onlooker that Roderigo has no chance of ever being Desdemona's lover. Yet Iago convinces him that he does, and that Desdemona's new marriage will soon cool, allowing Roderigo the opportunity to make his move and 'enjoy' Desdemona himself (359).

Roderigo, having heard of Desdemona's marriage, is ready to kill himself. But Iago convinces him not only to go on living but sell as his land and sail to Cyprus. This is an exceptional feat of persuasion, one in which Iago repeats the phrase 'put money in thy purse', or variants thereof, again and again, as if he is hypnotising Roderigo or verbally beating him into submission.

A BRILLIANT ACTOR

This scene also showcases Iago's remarkable powers of deception. He thinks of Roderigo as a worthless creature and associates with him only to use him for 'sport' and for financial gain: 'Thus do I ever make my fool my purse' (381). Yet Roderigo is convinced that Iago is on his side and will assist him in the winning of Desdemona. He will sell his land to raise money that Iago – not himself – will make use of: 'I am changed: I'll go sell all my land' (378-9).

Othello too is taken in. He is convinced that Iago is completely trustworthy and even entrusts Desdemona to his care: 'A man he is of honest and trust / To his conveyance I assign my wife' (285-6). No one, then, sees through Iago's trustworthy exterior to the malignant schemer that lies within. No one has any inkling of the plans he draws against them.

IAGO'S SENSE OF SUPERIORITY

This scene highlights Iago's confidence and sense of superiority to those around him. He thinks of Roderigo as a 'snipe' and of Othello as an 'ass' (383-400).

He tells Roderigo that his 'wit' will find a way to drive a wedge between Desdemona and Othello (356-9). He is convinced that he can use his powers of deception to bamboozle the moor: Othello, he declares, 'will as tenderly be led by the nose / As asses are' (399-400).

IAGO'S LACK OF RESPECT FOR CONVENTIONAL VALUES

Roderigo displays a very traditional and romantic attitude toward love. Believing he has lost Desdemona, he lapses into despair and threatens to commit suicide: 'I will incontinently drown myself' (305). Iago, however, has no such romantic view, regarding love as little more than a bodily function: 'It is merely a lust of the blood and a permission of the will (335-6).

In a memorable speech he compares the body to a garden and human will to a gardener. Our wills, he believes, can control the emotions that flourish within us (319-27). Our reason can 'cool' or control the emotions and urges we experience, including love itself: 'we have reason to cool our raging motions' (330-1).

IAGO'S SHIFTING MOTIVATIONS

In this scene we get another insight into Iago's motives. By destroying Cassio he will be able to take what he sees as his rightful place as lieutenant (391). His hatred for Othello, meanwhile, is said to stem from a rumour that Othello has slept with his wife Emilia (385-6).

Iago doesn't know if this rumour is true or not. But he plans to act as if it is true and exact a terrible revenge on the Moor. It is important to note, however, that the motivations behind Iago's malice are shifting, complex and difficult to pin down precisely.

DESDEMONA

Brabantio describes Desdemona as a quiet, gentle and timid girl: 'A maiden never bold' (98-100). Desdemona, it seems, had a sheltered and privileged upbringing, so much so that she had never seen a black person and was frightened by Othello's appearance the first time she met him (96). Perhaps Desdemona's sheltered background made her more likely to be won over by Othello's exotic background and colourful tales of faraway lands. Though, as the Duke points out, such a powerful story would charm any woman.

Yet it must be noted that in this scene Desdemona comes across as strong-willed and assertive. She isn't afraid to speak her mind to her father, the Duke and the assembled dignitaries:

- She acknowledges the great debt of loyalty and gratitude she owes her father but asserts that her first duty must be to Othello because he is now her husband (180-9).
- She expresses her reluctance stay in her father's house now that Othello's going to war: 'Nor I; I would not there reside' (243).
- She is forthright in asking to accompany Othello to Cyprus: 'Let me go with him' (260).
- It could be argued that we see her independent spirit when Othello describes how she would quickly finish her household chores in order to spend time with him (147-50).
- It is similarly evident when she drops some very strong hints that he should make an effort to woo her (164-6).

'With such accommodation and besort / As levels with her breeding' (238-9). The Duke ventures that Desdemona might stay with her father (241). No one, however, is happy with this suggestion (241-3).

Desdemona requests permission to accompany Othello on his expedition: 'Let me go with him' (260). After all she married Othello in order to be with him: 'I did love the Moor to live with him' (249). If they are separated then what is the point of the marriage rites they entered into? 'if I be left behind… The rites for which I love him are bereft me' (256-8).

Othello agrees with Desdemona. He wants her to be with him on the campaign not for reasons of sexual desire but so that he might be 'free and bounteous to her mind' (261-6). He also stresses that her presence in Cyprus will not distract him from military matters and his duties as commander (267-75). The Duke is happy enough with this arrangement (276).

It is decided that Othello will leave for Cyprus that very night (278). Iago will follow tomorrow with Othello's formal commission or seal of office and various other things of 'quality and respect' that the council sees fit to grant him (285-8). Desdemona will travel with Iago rather than with Othello, presumably so that she has time to prepare for such a long journey (295-6).

The council of war breaks up. The lords agree to reconvene at nine the following morning to finalise their plans (280). Othello and Desdemona depart

to spend an 'hour / Of love' together before Othello must leave for Cyprus (299-301). Only Iago and Roderigo remain in the council chamber.

▶ LINES 299-370: IAGO BAMBOOZLES RODERIGO

Roderigo is filled with sorrow because he seems to have lost Desdemona. Now that she is married to Othello he feels he can never have her. His despair is such that he threatens to drown himself: 'It is silliness to live when to live is torment' (308).

Iago convinces Roderigo that Desdemona can still be his:

- Roderigo, he says, should travel with the fleet to Cyprus: 'follow thou the wars' (341).
- Eventually, he says, Desdemona will tire of her relationship with Othello: 'It cannot be that Desdemona should long continue her love to the Moor' (342-4).
- Othello, too, will tire of the marriage: 'These Moors are changeable in their wills' (347-8).
- Iago is convinced his 'wits' will drive the couple apart, allowing Roderigo to make his move (357-9).
- He repeatedly urges Roderigo to sell all his assets in order to fund their expedition.

Iago reassures Roderigo that he can trust him, that they are both on the same side (365). Both of them, for various reasons, hate Othello (367-8). Their revenge, therefore, should be 'conjunctive', meaning they should work together (368-9). Iago claims he would be delighted if Roderigo managed to 'cuckold' Othello by sleeping with Desdemona

CHARACTER DEVELOPMENT

DESDEMONA

behind his back (369-70). Roderigo, convinced that Iago is on his side, agrees to meet the following morning and goes off to sell all his land (374, 379).

▶ LINES 372-393:
IAGO COMES UP WITH A PLAN OF 'DOUBLE KNAVERY'

Iago reveals that he's only using Roderigo. He regards Roderigo as no more than a 'snipe', a foolish and useless creature (383). Iago says he's 'profaning' or going against his own wisdom, his own 'gained knowledge', by spending time with such a person (382-3). Yet he does so for 'sport and profit' (384). He wishes to use Roderigo as a pawn in his schemes. He also wants access to Roderigo's money: 'Thus do I ever make my fool my purse' (381).

Iago also reveals more about why he hates Othello. As we've noted Iago hates Othello for not giving him the job of lieutenant. Yet Iago has also heard a rumour that Othello slept with his wife behind his back: 'And it is thought abroad, that 'twixt my sheets/ He has done my office' (385-6). Iago doesn't know if this rumour is true but he's determined to punish Othello as if it were (387-8).

Iago is also determined to destroy Cassio. He wants to 'get his place' (391), to take Cassio's position as lieutenant, a position he feels should have been his to begin with. What Iago desires, then, is a plan of 'double knavery' (392) or double villainy, a plan that will take down his two targets at the same time (391-2).

He decides to convince Othello that Cassio is sleeping with Desdemona: 'to abuse Othello's ear/ That he is too familiar with his wife' (393-4). Iago is convinced that this plan will work. Cassio, he says, is 'proper' or handsome and has a 'smooth' or charming manner (390, 395). It would be easy to believe how Desdemona could fall for such a person: 'He hath a person and a smooth dispose/ To be suspected' (395-6).

RODERIGO

This scene reinforces our sense of Roderigo's extreme gullibility. Roderigo threatens suicide but Iago convinces him instead to sail with the fleet to Cyprus.

He convinces Roderigo that they are both on the same side and that he will do everything in his power to ensure Roderigo and Desdemona become lovers. In reality, of course, Iago merely intends to use Roderigo as a pawn in his various schemes. Iago also convinces him to sell all his land. Iago, of course, will spend the money Roderigo raises himself.

In this scene Roderigo is once again revealed to be a hopeless romantic, a man absolutely besotted with Desdemona, the object of his obsessive affection. When he learns that Desdemona's marriage to Othello is valid and genuine he is filled with such despair that he threatens suicide. He is so much in love with Desdemona that he sees hope where it's obvious to the audience there is none. By the end of the scene we find him clinging to the faint hope, sneakily fostered by Iago, that the love between Othello and Desdemona will soon fade, allowing him the possibility to be her lover.

Furthermore, Iago knows that Othello has a very trusting nature: 'The Moor is of a free and open nature,/ That thinks men honest that but seem to be so' (396-8). In particular, it seems, Othello trusts Iago himself: 'He holds me well' (388). It will be easy to lead him into such a trap: Othello 'will as tenderly be led by the nose/ As asses are' (399-400). The scene concludes with Iago declaring that his terrible plan has been conceived: 'I have't. It is engender'd' (401). ◆

💬THINK ABOUT IT
Othello promises the assembled lords that he does not want Desdemona to accompany him because of sexual desire, for the 'heat' and 'proper satisfaction' of youthful love. He claims to have outgrown such 'young affects': 'Nor to comply with heat – the young affects /In me defunct – and proper satisfaction' (263-4).

He also swears that Desdemona's presence in Cyprus will not distract him from his duties, will not 'corrupt and taint [his] business' on the island (267-75). We will see as the play goes on just how difficult Othello finds it keep his passion and emotions in check and his mind upon his military responsibilities.

ACT 2 SCENE 1

Cyprus. A quayside

Enter MONTANO and two Gentlemen

MONTANO	What from the cape can you discern at sea?
First Gentleman	Nothing at all; it is a high-wrought flood;
	I cannot 'twixt the heaven and the main
	Descry a sail.
MONTANO	Methinks the wind hath spoke aloud at land –
	A fuller blast ne'er shook our battlements;
	If it hath ruffianed so upon the sea,
	What ribs of oak, when mountains melt on them,
	Can hold the mortise? What shall we hear of this?
Second Gentleman	A segregation of the Turkish fleet:
	For do but stand upon the foaming shore,
	The chidden billow seems to pelt the clouds,
	The wind-shaked surge with high and monstrous mane
	Seems to cast water on the burning Bear,
	And quench the guards of th'ever-fixed Pole:
	I never did like molestation view
	On the enchafed flood.
MONTANO	If that the Turkish fleet
	Be not ensheltered and embayed, they are drowned:
	It is impossible they bear it out.

Enter a third Gentleman

Third Gentleman	News, lads! Our wars are done:
	The desperate tempest hath so banged the Turks
	That their designment halts. A noble ship of Venice
	Hath seen a grievous wrack and sufferance
	On most part of their fleet.
MONTANO	How? Is this true?
Third Gentleman	The ship is here put in,
	A Veronese; Michael Cassio,
	Lieutenant to the warlike Moor Othello,
	Is come on shore; the Moor himself at sea,
	And is in full commission here for Cyprus.
MONTANO	I am glad on't; 'tis a worthy governor.
Third Gentleman	But this same Cassio, though he speak of comfort
	Touching the Turkish loss, yet he looks sadly
	And prays the Moor be safe; for they were parted
	With foul and violent tempest.
MONTANO	Pray heavens he be!
	For I have served him, and the man commands
	Like a full soldier. Let's to the seaside, ho! –
	As well to see the vessel that's come in
	As to throw out our eyes for brave Othello,
	Even till we make the main and th'aerial blue
	An indistinct regard.

Line numbers: 5, 10, 15, 20, 25, 30, 35, 40

Glossary
2 *high-wrought:* furiously agitated
3 *main:* the open sea
4 *Descry:* catch sight of
7 *ruffianed:* raged
8 *ribs of oak:* framing timbers of a ship
8 *mountains:* mountainous seas
9 *mortise:* joints that hold a ship's timber together
10 *segregation:* a splitting up
12 *chidden:* an older form of the past tense of 'chide'
13 *monstrous mane:* here the seas are compared to a wild beast
14 *the burning Bear:* a constellation, probably Ursa Minor (meaning 'Little Bear')
15 *th'ever-fixed Pole:* the Pole star, used by sea-farers to navigate
16 *molestation:* disturbance, turbulence
17 *enchafed flood:* furious flood
18 *embayed:* protected by a bay
22 *designment:* undertaking
23 *wrack:* destruction
23 *sufferance:* damage
27 *Veronesa:* presumably this was a vessel fitted out by Verona, which belonged to Venice
33 *Touching:* concerning
35 *tempest:* wild storm, commotion
39 *throw out our eyes for:* look for
40 *th'aerial blue:* the sky.
41 *An indistinct regard:* indistinguishable

Third Gentleman	Come, let's do so:
	For every minute is expectancy
	Of more arrivance.

Enter CASSIO

CASSIO	Thanks, you the valiant of this warlike isle
	That so approve the Moor. O, let the heavens	45
	Give him defence against the elements,
	For I have lost him on a dangerous sea.
MONTANO	Is he well shipped?
CASSIO	His barque is stoutly timbered, and his pilot
	Of very expert and approved allowance;	50
	Therefore my hopes, not surfeited to death,
	Stand in bold cure.
Voices *(shouting within)*	A sail, a sail, a sail!
CASSIO	What noise?
Second Gentleman	The town is empty; on the brow o' th' sea	55
	Stand ranks of people, and they cry 'A sail!'
CASSIO	My hopes do shape him for the governor.

A shot is heard

Second Gentlemen	They do discharge their shot of courtesy:
	Our friends, at least.
CASSIO	I pray you, sir, go forth,	60
	And give us truth who 'tis that is arrived.
Second Gentleman	I shall.

Exit

MONTANO	But, good lieutenant, is your general wived?
CASSIO	Most fortunately: he hath achieved a maid
	That paragons description and wild fame,
	One that excels the quirks of blazoning pens,	65
	And in th'essential vesture of creation,
	Does tire the ingener.

Enter second Gentleman

	How now! Who has put in?
Second Gentleman	'Tis one Iago, ensign to the general.
CASSIO	He's had most favourable and happy speed:
	Tempests themselves, high seas, and howling winds,	70
	The guttered rocks and congregated sands
	(Traitors ensteeped to clog the guiltless keel)
	As having sense of beauty, do omit
	Their mortal natures, letting go safely by
	The divine Desdemona.
MONTANO	What is she?	75
CASSIO	She that I spake of: our great captain's captain,
	Left in the conduct of the bold Iago,
	Whose footing near anticipates our thoughts
	A sennight's speed. Great Jove, Othello guard,
	And swell his sail with thine own powerful breath,	80
	That he may bless this bay with his tall ship,
	Make love's quick pants in Desdemona's arms,
	Give renewed fire to our extinct spirits

Enter DESDEMONA, EMILIA, IAGO, RODERIGO, and Attendants

	And bring all Cyprus comfort– O, behold,
	The riches of the ship is come on shore!	85
	Ye men of Cyprus, let her have your knees.

Glossary (right margin):

42 *expectancy:* expectation

43 *more arrivance:* arrival of more ships

49 *barque:* a ship, typically with three sails

50 *allowance:* reputation

51-52 *Therefore my hopes... bold cure:* without indulging in blind hope, Cassio is confident that Othello will survive the seas

57 *My hopes do shape him for:* I hope it is

64-67 *That paragons... ingener:* both her inner and outer beauty exceeds description

71 *guttered:* jagged

72 *ensteeped:* submerged

73-74 *do omit Their mortal natures:* refrain from indulging their deadly natures

79 *sennight:* a week

83 *extincted:* extinguished

41

Hail to thee, lady; and the grace of heaven,
Before, behind thee, and on every hand,
Enwheel thee round!

DESDEMONA   I thank you, valiant Cassio.
What tidings can you tell me of my lord?

CASSIO He is not yet arrived: nor know I aught
But that he's well and will be shortly here.

DESDEMONA O, but I fear – how lost you company?

CASSIO The great contention of the sea and skies
Parted our fellowship.

Voices shout within: 'A sail, a sail!'

               But, hark – a sail!

[A shot is heard]

Second Gentleman They give their greeting to the citadel:
This likewise is a friend.

CASSIO   See for the news.

Exit Second Gentleman

Good ensign, you are welcome. Welcome, mistress!

He kisses Emilia

Let it not gall your patience, good Iago,
That I extend my manners. 'Tis my breeding
That gives me this bold show of courtesy.

IAGO Sir, would she give you so much of her lips
As of her tongue she oft bestows on me,
You'd have enough.

DESDEMONA Alas, she has no speech.

IAGO In faith, too much!
I find it still when I have leave to sleep.
Marry, before your ladyship, I grant,
She puts her tongue a little in her heart,
And chides with thinking.

EMILIA   You have little cause to say so.

IAGO Come on, come on! You are pictures out of doors;
Bells in your parlours; wild-cats in your kitchens;
Saints in your injuries; devils being offended;
Players in your housewifery; and housewives
In your beds.

DESDEMONA   O, fie upon thee, slanderer!

IAGO Nay, it is true, or else I am a Turk:
You rise to play, and go to bed to work.

EMILIA You shall not write my praise.

IAGO   No, let me not.

DESDEMONA What wouldst thou write of me, if thou shouldst
     praise me?

IAGO O gentle lady, do not put me to't,
For I am nothing if not critical.

DESDEMONA Come on, assay – there's one gone to the harbour?

IAGO Ay, madam.

DESDEMONA I am not merry; but I do beguile
The thing I am by seeming otherwise.
Come, how wouldst thou praise me?

IAGO I am about it; but indeed my invention
Comes from my pate as birdlime does from frieze –
It plucks out brains and all. But my Muse labours,

---

89   *Enwheel:* encircle

90

95

100

102   *extend my manners:* take such unusual freedoms in
my behaviour

105

109   *still:* always

110

112   *and chides with thinking:* does not utter
her shrewish thoughts
113-117
  You are pictures... beds: Iago here describes women
as quiet in public, noisy and troublesome in the
home, domestically delinquent, and sexually
unprincipled

115

120

122   *put me to't:* put me to the test

124   *assay:* try

125

126   *beguile:* in this context, beguile meant to divert
attention from

130   130   *pate... frieze:* pate is an archaic word for head.
Birdlime was a sticky substance used to trap small
birds. Frieze was a type of coarse fabric

	And thus she is delivered.	
	If she be fair and wise: fairness and wit,	
	The one's for use, the other useth it.	
DESDEMONA	Well praised! How if she be black and witty?	135
IAGO	If she be black and thereto have a wit,	
	She'll find a white that shall her blackness hit.	
DESDEMONA	Worse and worse.	
EMILIA	How if fair and foolish?	
IAGO	She never yet was foolish that was fair,	
	For even her folly helped her to an heir.	140
DESDEMONA	These are old fond paradoxes to make fools	
	laugh i'th alehouse. What miserable praise hast	
	thou for her that's foul and foolish?	
IAGO	There's none so foul and foolish thereunto,	
	But does foul pranks which fair and wise ones do.	145
DESDEMONA	O heavy ignorance! Thou praisest the worst best.	
	But what praise couldst thou bestow on a deserving	
	woman indeed? One that, in the authority of her	
	merit, did justly put on the vouch of very malice itself?	
IAGO	She that was ever fair and never proud,	150
	Had tongue at will and yet was never loud,	
	Never lacked gold and yet went never gay,	
	Fled from her wish and yet said 'Now I may';	
	She that being angered, her revenge being nigh,	
	Bade her wrong stay and her displeasure fly;	155
	She that in wisdom never was so frail	
	To change the cod's head for the salmon's tail;	
	She that could think and ne'er disclose her mind,	
	See suitors following and not look behind:	
	She was a wight – if ever such wight were –	160
DESDEMONA	To do what?	
IAGO	To suckle fools and chronicle small beer.	
DESDEMONA	O most lame and impotent conclusion! Do not learn of	
	him, Emilia, though he be thy husband. How say you,	
	Cassio, is he not a most profane and liberal counsellor?	165
CASSIO	He speaks home, madam: you may relish him more	
	in the soldier than in the scholar.	
IAGO	(aside) He takes her by the palm – ay, well said, whisper! –	
	with as little a web as this will I ensnare as great a	
	fly as Cassio. – Ay, smile upon her, do! I will gyve	170
	thee in thine own courtship. – You say true, 'tis so,	
	indeed. – If such tricks as these strip you out of your	
	lieutenantry, it had been better you had not kissed	
	your three fingers so oft, which now again you are	
	most apt to play the sir in. – Very good, well kissed,	175
	and excellent courtesy! 'Tis so, indeed. – Yet again,	
	your fingers to your lips? Would they were	
	clyster-pipes for your sake.	
	Trumpets within	
	(Aloud) The Moor! I know his trumpet.	
CASSIO	'Tis truly so.	
DESDEMONA	Let's meet him and receive him.	
CASSIO	Lo, where he comes!	180

Glossary:

135 *black:* dark-haired
135 *witty:* clever

140 *folly:* wantonness
141 *fond:* foolish

143 *foul:* ugly or sluttish

145 *pranks:* sexual tricks
146 *heavy:* intense

149 *put on the vouch:* compel the approval

152 *gay:* showily dressed
153 *Fled from her...'Now I may':* turned her back on her desires despite knowing she was in a position to fulfil them

155 *Bade her wrong stay:* restrained her sense of injustice
156 *frail:* morally weak

160 *wight:* person

162 *small beer:* trivial events

165 *profane:* worldly

166-167 *relish him more in:* appreciate him more in the role of

170 *gyve:* fetter, ensnare

173-74 *kissed your three fingers:* a courtly gesture of flirtation

178 *clyster-pipes:* tubes used for injection

Enter OTHELLO and Attendants

OTHELLO	O, my fair warrior!
DESDEMONA	My dear Othello!
OTHELLO	It gives me wonder great as my content

To see you here before me. O my soul's joy,
If after every tempest come such calms,
May the winds blow till they have wakened death,   185
And let the labouring barque climb hills of seas
Olympus-high, and duck again as low
As hell's from heaven. If it were now to die,
'Twere now to be most happy; for I fear
My soul hath her content so absolute   190
That not another comfort like to this
Succeeds in unknown fate.

DESDEMONA   The heavens forbid
But that our loves and comforts should increase
Even as our days do grow.

OTHELLO   Amen to that, sweet powers!
I cannot speak enough of this content: 195
It stops me here, it is too much of joy.
They kiss
And this, and this the greatest discords be
That e'er our hearts shall make.

IAGO   *(aside)*   O, you are well tuned now!
But I'll set down the pegs that make this music,
As honest as I am.

OTHELLO   *(To Desdemona)*   Come, let us to the castle.   200
(To the rest)   News, friends: our wars are done, the Turks
are drowned.
How does my old acquaintance of this isle?–
Honey, you shall be well desired in Cyprus;
I have found great love amongst them. O my sweet,
I prattle out of fashion, and I dote   205
In mine own comforts! – I prithee, good Iago,
Go to the bay and disembark my coffers.
Bring thou the master to the citadel;
He is a good one, and his worthiness
Does challenge much respect. – Come, Desdemona,   210
Once more well met at Cyprus!

Exeunt OTHELLO, DESDEMONA, and Attendants

IAGO *(To a departing attendant)* Do thou meet me presently at the harbour.
(To Roderigo) Come hither, if thou be'st valiant – as they say base
men being in love have then a nobility in their
natures more than is native to them – list me: 215
the lieutenant tonight watches on the court of
guard. First, I must tell thee this: Desdemona is
directly in love with him.

RODERIGO   With him? Why, 'tis not possible.

IAGO   Lay thy finger thus, and let thy soul be instructed: 220
mark me with what violence she first loved the
Moor but for bragging, and telling her fantastical
lies. To love him still for prating? Let not

181 *fair warrior:* Othello is referring to her courage in accompanying him to the wars

187 *Olympus:* the mountain on which Greek gods were supposed to dwell

192 *Succeeds in unknown fate:* can possibly ensue in our unknowable, yet predetermined future

194 *as our days do grow:* as we grow older

199 *set down the pegs:* slacken the strings

205 *out of fashion:* unbecomingly
205-206 *I dote In mine own comforts!:* I am besotted with sheer happiness
207 *disembark my coffers:* unload my chests and trunks
208 *master:* ship's captain

210 *challenge:* claim
211 *well met at:* welcome to
212 *presently:* at once
213 *base men:* low-born men

220 *thus:* on the lips

thy discreet heart think it! Her eye must be fed.
And what delight shall she have to look on the
devil? When the blood is made dull with the act of
sport, there should be a game to inflame it, and (to
give satiety a fresh appetite) loveliness in favour,
sympathy in years, manners, and beauties – all which
the Moor is defective in. Now, for want of these
required conveniences, her delicate tenderness will
find itself abused, begin to heave the gorge,
disrelish and abhor the Moor; very nature will
instruct her in it, and compel her to some second
choice. Now sir, this granted (as it is a most
pregnant and unforced position), who stands so
eminent in the degree of this fortune, as Cassio
does – a knave very voluble, no further
conscionable than in putting on the mere form of
civil and humane seeming for the better compass
of his salt and most hidden loose affection? Why
none, why, none – a slipper and subtle knave, a
finder of occasion, that has an eye can stamp and
counterfeit advantages (though true advantage never
present itself), a devilish knave! Besides, the
knave is handsome, young, and hath all those
requisites in him that folly and green minds look
after – a pestilent complete knave, and the woman
hath found him already.

RODERIGO   I cannot believe that in her: she's full of most blessed
                condition.

IAGO   Blessed fig's end! The wine she drinks is made of
                grapes. If she had been blest, she would never
                have loved the Moor. Blest pudding! Didst thou
                not see her paddle with the palm of his hand?
                Didst not mark that?

RODERIGO   Yes, that I did – but that was but courtesy.

IAGO   Lechery, by this hand! – an index and obscure prologue
                to the history of lust and foul thoughts. They met
                so near with their lips that their breaths embraced
                together. Villanous thoughts, Roderigo! When these
                mutualities so marshal the way, hard at hand comes
                the master and main exercise, th'incorporate
                conclusion. Pish! But sir, be you ruled by me – I
                have brought you from Venice. Watch you tonight.
                For the command, I'll lay't upon you: Cassio knows
                you not; I'll not be far from you; do you find
                some occasion to anger Cassio, either by speaking
                too loud or tainting his discipline, or from what
                other course you please, which the time shall more
                favourably minister.

RODERIGO   Well.

IAGO   Sir, he's rash and very sudden in choler, and haply
                with his truncheon may strike at you – provoke him
                that he may; for even out of that will I cause these of
                Cyprus to mutiny, whose qualification shall come into
                no true taste again but by the displanting of Cassio.

225

227   *sport:* copulation

228   *satiety:* surfeit, feeding, indulgence

230

231   *conveniences:* points of fitness

232   *heave the gorge:* retch

233   *disrelish:* find disgusting

235

236   *pregnant:* cogent
236-237
       who...fortune: who is better placed to benefit from
       this turn of events
236   *voluble:* full of smooth-talking eloquence
239   *conscionable:* conscientious
240 240 *humane:* polite

242   *slipper:* slippery, deceitful
243   *stamp:* coin

245

250 250 *condition:* characteristics
251   *fig's end:* a worthless thing

254   *paddle with:* stroke
255

260

261   *mutualities:* exchanges of intimacy

265

268   *tainting:* sneering at

270

272   *choler:* angry
273   *truncheon:* officer's baton

275 275 *qualification:* dilution, appeasement

Iago constantly refers to O as a base creature

when she is sick of O she'll move away from the moor

Cassio was [ ] up well

she's the same as every one else

Cassio has a quick temper Iago knows this is easy to provoke

So shall you have a shorter journey to your desires by
the means I shall then have to prefer them; and the
impediment most profitably removed, without the
which there were no expectation of our prosperity.   280

RODERIGO   I will do this, if I can bring it to any opportunity.

IAGO   I warrant thee. Meet me by and by at the citadel.
I must fetch his necessaries ashore. Farewell.

RODERIGO   Adieu.

Exit

IAGO   That Cassio loves her, I do well believe't;   285
That she loves him, 'tis apt and of great credit.
The Moor (howbeit that I endure him not)
Is of a constant, loving, noble nature;
And I dare think he'll prove to Desdemona
A most dear husband. Now I do love her too,   290
Not out of absolute lust (though peradventure
I stand accountant for as great a sin)
But partly led to diet my revenge,
For that I do suspect the lusty Moor
Hath leapt into my seat – the thought whereof   295
Doth, like a poisonous mineral, gnaw my inwards;
And nothing can or shall content my soul
Till I am evened with him, wife for wife;
Or, failing so, yet that I put the Moor
At least into a jealousy so strong   300
That judgment cannot cure – which thing to do,
If this poor trash of Venice, whom I trace
For his quick hunting, stand the putting on,
I'll have our Michael Cassio on the hip,
Abuse him to the Moor in the rank garb   305
(For I fear Cassio with my nightcap too)
Make the Moor thank me, love me, and reward me
For making him egregiously an ass
And practising upon his peace and quiet
Even to madness. 'Tis here, but yet confused: 310
Knavery's plain face is never seen till used.

Exit

A wife for a wife

---

282 *I warrant thee:* I assure you

283 *his necessaries:* his luggage

286 *'tis apt and of great credit:* fitted to the facts
and entirely credible

291 *peradventure:* 'as it happens' or
'it may be the case that'
292 *accountant:* accountable
293 *diet:* feed

295 *leapt into my seat:* had a romantic relationship
with his wife

302 *trash:* worthless person

303 *stand the putting on:* do what I incite him to

304 *on the hip:* at my mercy

305 *rank garb:* gross manner

308 *egregiously:* outrageously

309 *practising upon:* plotting against

A terrible storm rages on the island of Cyprus. Cassio arrives with news that Turkish fleet has been destroyed by the tempest. The ship carrying Iago, Desdemona and Emilia also makes it through the storm. There is some witty banter as they wait nervously for the ship carrying Othello. Othello finally does appear on the quayside. He rejoices that the Turkish threat has passed and is overjoyed to be reunited with Desdemona.

Iago persuades Roderigo that Cassio and Desdemona are in love. He convinces Roderigo to assist in a plan to undo Cassio. While Cassio stands guard that night Roderigo will insult or attack him, provoking the quick-tempered Cassio to abandon his post. Iago will use this slip-up to have Cassio stripped of the lieutenantship. Iago also considers the possibility of destroying Othello's 'peace and quiet' and driving him into an insanely jealous rage.

ACTION

LINE BY LINE

▶ LINES 1-43: A RAGING TEMPEST

This scene takes place on a quayside in Cyprus, whose people fear invasion by the approaching Turkish fleet. Also on their way to Cyprus, of course, are a number of ships containing Othello and his companions. (One ship carries Cassio; another carries Iago and Desdemona, while a third belongs to Othello). A terrible storm is raging.

Montano, the governor of Cyprus, and some of his gentlemen discuss the tempest. Montano claims that it is the worst storm ever to hit Cyprus. The island's battlements, he suggests, have never felt such ferocious wind: 'a fuller blast ne'er shook our battlements' (6). The storm, according to one of the gentlemen, is so ferocious that 'Nothing at all' (2) can be seen at sea. Another gentlemen describes how the 'enchafed' or furious waters seem to threaten even the stars themselves (10-7).

Montano speculates that the Turkish fleet must have been 'drowned' in the stormy conditions (17-9). Another gentleman confirms this. He has spoken to Cassio, whose ship has survived the storm and reached Cyprus safely. Cassio witnessed how the 'desperate tempest' brought 'wrack and sufferance' to the Turkish ships, forcing them to halt their invasion plans (20-4). The elements, therefore, seem to have saved Cyprus from the Turkish hordes: 'Our wars are done' (20).

▶ LINES 44-: CASSIO ARRIVES

Cassio himself arrives. He is worried because Othello's ship has become lost on the stormy ocean: 'I have lost him on a dangerous sea' (47). He prays that Othello will survive the storm: 'O, let the heavens / Give him defence against the elements' (45-6). The fact that Othello's ship is 'stoutly timber'd' and has an 'expert' pilot gives him hope (49-50).

IAGO

BACKGROUND

This scene also reinforces our sense of the 'class difference' between Iago and the other characters. While they are noble lords and ladies he is a humble soldier. Cassio suggests that he lacks a gentleman's scholarly education: 'you may relish him more in the soldier than in the scholar' (166-7). According to Cassio, he 'speaks home', suggesting that his manner of speech is plain or common, and lacks a gentleman's finesse (166). In lines 101-2 Cassio seems to hint that Iago lacks the 'breeding' he himself possesses.

Iago takes delight in simple, vulgar rhymes that would be deemed inappropriate for a lord or lady. According to Desdemona these little poems are a basic form of entertainment aimed at the lower classes, designed 'to make fools laugh i'th'alehouse' (141-2).

A BRILLIANT ACTOR

Once again we note in this scene how no one suspects what Iago is up to or identifies the malevolent and malicious nature of his personality. Cassio and Othello refer to their nemesis as 'good ensign' and 'good Iago' reinforcing our sense of how greatly they have misjudged his character (100, 101, 206).

Indeed Cassio and Desdemona regard him as being 'honest' in the sense of simple or unsophisticated. To them he is little more than an amusing character with his simple rhymes and bad jokes from the alehouse. Little do they suspect that this soldier will bring ruin to them all: 'But I'll set down the pegs that make this music,/ As honest as I am' (199-200).

A MASTER PLOTTER

In this scene Iago once again emerges as a master plotter of persuasion and manipulation. He overcomes Roderigo's misgivings and persuades him that Cassio and Desdemona are in love. He also manipulates Roderigo into insulting or attacking Cassio that evening while the latter is on guard duty.

Yet this scene also reinforces our sense that Iago's schemes work more through brilliant improvisation than meticulous planning. Indeed he seems to be juggling several plots or potential plots at the same time:

- He would also be avenged by sleeping with Desdemona (287-8).
- Othello, he believes, has slept with Emilia. He would be avenged by driving Othello insane with jealousy (299-301).
- Cassio, he believes, is in love with Desdemona. He will use this to 'ensnare' Cassio and bring him down (168-70).
- He will provoke Cassio into behaving badly while on guard duty ensuring Cassio is stripped of the lieutenantship.

By the scene's end he has a rough plan regarding how to proceed against Othello. Yet his scheme's outlines are still somewhat blurred and out of focus: ''Tis here, but yet confused' (310). It is only when he actually puts his plan into practise that its fine details will emerge: 'Knavery's plain face is never seen till used' (311).

no body suspects the villian until he reveals themself

A SENSE OF SUPERIORITY

Iago's extreme self-belief is once again in evidence throughout this scene. He boldly declares to the audience that he will 'ensnare' Cassio and detune the instruments that make the music of Othello's newfound joy: 'O, you are well tuned now! / But I'll set down the pegs that make this music' (168-70, 198-9).

He is sure he can cause the local people of Cyprus to 'mutiny' and demand Cassio's removal as lieutenant (274-6). He is certain that Othello, too, will be manipulated in this regard, 'making him egregiously an ass' (308). He is equally confident that he will be able to manipulate Othello's mental state, destroying his 'peace and quiet' by filling his mind with jealousy.

IAGO'S LACK OF RESPECT FOR CONVENTIONAL VALUES

Iago has little time for any romantic or idealistic idea of love. He regards women as untrustworthy and sexually promiscuous, his sexist attitude highlighted in the rhymes and witty banter he shares with Desdemona. Loving relationships, he suggests, are inclined to fizzle out once sexual satisfaction has been achieved (226-7).

This cynical attitude toward love is also suggested when he describes how Desdemona's 'violent' passions must soon change again and when he suggests that her 'eye must be fed' with physical beauty if her interest in the relationship is to be maintained (224). He has no time for the view that Desdemona is 'full of the most blessed condition',

IAGO

is a particularly noble or virtuous person. In his view she's as changeable and untrustworthy as anybody else. Like everyone else 'The wine she drinks is made of grapes' (251-2).

IAGO'S SHIFTING MOTIVATIONS

Iago once again refers to his suspicion that Othello has slept with his wife Emilia (294-5). The thought of this betrayal, he says, eats him up inside: 'the thought whereof/ Doth, like a poisonous mineral,/gnaw my inwards' (295-6). He is determined, then, to get his revenge on Othello 'wife for wife' (298). Many readers, however, find Iago's motivations too shifting and complex to be pinned down by even this straightforward statement of intent.

The townspeople have gathered on a nearby cliff to watch for vessels that might have survived the storm (55-6). A ship is spotted in the distance and discharges its 'shot of courtesy', the signal that it is friend rather than foe (58-9). Hopeful that it might be Othello's vessel Cassio sends one of the gentlemen to investigate (60-1). It turns out, however, that this is the ship carrying Iago and Desdemona (68, 74).

▶ LINES: DESDEMONA, IAGO AND EMILIA ARRIVE

Cassio greets the new arrivals. Desdemona, naturally, is concerned as to the whereabouts of her husband (90).Cassio tells how he and Othello became separated by the storm but assures her that everything will be all right: 'nor know I aught/ But that he's well and will be shortly here' (91-2). At that moment yet another ship is sighted and a gentleman goes to investigate (96-8).

Cassio makes much of Desdemona's beauty:
• Before she arrives he describes her to Montano as a woman whose beauty is beyond description: 'A maid/ that paragons description and wild fame' (63-4).
• Her good looks, he says, cannot be captured by the words of poets: it 'excels the quirks of blazoning pens' (65).
• When she reaches the quay he greets her with extravagant praise: 'Hail to thee, lady! And the grace of heaven/ Before, behind thee, and on every hand' (87-8).
• He describes her as the precious cargo of the ship that carried her: 'The riches of the ship is come on shore!' (85).

• He urges the men of Cyprus to kneel before this divinely beautiful creature: 'Ye men of Cyprus, let her have your knees' (86).
• He even suggests that the raging elements, the 'high seas, and howling winds', were calmed by the sight of her beauty and went against their own destructive natures, allowing her ship safe passage: 'As having sense of beauty, do omit/ Their mortal natures, letting go safely by/ The divine Desdemona' (73-5).

▶ LINES 81-175: A NERVOUS WAIT

The assembled characters wait nervously, hoping that the latest ship to be sighted is indeed Othello's. There is some idle banter. Iago makes a variety of witty yet sexist jokes about women and wives:
• He describes how his wife Emilia nags and berates him with her cutting tongue (104-6).
• He describes women in general as being hypocritical, nagging, untrustworthy and sexually promiscuous (113-07).
• He recites or composes a variety of rhymes wittily describing different types of women, for example a woman who is 'black and witty' or a woman who is 'foolish and fair' (129-62).

Desdemona banters freely with Iago, both egging him on and playfully criticising his sexist rhymes. Yet she joins this light-hearted conversation only to take her mind off the nervous wait for Othello: 'I am not merry, but I do beguile/ The thing I am by seeming otherwise' (126-7). By verbally sparring with Iago she hopes to 'beguile' or assuage her tension and apprehension.

Iago notices how Cassio treats Desdemona with 'courtship', with the exaggerated respect and courtesy a knight might show his lady: 'Very good, well kissed, and excellent courtesy!' (175-6). He watches Cassio 'play the sir', taking Desdemona's hand, smiling at her and repeatedly kissing his own three finges in a gesture of courtly respect (173-7).

Iago feels he can use this display of courtly charm against Cassio and have him stripped of the office of lieutenant: 'with as little a web as this will I/ensnare as great a fly as Cassio' (169-70).

▶ LINES 175-207:
OTHELLO HIMSELF FINALLY ARRIVES

Iago hears a trumpeter blow Othello's distinctive signal, indicating that the ship recently arrived in the harbour does indeed belong to the Moor (174). Othello reaches the quay and there is a joyful reunion between him and Desdemona.

Othello says that if he died now he would do so a happy man, having seen Desdemona once again: 'If it were now to die, / 'Twere now to be most happy' (188-9). He fears that he will never know such 'content' again (189-92). If every storm had such a blissful conclusion he would be happy for the winds to blow until they have waken the dead themselves (184-5). Desdemona prays that their happiness will only grow as their years together pass (192-4).

Othello declares to those assembled that 'our wars are done' (201) because the Turks have all 'drowned' in the storm (201-2). Yet because there is still business to be taken care of he departs for the citadel. Iago is instructed to follow, bringing with him Othello's 'coffers' and the 'master' or captain of his ship (206-8).

▶ LINES 208-248: IAGO BAMBOOZLES RODERIGO

Iago is left alone with Roderigo once again. He tells him that Cassio and Desdemona are in love or are in the process of falling in love. He gives several reasons for why he believes this:
• The suddenness or 'violence' with which she fell in love with Othello means she could fall equally suddenly in love with Cassio: 'mark me with what violence she first loved the Moor' (221-2).

OTHELLO

OTHELLO AS SOLDIER

Though Othello only briefly appears in this scene, we still learn much about his character from the remarks of others. The scene reinforces our sense of Othello as 'the warlike Moor', as a fierce warrior and gifted general (28).

All of Cyprus, it seems, holds Othello in very high esteem. Othello himself mentions how he has 'found great love' there (204). Cassio describes how Cyprus does 'approve the Moor' and how his arrival will lift the spirits of the entire island: 'That he may bless this bay with his tall ship… And bring all Cyprus comfort' (45, 81-4).

Montano, currently in charge of Cyprus, praises Othello's military leadership: 'For I have served him, and the man commands/ Like a full soldier' (36-7). He seems glad that Othello will be taking over as governer: 'I am glad on't; 'tis a worthy governor' (31). Othello clearly takes his duties as military commander very seriously. His wastes little time on his arrival but heads straight to the citadel to take care of business (200).

OTHELLO'S FUNDAMENTAL DECENCY

In his soliloquy Iago refers to the fundamentally decent nature of Othello's personality. He hates the Moor but admits that he is 'of a constant, loving, noble nature' (288). Othello, he feels, will be a great husband to Desdemona: 'And I dare think he'll prove to Desdemona/ A most dear husband' (289-90).

We see this sweet and gentle side of Othello's nature when he comes ashore. He is presented as a loving husband who cares deeply about Desdemona. He is obviously overjoyed to see his new wife, referring to her as 'my soul's joy' (183). The happiness she brings him is too great for words 'I cannot speak enough of this content; / It stops me here; it is too much of joy' (195-6). It is perhaps his noble and admirable nature as much as his military prowess that has won Othello such approval from the people of Cyprus and Venice.

OTHELLO'S ELOQUENCE

In the play's first act Othello spoke with extraordinary eloquence, in a formal and deliberate style well suited to a courtier or a noble man. His manner of speech throughout the act was extremely elaborate, poetic and controlled. In this scene, however, emotion causes Othello's eloquence to break down somewhat. He is so overcome with joy on seeing Desdemona that he 'prattles' or babbles in manner he considers 'out of fashion' or unbecoming to his station as general (205). We shall see as the play goes on how extreme emotion continues to negatively affect his eloquence.

- Othello's foreign appearance means he isn't handsome enough to sustain Desdemona's interest: 'Her eye must be fed. And what delight shall she have to look on the devil?' (224-6).
- Othello lacks the qualities attractive to a youthful or 'green' person like Desdemona: 'loveliness in favour, sympathy in years, manners, and beauties – all which the Moor is defective in' (228-30).

Cassio, however, does possess such qualities: 'Besides, the knave is handsome, young, and hath all those requisites in him that folly and green minds look after' (245-8). He claims Desdemona's attraction to Cassio was obvious by the way they held hands while waiting nervously for Othello to arrive: 'Didst thou not see her paddle with the palm of his hand? Didst not mark that?' (253-5).

Their lips, he says, almost touched when they were speaking: 'They met so near with their lips that their breaths embraced together' (258-60). Roderigo is initially sceptical that Desdemona is in love with Cassio: 'With him? Why, 'tis not possible' (219). He feels they held hands because of 'courtesy' rather that sexual desire (256). Desdemona, he believes, is simply not the kind of person who quickly tires of a lover and seeks satisfaction elsewhere: 'I cannot believe that in her: she's full of most blessed condition' (250).

Iago, however, is adamant that Cassio and Desdemona are filled with lustful or lecherous thoughts toward one another: 'Lechery, by this hand! – an index and obscure prologue to the history of lust and foul thoughts' (257-8). Cassio, he maintains, is an obstacle or 'impediment' that prevents Roderigo gaining Desdemona's affection, just as he stands in the way of Iago gaining the lieutenantship: 'and the impediment most profitably removed, without the which there were no expectation of our prosperity' (278-80).

▶ LINES 249-275: IAGO'S PLAN TO UNDO CASSIO

He tells Roderigo of his plan to remove Cassio from the equation. Cassio, he says, will be on guard duty that very night: 'the lieutenant tonight watches on the court of guard' (216-7). He tends to behave rashly and exhibit bad judgement when angered: 'Sir, he's rash and very sudden in choler' (272). Roderigo, who is a stranger to Cassio, must find some way of insulting and provoking him while he stands watch: 'do you find some occasion to anger Cassio, either by speaking too loud or tainting his discipline' (266-8).

OTHELLO AND DESDEMONA

DESDEMONA

This scene reinforces our sense of Desdemona as a great beauty. Cassio describes how she is too beautiful for words and declares that raging elements must have calmed in tribute to her beauty. We already know that Othello loves her deeply and that she is the object of Roderigo's obsession. In this scene Iago, too, admits that he lusts for her (290).

And there is the possibility that Cassio has feelings for her as well.

She seems to be genuinely in love with her new husband. The first thing she does when she reaches the quay is to ask about his whereabouts (90). She waits nervously for news of Othello, bantering with Iago in order to distract herself from the nervous tension that fills her (126-7). She seems overjoyed when Othello finally arrives, declaring her hope that there 'loves and comforts' will increase as they grow old together (192-4).

Yet in this scene, as in the previous one, Desdemona comes across as strong-willed and assertive. We get the sense that Desdemona is no mere gentle princess. She seems a worthy verbal sparring partner for Iago, simultaneously encouraging and playfully criticising his bawdy rhymes. She seems unfazed and unembarrassed by this somewhat crude banter suited to men sitting around in the 'alehouse'.

CASSIO

This scene once again stresses once again Cassio's noble background. He is a man, as he declares himself, of 'breeding' (102). He perhaps has his own first class education in mind when he refers to Iago as a soldier rather than a scholar (166-7). He has been brought up to treat women in an extremely chivalrous and courteous manner. We see this when he kisses Emilia as she arrives at the quayside (101-3). It is also evident in how he treats Desdemona as they nervously wait for Othello to arrive, with Iago bitterly remarking how Cassio exhibits great 'courtship' or courtesy and 'play the sir' (171, 175).

Cassio clearly has the greatest of regard and respect for Othello. On arrival he praises the people of Cyprus because they 'approve the Moor' (44-5). He hopes that the ship sighted in the bay belongs to Othello and prays that the Moor will reach the island safely: 'Great Jove, Othello guard, / And swell his sail with thine own powerful breath' (57, 79-80). He is convinced that Othello's arrival will 'bring all Cyprus comfort' (84).

We are also reminded that Cassio is something of ladies' man or, at the very least, is highly attractive to the opposite sex. Iago stresses that Cassio has all the qualities young ladies look for in a man: 'Besides, the knave is handsome, young, and hath all those requisites in him that folly and green minds look after' (245-8).

Yet Iago also refers to a darker aspect of Cassio's character: he has a quick temper and often exhibits rashness and poor decision making when angry: 'Sir he's rash and very sudden in choler' (272).

TALK ABOUT IT

Iago describes Cassio as a 'pestilent complete knave', as a 'devilsih', wicked and dishonest person (245, 248). Cassio he says is a sneaky person, a 'slipper and subtle knave', who hides his lusts and other failings behind a 'civil and humane' exterior (240, 242). According to Iago, Cassio is always on the lookout for personal advantage, for occasions to get what he wants: 'a finder of occasion, that has an eye can stamp and counterfeit advantages' (242-4). Based on what you've read so far do you think there's evidence to support Iago's damning view of Cassio's personality? Or is Iago's judgment here coloured by jealousy and resentment?

This, he says, will cause Cassio to act unprofessionally, in a manner unbecoming the role of night watch man: 'haply with his truncheon may strike at you' (272-3). Iago is confident he will be able to use such a slip up against Cassio, by getting the local officers of Cyprus to demand his removal as lieutenant (274-6). Roderigo, despite his earlier misgivings, agrees to participate in this scheme (281).

▶ LINES 276-: IAGO REVEALS MORE OF HIS THINKING

In a soliloquy Iago reveals more about his plotting. He will use Roderigo, this 'poor trash of Venice', to get Cassio 'on the hip' or in a weak and vulnerable position (302-4). He will then criticise or 'abuse' Cassio to Othello, ensuring that Cassio loses the lieutenantship (305). Iago is confident that Othello will reward him for his efforts even though all the while he is being manipulative and deceitful: 'Make the Moor thank me, love me, and reward me / For making him egregiously an ass' (307-8).

As we have seen, he suspects that Othello has slept with his wife Emilia: 'For that I do suspect the lusty Moor / Hath leapt into my seat' (294-5). The thought tortures him, filling him with a jealous rage: 'the thought whereof / Doth, like a poisonous mineral, gnaw my inwards' (295-6). He is determined to get even: 'And nothing can or shall content my soul / Till I am evened with him, wife for wife' (297-8).

He considers the possibility of sleeping with Desdemona himself. As it happens ('peradventure') (291) he does have lustful feelings toward her: 'I stand accountant for as great a sin' (292). He would sleep with her but mainly out of his desire for revenge, to do to Othello what he thinks Othello did to him: 'But partly led to diet my revenge' (293).

Yet he also considers another route to vengeance. If he cannot sleep with Desdemona he can at least make Othello insane with jealousy: 'Or, failing so, yet that I put the Moor / At least into a jealousy so strong / That judgment cannot cure' (299-301). He will gnaw away at Othello's 'peace and quiet' (309) until the Moor is demented with rage: 'And practising upon his peace and quiet / Even to madness'(309-10). ◆

OTHELLO AND DESDEMONA

CHARACTER DEVELOPMENT

RODERIGO

In this scene Roderigo comes across once more as Iago's gullible dupe. Iago convinces him that Cassio and Desdemona are in love, overcoming his misgivings on the matter wth relative ease. He persuades him to provoke Cassio while he stands guard that night, with a view to getting Cassio disgraced and removed from office. Roderigo agrees to participate in this scheme, believing Iago when he tells him that Cassio's fall will leave him with a 'shorter journey' (277) to Desdemona's affections: 'I will do this, if I can bring it to any opportunity' (281).

✎ WRITE ABOUT IT

Iago seems to genuinely believe that Cassio and Desdemona are in love: 'That Cassio loves her, I do well believe't; / That she loves him, 'tis apt and of great credit' (285-6). Do you agree with his assessment? Write a couple of paragraphs outlining the reasons for your answer.

You may wish to consider the following:
• Cassio's exaggerated praise of Desdemona's beauty.
• His declaration of hope that Othello will soon arrive to make 'love's quick pants' in Desdemona's arms.
• The display of courtly affection whereby Cassio takes Desdemona's hand.
• The various subtle possibilities that exist for the actors playing these two parts.

ACT 2

SCENE 2

A street

Enter Othello's herald with a proclamation

HERALD   *(reads)* 'It is Othello's pleasure, our noble and valiant
general, that, upon certain tidings now arrived,
importing the mere perdition of the Turkish fleet,
every man put himself into triumph: some to dance,
some to make bonfires, each man to what sport and
revels his addiction leads him; for, besides these
beneficial news, it is the celebration of his
nuptial.' – So much was his pleasure should be
proclaimed. All offices are open and there is full
liberty of feasting from this present hour of five
till the bell have told eleven. Heaven bless the
isle of Cyprus and our noble general, Othello!

Exit

3   *mere perdition:* absolute destruction

4   *put himself into triumph:* prepare himself for
public celebration

5

9   *offices:* rooms in a house, castle or public palace
devoted to domestic services. e.g. kitchens, pantries etc.

10

A celebrations of the defeat of
the turks & Othellos wedding

ACT 2 SCENE 3

A hall in the castle

Enter OTHELLO, DESDEMONA, CASSIO, and attendants

OTHELLO	Good Michael, look you to the guard tonight.
	Let's teach ourselves that honourable stop
	Not to out-sport discretion.
CASSIO	Iago hath direction what to do;
	But notwithstanding, with my personal eye
	Will I look to't.
OTHELLO	Iago is most honest.
	Michael, good night. Tomorrow with your earliest,
	Let me have speech with you. – Come, my dear love,
	The purchase made, the fruits are to ensue:
	That profit's yet to come 'tween me and you.
	Good night.

Exeunt OTHELLO, DESDEMONA, and Attendants
Enter IAGO

CASSIO	Welcome, Iago. We must to the watch.
IAGO	Not this hour, lieutenant: 'tis not yet ten o' th' clock. Our general cast us thus early for the love of his Desdemona – who let us not therefore blame: he hath not yet made wanton the night with her, and she is sport for Jove. JUPITOV
CASSIO	She's a most exquisite lady.
IAGO	And, I'll warrant her, full of game.
CASSIO	Indeed, she's a most fresh and delicate creature.
IAGO	What an eye she has! Methinks it sounds a parley to provocation.
CASSIO	An inviting eye – and yet methinks right modest.
IAGO	And when she speaks, is't not an alarum to love?
CASSIO	She is indeed perfection.
IAGO	Well, happiness to their sheets! Come, lieutenant, I have a stoup of wine, and near without are a brace of Cyprus gallants that would fain have a measure to the health of black Othello.
CASSIO	Not tonight, good Iago: I have very poor and unhappy brains for drinking. I could well wish courtesy would invent some other custom of entertainment.
IAGO	O, they are our friends! But one cup – I'll drink for you.
CASSIO	I have drunk but one cup tonight – and that was craftily qualified too – and behold what innovation it makes here. I am unfortunate in the infirmity, and dare not task my weakness with any more.
IAGO	What, man? 'Tis a night of revels; the gallants desire it.

5

10

14 *cast:* dismissed

15

✳ 17 *Jove:* Classical mythology is full of stories of Jupiter's amours with mortal women

20

21-2 *sounds a parley to provocation:* arouses lustful thoughts

7 *with your earliest:* at your earliest convenience

9 *the fruits are to ensue:* The marriage has not yet been consummated

25

26 *stoup:* jug

27-8 *would fain have a measure to the health:* want a measure (of wine) to toast the health

29-30 *I have very poor and unhappy brains for drinking:* I have a bad head for liquor

30

33 *I'll drink for you:* I'll drink in your place

35

35 *qualified:* mixed with water

CASSIO	Where are they?	40
IAGO	Here at the door. I pray you call them in.	
CASSIO	I'll do't, but it dislikes me.	
Exit		
IAGO	If I can fasten but one cup upon him,	

43 *fasten:* force

With that which he hath drunk tonight already,
He'll be as full of quarrel and offence   45
As my young mistress' dog. Now my sick fool
  Roderigo,
Whom love hath turned almost the wrong side out,
To Desdemona hath tonight caroused
Potations pottle-deep; and he's to watch.

49 *pottle-deep:* to the bottom of a two-quart tankard

Three else of Cyprus – noble, swelling spirits   50

50 *swelling:* lively

That hold their honours in a wary distance,

51 *hold their honours in a wary distance:* are quick to take offence at any suspected insult

The very elements of this warlike isle–
Have I tonight flustered with flowing cups,
And they watch too. Now 'mongst this flock of
  drunkards
Am I to put our Cassio in some action   55

55 *put our Cassio in some action:* push our friend Cassio into some fight

That may offend the isle. But here they come.

Enter CASSIO, MONTANO and Gentlemen

If consequence do but approve my dream,

57 *consequence:* what happens

My boat sails freely, both with wind and stream.

CASSIO	Fore God, they have given me a rouse already.	

59 *rouse:* large glass

MONTANO	Good faith, a little one – not past a pint,	60
	As I am a soldier!	
IAGO	Some wine, ho!	
(sings)	And let me the canakin clink, clink,	

63 *canakin:* small can

       And let me the canakin clink.

63-7 *And let...soldier drink:* possibly a popular drinking song of the time

         A soldier's a man;   65
         O, man's life's but a span–
         Why, then, let a soldier drink.
Some wine, boys!

CASSIO	Fore God, an excellent song!	
IAGO	I learned it in England, where indeed, they are	

most potent in potting. Your Dane, your German, and   70

70 *potting:* drinking

your swag-bellied Hollander – drink, ho! – are nothing

71 *swag-bellied:* having a great swaying paunch

to your English. C C

CASSIO	Is your Englishman so expert in his drinking?	
IAGO	Why, he drinks you, with facility your Dane dead	

drunk; he sweats not to overthrow your Almain; he   75

75 *Almain:* German

gives your Hollander a vomit ere the next pottle
can be filled.

CASSIO	To the health of our general!	
MONTANO	I am for it, lieutenant; and I'll do you justice.	
IAGO	O sweet England!	80
(sings)	King Stephen was a worthy peer,	

    His breeches cost him but a crown;
He held them sixpence all too dear,
    With that he called the tailor lown.

84 *lown:* loon, rogue

He was a wight of high renown,   85
    And thou art but of low degree:
'Tis pride that pulls the country down,

	Then take thy old cloak about thee.	
	Some wine, ho!	
CASSIO	Fore God, this is a more exquisite song than the other!	90
IAGO	Will you hear't again?	
CASSIO	No, for I hold him to be unworthy of his place that	
	does those things. Well, God's above all, and there	
	be souls must be saved, and there be souls must not	
	be saved.	95
IAGO	It's true, good lieutenant.	
CASSIO	For mine own part – no offence to the general, nor	
	any man of quality – I hope to be saved.	
IAGO	And so do I too, lieutenant.	
CASSIO	Ay; but, by your leave, not before me: the	100
	lieutenant is to be saved before the ensign. Let's	
	have no more of this: let's to our affairs. God forgive	
	us our sins! Gentlemen, let's look to our business.	
	Do not think, gentlemen, I am drunk: this is my	
	ensign; this is my right hand, and this is my left.	105
	I am not drunk now: I can stand well enough, and	
	Ispeak well enough.	
Gentlemen	Excellent well.	
CASSIO	Why, very well then – you must not think, then, that I	
	am drunk.	

Exit

MONTANO	To th'platform, masters, come: let's set the watch.	
IAGO	You see this fellow that is gone before?	110
	He's a soldier fit to stand by Caesar	
	And give direction; and do but see his vice–	
	'Tis to his virtue a just equinox,	
	The one as long as th'other. 'Tis pity of him:	
	I fear the trust Othello puts him in,	115
	On some odd time of his infirmity,	
	Will shake this island.	
MONTANO	But is he often thus?	
IAGO	'Tis evermore the prologue to his sleep:	
	He'll watch the horologe a double set	120
	If drink rock not his cradle.	
MONTANO	It were well	
	The general were put in mind of it.	
	Perhaps he sees it not, or his good nature	
	Prizes the virtue that appears in Cassio,	
	And looks not on his evils: is not this true?	125

Enter RODERIGO

IAGO	*(aside to Roderigo)* How now, Roderigo!	
	I pray you, after the lieutenant go.	

Exit RODERIGO

MONTANO	And 'tis great pity that the noble Moor	
	Should hazard such a place as his own second	
	With one of an ingraft infirmity:	130
	It were an honest action to say	
	So to the Moor.	
IAGO	Not I, for this fair island!	
	I do love Cassio well, and would do much	
	To cure him of this evil–	

92-5 *No, for I hold him to be unworthy...souls must not be saved:* Cassio is already drunk, as Shakespeare indicates by his moralizing and theology

116 *On some odd time of his infirmity:* at some unpredictable moment when he is overcome by his weakness

120 *He'll watch the horologe a double set:* He will stay awake for two complete revolutions of the clock

	Voices within cry 'Help! Help!'	
	But, hark! what noise?	135

Enter CASSIO driving in RODERIGO

CASSIO	'Swounds, you rogue, you rascal!	
MONTANO	What's the matter, lieutenant?	
CASSIO	A knave teach me my duty! I'll beat the knave into a	
	twiggen bottle!	
RODERIGO	Beat me?	
CASSIO	Dost thou prate, rogue?	140
	Striking RODERIGO	
MONTANO	Nay, good lieutenant! I pray you, sir, hold your hand.	
CASSIO	Let me go, sir, or I'll knock you o'er the mazard.	
MONTANO	Come, come, you're drunk.	
CASSIO	Drunk?	
	They fight	145
IAGO *(Aside to Roderigo)*	Away, I say! Go out and cry 'a mutiny!'	146

Exit RODERIGO

	Nay, good lieutenant! God's will, gentlemen!	
	Help, ho! Lieutenant! Sir Montano! Sir!	
	Help, masters! Here's a goodly watch indeed!	
	A Bell rings	
	Who's that which rings the bell? Diablo!– Ho!	150
	The town will rise. God's will, lieutenant, hold!	
	You'll be ashamed for ever!	

Enter OTHELLO, and attendants with weapons

OTHELLO	What is the matter here?	
MONTANO	'Swounds, I bleed still!	
	I am hurt to the death.	155
(Lunging at Cassio)	He dies!	
OTHELLO	Hold, for your lives!	
IAGO	Hold, ho! Lieutenant! Sir Montano! Gentlemen!	
	Have you forgot all sense of place and duty?	
	Hold! The general speaks to you; hold, for shame!	
OTHELLO	Why, how now! Ho! From whence ariseth this?	160
	Are we turned Turks, and to ourselves do that	
	Which Heaven hath forbid the Ottomites?	
	For Christian shame, put by this barbarous brawl!	
	He that stirs next to carve for his own rage	
	Holds his soul light: he dies upon his motion.	165
	Silence that dreadful bell: it frights the isle	
	From her propriety. What is the matter, masters?	
	Honest Iago, that looks dead with grieving,	
	Speak: who began this?– On thy love I charge thee!	
IAGO	I do not know. Friends all, but now, even now,	170
	In quarter and in terms like bride and groom	
	Divesting them for bed; and then but now,	
	As if some planet had unwitted men,	
	Swords out, and tilting one at other's breasts	
	In opposition bloody. I cannot speak	175
	Any beginning to this peevish odds;	
	And would in action glorious I had lost	
	Those legs that brought me to a part of it!	
OTHELLO	How comes it, Michael, you are thus forgot?	
CASSIO	I pray you pardon me, I cannot speak.	180

138   *twiggen-bottle:* bottle cased in wicker-work

142   *mazard:* head

146   *mutiny:* riot; revolt against authority

150   *bell:* church bells were customarily rung as a public alarm
150   *Diablo:* the devil

164   *He that stirs next to carve for his own rage:* Othello literalizes the proverbial expression 'To carve for oneself', meaning to please or help oneself, in this case he means to satisfy his personal outrage by stabbing as he pleases
165   *upon his motion:* the instant he moves

171   *quarter:* friendship
172   *Divesting them:* undressing

176   *peevish odds:* foolish quarrel

OTHELLO   Worthy Montano, you were wont be civil;
The gravity and stillness of your youth
The world hath noted; and your name is great
In mouths of wisest censure. What's the matter,
That you unlace your reputation thus,   185
And spend your rich opinion for the name
Of a night-brawler? Give me answer to it.

MONTANO   Worthy Othello, I am hurt to danger:
Your officer Iago can inform you –
While I spare speech, which something now
     offends me –   190
Of all that I do know; nor know I aught
By me that's said or done amiss this night –
Unless self-charity be sometimes a vice,
And to defend ourselves it be a sin
When violence assails us.

OTHELLO   Now, by heaven,   195
My blood begins my safer guides to rule,
And passion, having my best judgment collied,
Assays to lead the way. 'Swounds, if I stir,
Or do but lift this arm, the best of you
Shall sink in my rebuke. Give me to know   200
How this foul rout began, who set it on,
And he that is approved in this offence –
Though he had twinned with me, both at a birth –
Shall lose me. What, in a town of war
Yet wild, the people's hearts brim-full of fear,   205
To manage private and domestic quarrel?
In night, and on the court and guard of safety?
'Tis monstrous! Iago, who began't?

MONTANO   If partially affined or leagued in office,
Thou dost deliver more or less than truth,   210
Thou art no soldier.

IAGO   Touch me not so near –
I had rather have this tongue cut from my mouth
Than it should do offence to Michael Cassio;
Yet I persuade myself to speak the truth
Shall nothing wrong him. Thus it is, general: 215
Montano and myself being in speech,
There comes a fellow crying out for help,
And Cassio following him with determined sword
To execute upon him. Sir, this gentleman
Steps in to Cassio and entreats his pause;   220
Myself the crying fellow did pursue,
Lest by his clamour (as it so fell out)
The town might fall in fright. He, swift of foot,
Outran my purpose; and I returned then, rather
For that I heard the clink and fall of swords   225
And Cassio high in oath, which till tonight
I ne'er might say before. When I came back –
For this was brief – I found them close together
At blow and thrust, even as again they were
When you yourself did part them.   230
More of this matter cannot I report.

---

184   *censure:* judgement

186   *spend your rich opinion:* squander the high esteem in which you are held

198   *collied:* blackened

201   *rout:* brawl
202   *approved:* proven guilty

209   *leagued in office:* unwilling to testify against a superior

211   *Touch me not so near:* be careful not to wound my honour so intimately

220   *entreats his pause:* begs him to stop

But men are men: the best sometimes forget.
Though Cassio did some little wrong to him,
As men in rage strike those that wish them best,
Yet surely Cassio, I believe, received 235
From him that fled some strange indignity,
Which patience could not pass.

OTHELLO   I know, Iago,
Thy honesty and love doth mince this matter,
Making it light to Cassio. – Cassio, I love thee;
But never more be officer of mine. 240

Enter DESDEMONA attended

Look if my gentle love be not raised up!
I'll make thee an example.

DESDEMONA   What's the matter, dear?

OTHELLO   All's well now, sweeting:
Come away to bed. *(To Montano)* Sir, for your hurts
Myself will be your surgeon. Lead him off. 245

MONTANO is led off

Iago, look with care about the town,
And silence those whom this vile brawl distracted.
Come, Desdemona: 'tis the soldiers' life
o have their balmy slumbers waked with strife.

Exeunt all but IAGO and CASSIO

IAGO   What, are you hurt, lieutenant? 250

CASSIO   Ay, past all surgery.

IAGO   Marry, God forbid!

CASSIO   Reputation, reputation, reputation! O, I have lost
my reputation! I have lost the immortal part of
myself, and what remains is bestial. My reputation, 255
Iago, my reputation!

IAGO   As I am an honest man, I thought you had received
some bodily wound; there is more sense in that than
in 'reputation'. 'Reputation' is an idle and most false
imposition, oft got without merit, and lost without 260
deserving. You have lost no reputation at all,
unless you repute yourself such a loser. What, man!
there are ways to recover the general again. You
are but now cast in his mood – a punishment more in
policy than in malice, even so as one would beat his 265
offenceless dog to affright an imperious lion. Sue
to him again and he's yours.

CASSIO   I will rather sue to be despised than to deceive so
good a commander with so slight, so drunken, and
so indiscreet an officer. Drunk, and speak parrot, 270
and squabble? Swagger, swear, and discourse
fustian with one's own shadow? O, thou invisible
spirit of wine, if thou hast no name to be known by,
let us call thee devil!

IAGO   What was he that you followed with your sword? What 275
had he done to you?

CASSIO   I know not.

IAGO   Is't possible?

CASSIO   I remember a mass of things, but nothing distinctly–
a quarrel, but nothing wherefore. O God, that men 280

238   *mince:* make light of

265-6 *beat his offenceless dog to affright an imperious lion:*
punish the innocent to deter the great criminal

269   *slight:* worthless

270   *parrot:* nonsense

271   *fustian:* inflated nonsense

278   *Is't possible:* this question will become a recurrent
motif in the next two acts, as though the play were
confessing its own improbabilities and there-by
pre-empting the audience's incredulity

should put an enemy in their mouths to steal away their brains; that we should, with joy, pleasance, revel, and applause, transform ourselves into beasts!

IAGO   Why, but you are now well enough: how came you thus recovered?

CASSIO   It hath pleased the devil drunkenness to give place to the devil wrath; one unperfectness shows me another to make me frankly despise myself.

IAGO   Come, you are too severe a moraller. As the time, the place, and the condition of this country stands, I could heartily wish this had not so befallen; but, since it is as it is, mend it for your own good.

CASSIO   I will ask him for my place again, he shall tell me I am a drunkard. Had I as many mouths as Hydra, such an answer would stop them all. To be now a sensible man, by and by a fool, and presently a beast – O strange! Every inordinate cup is unblessed, and the ingredient is a devil.

IAGO   Come, come, good wine is a good familiar creature if it be well used: exclaim no more against it. And, good lieutenant, I think you think I love you.

CASSIO   I have well approved it, sir – I drunk?

IAGO   You, or any man living, may be drunk, at a time, man. I tell you what you shall do: our general's wife is now the general. I may say so in this respect, for that he hath devoted and given up himself to the contemplation, mark, and denotement of her parts and graces. Confess yourself freely to her; importune her help to put you in your place again. She is of so free, so kind, so apt, so blessed a disposition, she holds it a vice in her goodness not to do more than she is requested. This broken joint between you and her husband entreat her to splinter. And – my fortunes against any lay worth naming! – this crack of your love shall grow stronger than it was before.

CASSIO   You advise me well.

IAGO   I protest, in the sincerity of love and honest kindness.

CASSIO   I think it freely; and betimes in the morning I will beseech the virtuous Desdemona to undertake for me. I am desperate of my fortunes if they check me here.

IAGO   You are in the right. Good night, lieutenant: I must to the watch.

CASSIO   Good night, honest Iago.

Exit

IAGO   And what's he then that says I play the villain,
When this advice is free I give, and honest,
Probal to thinking, and indeed the course
To win the Moor again? For 'tis most easy
Th'inclining Desdemona to subdue
In any honest suit. She's framed as fruitful
As the free elements; and then for her
To win the Moor – were't to renounce his baptism,
All seals and symbols of redeemed sin–
His soul is so enfettered to her love

---

282 *pleasance:* pleasure

285

290

293 *Hydra:* snake with many heads, slain by Hercules

295

298 *familiar creature:* friendly spirit

300

305

309 *free:* open

310

312 *splinter:* to put a splint on

315

318 *I am desperate of my fortunes if they check me here:* I shall think my fortunes are quite hopeless if I am rebuffed

320

324 *Probal:* reasonable

325

326 *subdue:* persuade

327 *fruitful:* generous

329 *renounce his baptism:* one of several references to Othello's faith

330 *seals:* tokens, signs, or symbols authenticating a covenant

61

That she may make, unmake, do what she list,
Even as her appetite shall play the god,
With his weak function. How am I then a villain
To counsel Cassio to this parallel course   335
Directly to his good? Divinity of hell!
When devils will the blackest sins put on,
They do suggest at first with heavenly shows,
As I do now. For, whiles this honest fool
Plies Desdemona to repair his fortune,   340
And she for him pleads strongly to the Moor,
I'll pour this pestilence into his ear:
That she repeals him for her body's lust;
And by how much she strives to do him good
She shall undo her credit with the Moor.   345
So will I turn her virtue into pitch,
And out of her own goodness make the net
That shall enmesh them all.

Enter RODERIGO

                            How now, Roderigo?

RODERIGO   I do follow here in the chase, not like a hound that
hunts, but one that fills up the cry. My money is   350
almost spent; I have been tonight exceedingly well
cudgelled; and I think the issue will be, I shall
have so much experience for my pains, and so, with
no money at all and a little more wit, return again
to Venice.   355

IAGO   How poor are they that have not patience!
What wound did ever heal but by degrees?
Thou know'st we work by wit and not by witchcraft,
And wit depends on dilatory time.
Does't not go well? Cassio hath beaten thee,   360
And thou by that small hurt hast cashiered Cassio.
Though other things grow fair against the sun,
Yet fruits that blossom first will first be ripe.
Content thyself awhile. By th'mass, 'tis morning:
Pleasure and action make the hours seem short!   365
Retire thee, go where thou art billeted.
Away, I say! thou shalt know more hereafter–
Nay, get thee gone!

Exit RODERIGO

                        Two things are to be done:
My wife must move for Cassio to her mistress–
I'll set her on–   370
Myself a while to draw the Moor apart
And bring him jump when he may Cassio find
Soliciting his wife. Ay, that's the way:
Dull not device by coldness and delay.

Exit

---

333 *her appetite:* his desire for her

335 *parallel:* To Iago's plot
336 *Divinity:* Theology

350 *cry:* pack

374 *Dull not device by coldness:* don't let my plots lose their impetus through lack of enthusiasm

CASSIO AND IAGO

Othello leaves Cassio in charge of the night watch. Though he has 'poor brains for drinking' he is persuaded to drink for a while with Iago, Montano and some gentlemen before taking up his position on guard.

Rendered aggressive by alcohol, Cassio is easily provoked into attacking Roderigo. When Montano intervenes he attacks him as well. An enraged Othello and some guards arrive to investigate. When he discovers that Cassio is responsible for the brawl he fires him on the spot. Iago persuades a distraught Cassio to go to Desdemona for help in getting his job back. Desdemona, he says, can plead with Othello on Cassio's behalf.

Iago plans to convince Othello that Cassio and Desdemona are having an affair. Getting Desdemona to intercede on behalf of Cassio is part of this scheme. He will convince Othello that she does so because she is secretly in love with the recently fired lieutenant.

ACTION

LINE BY LINE

▶ LINES 1-59: IAGO AND CASSIO SPEAK

Othello asks Cassio to take charge of the night watch and to ensure that the party does not get out of control (1-3). Cassio tells him that although Iago has already been given the necessary instructions, he will anyway see to it personally: 'Iago hath direction what to do;/ But notwithstanding, with my personal eye/ Will I look to't' (4-6). Othello then departs for bed with Desdemona.

When Iago arrives Cassio suggests that they set about the night's watch, but Iago says it is early yet - ''tis not yet ten o'th' clock' (13-4). He suggests Othello was quick to give orders this night as he was eager to get to bed with his wife: 'Our general cast us thus early for the love of his Desdemona' (14-5).

Iago begins to speak about Desdemona in a rather lewd manner, hoping to get Cassio to do the same:
• He says that Desdemona is eager to make love: 'she is sport for Jove' and 'full of game' (17-9).

IAGO

BACKGROUND

This scene again reinforces our sense of the 'class difference' between Iago and the other characters. Iago sings a number of drinking songs that are unfamiliar to Cassio, but which the lieutenant finds most entertaining. He tells the lieutenant that he picked up one of the songs in England, possibly in some working-class taverns that people like Cassio or Roderigo would never frequent: 'I learned it in England, where indeed they are most potent in potting' (69-70).

Iago also plays up to the role of being a simple, humble man, knowing that if people see him as such he will be able to get away with more than he ever could if they thought him cunning and clever. When Cassio cries out that he is wounded 'past all surgery' (251) Iago says that, being a simple fellow, he took him at his word and thought him physically hurt: 'As I am an honest man, I thought you had received some bodily wound' (257-8).

Cassio rather cruelly alludes to Iago's lowly status when he is drunk, reminding the ensign of his superiority as lieutenant: 'the lieutenant is to be saved before the ensign' (100-1).

A BRILLIANT ACTOR

In this scene Iago must act as though he cares deeply for Cassio, whilst simultaneously managing the lieutenant's downfall. He tells Montano that he would hate to inform Othello of his lieutenant's drink problem, preferring instead to do all he can to help his friend: 'I do love Cassio well and would do much/ To cure him of this evil' (133-4). Iago also brilliantly fakes reluctance to tell Othello that Cassio was responsible for starting the fight (though this is exactly what he goes on to tell the general): 'I had rather have this tongue cut from my mouth/ Than it should do offence to Michael Cassio' (212-3).

Having instigated the chaos that he desired, Iago also pretends to find the commotion and unruly behaviour upsetting and shocking. He expertly fakes distress at the fight between Cassio and Montano and acts as if he wishes to stop the brawl: 'Help, ho! Lieutenant! Sir Montano! Sir!' (157). When Othello arrives he continues to act as though he is appalled at the men's behaviour: 'Have you forgot all sense of place and duty?' (158). He also manages to look so upset that according to Othello he appears 'dead with grieving' (168).

A MASTER PLOTTER

In this scene Iago once again emerges as a master of persuasion and manipulation. He manages to convince Cassio to have another drink, even though Cassio already knows he's had enough, telling him that it is a night of celebration and the locals wish him to join in the fun: ''Tis a night of revels; the gallants desire it' (38-9). He also gets the lieutenant to fetch the men waiting outside who are eager to drink and party. Though Cassio is Iago's superior and says he is unhappy to do this, he follows Iago's instructions: 'I'll do't, but it dislikes me' (42).

Iago manages to convince Montano that Cassio has a drink problem, saying that the lieutenant can no longer sleep at night if he has not had a drink: ''Tis evermore the prologue to his sleep' (119). He knows that these words may well compromise Cassio's fitness for the role as Othello's lieutenant.

Iago also continues to manipulate the 'sick fool Roderigo' (46), using him as a pawn in his various schemes:
- Once Cassio is drunk enough, Roderigo is sent immediately to antagonise him.
- When Cassio has been wound up and a fight has broken out Iago quickly directs Roderigo to go out and scream that a riot has started on the island: 'Away, I say! Go out and cry 'a mutiny'! (145)'
- When Roderigo appears at the end of the scene in a pathetic state, saying that he is almost broke and wishes to go home, Iago convinces him to stick around, telling him to have patience and that things are going according to plan (356-68).

This scene also shows how Iago works to keep his various plots in motion, looking to act swiftly to ensure that momentum is not lost: 'Ay, that's the way:/ Dull not device by coldness and delay' (373-4). Once Cassio has been fired, Iago immediately convinces him to seek Desdemona's help. He knows that Desdemona will do her best to convince Othello to forgive Cassio, and that he will find a way to make the Moor suspicious of the relationship between his wife and his lieutenant. His fiendish plans to destroy the people that he despises now seem to be coming to fruition and it won't be long before the 'net' he is weaving 'shall enmesh them all' (347-8).

We also, again, get the sense that Iago's schemes work more through brilliant improvisation than meticulous planning. Iago knows that if he gets everyone drunk, chances are he will find a way to get Cassio in trouble.

But his plan is remains somewhat loose and requires a deal of good luck and fortune if it is to succeed. He knows this is the case, calling upon 'consequence' to 'approve [his] dream' (57). Luckily things go his way and he is quick to respond to events as they unfold, directing Roderigo to provoke Cassio as soon as the opportunity arises and then waking Othello with shouts that a riot is taking place on the island.

Iago's lack of respect for conventional values
Iago once again displays total disregard for the values that most people hold important. When Cassio says that his reputation is now in tatters, Iago tells him that he ought not to be concerned about this. Reputation, he argues, is a fickle notion, something that is quickly gained and lost, often without merit or reason: '"Reputation' is an idle and most false imposition, oft got without merit, and lost without deserving' (259-261).

Iago also displays a sexist and disrespectful attitude toward women. We see this in his vulgar comments about Desdemona at the beginning of the scene. He suggests that she is lustful ('I'll warrant her full of game' (19)) and that she deliberately attempts to provoke men's sexual desires: 'What an eye she has! Methinks it sounds a parley to provocation' (21). He encourages Cassio to see her as nothing more than a common prostitute ('And when she speaks, is't not an alarum to love?' (23)) but the lieutenant refuses to speak of her in these terms.

IAGO'S SHIFTING MOTIVATIONS
As we have noted previously, Iago's goals and motivations are shifting and seem at times amorphous, even to the man himself. Although he achieved one of his main objectives – to destroy Cassio's reputation and have him lose the position of lieutenant – Iago is anything but satisfied. The position of lieutenant that he coveted is now surely set to be his, but he is not content to let things rest, immediately turning his thoughts to how he can get Cassio to entreat Desdemona to speak to Othello on his behalf. He will meanwhile poison Othello's mind with thoughts that something is happening between Desdemona and Cassio. If things go according to plan he will have destroyed any happiness and contentment that the Moor and his wife possess and further damaged Cassio's reputation. Will he then be satisfied? We are beginning to get the impression that this is a man without an absolutely clear goal, someone driven by a desire to do evil, to push things as far as he can, whatever the consequences.

- He says that Desdemona has a provocative eye that arouses lustful thoughts: 'it sounds a parley to provocation' (21).
- He says that when she speaks her voice is like call to make love: 'And when she speaks, is't not an alarum to love?'(23).

Cassio refuses to be drawn in this direction and speaks of Desdemona only in respectful, admiring terms. He says that she is a 'most exquisite lady' (18) and a 'most fresh and delicate creature' (20). Her eye may be 'inviting' but it also 'modest' (22).

Iago has brought a jug of wine with him and he tells Cassio that there are a group of Cyprus gentlemen outside waiting to drink with them: 'I have a stoup of wine, and near without are a brace of/ Cypriot gallants' (25-7). He wishes Cassio to drink with him but Cassio refuses, saying that he has a poor constitution for drink: 'I have very poor and unhappy brains for drinking' (29-30). Cassio has already drunk one cup of wine and, though it was diluted, this has made him a little tipsy: 'I have drunk but one cup tonight – and that was craftily qualified too – and behold what innovation it makes here' (34-6). However, Iago persists, saying that it is a night for merrymaking and that the local gentlemen of Cyprus are eager to celebrate. He asks Cassio to go and call them in: 'I pray you call them in' (41). Cassio is not happy about any of this, but agrees to do as Iago asks: 'I'll do't, but it dislikes me' (42).

While Cassio is fetching the waiting men, Iago outlines a plan to get him in trouble:
- He knows that if he can get Cassio to drink just one more cup of wine the lieutenant will be drunk enough to get quarrelsome: 'If I can fasten but one cup upon him…He'll be as full of quarrel and offence/ As my young mistress' dog' (43-6).
- The heartbroken Roderigo has already drunk plenty and is ready to provoke Cassio when the time is right.
- Iago has also gotten three other Cypriot men drunk. These men, Iago says, are quintessential men of Cyprus – proud and quick to take offence and fight if provoked: 'Three else of Cyprus – noble, swelling spirits/ That hold their honours in a wary distance' (50-1).
- All Iago needs to do is get these drunken, quick-tempered men together and have Cassio cause offence: 'Now 'mongst this flock of drunkards/ Am I to put our Cassio in some action/ That may offend the isle' (54-6).

▶ LINES 59 -154: A DRUNKEN CASSIO BRAWLS

Cassio returns with Montano and two other gentlemen. He declares that these men have already given him a large glass of wine to drink: 'Fore God, they have given me a rouse already' (59). Iago is delighted to hear this – the first element of his plan is now in place. He sings a drinking song to get the party going and jokes about the drinking abilities of different nations. Cassio is beginning to get quite drunk now and is enjoying himself. He declares that he finds Iago's songs delightful and raises a toast to Othello: 'To the health of our general!' (78). When Iago offers to sing some more, however, Cassio says it is best that he doesn't. He tries to collect himself, but his drunkenness is now very apparent:

- He speaks in a rambling manner, moralising about appropriate and inappropriate behaviour and suggesting that some souls are not worthy enough to be saved by God: 'Well, God's above all, and there be souls must be saved, and there be souls must not be saved' (93-5).

- When Iago says that he desires that his soul will be saved, Cassio acts in an unpleasantly superior manner, stating that the lieutenant's soul will be saved before the ensign's: 'Ay: but, by your leave, not before me: the lieutenant is to be saved before the ensign' (101).

- He repeatedly insists that he is not drunk (a clear indication always that someone is drunk): 'I am not drunk now...you must not think, then, that I am drunk' (104-6).

Cassio realises that he is drunk and makes an effort to check himself, calling on the men to attend to their duties: 'Let's have no more of this: let's to our affairs' (101-3). When he leaves to take charge of the watch, Iago tells Montano that although Cassio is a great solider, he has a problem with drink: 'He's a solider fit to stand by Caesar/ And give direction; and do but see his vice' (111-2). He says that he fears Cassio's drinking will eventually cause serious trouble and that the lieutenant will ultimately betray the trust that Othello has placed in him: 'I fear the trust Othello puts him in,/ On some odd time of his infirmity,/ Will shake this island' (115-7). Montano is shocked to hear this and suggests that Othello ought to be informed of his lieutenant's behaviour: 'It were well/ The general were put in

mind of it' (121-2). Iago claims that he could not do this to Cassio, that he is fond of the lieutenant and would prefer to do what he can to cure him of his drink problem: 'I do love Cassio well, and would do much/ To cure him of this evil' (133-4).

While this conversation is taking place, Roderigo appears. Iago quickly tells him to go after Cassio, that now is the time to provoke the lieutenant: 'I pray you, after the lieutenant go' (127). Roderigo is quick to act and it is not long before he reappears screaming for help and being chased by an infuriated Cassio. Roderigo has obviously said something to upset Cassio and the lieutenant is threatening to give him a severe beating: 'I'll beat the knave into a twiggen bottle' (138). Montano tries to intervene and restrain Cassio but the lieutenant is so drunk and enraged that he threatens to clock the governor over the head. When Montano tells Cassio that he is drunk, it is more than the lieutenant can take and the two men start fighting.

Iago's plan is working perfectly. All he needs now is to have Othello witness his lieutenant's drunken, disorderly behaviour. He tells Roderigo to go outside and start screaming that a riot is taking place: 'Away, I say! Go out and cry 'a mutiny'!' (145). Iago then turns his attention to the brawling men, acting as though he wishes to restore order: 'Nay, good lieutenant! God's will, gentlemen!' (146).

▶ LINES 145-249: OTHELLO RESTORES ORDER

This ruckus disturbs the entire town, bringing Othello and some guards rushing to investigate. Othello is enraged and disgusted by this disturbance of the peace. He warns that the next person to make an aggressive move will die: 'He that stirs next to carve for his own rage/ Holds his soul light: he dies upon his motion' (164-5). Such brawling, he says, is inappropriate for Christian gentlemen. It would disgrace even the barbaric Turks: 'Are we turned Turks… For Christian shame, put by this barbarous brawl' (163).

Othello demands to know how the ruckus began, asking each of those present in turn (169-208). Iago lies brilliantly, denying any knowledge of how the fight began: 'I cannot speak/ Any beginning to this peevish odds' (175-6). Cassio, it seems, is unable to speak, overcome by rage, alcohol or physical

💬 TALK ABOUT IT

Othello places a great deal of trust in Iago and thinks him a very reliable person. Do you think that Iago has earned this trust through honest actions in the past or do you think the ensign has always hated Othello and only ever pretended to be loyal and true?

exertion (180). Montano, too, claims to find speech difficult but declares he did nothing 'amiss' and acted only in self-defence (191-4).

This lack of information further enrages Othello. He describes how his anger, his 'blood' and 'passion', is on the verge of overcoming his reason or 'best judgement' (196-8). He threatens those present with terrible consequences and demands once again to know who began this 'foul rout: ' Swounds, if I stir, / Or do but lift this arm, the best of you / Shall sink in my rebuke. (198-200).

OTHELLO AND IAGO

CHARACTER DEVELOPMENT

OTHELLO

OTHELLO AS SOLDIER

Throughout this scene Othello comes across as a responsible military commander. Before retiring for a night of pleasure with his new bride he ensures that the town's defences are left in the hands of his trusted lieutenant: 'Good Michael, look you to the guard tonight' (1).

Othello is a stern military commander who places a great value on discipline. He takes immediate and decisive action when roused by the sound of the brawl. He puts an immediate stop to this fracas, threatening the next person to raise a hand with immediate execution (164-5). He fairly quickly gets to the bottom of what caused the disturbance and fires Cassio on the spot for his indiscretion (240). Indeed, Cassio suspects that Othello will never forgive him this drunken lapse and return him to the post of lieutenant.

Othello is also highly concerned that the island under his command remain calm, peaceful and stable: 'Silence that dreadful bell: it frights the isle / From her propriety' (166-7). He sends Iago to reassure the townspeople in the wake of this disturbance of the peace (246-7). This, after all, is a 'town of war' that was recently threatened with invasion and whose people are 'brim-full of fear' (204-5).

DIGNITY AND SELF-POSSESSION

In this scene we get our first real glimpse of Othello's tendency towards anger and rage. For the first time we see his trademark composure and self-possession begin to slip.

He reacts furiously to the brawl that has broken out between Cassio and Montano. And while he contains his anger on this occasion he declares that his passion and his emotions ('his blood') are in danger of getting the better of his reason (his 'best judgement'). Othello's tendency to be guided by his emotions rather than by his reason will contribute to the play's tragic conclusion.

OTHELLO'S LOVE FOR DESDEMONA

Othello's love for his new bride is evident at the beginning of the scene when he takes obvious delight at the prospect of spending a night with her (8-10). It also shows in his obvious irritation that her sleep has been disturbed by the noise of the brawl: 'Look if my gentle love be not raised up!' (241). Iago, too, refers to Othello's great affection for his new wife, describing how he is 'enfettered' or chained by his great love for her. In Othello's eyes, he declares, Desdemona can do no wrong and he would do anything to please her (331-4).

OTHELLO'S TRUSTING NATURE

Othello continues to trust Iago completely, viewing him as 'most honest' and turning to him for a full and honest account of the brawl and its causes (208). He is taken in completely by Iago's acting, believing him to be 'dead with grieving' at this breakdown of discipline (168). When he returns to bed he leaves Iago in charge, telling him to 'look with care about the town, / And silence those whom this vile brawl distracted' (246-7).

CASSIO AND MONTANO FIGHTING

CHARACTER DEVELOPMENT

💬 TALK ABOUT IT

- He has one drink when he goes to fetch Montano and the gentlemen: 'Fore God, they have given me a rouse already' (60).
- He has at least one more, presumably, during the singing. But some productions show Iago or the others constantly refilling his cup.
- He claims to have had only one watered down drink earlier in the night. But is he being honest here or is he actually downplaying his alcohol consumption?

CASSIO

CASSIO AND ALCOHOL

Cassio, in this scene, comes across as an extremely bad drunk. He acknowledges as much at the beginning of the scene: 'I have very poor and unhappy brains for drinking' (30). Alcohol tends to make Cassio aggressive and quarrelsome. As Iago points out, a few cups of wine will make him 'as full of quarrel and offence As my young mistress' dog' (45-6).

We might detect a hint of this aggression even when he repeatedly denies being drunk to Montano and the other gentlemen, in lines that offer an actor great comic potential: 'Do not think, gentlemen, I am drunk: this is my ensign; this is my right hand, and this is my left. I am not drunk now' (104-6). We see it more clearly when he is easily provoked into attacking Roderigo, abandoning his post and chasing after him (136). It is also evident when he assualts Montano, who is merely trying to keep the peace (145).

Alcohol is presumably at least in part responsible for his inability to speak after the brawl (180). It also tends to cause Cassio severe memory loss, erasing his recollections how the brawl and how it was provoked: 'I remember a mass of things, but nothing distinctly– a quarrel, but nothing wherefore' (279-80).

Iago tells Montano that Cassio is an alcoholic. Iago is untrustworthy and has his own reasons for destroying Cassio's reputation. Yet perhaps there's some truth to this accusation. Cassio, after all, can't resist joining the drinking session even though he knows he's a bad drunk and has responsibilities that night. Perhaps his repeated claims, toward the scene's end, that alcohol is a 'devil' also suggests such an addiction. Othello's warning that they not enjoy themselves too much might also hint at previous overindulgence on Cassio's part: 'Let's teach ourselves that honourable stop / Not to out-sport discretion' (3).

CASSIO'S BACKGROUND

Cassio, we must remember, is a member of the noble classes, man who places great stock in manners, chivalry and breeding. This is perhaps evident at the conclusion of the scene when he displays great concern for the damage his night-time brawling has done to his reputation (253). Reputation, to Cassio, is all. It is the soul or immortal part of each person. Everything else is 'bestial', is animalistic and unimportant: 'I have lost the immortal part of myself, and what remains is bestial' (254-5).

CASSIO'S DEVOTION TO OTHELLO

Cassio, however, also demonstrates great devotion to Othello throughout this scene. Even when he drinks it is in honour of Othello: 'To the health of our general!' (78). He shows no bitterness toward Othello for firing him, instead blaming himself for what has happened. His drunken indiscretion, he feels, makes him unworthy to serve such a great leader: 'I will rather sue to be despised than to deceive so good a commander with so slight, so drunken, and so indiscreet an officer' (268-70).

Iago finally reveals that Cassio was responsible for the fracas. He describes firstly how Cassio with his 'determined sword' (218) pursued an unknown 'fellow crying out for help' (217). He then describes how Cassio came to blows with Montano when the latter tried to calm him down (219-30).

Othello has heard enough. He fires Cassio from his post as lieutenant: 'Cassio, I love thee, / But never more be officer of mine' (239-40). He instructs Iago to ensure the town's calm is restored and departs with Desdemona, who appears briefly having been awoken by the brawl (243).

▶ LINES 250-321: IAGO ADVISES CASSIO

Iago is left alone with Cassio, who is understandably devastated at having lost his position. His reputation, he feels, has been ruined by his brawling and by his dismissal from his post. His despair is evident in the way he repeats the word 'reputation' over and over again: 'Reputation, reputation, reputation! / O, I have lost my reputation!' (253-55).

He feels he has let Othello down and is unworthy to serve as his officer: 'I will rather sue to be despised than to deceive so good a commander with so slight, so drunken, and so indiscreet an officer' (268-70). He is disgusted at his own drunken behaviour (271-2). He repeatedly curses alcohol itself for leading him astray: 'O, thou invisible spirit of wine, if thou hast no name to be known by, let us call thee devil!' (272-4).

Cassio, due to his low tolerance for drink, has no clear memory of why the brawl started or of being goaded by Roderigo: 'I remember a mass of things but nothing distinctly: a quarrel, but nothing wherefore' (279-80). The anger into which he was provoked, however, has caused him to sober up somewhat: 'It hath pleased the devil drunkenness to give place to the devil wrath' (285-86).

Iago warns Cassio that he's being too hard on himself: 'Come, you are too severe a moraller' (297). Reputations, he says, are fickle and are often won and lost undeservedly (259-60). Othello, he goes on, fired Cassio not for reasons of personal 'malice' but because he had to be seen to do so (264-5). Iago declares that Cassio can easily 'mend' the breach that has come between them by asking for

DESDEMONA

Though Desdemona makes only two brief appearances in this scene, we still manage to learn about her through the remarks of other characters. Her physical beauty is stressed at the scene's beginning, with Cassio describing her as an 'exquisite lady', 'a most fresh and delicate creature' and 'perfection'. Iago, meanwhile, describes as a fitting partner for the great god Jove himself (17).

The conclusion of the scene, meanwhile, emphasises Desdemona's kindness and decency. Cassio refers to her as the 'virtuous Desdemona' and Iago reminds him that she's inclined to respond to any honest request that's made of her: 'She is of so free, so kind, so apt, so blessed a disposition, she holds it a vice in her goodness not to do more than she is requested' (308-11).

He makes this point once again in his venomous final soliloquy, describing how Desdemona is as generous and giving as nature itself: 'She's framed as fruitful / As the free elements' (327-8). Iago, however, is determined to use her virtue and her goodness to destroy the other characters.

🗨 THINK ABOUT IT

Throughout this inquisition Iago's acting skills are superbly on display:

• He claims to be baffled by the fact that these men, 'Friends all', somehow ended up with 'Swords out, and tilting one at other's breasts / In opposition bloody' (174-5).
• He pretends to be deeply saddened by this turn of events, with Othello remarking how he looks 'dead with grieving' (168).
• Iago pretends to reveal Cassio's guilt only with the greatest of reluctance: 'I had rather have this tongue cut from my mouth / Than it should do offence to Michael Cassio' (212-3).
• He even makes excuses for Cassio's bad behaviour, declaring that even the best of men sometimes make such mistakes and speculating that Cassio must have been gravely insulted by the man he pursued.

All the while, of course, the audience knows that he provoked the entire affair.

forgiveness 'What, man! there are ways to recover the general again' (262-3).

Iago tells Cassio that the best way to regain his position is by asking Desdemona to plead with Othello on his behalf: 'Confess freely to her, importune her help to put you in your place again' (307-8). Othello, he claims, will be guided by Desdemona's opinion in relation to this matter: 'Our general's wife is now the general. I may say so in this respect' (303-4).

Initially Cassio is reluctant to ask for his job back. He feels unworthy to serve Othello given his disgraceful behaviour and fears rejection from this man he admires so much. (292-7) Yet he is swayed by Iago's words and says that in the morning he will ask Desdemona to intercede with Othello on his behalf: 'in the morning I will / beseech the virtuous Desdemona to undertake for me' (317-8).

▶ LINES 322-348: IAGO SCHEMES

Cassio exits and in a soliloquy Iago expands upon his plans. In a sense, the advice he's just given Cassio isn't villainous at all (322-5). Desdemona, he says, is kind-hearted and would help anyone who approached her with an honets plea for help: For 'tis most easy / Th'inclining Desdemona to subdue / In any honest suit' (325-7). Othello, in turn, is so 'enfettered to her love' that he might well listen to her pleas (331-2).

On the surface, then. Iago's advice seems helpful, fair and reasonable: 'this advice is free I give, and honest,/ Probal to thinking, and indeed the course/ To win the Moor again' (323-4). He has pointed Cassio down the right road to regaining his position: 'How am I then a villain/ To counsel Cassio to this parallel course/ Directly to his good?' (334-6).

Yet Iago has a deeper and a darker purpose. In this he resembles devils who appear good and noble at first, all the better to tempt their victims toward the 'blackest' sins: 'When devils will the blackest sins put on,/ They do suggest at first with heavenly shows' (337-8).

He aims to convince Othello that Cassio and Desdemona are having an affair: 'I'll pour this pestilence into his ear' (342). Desdemona's goodness means she'll plead for Cassio to get his job back (341). Iago will convince Othello that she does so only because she's sleeping with Cassio behind his back: That she repeals him for her body's lust '(343).

The more Desdemona pleads on Cassio's behalf the more it will seem to Othello that the affair is real: 'And by how much she strives to do him good/ She shall undo her credit with the Moor' (344-5). Iago, therefore, intends to use Desdemona's fundamental kindness to destroy everyone: 'And out of her own goodness make the net/ That shall enmesh them all' (347-8).

▶ LINES 349-374: RODERIGO COMPLAINS TO IAGO

Roderigo enters, cutting a somewhat pathetic figure. His money has almost all been spent and he has been beaten severely in the brawl (351-2). He is on the verge of returning of Venice.

Iago, however, convinces him to be patient and remain on Cyprus: 'How poor are they that have not patience!' (356). While he's taken a beating his wounds will heal and by this 'small hurt' he has manged to get Cassio 'cashiered' or fired (361). Iago tells Roderigo that the seeds of other great schemes have been planted: 'Though other things grow fair against the sun' (362). He sends Roderigo back to his lodging, promising him he'll more of these plans later (366-8).

Iago returns to the details of his plan. He will use his wife to make sure that Desdemona pleads with Othello on Cassio's behalf: 'My wife must move for Cassio to her mistress –/ I'll set her on'. (369-70). He also wants to make sure that Othello sees Cassio and Desdemona together when Cassio goes to see her in the morning: 'Myself the while to draw the Moor apart,/ And bring him jump when he may Cassio find/ Soliciting his wife' (371-4). ◆

ACT 3 SCENE 1

Cyprus. Before the castle.

Enter Cassio with Musicians

CASSIO: Masters, play here – I will content your pains –
Something that's brief; and bid 'Good morrow, general!'

They play. Enter Clown

Clown: Why, masters, have your instruments been in Naples
that they speak i'th' nose thus?

Boy Musician: How, sir? how?

Clown: Are these, I pray you, wind instruments?

Boy Musician: Ay, marry are they, sir.

Clown: O, thereby hangs a tail.

Boy Musician: Whereby hangs a tale, sir?

Clown: Marry, sir, by many a wind instrument that I know.
But, masters, here's money for you; and the general
so likes your music that he desires you, for love's
sake, to make no more noise with it.

Boy Musician: Well, sir, we will not.

Clown: If you have any music that may not be heard, to't
again – but (as they say) to hear music the general
does not greatly care.

Boy Musician: We have none such, sir.

Clown: Then put up your pipes in your bag, for I'll away.
Go, vanish into air, away!

Exeunt Musicians

CASSIO: Dost thou hear, mine honest friend?

Clown: No, I hear not your honest friend – I hear you.

CASSIO: Prithee, keep up thy quillets – there's a poor piece
of gold for thee: if the gentlewoman that attends
the general's wife be stirring, tell her there's
one Cassio entreats her a little favour of speech.
Wilt thou do this?

Clown: She is stirring, sir: if she will stir hither, I shall seem
to notify unto her.

CASSIO: Do, my good friend.

Exit Clown
Enter IAGO

In happy time, Iago.

IAGO: You haven't been a-bed then?

CASSIO: Why, no: the day had broke
Before we parted. I've made bold, Iago,
To send in to your wife. My suit to her
Is that she will to virtuous Desdemona
Procure me some access.

IAGO: I'll send her to you presently:
And I'll devise a mean to draw the Moor
Out of the way, that your converse and business
May be more free.

---

1   *I will content your pains:* I will reward you for your troubles
2   *Good morrow:* after the wedding night, songs and music were customarily performed outside the bridal chamber to greet the dawn. Donne's lyric 'The Good-Morrow' is a sophisticated imitation of this folk ritual
3   *have your instruments been in Naples:* an allusion to the results of the pox

6   *wind instruments:* anus

12-13 *for love's sake:* for the sake of any affection you may have for him

19   *put up your pipes:* put away your pipes
19   *in your bag:* presumably the bag in which they carried their instruments

23   *quillets:* quibbles
24   *attends:* serves

28   *stirring:* sexually arousing

30   *In happy time:* you have arrived at the right moment

35   *Procure:* obtain
35   *presently:* forthwith

Exit

CASSIO

I humbly thank you for't.
I never knew a Florentine more kind and honest!

Enter EMILIA

EMILIA

Good morrow, good lieutenant. I am sorry
For your displeasure, but all will sure be well.
The general and his wife are talking of it,
And she speaks for you stoutly. The Moor replies
That he you hurt is of great fame in Cyprus
And great affinity; and that in wholesome wisdom
He might not but refuse you. But he protests he loves you
And needs no other suitor but his likings
To take the safest occasion by the front
To bring you in again.

CASSIO

Yet I beseech you,
If you think fit, or that it may be done,
Give me advantage of some brief discourse
With Desdemona alone.

EMILIA

Pray you, come in:
I will bestow you where you shall have time
To speak your bosom freely.

CASSIO

I am much bound to you.

Exeunt

---

39   *Florentine:* Cassio is surprised that Iago, a Venetian, should be as kind as one of his own fellow-countrymen

40

41   *your displeasure:* the disfavour into which you have fallen

43   *stoutly:* resolutely, vigorously

45   *great affinity:* he has powerful family connections
45   *wholesome wisdom:* prudent common sense
46   *might not but:* had no option but to

48   *take the safest occasion by the front:* seize on the first safe occasion
49   *To bring you in again:* to reinstate you in your office

50

54   *To speak your bosom freely:* to utter your most intimate thoughts

---

CASSIO

Cassio is obviously very upset at losing the position of lieutenant and disappointed by the fact that he let Othello, a man he greatly admires, down so badly. He hasn't gone to bed at all and has decided to follow Iago's suggestion that he talk to Emilia and arrange a meeting with Desdemona. When he hears from Emilia that Othello has spoken well of him and will look to reinstate him as lieutenant when the time is right, Cassio still pushes for this meeting with Desdemona. It seems that he is so desperate to have Othello think well of him again that he feels he must do all he can to restore his character.

We get the impression throughout the play that Cassio is something of a ladies' man. In this scene he seems confident that if he can get to speak with Emilia she will arrange the meeting he desires with Desdemona. He then plans to convince Desdemona to speak to her husband on his behalf. The fact that he has chosen this route to get back on good terms with Othello suggests that he is confident of his ability to charm women. We also get the sense that Cassio is attractive and sympathetic to the opposite sex. We hear that Desdemona has spoken 'stoutly' in his defence to her husband (43). Emilia is also very willing to assist him, offering to bring him to a private place where he can meet with her mistress. We might wonder if both women would be so supportive if Cassio was not so charming and pleasing on the eye.

Cassio has not gone to bed this night and has decided to follow Iago's suggestion that he speak to Emilia. He hopes that Emilia will arrange a meeting with Desdemona who will relay his plea to Othello. Iago is happy to hear that Cassio is doing as he hoped and arranges to have Emilia come to him immediately. Emilia tells Cassio that Othello and Desdemona are speaking favourably about him and that Othello wishes to have him reinstated as lieutenant when the time is right. She agrees to arrange a meeting between him and Desdemona.

ACTION

LINE BY LINE

▶ LINES 1-54: CASSION LOOKS TO MEET OTHELLO

It is the morning after the drunken party and Cassio is still awake. Musicians have arrived to awaken Othello and Desdemona with music. A clown is also present and he makes fun of the musicians. He tells them that their music has a nasal twang like the Neapolitan accent ('have your instruments been in/ Naples that they speak 'th' nose thus?' (3-4)) and that the general is so fond of their music he would be pleased if they made 'no more noise with it' (13).

Cassio gives the clown a gold piece and asks him to go to Emilia and tell her that he wishes to speak to her. Iago appears and Cassio tells him that he has asked to meet with his wife in the hope that she can gain him access to Desdemona: 'My suit to her/ Is that she will to virtuous Desdemona/ Procure me some access' (33-5). Iago says that he will make sure that Emilia comes to him very shortly and that he will find a way of keeping Othello busy so that Cassio can speak more freely with Desdemona when he gets a chance: 'I'll devise a mean to draw the Moor/ Out of the way, that your converse and business/ May be more free' (36-8). Cassio is very grateful for this and says that he has never met someone in Florence as 'kind and honest' as Iago (39).

Emilia comes to Cassio and tells him how sorry she is to hear of his misfortune. She tells him that at this very moment Othello and Desdemona are speaking of his recent dismissal and that Desdemona is vigorously defending him: 'The general and his wife are talking of it,/ And she speaks for you stoutly' (42-3). Othello is saying that the man Cassio wounded is well-known in Cyprus and that he had no option but to make an example of him and have him dismissed. However, the general likes Cassio and intends to reinstate him when the convenient moment arises: 'he protests he loves you/ And needs no other suitor but his likings/ To take the safest occasion by the front/ To bring you in again' (46-9).

Cassio asks Emilia if she can arrange for him to have a word with Desdemona. Anything, he says, that will improve his chances of being reappointed lieutenant is worth doing. Emilia offers to bring him inside and to position him in the best place to have a quiet word with Desdemona: 'I will bestow you where you shall have time/ To speak your bosom freely' (53-4). ◆

💬 TALK ABOUT IT

Emilia is Iago's wife and Desdemona's mistress. Her dual role means that she is set to become an important character in the play. What is your impression of her in this scene and what part do you think she will play in her husband's schemes?

IAGO

MASTER PLOTTER

Iago must be delighted when he hears that Cassio has followed through on his suggestion that he meet with Emilia. His plan to have Cassio speak with Desdemona is now in motion and he quickly has his wife meet with the former lieutenant to ensure that things progress (35). He promises Cassio that he will keep Othello distracted while this meeting takes place: 'I'll devise a mean to draw the Moor/ Out of the way' (36-7). This, he says, will allow Cassio to discuss matters freely with Desdemona: 'that your converse and business/ May be more free' (37-8). This, of course, is false – Iago now has the perfect opportunity to have Othello happen upon a meeting between his wife and Cassio and to sow seeds of doubt about Desdemona's fidelity in the general's mind.

ACT 3

SCENE 2

A room in the castle.

Enter Othello, Iago, and Gentlemen

OTHELLO   These letters give, Iago, to the pilot,
And by him do my duties to the Senate:
That done, I will be walking on the works:
Repair there to me.

IAGO   Well, my good lord, I'll do't.

OTHELLO   This fortification, gentlemen, shall we see't?

Gentleman   We'll wait upon your lordship.

Exeunt

2   *do my duties:* offer my dutiful service

3   *works:* fortifications

5

6   *wait upon:* attend (as servants 'attend' or 'wait upon' their masters)

ACT 3

SCENE 3

Before the castle.

Enter Desdemona, Cassio, and Emilia

DESDEMONA	Be thou assured, good Cassio, I will do
	All my abilities in thy behalf.
EMILIA	Good madam, do: I warrant it grieves my husband,
	As if the case were his.
DESDEMONA	O, that's an honest fellow. Do not doubt, Cassio,
	But I will have my lord and you again
	As friendly as you were.
CASSIO	Bounteous madam,
	Whatever shall become of Michael Cassio,
	He's never any thing but your true servant.
DESDEMONA	I know't. I thank you. You do love my lord;
	You have known him long; and be you well assured
	He shall in strangeness stand no further off
	Than in a politic distance.
CASSIO	Ay, but, lady,
	That policy may either last so long,
	Or feed upon such nice and waterish diet,
	Or breed itself so out of circumstance,
	That, I being absent and my place supplied,
	My general will forget my love and service.
DESDEMONA	Do not doubt that: before Emilia here
	I give thee warrant of thy place. Assure thee,
	If I do vow a friendship, I'll perform it
	To the last article. My lord shall never rest,
	I'll watch him tame and talk him out of patience;
	His bed shall seem a school, his board a shrift;
	I'll intermingle every thing he does
	With Cassio's suit. Therefore be merry, Cassio;
	For thy solicitor shall rather die
	Than give thy cause away.

Enter OTHELLO and IAGO

EMILIA	Madam, here comes my lord.
CASSIO	Madam, I'll take my leave.
DESDEMONA	Why stay, and hear me speak.
CASSIO	Madam, not now: I am very ill at ease,
	Unfit for mine own purposes.
DESDEMONA	Well, do your discretion.

Exit CASSIO

IAGO	Ha? I like not that.
OTHELLO	What dost thou say?
IAGO	Nothing, my lord; or if – I know not what.
OTHELLO	Was not that Cassio parted from my wife?
IAGO	Cassio, my lord? – No, sure, I cannot think it

(handwritten note in margin): She seems exceptionally eager to help Cassio

5

10

12-13 *He shall in strangeness stand no further off / Than in a polite distance:* the estranged distance he puts between you will be no greater than practical wisdom requires

15 *nice:* thin

16 *breed itself so out of circumstance:* be so long delayed

17 *supplied:* filled up

19 *doubt:* fear

20 *give thee warrant of:* guarantee

22 *My lord shall never rest:* Desdemona, however charmingly, is proposing to nag Othello until she gets her way

23 *watch him tame:* prevent him from sleeping

24 *shrift:* place of confession or penance

25

27 *solicitor:* advocate

28 *give thy cause away:* abandon your case

30

32 *do your discretion:* behave as you think wise

33 *Ha?:* In Shakespeare's time a question mark was often used where we would expect an exclamation mark; editors normally assume that such is the case here

33 *I like not that:* Iago begins his temptation

35

	That he would steal away so guilty-like,
	Seeing you coming.
OTHELLO	I do believe 'twas he.	40
DESDEMONA	How now, my lord?
	I have been talking with a suitor here,
	A man that languishes in your displeasure.
OTHELLO	Who is't you mean?
DESDEMONA	Why, your lieutenant, Cassio – good my lord,	45
	If I have any grace or power to move you,
	His present reconciliation take;
	For if he be not one that truly loves you,
	That errs in ignorance and not in cunning,
	I have no judgment in an honest face:	50
	I prithee call him back.
OTHELLO	Went he hence now?
DESDEMONA	Yes, faith; so humbled
	That he hath left part of his grief with me,
	To suffer with him. Good love, call him back.	55
OTHELLO	Not now, sweet Desdemona – some other time.
DESDEMONA	But shall't be shortly?
OTHELLO	The sooner, sweet, for you.
DESDEMONA	Shall't be tonight at supper?
OTHELLO	No, not tonight.
DESDEMONA	Tomorrow dinner, then?
OTHELLO	I shall not dine at home:
	I meet the captains at the citadel.	60
DESDEMONA	Why then tomorrow night, or Tuesday morn,
	On Tuesday noon, or night, or Wednesday morn –
	I prithee name the time, but let it not
	Exceed three days. I'faith he's penitent;
	And yet his trespass, in our common reason –	65
	Save that they say the wars must make examples
	Out of her best – is not almost a fault
	T'incur a private check. When shall he come?
	Tell me, Othello! I wonder in my soul
	What you would ask me, that I should deny	70
	Or stand so mamm'ring on. What? Michael Cassio,
	That came a-wooing with you, and so many a time,
	When I have spoke of you dispraisingly,
	Hath ta'en your part; to have so much to do
	To bring him in? By'r Lady, I could do much, –	75
OTHELLO	Prithee, no more: let him come when he will –
	I will deny thee nothing.
DESDEMONA	Why, this is not a boon:
	'Tis as I should entreat you wear your gloves,
	Or feed on nourishing dishes, or keep you warm,
	Or sue to you to do a peculiar profit	80
	To your own person. Nay, when I have a suit
	Wherein I mean to touch your love indeed,
	It shall be full of poise and difficult weight,
	And fearful to be granted.
OTHELLO	I will deny thee nothing:
	Whereon, I do beseech thee, grant me this:	85
	To leave me but a little to myself.

46 *grace:* pleasing quality, beauty; favour
47 *present:* immediate
48 *in cunning:* knowingly; because of his crafty nature
65 *trespass:* offence
67 *her best:* the most distinguished, highest ranking soldiers
68 *check:* reprimand
71 *mamm'ring:* stammering, hesitating
75 *bring him in:* get him reinstated
80-81 *do a peculiar profit To your own person:* do yourself a special favour
82 *touch:* put to the test
83 *poise:* weight, gravity, importance

DESDEMONA	Shall I deny you? No! Farewell, my lord.	
OTHELLO	Farewell, my Desdemona: I'll come to thee straight.	88 *straight:* at once
DESDEMONA	Emilia, come. *(To Othello)* Be as your fancies teach you:	
	Whate'er you be, I am obedient.	90

Exeunt DESDEMONA and EMILIA

OTHELLO	Excellent wretch, perdition catch my soul	91 *wretch:* term of endearment
	But I do love thee! And when I love thee not,	92 *But I do:* If I do not
	Chaos is come again.	
IAGO	My noble lord –	
OTHELLO	What dost thou say, Iago?	95
IAGO	Did Michael Cassio, when you wooed my lady,	
	Know of your love?	
OTHELLO	He did, from first to last –	
	Why dost thou ask?	
IAGO	But for a satisfaction of my thought,	
	No further harm.	
OTHELLO	Why of thy thought, Iago?	100
IAGO	I did not think he had been acquainted with her.	
OTHELLO	Oh yes, and went between us very oft.	
IAGO	Indeed?	
OTHELLO	Indeed? Ay, indeed: Discern'st thou aught in that?	
	Is he not honest?	
IAGO	Honest, my lord?	105
OTHELLO	Honest? Ay, honest.	
IAGO	My lord, for aught I know.	
OTHELLO	What dost thou think?	
IAGO	Think, my lord?	
OTHELLO	'Think, my lord'? By heaven, thou echo'st me,	
	As if there were some monster in thy thought	110 *monster:* deformed, unnatural creature
	Too hideous to be shown. Thou dost mean something:	
	I heard thee say even now thou likedst not that,	
	When Cassio left my wife. What didst not like?	
	And when I told thee he was of my counsel	114 *of my counsel:* in my confidence
	In my whole course of wooing, thou criedst 'Indeed?'	115
	And didst contract and purse thy brow together,	
	As if thou then hadst shut up in thy brain	
	Some horrible conceit. If thou dost love me,	118 *conceit:* idea
	Show me thy thought.	
IAGO	My lord, you know I love you.	120
OTHELLO	I think thou dost;	
	And, for I know thou'rt full of love and honesty,	
	And weigh'st thy words before thou giv'st them breath,	
	Therefore these stops of thine fright me the more –	124 *stops:* pauses
	For such things in a false disloyal knave	125
	Are tricks of custom, but in a man that's just	126 *tricks of custom:* customary habits
	They are close dilations, working from the heart	127 *close dilations:* involuntary delays
	That passion cannot rule.	128 *That passion cannot rule:* that passion is unable to control
IAGO	For Michael Cassio,	
	I dare be sworn, I think, that he is honest.	
OTHELLO	I think so too.	
IAGO	Men should be what they seem –	130
	Or those that be not, would they might seem none.	131 *none:* not to be men
OTHELLO	Certain, men should be what they seem.	
IAGO	Why, then I think Cassio's an honest man.	

OTHELLO   Nay, yet there's more in this!

I prithee speak to me as to thy thinkings,

As thou dost ruminate, and give thy worst of thoughts 135

The worst of words.

IAGO   Good my lord, pardon me:

Though I am bound to every act of duty,

I am not bound to that all slaves are free to –

Utter my thoughts? Why, say they are vile and false – 140

As where's that palace whereinto foul things

Sometimes intrude not? – who has a breast so pure,

where no uncleanly apprehensions

Keep leets and law-days and in session sit

With meditations lawful? 145

OTHELLO   Thou dost conspire against thy friend, Iago,

If thou but think'st him wrong'd, and mak'st his ear

A stranger to thy thoughts.

IAGO   I do beseech you –

Though I perchance am vicious in my guess,

(As I confess it is my nature's plague 150

To spy into abuses), and oft my jealousy

Shapes faults that are not – that your wisdom yet,

From one that so imperfectly conjects,

Would take no notice, nor build yourself a trouble

Out of his scattering and unsure observance. 155

It were not for your quiet, nor your good,

Nor for my manhood, honesty, and wisdom,

To let you know my thoughts.

OTHELLO   What dost thou mean?

IAGO   Good name in man – and woman – dear my lord,

Is the immediate jewel of their souls: 160

Who steals my purse, steals trash; 'tis something, nothing;

'Twas mine, 'tis his, and has been slave to thousands:

But he that filches from me my good name

Robs me of that which not enriches him,

And makes me poor indeed.

OTHELLO   By heaven, I'll know thy thoughts! 165

IAGO   You cannot, if my heart were in your hand;

Nor shall not, whilst 'tis in my custody.

OTHELLO   'Swounds!

IAGO   O, beware, my lord, of jealousy;

It is the green-eyed monster which doth mock

The meat it feeds on. That cuckold lives in bliss 170

Who, certain of his fate, loves not his wronger;

But, O, what damnèd minutes tells he o'er,

Who dotes yet doubts, suspects yet soundly loves!

OTHELLO   O misery!

IAGO   Poor and content is rich, and rich enough, 175

But riches fineless, is as poor as winter,

To him that ever fears he shall be poor.

Good God the souls of all my tribe defend

From jealousy!

OTHELLO   Why? Why is this?

Think'st thou I'ld make a lie of jealousy, 180

To follow still the changes of the moon

---

139 *that all slaves are free to:* that which even slaves are free to do

143 *uncleanly apprehensions:* foul ideas

144 *leets:* days on which courts are held

146 *thy friend, Iago:* an important moment: responding to Iago's protestation of 'love', Othello elevates him from the servantly role defined by his rank to the intimate status of 'friend'

151 *jealousy:* suspicious nature

153 *conjects:* conjectures

155 *scattering:* random

160 *immediate:* nearest the heart

170 *The meat it feeds on:* its victim

171 *his wronger:* his adulterous wife

173 *soundly:* to the full

176 *fineless:* limitless

181-182
To follow still the changes of the moon
With fresh suspicions: Indulge in new suspicions
several times a month

With fresh suspicions? No: to be once in doubt
Is once to be resolved. Exchange me for a goat
When I shall turn the business of my soul
To such exsufflate and blown surmises,   185
Matching thy inference. 'Tis not to make me jealous
To say my wife is fair, feeds well, loves company,
Is free of speech, sings, plays and dances well –
Where virtue is, these are more virtuous –
Nor from mine own weak merits will I draw   190
The smallest fear or doubt of her revolt,
For she had eyes and chose me. No, Iago,
I'll see before I doubt; when I doubt, prove;
And on the proof, there is no more but this:
Away at once with love or jealousy!   195

IAGO   I am glad of this, for now I shall have reason
To show the love and duty that I bear you
With franker spirit. Therefore – as I am bound –
Receive it from me. I speak not yet of proof:
Look to your wife; observe her well with Cassio;   200
Wear your eye thus: not jealous, nor secure –
I would not have your free and noble nature,
Out of self-bounty be abused – look to't.
I know our country disposition well:
In Venice they do let heaven see the pranks   205
They dare not show their husbands; their best conscience
Is not to leave't undone, but keep't unknown.

OTHELLO   Dost thou say so?

IAGO   She did deceive her father, marrying you;
And when she seem'd to shake and fear your looks,   210
She loved them most.

OTHELLO   And so she did.

IAGO   Why, go to then!
She that, so young, could give out such a seeming
To seal her father's eyes up close as oak –
He thought 'twas witchcraft - But I am much to blame;
I humbly do beseech you of your pardon   215
For too much loving you.

OTHELLO   I am bound to thee for ever.

IAGO   I see this hath a little dashed your spirits.

OTHELLO   Not a jot, not a jot.

IAGO   I' faith, I fear it has.
I hope you will consider what is spoke
Comes from my love. But I do see you're moved.   220
I am to pray you not to strain my speech
To grosser issues nor to larger reach
Than to suspicion.

OTHELLO   I will not.

IAGO   Should you do so, my lord,   225
My speech should fall into such vile success
As my thoughts aim not at. Cassio's my worthy friend –
My lord, I see you're moved.

OTHELLO   No, not much moved:
I do not think but Desdemona's honest.

IAGO   Long live she so! -And long live you to think so!   230

182-183
No: to be once in doubt Is once to be resolved:
If I once doubt, I will settle the question one way or the other

185   *exsuffilate and blown:* inflated and blown up

186   *inference:* conclusion

203   *self-bounty:* inherent generosity

205-207
In Venice they do let...keep't unknown: **Othello starts to worry here because of his comparative ignorance of Venetian society**

213   *seal:* blind

216   *bound to thee:* indebted to you

222   *issues:* conclusions

226   *success:* result

229   *honest:* chaste

OTHELLO   And yet, how nature erring from itself –

IAGO   Ay, there's the point! As – to be bold with you –

Not to affect many proposed matches

Of her own clime, complexion, and degree,

Whereto we see in all things nature tends –   235

Foh! One may smell in such a will most rank,

Foul disproportion, thoughts unnatural –

But pardon me; I do not in position

Distinctly speak of her – though I may fear

Her will, recoiling to her better judgment,   240

May fall to match you with her country forms,

And happily repent.

OTHELLO   Farewell, farewell.

If more thou dost perceive, let me know more:

Set on thy wife to observe. Leave me, Iago:

IAGO   *[going]*   My lord, I take my leave.   245

OTHELLO   Why did I marry? This honest creature doubtless

Sees and knows more, much more than he unfolds.

IAGO   *[returning]*   My lord, I would I might entreat your honour

To scan this thing no further; leave it to time.

Although 'tis fit that Cassio have his place –   250

For sure he fills it up with great ability –

Yet, if you please to hold him off a while,

You shall by that perceive him and his means:

Note, if your lady strain his entertainment

With any strong or vehement importunity;   255

Much will be seen in that. In the meantime,

Let me be thought too busy in my fears

(As worthy cause I have to fear I am)

And hold her free, I do beseech your honour.

OTHELLO   Fear not my government.

IAGO   I once more take my leave.   260

Exit

OTHELLO   This fellow's of exceeding honesty,

And knows all qualities, with a learned spirit

Of human dealings. If I do prove her haggard,

Though that her jesses were my dear heart-strings,

I'd whistle her off and let her down the wind   265

To prey at fortune. Haply, for I am black

And have not those soft parts of conversation

That chamberers have, or for I am declined

Into the vale of years – yet that's not much –

She's gone, I am abused, and my relief   270

Must be to loathe her. O curse of marriage,

That we can call these delicate creatures ours,

And not their appetites! I had rather be a toad

And live upon the vapour of a dungeon,

Than keep a corner in the thing I love   275

For others' uses. Yet, 'tis the plague of great ones:

Prerogatived are they less than the base.

'Tis destiny unshunnable, like death:

Even then this forked plague is fated to us

When we do quicken. Look where she comes –   280

Enter DESDEMONA and EMILIA

---

233   *affect:* like

234   *clime:* region; latitude

236-237
    Foh! One may smell...thoughts unnatural: This mention of the difference of colour is Iago's strongest card

238   *in position:* positively

240   *recoiling:* returning

241   *fall to match:* happen to compare

242   *happily:* maybe

250-251
    place...fills it up: an obscene innuendo

253   *means:* to recover his post

254   *strain his entertainment:* insist his reinstatement

257   *busy:* interfering

259   *free:* innocent

260   *government:* self-control

263   *haggard:* wild

264   *jesses:* these were straps tied to the legs of hawks

266   *prey at fortune:* fend for herself

266   *Haply:* perhaps

267   *soft parts:* pleasant arts

268   *chamberers:* gallants

273   *toad:* here we see Othello begin to use the animal imagery characteristic of Iago

277   *Prerogatived:* privileged

279   *forked plague:* cuckold's horns

280   *do quicken:* are conceived

	If she be false, O then heaven mocks itself:	
	I'll not believe't.	
DESDEMONA	How now, my dear Othello!	
	Your dinner, and the generous islanders	*generous*: noble (283)
	By you invited, do attend your presence.	
OTHELLO	I am to blame.	
DESDEMONA	Why do you speak so faintly?	285
	Are you not well?	
OTHELLO	I have a pain upon my forehead, here.	
DESDEMONA	Faith, that's with watching: 'twill away again.	*watching*: not obtaining enough sleep (288)
	Let me but bind it hard, within this hour	
	It will be well.	
OTHELLO	Your napkin is too little.	290 *napkin*: handkerchief (290)

She drops her handkerchief

| | Let it alone. Come, I'll go in with you. | |
| DESDEMONA | I am very sorry that you are not well. | |

Exeunt OTHELLO and DESDEMONA

EMILIA	I am glad I have found this napkin:	
	This was her first remembrance from the Moor;	
	My wayward husband hath a hundred times	295
	Wooed me to steal it; but she so loves the token –	
	For he conjured her she should ever keep it –	
	That she reserves it evermore about her	
	To kiss and talk to. I'll have the work ta'en out,	*ta'en out*: copied, duplicated (299)
	And give't Iago: what he will do with it	300
	Heaven knows, not I –	
	I nothing, but to please his fantasy.	*I nothing, but*: I know nothing except (302) / *fantasy*: whim (302)

Enter Iago

IAGO	How now? What do you here alone?	
EMILIA	Do not you chide: I have a thing for you.	
IAGO	You have a thing for me? It is a common thing –	305
EMILIA	Hah?	
IAGO	To have a foolish wife.	
EMILIA	O, is that all? What will you give me now	
	For that same handkerchief?	
IAGO	What handkerchief?	
EMILIA	What handkerchief?	310
	Why that the Moor first gave to Desdemona,	
	That which so often you did bid me steal.	
IAGO	Hast stolen it from her?	
EMILIA	No, faith, she let it drop by negligence,	
	And, to th'advantage, I, being here, took't up:	315
	Look, here it is.	
IAGO	A good wench! Give it me.	

[He snatches it]

EMILIA	What will you do with it, that you have been	
	So earnest to have me filch it?	
IAGO	Why, what's that to you?	
EMILIA	If it be not for some purpose of import,	*import*: importance (319)
	Give't me again. Poor lady, she'll run mad	320
	When she shall lack it.	*lack*: miss (321) / *Be not acknown on't*: don't acknowledge anything about it (321)
IAGO	Be not acknown on 't:	
	I have use for it. Go, leave me.	

Exit EMILIA

I will in Cassio's lodging lose this napkin,
And let him find it. Trifles light as air
Are to the jealous confirmations strong   325
As proofs of holy writ. This may do something.
The Moor already changes with my poison:
Dangerous conceits are in their natures poisons,   328 *conceits:* ideas
Which at the first are scarce found to distaste,   329 *distaste:* be distasteful
But with a little act upon the blood,   330   330 *act:* action
Burn like the mines of sulphur. I did say so.

Enter OTHELLO

Look where he comes. Not poppy, nor mandragora,   332 *poppy:* opium (derived from the poppy)
Nor all the drowsy syrups of the world   332 *mandragora:* narcotic plant
Shall ever medicine thee to that sweet sleep   333 *drowsy:* causing sleep
Which thou owedst yesterday.

OTHELLO   Ha, ha, false to me?   335   335 *owedst:* didst own
IAGO   Why, how now, general? No more of that!
OTHELLO   Avaunt, be gone! Thou hast set me on the rack: 337 *Avaunt:* away with you
I swear 'tis better to be much abused
Than but to know't a little.

IAGO   How now, my lord?
OTHELLO   What sense had I in her stolen hours of lust? 340
I saw't not, thought it not – it harm'd not me;
I slept the next night well, fed well, was free, and merry;   342 *free:* untroubled
I found not Cassio's kisses on her lips.
He that is robbed, not wanting what is stolen,   344 *wanting:* missing
Let him not know't, and he's not robbed at all.   345
IAGO   I am sorry to hear this.
OTHELLO   I had been happy if the general camp,   347 *general camp:* whole army
Pioneers and all, had tasted her sweet body,   348 *Pioneers:* sappers
So I had nothing known. O, now for ever   349 *So:* if
Farewell the tranquil mind; farewell content;   350
Farewell the plumed troops, and the big wars
That make ambition virtue – O, farewell!
Farewell the neighing steed, and the shrill trump,
The spirit-stirring drum, th'ear-piercing fife,
The royal banner, and all quality,   355
Pride, pomp, and circumstance of glorious war;   356 *circumstance:* pageantry
And O you mortal engines, whose rude throats   357 *mortal engines:* deadly instruments
Th'immortal Jove's dread clamours counterfeit,   358 *Jove's dread clamours:* thunder
Farewell! Othello's occupation's gone!
IAGO   Is't possible, my lord?   360
OTHELLO   Villain, be sure thou prove my love a whore!
Be sure of it; give me the ocular proof;
[He seizes Iago by the throat]
Or, by the worth of mine eternal soul,
Thou hadst been better have been born a dog
Than answer my waked wrath!
IAGO   Is't come to this?   365
OTHELLO   Make me to see't; or, at the least, so prove it   367 *probation:* proof
That the probation bear no hinge nor loop
To hang a doubt on – or woe upon thy life!
IAGO   My noble lord –
OTHELLO   If thou dost slander her and torture me,   370
Never pray more! Abandon all remorse,

On horror's head horrors accumulate,
Do deeds to make heaven weep, all earth amazed!
For nothing canst thou to damnation add
Greater than that.

IAGO   O grace! O heaven forgive me!   375
Are you a man? Have you a soul or sense?
God by you, take mine office – O wretched fool
That lov'st to make thine honesty a vice!
O monstrous world! Take note, take note, O world,
To be direct and honest is not safe!–   380
I thank you for this profit, and from hence
I'll love no friend, sith love breeds such offence.

OTHELLO   Nay, stay. Thou shouldst be honest.

IAGO   I should be wise; for honesty's a fool,
And loses that it works for.

OTHELLO   By the world,   385
I think my wife be honest, and think she is not;
I think that thou art just, and think thou art not:
I'll have some proof. Her name, that was as fresh
As Dian's visage, is now begrimed and black
As mine own face. If there be cords, or knives,   390
Poison, or fire, or suffocating streams,
I'll not endure it. Would I were satisfied!

IAGO   I see, sir, you are eaten up with passion:
I do repent me that I put it to you.
You would be satisfied?

OTHELLO   Would? Nay, and I will!   395

IAGO   And may – but how? How 'satisfied', my lord?
Would you the supervisor grossly gape on?
Behold her tupped?

OTHELLO   Death and damnation! O!

IAGO   It were a tedious difficulty, I think,
To bring them to that prospect. Damn them, then,   400
If ever mortal eyes do see them bolster
More than their own. What then? How then?
What shall I say? Where's satisfaction?
It is impossible you should see this,
Were they as prime as goats, as hot as monkeys,   405
As salt as wolves in pride, and fools as gross
As ignorance made drunk. But yet, I say,
If imputation and strong circumstances,
Which lead directly to the door of truth,
Will give you satisfaction, you might have't.   410

OTHELLO   Give me a living reason she's disloyal.

IAGO   I do not like the office;
But sith I am entered in this cause so far,
Pricked to't by foolish honesty and love,
I will go on: I lay with Cassio lately;   415
And, being troubled with a raging tooth,
I could not sleep. There are a kind of men
So loose of soul that in their sleeps will mutter
Their affairs – one of this kind is Cassio:
In sleep I heard him say 'Sweet Desdemona,   420
Let us be wary, let us hide our loves';

---

378   *to make thine honesty a vice:* **by carrying it to the excess**

382   *sith:* **since**

387   *just:* **true**

389   *Dian's:* **Diana (goddess of chastity)**

390-392:   *If there be cords, or knives...I'll not endure it:* **Here Othello contemplates suicide**

397   *supervisor:* **on-looker**

405   *prime:* **lecherous**
406   *salt:* **lustful**
406   *pride:* **heat**

408   *imputation and strong circumstances:* **strong circumstantial evidence**

414   *Pricked:* **spurred on**

415   *lay with:* **Beds being expensive items, were commonly shared by same sex friends and by members of the family**

418   *loose of soul:* **careless about their most inward secrets**

And then, sir, would he gripe and wring my hand,
Cry 'O, sweet creature!', and then kiss me hard,
As if he plucked up kisses by the roots
That grew upon my lips, then laid his leg   425
Over my thigh, and sighed, and kissed, and then
Cried 'Cursed fate that gave thee to the Moor!'

OTHELLO   O monstrous! Monstrous!

IAGO   Nay, this was but his dream.

OTHELLO   But this denoted a foregone conclusion.

IAGO   'Tis a shrewd doubt, though it be but a dream;   430
And this may help to thicken other proofs,
That do demonstrate thinly.

OTHELLO   I'll tear her all to pieces!

IAGO   Nay, yet be wise: yet we see nothing done –
She may be honest yet. Tell me but this,
Have you not sometimes seen a handkerchief   435
Spotted with strawberries in your wife's hand?

OTHELLO   I gave her such a one – 'twas my first gift.

IAGO   I know not that; but such a handkerchief –
I am sure it was your wife's – did I today
See Cassio wipe his beard with.   440

OTHELLO   If it be that—

IAGO   If it be that, or any, that was hers.
It speaks against her with the other proofs.

OTHELLO   O, that the slave had forty thousand lives –
One is too poor, too weak for my revenge!   445
Now do I see 'tis true. Look here, Iago:
All my fond love thus do I blow to heaven – 'tis gone!
Arise, black Vengeance from thy hollow hell,
Yield up, O Love, thy crown and hearted throne
To tyrannous Hate! Swell, bosom, with thy fraught,   450
For 'tis of aspics' tongues.

IAGO   Yet be content.

[Othello kneels]

OTHELLO   O, blood, blood, blood!

IAGO   Patience, I say: your mind perhaps may change.

OTHELLO   Never, Iago. Like to the Pontic Sea,
Whose icy current and compulsive course,   455
Ne'er feels retiring ebb, but keeps due on
To the Propontic and the Hellespont,
Even so my bloody thoughts, with violent pace,
Shall ne'er look back, ne'er ebb to humble love,
Till that a capable and wide revenge   460
Swallow them up. Now, by yon marble heaven,
In the due reverence of a sacred vow,
I here engage my words.

IAGO   Do not rise yet.

[Iago kneels]

Witness, you ever-burning lights above,
You elements that clip us round about,   465
Witness that here Iago doth give up
The execution of his wit, hands, heart,
To wronged Othello's service. Let him command,
And to obey shall be in me remorse,

429 *foregone conclusion:* previous copulation

430 *shrewd doubt:* cursed suspicion

433 *yet we see nothing done:* refers to Othello's demand for ocular proof

449 *hearted:* seated in the heart

450 *fraught:* burdened

451 *aspics':* venomous snakes'

454 *Pontic Sea:* the Black Sea

457 *Propontic:* Sea of Marmora
457 *Hellespont:* Dardanelles

460 *capable:* ample

465 *clip:* encompass

467 *execution:* activities
467 *wit:* intelligence
468 *remorse:* compassion

	What bloody business ever.	470
OTHELLO	I greet thy love,	
	[They rise]	
	Not with vain thanks, but with acceptance bounteous;	
	And will upon the instant put thee to't.	
	Within these three days let me hear thee say	
	That Cassio's not alive.	
IAGO	My friend is dead:	475
	'Tis done at your request. But let her live.	
OTHELLO	Damn her, lewd minx! O, damn her, damn her!	
	Come, go with me apart; I will withdraw	
	To furnish me with some swift means of death	
	For the fair devil. Now art thou my lieutenant.	480
IAGO	I am your own for ever.	
Exeunt		

IAGO AND OTHELLO

Desdemona promises Cassio that she will do all she can to convince her husband to reinstate him. Iago tries to make Othello suspicious about the nature of his wife's relationship with his former lieutenant, drawing Othello's attention to Cassio's hurried departure but the Moor initially thinks nothing of it. However, when the ensign pretends to know something that he is reluctant to reveal and reminds the Moor how Desdemona deceived her own father when she married him, Othello starts to think that there is something to Iago's suspicions. Emilia finds a handkerchief that Desdemona drops and, knowing that it was a gift from Othello, plans to return it to her mistress. However, Iago snatches it from her and plans to leave it in Cassio's lodgings.

When Iago later meets Othello again it is clear that the Moor's mind is greatly agitated. He tells Iago that his mind is tortured with thoughts of wife being with Cassio and demands to be given proof of the affair. When Iago says that he heard Cassio speak of Desdemona in his sleep, Othello vows bloody vengeance. Iago then mentions that he saw Cassio wipe his face with Desdemona's handkerchief. Othello is so enraged that he asks Iago to have Cassio killed. He vows to kill Desdemona and appoints Iago lieutenant.

ACTION

LINE BY LINE

▶ LINES 1-90:
CASSION SPEAKS WITH DESDEMONA

Acting on Iago's advice Cassio has come to speak with Desdemona. He wants her to intercede with Othello on his behalf. Desdemona, he hopes, can persuade Othello to give him back his job as lieutenant.

Desdemona acknowledges that Cassio has served Othello well: 'You do love my lord:/ You have known him long' (10-1). She promises to plead Cassio's case with the Moor, saying she would rather die than let him down: 'I will do/ All my abilities in thy behalf' (1-2). She will do so to 'the last article' (22), pleading with Othello constantly until he relents and restores Cassio to the lieutenantship: 'I'll intermingle every thing he does/ With Cassio's suit' (21-5). She seems confident that the breach between the two will soon be healed: (5-7).

Othello and Iago enter the garden. Cassio, however, does not stay to hear Desdemona press his case. Given the previous night's drunken lapse he feels awkward and embarrassed to be around Othello and slips quietly away (30-1).

Desdemona immediately raises the matter of Cassio's suit: 'I have been talking with a suitor here, / A man that languishes in your displeasure' (42-3). Cassio, she says, made an honest mistake and 'errs in ignorance and not in cunning' (49).

She asks Othello to call him back and make peace with him (55). Though Othello is unwilling to do so Desdemona persists, repeatedly pleading with Othello to rehire him as soon as possible: 'I prithee, name the time, but let it not / Exceed three days' (61-5). Othello, initially reluctant and non-committal, is eventually ruled by his love for Desdemona. Cassio, he says, may visit him anytime to be reinstated as lieutenant (76). He can deny his beautiful new wife nothing (77).

Othello asks to be left alone and Desdemona obliges, stressing that she will be obedient to Othello, no matter what moods, notions or 'fancies' take hold of him: 'Be as your fancies teach you; / Whate'er you be, I am obedient' (89-90). As she departs Othello again stresses his deep affection for her, saying how only his love for Desdemona saves him from chaos and perdition or hell (91-3).

► LINES 91-135: IAGO SOWS THE FIRST SEEDS OF DOUBT

Iago, as he revealed in Act 2 Scene 3, plans to drive Othello insane with jealousy by convincing him that Desdemona is having an affair with Cassio. He now begins to execute this plan.

He sows the first seeds of doubt when Cassio slips guiltily away as he and Othello approach. He pretends to be disturbed by this sight: 'Ha? I like not that' (33). He says it can't have been Cassio departing because Cassio has no reason to react guiltily at Othello's approach (37-9). By doing so, of course, he creates the first faint association between Cassio and guilt in Othello's mind.

He then asks a simple, seemingly harmless question, wondering if Cassio knew of the courtship between Othello and Desdemona: 'Did Michael Cassio, when you woo'd my lady, / Know of your love?' (96-7). Cassio, Othello responds, not only knew of their relationship but acted as their go-between (97, 102).

Iago's brilliance here lies not in what he says but in what he doesn't say. His seemingly innocent

question catches Othello's attention, arousing his curiosity and suspicion. Iago, however, pretends to be reluctant to discuss the matter any further:

- He claims to have raised it only out of idle curiosity: 'But for a satisfaction of my thought' (99).
- He response to Othello, 'Indeed!', is enigmatic and suggests Iago knows more than he's letting on.
- He echoes Othello's questions rather than reply to them directly: 'Honest, my lord!', 'Think, my lord!' (105, 108).
- He repeatedly states his belief in Cassio's honesty but does so in a half-hearted manner intended to arouse suspicion (107, 128-9).

Iago's evasive and one-word responses are designed to further enflame Othello's curiosity, which of course they do. After all, we are never more curious that when someone knows a secret but refuses to reveal it.

Othello begins to suspect that Iago must know something horrible about Cassio and Desdemona, a secret too terrible to mention: 'As if there were some monster in thy thought / Too hideous to be shown' (110-1). He feels that Iago's wisdom and sense of justice prevent him from speaking freely, something that deeply unsettles him: 'Therefore these stops of thine fright me the more' (122-8). He repeatedly demands to know what's on Iago's mind: 'if thou dost love me, / Show me thy thought', 'I prithee, speak to me as to thy thinkings' (118-9, 135).

💬 THINK ABOUT IT

Iago's abilities as an actor
Iago is engaged in a brilliant form of 'double pretence' here. He pretends to know about a secret affair that is not actually taking place. He also pretends to be reluctant to discuss the 'affair' when he is actually eager to convince Othello that it is real. He knows that such a show of reticence will make his accusation seem all the more convincing.

► LINES 136 -178: IAGO CONTINUES TO BE EVASIVE

Iago continues in his refusal to reveal his thoughts about Cassio and Desdemona, giving a variety of reasons for doing so:

- Though Iago, as Othello's ensign, is 'bound' to him in all things he cannot be made speak about this matter. Even slaves, after all, cannot be compelled to reveal their innermost thoughts (137-40).
- There is the possibility that his suspicions are 'vile and false' (140). After all, he says, no one has a 'breast so pure' that they escape all such 'uncleanly' doubts about other people's character and behaviour (141-5).

OTHELLO

OTHELLO AS SOLDIER

Othello is someone who has spent much of his life on the battlefield. He has only ever known war and it is in this environment that he seems to feel most in control and at ease. Of the battlefield he is a master but when it comes to social games he feels unqualified and ill-at-ease. He, therefore, places great trust in Iago's knowledge of these matters. His ensign, he says, 'knows all qualities, with a learned spirit/ Of human dealings' (262-3).

The qualities that make Othello such a great military leader are evident in this scene. We see his decisiveness and commitment to a course of action once he has made a decision. When he is sure that his wife is having an affair with Michael Cassio he vows bloody revenge, telling Iago that, now that he has made up his mind there is no going back. He compares his resolve to the sea's current that flows compulsively until it reaches its destination. Othello also seems to view his revenge as if it is a military campaign, vowing to execute a 'capable and wide revenge' (260). He gives Iago his orders to have Cassio killed in no more than three days and withdraws to think about how best to kill his wife: 'I will withdraw/ To furnish me with some swift means of death/ For the fair devil' (478-80).

OTHELLO

We also get to see just what being a soldier means to Othello. When he believes that his wife is unfaithful he thinks that his life is over and his career is at an end. He thinks about the things that once meant so much to him: the soldiers in their immaculate uniforms; the 'big wars' (351) that can do honour to a man's ambition; the sounds of the horses, the trumpets and drums; the magnificent splendour of battle and the pride and glory that accompanies it. This is the world that he knows and loves and he feels that all is now lost.

DIGNITY AND SELF-POSSESSION

Though Othello begins the scene in a composed and self-possessed manner it is not long before these qualities give way to agitation, anger and self-doubt. Iago maddens him by hinting at knowing something terrible but not revealing exactly what it is that he knows. Othello initially seems untroubled by his ensign's suspicions, saying that he is not someone prone to jealousy, but very soon he is demanding to know exactly what Iago is thinking: 'By heaven, I'll know thy thoughts' (165). Before long the suspicions that Iago introduces into his mind are torturing him: 'Thou hast set me on the rack' (337). His words and actions become increasingly brutal and violent: 'Villain, be sure thou prove my love a whore...Or by the worth of mine eternal soul,/ Thou hadst been better have been born a dog' (361-4). He seizes Iago by the neck and later threatens to tear Desdemona 'all to pieces' (432).

What is perhaps most surprising in this scene is how rapidly Othello becomes dispirited and morose. For the first time in the play we glimpse Othello's vulnerabilities and self-doubts:
- He wonders why he ever married (246).
- He considers the fact that he is not of Venetian society and that he is old and unsophisticated: 'for I am black/ And have not those soft parts of conversation/ That chamberers have, or for I am declined/ Into the vale of years' (266-9)
- At one point he says he would rather be a toad in a dungeon than the husband of an unfaithful wife: 'I had rather be a toad/ And live upon the vapour of a dungeon' (273-4).
- He seems to contemplate suicide: 'If there be chords, or knives,/ Poison, or fire, or suffocating streams,/ I'll not endure it' (390-2).

💬 **THINK ABOUT IT**

We perhaps see Iago's acting at its most audacious when Othello briefly turns on him. He is suffering, he declares, for being an honest and good friend, something this 'monstrous world' has no place for: 'To be direct and honest is not safe!' (375-80). He proclaims that it would have been wiser to be deceptive all along: 'I should be wise; for honesty's a fool, / And loses that it works for' (384-5). To the reader or audience member, of course, Iago's protests are outrageous in their irony.

Iago preys on these insecurities. He knows that Othello feels a little unsure of himself in Venetian society and that the Moor is unfamiliar with the customs of the city and ways of its people. He tells Othello that Venetian women are known to be unfaithful and that it is not something they are ashamed of. As long as their husbands are unaware of their behaviour they feel no remorse: 'In Venice they do let God see the pranks/ They dare not show their husbands; their best conscience/ Is not to leave't undone, but keep't unknown' (205-7).

Iago also contends that Desdemona chose to marry Othello because of his exotic looks and origins and that this was an unnatural choice for her to make: 'One may smell in such a will most rank,/ Foul disproportions, thoughts unnatural' (236-7). It is, Iago suggests, only a matter of time before Desdemona comes to her senses and gives Othello up for someone from her native land: 'I may fear/ Her will, recoiling to her better judgement,/ May fall to match you with her country forms' (239-42).

OTHELLO'S LOVE FOR DESDEMONA

At the beginning of the scene we see how affectionately Othello deals with his wife, addressing her as 'sweet Desdemona' (56). Though she harries him with her request to speak with Cassio, he does not lose his patience: 'I will deny thee nothing' (84). When he thinks he has been a little curt with her, he checks himself and reminds himself how much he loves her: 'Perdition catch my soul/ But I do love thee' (91-2). He imagines how terrible his life would be without her love: 'when I love thee not,/ Chaos is come again' (92-3).

It is not long, unfortunately, before this chaos has entered Othello's mind and the love that seemed so true and strong is being questioned. The 'poison' that Iago pours in the Moor's ear is quick to corrupt to thoughts. He is suddenly imagining Desdemona's 'stolen hours of lust' (340) and 'Cassio's kisses on her lips' (343). He talks of how he would feel if the entire army was bedding his wife: 'if the general camp,/ Pioneers and all, had tasted her sweet body' (347-8). In a very short period of time the woman that he once thought pure and innocent is 'begrimed' (389) with suspicions of infidelity. By the close of the scene, Othello considers her a 'lewd minx', a 'whore' and 'the fair devil' and wishes her dead (477-80).

OTHELLO'S TRUSTING NATURE

Othello's trusting nature is evident at the beginning of the scene. He finds nothing immediately suspicious about Cassio speaking to his wife, nor the fact that the former lieutenant slipped away when Othello arrived. Even when Iago characterises Cassio's behaviour as 'guilty-like' (38) the Moor barely takes notice. He has faith in people

and says that he thinks 'Cassio's an honest man' (133). He is also happy to have a wife who is 'fair, loves company,/ Is free of speech' (187-8) and claims that he is not someone prone to jealousy. His faith in those he loves is not fickle and he tells Iago that he will only doubt someone's good character when it has been clearly demonstrated that they have acted inappropriately: 'I'll see before I doubt; when I doubt, prove' (193).

Unfortunately it is the trust that he places in Iago that leads to Othello's doubting the woman he loves. Iago insists again and again throughout the scene that he loves the Moor and that his loyalty is absolute. Othello in turn considers Iago to be 'full of love and honesty' (122). It is for this very reason that Othello is alarmed by Iago's early hesitations and 'pursed brow' (116). If Iago fears something, Othello thinks, it must be a concern 'working from the heart' (127).

But Othello is not completely naive or blind to the possibility that Iago might be lying. In a moment of rage he takes Iago by the neck, telling him that he had better be speaking the truth or face the Moor's 'waked wrath': 'Villain, be sure thou prove my love a whore!/ Be sure of it' (361-2). Iago's feigned horror and hurt at the notion he would ever lie to Othello is, unfortunately, enough to ensure that Othello does not question him further. By the close of the scene Othello places complete faith in Iago, appointing him lieutenant and instructing him to kill Cassio.

OTHELLO'S ELOQUENCE

The eloquence of Othello's speech fades as his suspicions grow and as the scene progresses his language becomes increasingly brutal, violent and dark. The transformation in his manner of speech is shocking and tells of how disturbed Othello now is by the thought that his wife might not who he thought she was:

- He calls Iago a 'Villain' and demands that he prove Desdemona 'a whore' (361).
- He invokes 'black Vengeance' to rise up within him and for 'tyrannous Hate' to displace the love in his heart (448, 450).
- As Iago turns the screw and introduces ever stronger doubts into Othello's mind, the Moor can only respond with short exclamations of outrage and despair: 'O monstrous! Monstrous!' (428), 'O, blood, blood, blood!' (452).
- The scene closes with him damning his wife and calling her a whore: 'Damn her, lewd minx! O, damn her, damn her!' (477)

- By nature he's a jealous or suspicious person, who can't help seeing wrongdoings that are not actually there: 'and oft my jealousy / Shapes faults that are not' (151-2). A wise person like Othello, he feels, should and will 'take no notice' of his half-baked notions, of his 'scattering and unsure observance' (154-5).
- If his accusations or suspicions are false he will damage Cassio and Desdemona's good name, which is the most precious thing a person possesses: 'Good name in man and woman, dear my lord, / Is the immediate jewel of their souls' (159-60).
- He worries that his accusation will arouse Othello's jealousy, which is a very destructive emotion: 'O, beware, my lord, of jealousy; / It is the green-eyed monster' (168-9).
- Jealousy can make life miserable: a jealous man who loves his wife yet fears she's unfaithful will know only 'damnèd minutes' of misery, fear and suspicion (170-3).

Through all this Othello repeatedly demands to know what's on Iago's mind: 'By heaven, I'll know thy thoughts' (165). He declares that if Iago is truly his friend he'll tell him his suspicions (146-8). Iago, however, stubbornly refuses to budge, claiming that Othello can never know his innermost thoughts: 'You cannot, if my heart were in your hand' (166).

▶ LINES 179-260: IAGO PRETENDS TO RELUCTANTLY REVEAL WHAT'S ON HIS MIND

Othello reassures Iago that he will not be overcome with jealousy or ruled by his emotions. He trusts his wife and will require proof of any alleged wrong

doing on her behalf before acting against her (179-95). Iago, letting on he's reassured by this, pretends to finally and frankly reveal his suspicions. 'now I shall have reason / To show the love and duty that I bear you / With franker spirit' (196-8). Othello, he says, should fear an affair between Cassio and Desdmona: 'Look to your wife; observe her well with Cassio' (200). He gives several reasons for his suspicion:

- He knows Venice better than Othello and the city's women, he says, have a terrible tendency to be unfaithful, getting up to all kinds of 'pranks' in the bedroom when their husbands' backs are turned (204-7).
- He brings up the fact that Desdemona has a history of deception. After all she deceived her father when she courted and married Othello behind his back (209). Despite her youth she was more than able to pull the wool over her father's eyes: 'To seal her father's eyes up close as oak – / He thought 'twas witchcraft' (213-4).
- He pretends to fear that, because Othello is a foreigner, he will find it difficult to keep Desdemona, that she will eventually find herself falling for someone closer to herself in both race and upbringing (230-42).

Though Othello claims to be unmoved by these suspicions it seems obvious to Iago that he's badly shaken (217, 220, 228). He believes that Desdemona's honest but worries that she might go against her noble nature and betray him: 'And yet, how nature erring from itself' (229, 231). He also fears that Iago knows more than he's letting on (246-7).

DESDEMONA

Desdemona's kindness and decency are again evident in this scene. She seems to genuinely want to do her best for Cassio, promising the former lieutenant that she will do everything in her power to convince Othello to reinstate him: 'I will do / All my abilities in thy behalf' (1-2). She tells him that when she makes a promise to a friend she does everything she can to keep it: 'If I do vow a friendship I'll perform it / To the last article' (21-2).

Desdemona also displays a playfulness and fun-loving spirit. She tells Cassio that she will 'tame' (23) her powerful husband and turn their bedroom into a schoolroom and their lodgings into a confessional until Othello agrees to her demands: 'His bed shall

seem a school, his board a shrift' (24). When Othello appears she seems to tease him by telling him she has just been talking to a 'suitor' (42). She then playfully harasses him to meet with Cassio as soon as possible: 'Why then tomorrow night, or Tuesday morn, / On Tuesday noon, or night, on Wednesday morn' (61-2). However, perhaps Desdemona's behaviour reveals a certain immaturity on her part. She does not think for a moment that she might be interfering in military matters by lobbying for Cassio's reinstatement nor does she seem to show consideration for Othello's demanding role as general. Though he tells her that he is busy and cannot see Cassio immediately, she persists in her demand that he set a date. Her unfortunate reference to Cassio as a 'suitor' will also later add to Othello's suspicions that she is unfaithful to him.

OTHELLO AND DESDEMONA

Othello is clearly distressed and wishes to be alone. He asks Iago to keep him informed of any developments and to have Emilia spy on Desdemona: 'If more thou dost perceive, let me know more:/ Set on thy wife to observe' (243-4).

Iago departs with one final manipulative speech. Othello, he advises, at least for now shouldn't give Cassio back his post as lieutenant: 'Although 'tis fit that Cassio have his place…Yet, if you please to hold him off awhile' (250-2). This course of action will allow him to observe how Desdemona pleads on his behalf. If she does so too passionately it will indicate that the affair is actually taking place (254-6).

▶ LINES 261-292: OTHELLO IS FILLED WITH DOUBT

Othello is convinced of Iago's honesty and believes that his ensign is someone who knows much about human behaviour: 'knows all qualities, with a learned spirit/ Of human dealings'(262-3). The idea that Desdemona is not who he thought she was now seems very real. He considers the possibility that his wife is like some wild, untamed creature – a hawk that he has tethered with his own 'heart-strings'. If this is her true nature then he would prefer to release her and let her pursue what she desires: 'I'd whistle her off and let her down the wind/ To prey at fortune'(265-6).

The Moor begins to doubt the possibility that Desdemona could love a dark-skinned man such as he, someone who lacks the smooth tongue of the courtly young men: 'for I am black/ And have not those soft parts of conversation/ That chamberers

have' (266-8). He also considers the fact that he is considerably older than Desdemona: 'or for I am declined/ Into the vale of years' (268-9).

Suddenly his wife's seems lost to him and the only way he can console himself is by hating her: 'She's gone, I am abused, and my relief/ Must be to loathe her' (270-1). Marriage is a cursed affair – a man can acquire a wife but can never take control of her desires: 'we can call these delicate creatures ours,/ And not their appetites' (272-3). In a moment of utter despair Othello states that he would rather be a toad living in a filthy dungeon than the husband of a cheating wife, claiming but a small space in her affections: 'I had rather be a toad/ And live upon the vapour of a dungeon,/ Than keep a corner in the thing I love' (273-5). It is the fate of great men, Othello thinks, to be deceived in this manner by their wives: ''tis the plague to great ones' (276).

Just as Othello is torturing himself with these thoughts, Desdemona and Emilia arrive. Desdemona tells him that the guests he invited for dinner are awaiting him. Othello, still preoccupied with his thoughts, mutters something about only having himself to blame: 'I am to blame' (285). Desdemona sees that all is not right with her husband and asks him if he is feeling unwell. He tells her that he has a headache and when she looks to soothe his forehead with her handkerchief he tells her it is too small. Desdemona drops her handkerchief but Othello tells her to disregard it and that he will go to dinner with her: 'Let it alone. Come, I'll go in with you' (291).

IAGO

MALICIOUS, CALLOUS AND DESTRUCTIVE

Iago's intense malice is nowhere more evident than in this scene. He seems to take great pleasure in how Othello is consumed by jealousy, gloating that the Moor's poisoned mind will soon be beyond all help and will never know 'sweet sleep' (334) again, irrespective of whatever 'drowsy syrup' (333) he might take to aid his rest. By the scene's conclusion he has driven Othello practically demented with jealousy. Cassio and Desdemona, too, will suffer through Iago's malice, with Othello determined to have them both put to death.

A MASTER PLOTTER

Iago's mastery of scheming is evident throughout this scene:

- Act 3 Scene 3 suggests he's arranged things so that he and Othello arrive while Cassio and Desdemona are talking.
- He uses the fact that Cassio slips quietly and guiltily away to begin filling Othello's mind with doubts.
- He has urged Emilia 'a hundred times' to steal Desdemona's handkerchief, knowing he can use it for his own ends (295).
- He now plans to use the discarded handkerchief to further discredit Cassio in Othello's eyes, knowing that a jealous mind will find this relatively flimsy piece of evidence convincing: 'Trifles light as air / Are to the jealous confirmations strong / As proofs of holy writ' (324-6).
- He warns Othello to watch out for Desdemona pleading too vehemently on Cassio's behalf, knowing full well that such pleas are likely to occur.

Yet this scene stresses once again that Iago is a brilliant improviser rather than a meticulous planner. Iago operates more like a boxer, reacting skilfully to his opponent, than like a chess master who plots twenty steps ahead.

MANIPULATIVE AND PERSUASIVE

The scene also shows us Iago giving a master class of persuasion and manipulation. At the beginning of the scene Othello has no suspicions whatsoever that an affair might be taking place between Cassio and Desdemona. By its conclusion, however, he is convinced that the affair is real and threatens to kill them both. It is fascinating to watch how Iago gently leads Othello on this journey into suspicion, doubt and

jealous rage. For the most part he does so by dropping hints and sowing seeds of doubt while letting Othello's own imagination do most of the work.

Iago is much too clever to simply blurt out his false accusation. Instead he begins by sowing seeds of doubt regarding Cassio's relationship with Desdemona. He declares that he's troubled by the sight of Cassio skulking off as Othello arrives and asks if Cassio knew about the love between Othello and Desdemona when the couple were courting.

These simple statements naturally arouse Othello's curiosity. Yet Iago refuses to expand on them for as long as possible. At first he pretends not to know what Othello's getting at: 'Honest, my lord?', 'Think, my lord?' (105, 108). Then, when challenged more directly to reveal his suspicions, he comes up with a number of reasons not to do so, citing his over-active imagination, the possibility his suspicions might be false, the dangers of jealousy and his desire to avoid blackening anybody's name.

This reticence proves a brilliant tactic. It allows for Othello's doubts to sprout and flourish. It also causes the Moor's curiosity to reach fever pitch – after all we are never more curious than when someone is keeping a secret from us. Eventually, Othello is practically begging him to reveal what's on his mind. Furthermore, Iago's apparent caution and concern for others' good names make his accusation sound much more plausible when he finally reveals it.

In revealing his 'suspicion' Iago plays expertly on Othello's insecurities. As an outsider, he suggests, Othello doesn't know how promiscuous and untrustworthy the women of Venice actually are. He mentions the possibility that eventually Desdemona will find herself attracted to someone from her own race and background. He also brings up Desdemona's history of betrayal: the fact that she betrayed her father in marrying Othello means it's more likely she's betraying the Moor now.

Some time passes before the two continue their conversation, during which time Othello's doubts and suspicions continue to fester. As Iago puts it: 'The Moor already changes with my poison' (327). When the two meet again he lets Othello talk himself into a frenzy, leading him on with simple non-commital phrases like 'Is't possible, my lord?' and 'I am sorry to hear this' (346, 360).

It is important to note how long Iago delays in telling concrete and definite lies about other people. For most of the scene he refers to suspicions that he himself allegedly possesses. It is only toward the end of the scene, when Othello is on the verge of a jealous rage, that he drops in the story about Cassio talking in his sleep He has waited until precisely the right moment, until Othello's passions are enflamed to the extent that he is no longer thinking clearly.

Similarly, he responds very cleverly to Othello's demand for 'ocular proof' (362). It is unlikely, he tells the Moor, that it will be possible to catch Desdemona and Cassio in the act of making love (399-400). Yet perhaps there is some other way that satisfactory proof of their affair can be obtained. He pretends to ponder the matter before mentioning the handkerchief that has so recently come into his possession and describing how he saw Cassio 'wipe his beard' with it (438-40). These final barefaced lies are enough to overcome Othello's remaining doubts and tip him into a homicidal rage.

A BRILLIANT ACTOR

Iago's considerable acting skills are on display throughout the scene. He has managed to convince his wife Emilia that he's terribly distressed by Cassio's fall from grace: 'Good madam, do: I warrant it grieves my husband, / As if the case were his' (3-4). Desdemona, too, is deceived by him, being utterly convinced of his trustworthiness: 'O, that's an honest fellow' (5).

We are reminded that Othello, too, has been taken in by Iago, considering him an exceptionally honest person: 'for I know thou'rt full of love and honesty', 'This fellow's of exceeding honesty' (122, 261). He also has great respect for Iago's wisdom, considering him someone who has seen much of life and of human nature and who doesn't speak without carefully considering his words (123, 262-3)

Iago takes care to disguise his objectives and motivations. He repeatedly warns Othello not to be consumed by jealousy when such an outcome, of course, is his ultimate goal. Othello, he says, must be careful not to let his thougts run away with him: 'I am to pray you not to strain my speech / To grosser issues nor to larger reach / Than to suspicion' (221-3). When Othello does become jealous he repeatedly urges calm: 'Patience, I say: your mind perhaps may change' (453). He even declares he's sorry for bringing the matter up in the first place: 'I see, sir, you are eaten up with passion: / I do repent me that I put it to you' (393-4).

IAGO AND EMILIA
Act 2 Scene 1 showed how Iago and Emilia's relationship seemed marked by criticism and bickering, a trend that continues in this scene. Iago refers to her as a 'foolish wife' and a 'wench' (306, 316). He shows little gratitude when she gives him the handkerchief, refusing to tell her what he wants with it and rudely ordering her to leave (321-2).

As another smokescreen, Iago repeatedly urges Othello not to take his suspicions too seriously when, of course, that's exactly what he wants him to do. Othello, he says, should avoid jumping to conclusions for his fears will hopefully be proved false: 'In the meantime, / Let me be thought too busy in my fears....And hold her free' (256-9). He makes a similar point later in the scene: 'Nay, yet be wise: yet we see nothing done/ She may be honest yet' (433-4).

Throughout the scene, then, Iago convinces Othello that he's on his side, that the accusation he levels against Desdemona comes only from the love he bears for Othello. Again and again he mentions how he acts only out of loyalty and respect:
• My lord, you know I love you' (120).
• 'I humbly do beseech you of your pardon/ For too much loving you' (215-6)
• 'I shall have reason/ To show the love and duty that I bear you/ With franker spirit' (196-8).
• 'I hope you will consider what is spoke/ Comes from my love' (219-20).

In a final display of loyalty and brotherhood Iago kneels beside Othello in what can almost be described as an act of prayer, the two of them swearing by the heavens or the seas. Othello vows to be avenged, Iago vows to assist him in this 'bloody business', offering his himself to Othello's service (464-10).

Othello is completely taken in by this act of love and loyalty. He welcomes Iago's love and declares that he will be loyal to him in return: 'I greet thy love', 'I am bound to thee for ever' (471, 216). He even grants Iago Cassio's old position of lieutenant (480).

Iago uses a simple yet effective form of reverse psychology. He dangles some event, story or piece of evidence before Othello but denies its importance. Then when Othello insists that it's important after all, he agrees, making it seem as if Othello came to this conclusion independently. At first he dismisses Cassio's night-time behaviour, saying 'Nay, this was but his dream' (428). Then when Othello insists on its significance he agrees, declaring that, taken with other pieces of evidence, it might prove Desdemona's infidelity (431-2).

IAGO

▶ LINES 293 – 331:
EMILIA GIVES IAGO THE HANKERCHIEF

Emilia finds the handkerchief that Desdemona dropped. She recalls that this was the first gift Othello gave to his wife: 'This was her first remembrance from the Moor' (294). It is something that Othello hoped she would keep forever and Desdemona in turn treasured the handkerchief dearly. Emilia also says that Iago often expressed great interest in the item, asking her again and again if she could steal it for him. She decides that she will have an embroidered copy of the handkerchief made to give to Iago before she hands the original back to Desdemona: 'I'll have the work ta'en out, / And give't Iago' (299).

Iago appears and asks her what she is up to. She mentions that she has in her possession the handkerchief that 'the Moor first gave to Desdemona' (311). Iago is delighted by this good fortune and he snatches it off his wife. When Emilia asks him what he could possibly want with such an item he tells her to keep quiet about the matter and to leave him be: 'Be not acknown on't: / I have use for it. Go, leave me' (321-2).

Left alone Iago immediately hatches a plan involving the handkerchief. He decides that he will leave it in Cassio's lodging for him to find. He cannot predict exactly what the outcome will be, but knows that should an item such as this get into the hands of the man Othello suspects is having an affair with his wife, trouble will ensue. Othello is already showing signs of changing since Iago hinted at the possibility of his wife being unfaithful: 'The Moor already changes with my poison' (327). The ideas that he has planted in Othello's mind may now only be of slight discomfort to the Moor but if a few more insinuations are added to the mix his jealousy and anger will become greatly enflamed: 'with a little act upon the blood, / Burn like the mines of sulphur' (330-1).

▶ PHASE 4: LINES 332 - 411: IAGO TURNS THE SCREW

Iago sees Othello approaching and thinks how troubled the Moor's mind must now be. All the sedatives in the world, he thinks, could not now induce the peaceful sleep Othello enjoyed before he began to suspect his wife of being unfaithful: 'Not poppy, nor mandragora nor all the drowsy syrups of the world / Shall ever medicine thee to that sweet sleep / Which thou owedst yesterday' (332-4).

Othello still can't believe that Desdemona could cheat on him: 'Ha, ha, false to me?' (335). Iago tells him to let it alone and not think on it but Othello is in no mood to be calmed. He tells his ensign to get lost: 'Avaunt, be gone!' (337). Iago has tortured his mind with these suspicions. To know everything, no matter how bad, would be preferable to having these inklings of doubt: 'Thou hast set me on the rack: / I swear 'tis better to be much abused / Than but to know't a little' (337-9). Better still to be utterly ignorant of these matters: when he suspected nothing he slept and ate well and was 'free, and merry' (342). If Desdemona was sleeping with the whole army unbeknownst to him he could be content: 'I had been happy if the general camp...had tasted her sweet body, / So I had nothing known' (347-9). If a man is robbed and does not want what is stolen, don't tell him he is robbed and it will be to him as if he never was (344-5).

But Othello has been made to suspect his wife is unfaithful and these suspicions have destroyed any contentment he once enjoyed: 'O, now for ever / Farewell the tranquil mind' (349-50). The things that once mattered greatly to the Moor suddenly seem shorn of their value and importance: the soldiers in their immaculate uniforms; the 'big wars' (351) that can do honour to a man's ambition; the sounds of the horses, the trumpets and drums; the magnificent splendour of battle and the pride and glory that accompanies it – all these things now matter little to Othello. His career, he tells Iago, is over: 'Farewell! Othello's occupation's gone' (359).

In a fit rage Othello takes Iago by the throat and tells him that he had better prove Desdemona a 'whore' or face his 'wrath' (361-65). He demands to have physical proof of his wife's unfaithfulness: 'give me the ocular proof' (362). He wishes to see evidence or at least be so utterly convinced that no room for doubt can remain: 'Make me see't; or, at the least, so prove it / That the probation bear no hinge nor loop / To hang a doubt on' (366-8). If Iago cannot do this or, worse still, if his suspicions are proven false and he has slandered Desdemona and tortured Othello without proper reason, his behaviour will place him beyond forgiveness: 'For nothing canst thou to damnation add / Greater than that' (374-5).

Iago acts as though he is greatly wounded by such accusations and calls on Othello to dismiss him as his ensign if this is how he is viewed: 'God by you, take mine office' (377). He curses himself for being honest, saying that if honesty leads to such grief it must be considered a vice rather than a virtue: 'O wretched fool / That lov'st to make thine honesty a vice' (377-8). He thanks Othello for showing him the error of his ways and says that he now knows that it is a mistake to be 'direct and honest' (380).

Othello tells him to stay and that he should be honest. With all the Moor has heard recently he no longer knows what to think or believe. He thinks that Desdemona is faithful and also that she is not. He thinks Iago is fair and honest but he is equally unsure of this. What he desires is concrete proof so that he can be satisfied. To remain in a state of uncertainty is too painful and Othello would rather end his life than endure this further: 'I'll not endure it. Would I were satisfied' (392).

Iago asks him what he would need to be satisfied. Would he like to witness his wife making love to another man, gaping on while they complete the act? 'Would you the supervisor grossly gape on? / Behold her tupped?' (397-8). Surely, Iago suggests, it would be all but impossible to arrange it so that they could be viewed in this manner. Even if they were grossly lecherous and wanton in their desire it is unlikely they would ever be caught in the act. So what then will give the Moor the satisfaction he desperately requires? 'What then? How then? / What shall I say? Where's satisfaction?' (402-3).

► LINES 412 - 479: OTHELLO PLOTS HIS REVENGE

Iago thinks he has just the evidence that Othello needs. He claims that it is with great reluctance that he discloses this, but that having come this far, spurred on by honesty and love, he will continue. He tells Othello that he recently shared a bed with Cassio but due to the fact that he had a raging toothache, could not sleep. He says that during the night Cassio spoke in sleep, saying 'Sweet Desdemona, / Let us be wary, let us hide our loves' (420-1). Iago then claims that Cassio grasped him as though he were Desdemoa, planting passionate kisses on his lips and laying his leg over the ensign's thigh. He also cursed the fact that Desdemona should be wedded to Othello.

Othello is shocked and horrified at this tale of Iago's. Though Iago stresses that it was only a dream of Cassio's, Othello says it is proof enough that they made love on some occasion: 'But this denoted a foregone conclusion' (429). Wild with jealousy and rage, Othello says that

he will tear his wife 'all to pieces' (432). Iago now chooses to mention the handkerchief that Othello gave as a gift to Desdemona and that she recently dropped. He asks Othello if he knows of such an item and when Othello says he does, Iago tells him that he recently saw Cassio wipe his beard with this same handkerchief. Surely this is the 'ocular proof' that Othello needs: 'If it be that, or any, it was hers. / It speaks against her with the other proofs' (441-2).

The Moor has heard enough and is now absolutely convinced that his wife is having an affair with Michael Cassio. The love that he held for Desdemona has now evaporated and he wishes to enact great vengeance on his former lieutenant: 'O, that the slave had forty thousand lives – / One is too poor, too weak for my revenge' (443-4). He calls on his vengeance to rise up and for hate to take the place that love once occupied in his heart: 'Yield up, O Love, thy crown and hearted throne / To tyrannous Hate' (449-50). When Iago calls on him to calm down and suggests that he might yet change his mind, Othello says this is not a possibility. Now that he is set upon this vengeful path he cannot change course. Like a sea that only ever flows in one direction, the Moor's violent thoughts cannot be altered.

> ## 💬 THINK ABOUT IT
> Iago uses facial expressions to convey the apparent concern that lie behind his apparently innocent questions:
> • thou criedst *'Indeed! /
> And didst contract and purse thy brow together /
> As if thou then hadst shut up in thy brain'* (115-7).
> The possibilities for an actor here are endless. The actor is playing a malevolent character who's pretending to be a concerned friend who's pretending to mask his concern behind simple and innocuous comments. The scene presents us with Shakespeare at his most layered and complex.

Iago kneels down next to Othello and says that he is willing to to swear undying loyalty to the general. Whatever Othello commands of him he will do. The cruellest act will seem a kindness because it is done for the wronged Moor: 'Let him command, / And to obey shall be in me remorse, / What bloody business ever' (468-70). Othello welcomes his ensign's show of loyalty and immediately asks him to have Cassio murdered. Iago agrees to this command but asks that the Moor let Desdemona live: 'My friend is dead: / 'Tis done at your request. / But let her live (475-6). Othello damns his wife and says that he will plan how best to have her killed. Before he departs he appoints Iago his lieutenant: 'Now art thou my lieutenant' (480). ◆

ACT 3

SCENE 4

Before the castle.

Enter Desdemona, Emilia, and Clown

DESDEMONA	Do you know, sirrah, where Lieutenant Cassio lies?	
Clown	I dare not say he lies anywhere.	
DESDEMONA	Why, man?	
Clown	He's a soldier, and for me to say a soldier lies – 'tis stabbing.	
DESDEMONA	Go to! Where lodges he?	5
Clown	To tell you where he lodges, is to tell you where I lie.	
DESDEMONA	Can anything be made of this?	
Clown	I know not where he lodges; and for me to devise a lodging, and say he lies here, or he lies there, were to lie in mine own throat.	10
DESDEMONA	Can you enquire him out, and be edified by report?	
Clown	I will catechize the world for him – that is, make questions, and by them answer.	
DESDEMONA	Seek him, bid him come hither: tell him I have moved my lord on his behalf, and hope all will be well.	15
Clown	To do this is within the compass of man's wit, and therefore I will attempt the doing it.	

Exit

DESDEMONA	Where should I lose that handkerchief, Emilia?	
EMILIA	I know not, madam.	
DESDEMONA	Believe me, I had rather have lost my purse	20
	Full of crusadoes: and, but my noble Moor	
	Is true of mind and made of no such baseness	
	As jealous creatures are, it were enough	
	To put him to ill thinking.	
EMILIA	Is he not jealous?	
DESDEMONA	Who, he? I think the sun where he was born	25
	Drew all such humours from him.	
EMILIA	Look, where he comes	

Enter Othello

DESDEMONA	I will not leave him now till Cassio	
	Be called to him. How is't with you, my lord?	
OTHELLO	Well, my good lady. *(Aside)* O, hardness to	
	dissemble!–	
	How do you, Desdemona?	
DESDEMONA	Well, my good lord.	30
OTHELLO	Give me your hand. This hand is moist, my lady.	
DESDEMONA	It yet hath felt no age, nor known no sorrow.	
OTHELLO	This argues fruitfulness and liberal heart:	
	Hot, hot, and moist! This hand of yours requires	
	A sequester from liberty– fasting and prayer,	35
	Much castigation, exercise devout–	
	For here's a young and sweating devil here,	

Glossary / notes (right column):

1 *sirrah:* term of address to social inferiors

11 *edified:* instructed

12 *catechize:* interrogate

13 *by them answer:* 'by them be enabled to answer'

16 *compass:* reach

18 *should I lose:* could I have lost

19 *I know not:* Emilia's lie makes it difficult for her to explain matters after Othello has shown his jealousy

21 *crusadoes:* gold coins

26 *humours:* moods, dispositions

29 *hardness:* how hard it is

33 *argues:* indicates
33 *fruitfulness:* in this instance suggests that she's amorous or available for love
33 *liberal:* in this instance suggests she's lustful or licentious

35 *sequester:* removal, shutting away
36 *castigation:* chastisement
36 *exercise:* disciplinary suffering

37 *sweating:* labouring

	That commonly rebels. 'Tis a good hand,	
	A frank one.	
DESDEMONA	You may, indeed, say so;	40
	For 'twas that hand that gave away my heart	
OTHELLO	A liberal hand. The hearts of old gave hands,	
	But our new heraldry is hands, not hearts.	
DESDEMONA	I cannot speak of this. Come now, your promise.	
OTHELLO	What promise, chuck?	45
DESDEMONA	I have sent to bid Cassio come speak with you.	
OTHELLO	I have a salt and sorry rheum offends me:	
	Lend me thy handkerchief.	
DESDEMONA	Here, my lord.	
OTHELLO	That which I gave you.	
DESDEMONA	I have it not about me.	
OTHELLO	Not?	50
DESDEMONA	No, faith, my lord.	
OTHELLO	That is a fault: that handkerchief	
	Did an Egyptian to my mother give;	
	She was a charmer, and could almost read	
	The thoughts of people; she told her, while she kept it	55
	'Twould make her amiable and subdue my father	
	Entirely to her love– but if she lost it,	
	Or made gift of it, my father's eye	
	Should hold her loathed, and his spirits should hunt	
	After new fancies. She dying, gave it me	60
	And bid me, when my fate would have me wived,	
	To give it her. I did so; and, take heed on't,	
	Make it a darling like your precious eye:	
	To lose't or give't away were such perdition	
	As nothing else could match.	
DESDEMONA	Is't possible?	65
OTHELLO	'Tis true; there's magic in the web of it:	
	A sybil, that had numbered in the world	
	The sun to course two hundred compasses,	
	In her prophetic fury sewed the work;	
	The worms were hallowed that did breed the silk,	70
	And it was dyed in mummy, which the skilful	
	Conserved of maidens' hearts.	
DESDEMONA	I'faith, is't true?	
OTHELLO	Most veritable; therefore look to't well.	
DESDEMONA	Then would to God that I had never seen't!	
OTHELLO	Ha? Wherefore?	75
DESDEMONA	Why do you speak so startingly and rash?	
OTHELLO	Is't lost? Is't gone? Speak, is't out o'th' way?	
DESDEMONA	Heaven bless us!	
OTHELLO	Say you?	80
DESDEMONA	It is not lost; but what an if it were?	
OTHELLO	How?	
DESDEMONA	I say it is not lost	
OTHELLO	Fetch't, let me see't.	
DESDEMONA	Why, so I can, sir; but I will not now:	
	This is a trick to put me from my suit –	85
	Pray you, let Cassio be received again.	
OTHELLO	Fetch me the handkerchief; my mind misgives.	

Glossary (right column):

47   *salt and sorry rheum:* wretched running cold

54   *a charmer:* an enchantress

56   *amiable:* beloved

60   *fancies:* loves

63   *Make it a darling like your precious eye:* 'To love as one's own eye'
64   *perdition:* loss; ruin, damnation

66   *web:* warp; hence 'weaving'

67   *sybil:* prophetess
67-68   *that had numbered... two hundred compasses:* normally interpreted to mean she was two hundred years old. Extreme age was a frequent attribute of prophets

71   *mummy:* a dye prepared from the flesh and bandages from mummies

72   *maidens' hearts:* mummy prepared from the remains of virgins was thought especially effective and also thought of as a charm against jealousy

76   *rash:* rashly

77   *is't out o'th' way:* is it misplaced or missing

87   *misgives:* is suspicious

DESDEMONA	Come, come: you'll never meet a more sufficient man –	
OTHELLO	The handkerchief!	
DESDEMONA	I pray, talk me of Cassio-	90
OTHELLO	The handkerchief!	
DESDEMONA	– a man that all his time	
	Hath founded his good fortunes on your love,	
	Shared dangers with you –	
OTHELLO	The handkerchief!	
DESDEMONA	I'faith, you are to blame.	
OTHELLO	'Swounds!	95

Exit

EMILIA	Is not this man jealous?	
DESDEMONA	I ne'er saw this before.	
	Sure, there's some wonder in this handkerchief:	
	I am most unhappy in the loss of it.	
EMILIA	'Tis not a year or two shows us a man:	
	They are all but stomachs, and we all but food;	100
	To eat us hungerly, and when they are full	
	They belch us.	

Enter Iago and Cassio

	Look you, Cassio and my husband.	
IAGO	There is no other way: 'tis she must do't –	
	And, lo, the happiness! Go, and importune her.	
DESDEMONA	How now, good Cassio, what's the news with you?	105
CASSIO	Madam, my former suit: I do beseech you	
	That, by your virtuous means, I may again	
	Exist, and be a member of his love,	
	Whom I, with all the office of my heart	
	Entirely honour. I would not be delayed:	110
	If my offence be of such mortal kind	
	That nor my service past, nor present sorrows,	
	Nor purposed merit in futurity	
	Can ransom me into his love again –	
	But to know so must be my benefit;	115
	So shall I clothe me in a forced content,	
	And shut myself up in some other course	
	To fortune's alms.	
DESDEMONA	Alas, thrice-gentle Cassio,	
	My advocation is not now in tune:	
	My lord is not my lord; nor should I know him,	120
	Were he in favour as in humour altered.	
	So help me every spirit sanctified,	
	As I have spoken for you all my best,	
	And stood within the blank of his displeasure	
	For my free speech! you must awhile be patient:	125
	What I can do, I will; and more I will	
	Than for myself I dare. Let that suffice you.	
IAGO	Is my lord angry?	
EMILIA	He went hence but now,	
	And certainly in strange unquietness.	
IAGO	Can he be angry? I have seen the cannon	130
	When it hath blown his ranks into the air	
	And, like the devil, from his very arm	
	Puffed his own brother – and is he angry?	

Glossary (right margin):

88   *sufficient:* capable

90   *talk me of Cassio:* talk to me about Cassio#

97   *wonder:* supernatural property

100   *they are all but stomachs:* they consist only of apetite
101   *hungerly:* hungrily
102   *belch:* vomit up

104   *happiness:* good luck

109   *office of my heart:* loyal service of my heart
110   *would not:* do not wish to be
111   *mortal:* fatal

113   *purposed merit in futurity:* the merit I mean to demonstrate in the future
115   *to know so must be my benefit:* knowing the worst must be my only reward

117   *shut myself up:* confine myself

121   *favour:* appearance

124   *blank:* centre of target, range

129   *unquietness:* agitation

133   *Puffed:* blown, extinguished

Something of moment then: I will go meet him,
There's matter in't indeed, if he be angry.   135

DESDEMONA   I prithee, do so.

Exit Iago

             Something sure of state –
Either from Venice, or some unhatched practice
Made demonstrable here in Cyprus to him –
Hath puddled his clear spirit; and in such cases
Men's natures wrangle with inferior things,   140
Though great ones are their object. 'Tis even so;
For let our finger ache and it endues
Our other, healthful members even to a sense
Of pain. Nay, we must think men are not gods,
Nor of them look for such observancy   145
As fits the bridal. Beshrew me much, Emilia,
I was – unhandsome warrior as I am –
Arraigning his unkindness with my soul;
But now I find I had suborned the witness,
And he's indicted falsely.

EMILIA   Pray heaven it be   150
State matters, as you think, and no conception
Nor no jealous toy concerning you.

DESDEMONA   Alas the day! I never gave him cause.

EMILIA   But jealous souls will not be answered so;
They are not ever jealous for the cause,   155
But jealous for they're jealous. It is a monster
Begot upon itself, born on itself.

DESDEMONA   Heaven keep the monster from Othello's mind.

EMILIA   Lady, amen!

DESDEMONA   I will go seek him. Cassio, walk here about: 160
If I do find him fit, I'll move your suit
And seek to effect it to my uttermost.

CASSIO   I humbly thank your ladyship.

Exeunt Desdemona and Emilia
Enter Bianca

BIANCA   'Save you, friend Cassio.

CASSIO   What make you from home?
How is't with you, my most fair Bianca?   165
I' faith, sweet love, I was coming to your house.

BIANCA   And I was going to your lodging, Cassio.
What, keep a week away? Seven days and nights?
Eight-score eight hours? And lovers' absent hours
More tedious than the dial eight score times!   170
O weary reckoning!

CASSIO   Pardon me, Bianca:
I have this while with leaden thoughts been pressed;
But I shall, in a more continuate time
Strike off this score of absence. Sweet Bianca,
Take me this work out.   175

He gives her Desdemona's handkerchief

BIANCA   O Cassio, whence came this?
This is some token from a newer friend.
To the felt absence now I feel a cause.
Is't come to this? Well, well.

Glossary (right margin):

134   *moment:* importance

136   *Something sure of state:* it must be some matter of public affairs
137   *unhatched practise:* undisclosed plot
138   *Made demonstrable:* made evident, exposed
139   *puddled:* made muddy

142   *endues:* instructs

145   *observancy:* respectful and ceremonious attention
146   *bridal:* wedding
146   *Beshrew me:* may evil befall me (a mild oath that was often used playfully)
147   *unhandsome:* inadequate
149   *suborned:* corrupted

150-152   *Pray heaven it be... concerning you:* here we see Emilia feeling guilty about taking the handkerchief

170   *dial:* clock
171   *reckoning:* settling of accounts, judgement, punishment, revenge
172   *leaden:* as heavy as lead, depressing, burdensome
172   *pressed:* oppressed
173   *continuate:* uninterrupted
175   *Take me this work out:* copy this embroidery for me
177   *friend:* lover, mistress

[Handwritten annotations:]
- good example of Jealousy
- Theme of play → Jealousy
- Bianca - Cassio's lover very much in love with him
- Besotted
- Jealousy

CASSIO   Go to, woman!
Throw your vile guesses in the devil's teeth,   180
From whence you have them. You are jealous now
That this is from some mistress, some remembrance –
No, by my faith, Bianca.
BIANCA   Why, whose is it?
CASSIO   I know not, neither: I found it in my chamber.
I like the work well: ere it be demanded –   185
As like enough it will – I would have it copied.
Take it and do't; and leave me for this time.
BIANCA   Leave you? Wherefore?
CASSIO   I do attend here on the general,
And think it no addition nor my wish   190
To have him see me womaned.
BIANCA   Why, I pray you?
CASSIO   Not that I love you not.
BIANCA   But that you do not love me.
I pray you, bring me on the way a little,
And say if I shall see you soon at night.
CASSIO   'Tis but a little way that I can bring you,   195
For I attend here: but I'll see you soon.
BIANCA   'Tis very good – I must be circumstanced!
Exeunt

182 *remembrance:* keepsake, love-token

189 *attend here on:* wait for

191 *womaned:* accompanied by a woman

193 *bring:* accompany

197 *circumstanced:* I must give way to circumstance

10

OTHELLO AND DESDEMONA

CASSIO AND THE HANKERCHIEF

Desdemona sends the clown to fetch Cassio so he can make his case for reinstatement to Othello. She wonders where she has misplaced the handkerchief. Emilia denies all knowledge of its whereabouts.

Othello enters, attempting to disguise his suspicions about Desdemona and Cassio. To Othello, in a state of morbid jealousy and suspicion, Desdemona's moist hand seems a sign that she is filled with devilish lust. He asks Desdemona for the handkerchief, saying that is an exotic and magical family heirloom. Desdemona's inability to produce it makes him highly agitated, enfaming his suspicion of her infidelity. He repeatedly demands to seet it before storming off.

Cassio and Iago enter. Cassio, at Iago's urging, once again asks Desdemona to plead with Othello on his behalf. Desdemona promises to do so but stresses that Othello is not himself and that her efforts so far have brought her nothing but his displeasure.

Cassio has found the handkerchief in his chamber, where it has been planted by Iago. He has no idea of its importance nor of its owner's identity. He encounters Bianca, a woman with whom he has been having a casual relationship. He gives Bianca the handkerchief, asking her to copy its exquisite design before its rightful owner demands its return.

ACTION

LINE BY LINE

▶ LINES 1-101: OTHELLO QUESTIONS DESDEMONA

Desdemona is looking for Cassio. She wants to tell him that she has spoken to her husband as promised about his reinstatement and the time is right for him to make his case to Othello. She meets a clown who agrees to go and find the former lieutenant.

The lost handkerchief is troubling Desdemona. She can't think where she might have misplaced it and tells Emilia that she would rather have lost a purse full of gold coins than this item. Though her husband is not the jealous type, her losing this particular handkerchief is enough to put him to ill thinking. (24) When Emilia asks her if Othello is truly not the jealous type, Desdemona tells her that it is not in the Moor's nature to be such: 'Who, he? I think the sun where he was born/ Drew all such humours from him' (25-6).

When Desdemona sees Othello approaching she tells Emilia that she will not leave him until he has met with Cassio: 'I will not leave him now till Cassio/ Be called to him' (27-8). She greets her

OTHELLO

OTHELLO

DIGNITY AND SELF-POSSESSION

The last scene culminated with Othello raging against his wife and vowing to find a way to kill her. His mood was black and his speech violent and coarse. However, when Othello meets his wife in this scene he is initially composed and has his feelings under wraps. He greets her in a friendly manner: 'Well, my good lady' (29). But it only takes the mentioning of Cassio's name for Othello's composure to crack. He immediately asks for the handkerchief that he gave her as a first gift and when she says that she does not have it with her he gets increasingly agitated. When she refuses to produce the handkerchief and attempts to bring the conversation back around to Cassio's reinstatement, Othello storms off, cursing.

Desdemona is startled at his tone and manner of speech, asking him why he speaks 'so startingly and rash' (76). Earlier in the scene she had reminded us of the Moor's dignity and noble character when she told Emilia that he is 'true of mind' (22) and incapable of jealousy or other negative emotions: 'I think the sun where he was born / Drew all such humours from him' (25-6).

However, though Othello does lose his composure, we see how difficult the Moor finds it to not be completely honest or straightforward with Desdemona. He struggles to 'dissemble', or conceal his feelings and suspicions from her: 'O hardness to dissemble!' (29). Othello is therefore presented as a straightforward honest man to whom lying does not come naturally. The contrast between him and Iago could not be starker.

OTHELLO'S LOVE FOR DESDEMONA

There is a moment early in the scene when the love that Othello once felt for Desdemona seems to surface and his attitude towards her softens.

He refers to her affectionately as 'chuck' (45) and, though he initially considers her moist hand a sign of lustfulness, he cannot help but think that it is 'a good hand, / A frank one' (38-9).

However, his mind has been poisoned by Iago's words and the love he once felt for his wife tarnished. His view of her is now much influenced by Iago's general low opinion of women and he thinks that she is a lustful and promiscuous creature who craftily conceals her affairs from her husband. Othello tells her that 'there's a young and sweating devil' within her that urges her to 'rebel' and cheat on him (377-8). He suggests that she devote herself to 'fasting and prayer' (35) in order to keep her desires in check.

OTHELLO'S TRUSTING NATURE

Whereas once Othello seemed to trust his wife completely, his mind is now full of suspicions and doubts. He takes hold of her hand and, finding it warm and moist, thinks it a sign of her lascivious nature. When Desdemona mentions Cassio's name Othello immediately asks to see the handkerchief he gave her. In his mind her ability or inability to produce this item is now central to her guilt. When she tells him that she does not have the handkerchief with her and – worse still – when she says that she has not lost it but is reluctant to go and fetch it, it is all that Othello needs to reinforce and solidify the doubts that Iago has planted in his mind: 'my mind misgives' (87).

OTHELLO'S ELOQUENCE

We saw in the last scene how Othello's eloquence faded as his suspicions grew and as the scene progressed his language became increasingly brutal, violent and dark. Though he is much more subdued in this scene we again see how the eloquence that was so evident in the early scenes has given way to a more blunt and unpleasant manner of speech.

💬 THINK ABOUT IT

Othello's exotic origins
The story of the handkerchief emphasises the strange and exotic nature of Othello's character. His origins are not in the rational, orderly world of Venice but in the mysterious east, a land of myth and magic. According to Othello, a two hundred-year-old prophetess created the handkerchief from silk spun by enchanted worms and dye made form the dust of mummies. The tale of the handkerchief seems to startle Desdemona and she tells him that she wishes to God that she 'had never seen't' (74).

CHARACTER DEVELOPMENT

husband and he responds in a friendly manner, but he is struggling to conceal his true feelings and suspicions from her: 'O, hardness to dissemble' (29). He takes hold of her hand and comments on its moistness, saying that it indicates a free and amorous spirit: 'This argues fruitfulness and liberal heart' (33). To Othello, in a state of morbid jealousy and suspicion, this moistness seems a sign that Desdemona is filled with devilish lust: 'here's a young and sweating devil here' (37).

Desdemona does not register her husband's suspicions. Her hand is warm and moist, she says, because she is young and has known no sorrow (32). When he describes it as a 'frank' (39) hand, she takes this to mean 'honest' and agrees with him: 'You may indeed say so' (40). It was this hand, after all, that gave away her heart when they married. Othello says that there was a time when someone gave their hand in marriage they also gave their heart, but this is no longer the way: 'The hearts of old gave hands, / But our new heraldry is hands, not hearts' (42-3). However, he seems to soften and behaves in a more affectionate manner towards her, referring to her affectionately as 'chuck' (45).

But this affection is short lived. When Desdemona mentions Cassio's name Othello stiffens. He tells her that he has a cold and wishes to avail of her handkerchief. Desdemona offers him her handkerchief but it is not the one he gave her. When she tells him that she does not have it with her, he says that this is not a good thing – the handkerchief is a family heirloom with mysterious powers:

- It was given to his mother by an Egyptian enchanter (53).
- This woman told Othello's mother that while she kept the handkerchief it would make her desirable and keep her husband interested in her (55-6).
- If she ever lost the handkerchief or gave it away as a gift, her husband would loathe her and he would leave her for another woman (57-60).
- When Othello's mother was dying she gave the handkerchief to him, saying that when he got married to give it to his wife (62).
- She also told him to take great care of it and that if it ever should be lost great misfortune would result (63-5).
- There is also magic woven into the fabric of the handkerchief by a two hundred year old prophetess (68-9).
- The prophetess used the thread of scared silkworms and dye made from the dust of mummies (70-2).

DESDEMONA

Desdemona is fundamentally a good-natured individual. She has done as she promised and solicited Othello on Cassio's behalf. She now hopes that Cassio will meet her husband, make his case for reinstatement and that 'all will be well' (15). When she meets Othello she is eager that this happens and as soon as she can she raises the matter with him. Even though he is acting in a strange manner and is clearly upset about the handkerchief, she perseveres. Little does she know that every time she mention's Cassio's name it fuels Othello's suspicions that she is having an affair with his former lieutenant.

When Othello presses her about the handkerchief, asking her if it is lost, she lies and tells him that she knows where it is but does not wish to fetch it at this moment: 'It is not lost' (81). Perhaps it is Othello's disturbing behaviour that causes her to lie. Having just been informed that the handkerchief is a family heirloom with magical properties it is almost impossible for her to tell him that she has lost it.

Desdemona is amazed at this, asking twice if it is true. She denies that she has lost it: 'I say it is not lost' (83). Othello, clearly agitated by his suspicions of her infidelity, demands that she bring the handkerchief for him to look at: 'Fetch't, let me see't' (83). She says that she can fetch it for him, only that she won't do this now: 'Why, so I can, sir; but I will not now' (84). She tries to redirect the conversation back to talk of Cassio, but this, of course, only serves to strengthen Othello's suspicion that she is having an affair with him. Having repeatedly demanded to see the handkerchief, he eventually storms out cursing: 'Swounds!' (95).

▶ LINES 102-163: IAGO SPEAKS TO CASSIO

Iago and Cassio arrive. Iago once again urges Cassio to ask Desdemona about getting his job a lieutenant back. it si only by getting Desdemona to plead on his behalf that his old position will be restored: 'There is no other way; 'tis she must do't' (103). Cassio takes this advice and in an elaborate speech raises the matter of his 'former suit' (106).

IAGO

MALICIOUS, CALLOUS AND DESTRUCTIVE

In this scene Iago is only physically present for a brief moment. Yet his poison flows everywhere through it. Othello, due to his manipulations, is tortured with jealousy and suspicion, feverishly and almost incoherently demanding again and again to know the whereabouts of the handkerchief. Cassio, also a result of his plotting, is in a miserable state, filled with 'leaden thoughts' (172) as he futilely seeks a return to his old position as lieutenant.

Desdemona, too, has been wounded by his schemes; by the scene's end she is fending off worry, doubt and confusion regarding her marriage and its future. It could also be argued that Emilia's actions reveal the guilt she feels at being sucked into Iago's plans by giving him the handkerchief.

A MASTER PLOTTER

Iago's deft plotting, then, has begun to bring misery to all around him. Yet his machinations are far from complete. In this scene he encourages Cassio to keep pressing Desdemona about getting his job back. He stresses to Cassio that it's only through her intercession that Othello's mind can be changed. His real objective, of course, is to further convince Othello that Desdemona and Cassio are having an affair. If Desdemona continues to plead on Cassio's behalf it will convince Othello that the affair is real. He tells the others that he departs to investigate Othello's sudden change in temperament yet the audience knows he really intends to further poison the Moor's mind.

He longs to once again be in Othello's good graces, to 'be a member of his love' (108). However, if his 'offence' is too great for this to happen he wants to know. Knowing this awful truth will at least allow him to get on with his life: But to know so must be my benefit...' And shut myself up in some other course, / To fortune's alms' (115-8).

Desdemona replies that her pleas on his behalf have fallen on deaf airs: 'My advocation is not now in tune'(119). Othello does not seem to be himself: 'My lord is not my lord' (120). He has been acting strangely and is in 'humour altered' (121). She swears she has done her best for Cassio. Yet her efforts have brought her nothing but Othello's displeasure: 'As I have spoken for you all my best / And stood within the blank of his displeasure/ For my free speech' (123-5).

Iago suggests that something must be very much the matter if Othello's behaving in such an angry fashion: 'There's matter in't indeed, if he be angry'(135). He claims that Othello never gets angry, not even in the heat of battle when the cannon balls are flying and his brothers in arms are falling: 'I have seen the cannon' / 'When it hath blown his ranks into the air...and is he angry?' (130-3). Iago leaves, allegedly to discover what might be wrong with Othello. The audience, of course, knows that he really intends to further manipualte Othello's clouded mind.

Desdemona reassures herself that Othello must be upset by affairs of state rather than by anything that might be wrong with their marriage: 'Something sure of state…hath puddled his clear spirit' (136-9). She says that sometimes we deal with major concerns – like the affairs of state or government – by focusing on minor matters instead (140-4). Emilia urges her to pray that it is indeed political or 'state matters' (151) troubling Othello's mind rather than any jealous notion ('toy') he might have concerning her (150-2). The jealousy, she says, cannot be reasoned with in a rational or logical fashion (154). She describes jealousy as an emotion that feeds on itself, becoming stronger and stronger as those afflicted lapse ever further into bitterness and resentment (154-7). Desdemona says she never gave Othello any reason to be jealous and prays that the 'monster' of jealousy be kept from Othello's mind (153, 158). She goes off to find her husband,

💬 TALK ABOUT IT
How long has Othello been on Cyprus?

The events of 3.1, 3.2 and 3.3 all take place on the day after Othello reaches Cyprus, on the morning after the celebration that marks his arrival and the destruction of the Turkish fleer.

Yet how much passes between 3.3 and 3.4? Bianca suggests a fairly lengthy ongoing relationship between herself and Cassio, claiming that Cassio hasn't been to see her for over a week. Othello and his party, therefore, must have been on Cyprus long enough to allow Cassio become acquainted with Bianca and then ignore her for over a week. Several weeks, then, might have have lapsed between the end of 3.3 and the beginning of 3.4.

Readers of the play, however, usually get the impression that the events of 3.4 take place at most a few days after those of 3.3. How do we reconcile these two very different impressions of the play's time scheme?

EMILIA

Emilia shows herself to be somewhat less than honest when she denies any knowledge of the whereabouts of the handkerchief (20). She also comes across as a 'woman of the world', as someone who has much experience of relationships between men and women and has a cynical view of such matters. She seems to recognise that jealousy lies behind Othello's strange behaviour and his demands to see the handkerchief: 'Is he not jealous?' (25).

She urges Desdemona to pray that jealousy isn't the cause of Othello's outburst. Jealousy, she claims, is a 'monster' that can simply appear in a person's mind without cause or explanation. Her cynical attitude toward relationships is also evident in her comments about men and women: 'They are all but stomachs, and we all but food;/ they eat us hungrily' (100-1).

promising Cassio she'll continue to press his suit (160-2). We realise, of course, that these efforts will only serve to further enflame Othello's jealousy and suspicion.

► LINES 164-196: CASSIO MEETS BIANCA

Cassio encounters Bianca, a woman with whom he has been having a relationship. Bianca is angry with him because he hasn't visited her in over a week: 'What! Keep a week away? Seven days and nights?' (168). Cassio, somewhat unconvincingly, says he was just about to visit her (166). He claims to have been too preoccupied with worry to do so recently: 'I have this while with leaden thoughts been pressed' (172). He promises to renew the relationship at a more 'continuate' time, at a time when his life is less consumed and interrupted by worry (173).

Cassio gives Bianca Desdemona's handkerchief, asking her to copy its design for him before its owner looks for it back: 'Sweet Bianca,/ Take me this work out' (174-5). Bianca suspects the handkerchief it is a love token from a woman who has replaced her in Cassio's affections: 'This is some token form a newer friend' (176). Cassio chides her for her suspicious and jealous thoughts, saying he found the handkerchief in his bedroom and doesn't know who it belongs to: 'I know not neither; I found it in my chamber' (184). ◆

THINK ABOUT IT
Why doesn't Cassio want to be seen with Bianca?
Cassio doesn't want Othello to see him 'womaned'. What does he mean by this?
- Perhaps he fears that Othello will think him less of a man for keeping female company.
- Perhaps he doesn't want to give the impression that he's light-heartedly womanising and enjoying himself when he so recently lost his job. He wants to seem miserable, serious and completely focused on restoring his old position.
- Perhaps he's embarrassed to be seen with Bianca because she's from a lower social class than himself. Cassio, we remember, is something of an aristocrat.
- Perhaps he's embarrassed to be seen with Bianca because she has a reputation as a prostitute or some kind of 'loose woman'.

Cassio asks Bianca to leave because he doesn't want Othello to see them together (187-9). His desire for her to go, he says, indicates no lack of affection on his part: 'Not that I love you not' (192). Bianca looks for reassurance of his love, asking if he will soon recommence his night time visits to her chamber (193-4). Cassio replies in a non-committal fashion, saying only that he will see Bianca soon (195-6). ◆

CASSIO

CASSIO'S DEVOTION TO OTHELLO

In this scene Cassio once again demonstrates his deep devotion to Othello. He honours Othello with 'all the office of my heart' (109). and longs to be restored to his affections, that something might 'ransom me into his love again' (114). His mind, he says, has been filled with 'leaden thoughts' since he let Othello down (172). If he fails to mend the breach between himself and the Moor he will only sadly and reluctantly get on with his life: 'So shall I clothe me in a forced content/ And shut myself up in some other course' (116-7).

A LADIES' MAN

Earlier scenes have given us the impression that Cassio is popular with the opposite sex, that his good looks, smooth manner and noble upbringing make him something of a ladies' man. His relationship with Bianca reinforces this impression.

Yet their encounter shows Cassio in a somewhat less than favourable light. We get the distinct impression that he is using Bianca, that he sees her only when it suits him. After all he has stayed away for the past seven nights and makes only the vaguest commitment to visit her soon. His reasuarance of love for her is also far from convincing: 'Not that I love you not' (192). He also speaks to her very severely throughout the scene. He criticises her harshly when she suggests that the handkerchief is a token from some other lover: 'Go to woman!/ Throw your vile guesses in the devil's teeth' (179-80). He roughly orders her to leave him alone and to make a copy of the handkerchief: 'Take it and do't; and leave me for this time' (187).

ACT 4 SCENE 1

Cyprus. Before the castle

Enter Iago and Othello

IAGO Will you think so?
OTHELLO Think so, Iago?
IAGO What,
To kiss in private?
OTHELLO An unauthorized kiss!
IAGO Or to be naked with her friend in bed
An hour or more, not meaning any harm?
OTHELLO Naked in bed, Iago, and not mean harm?
It is hypocrisy against the devil.
They that mean virtuously, and yet do so,
The devil their virtue tempts, and they tempt heaven.
IAGO If they do nothing, 'tis a venial slip;
But if I give my wife a handkerchief –
OTHELLO What then?
IAGO Why, then 'tis hers, my lord; and, being hers,
She may, I think, bestow't on any man.
OTHELLO She is protectress of her honour too:
May she give that?
IAGO Her honour is an essence that's not seen,
They have it very oft that have it not.
But, for the handkerchief –
OTHELLO By heaven, I would most gladly have forgot it!
Thou saidst – O, it comes o'er my memory
As doth the raven o'er the infectious house:
Boding to all – he had my handkerchief.
IAGO Ay – what of that?
OTHELLO That's not so good now.
IAGO What
If I had said I had seen him do you wrong?
Or heard him say–as knaves be such abroad
Who, having, by their own importunate suit
Or voluntary dotage of some mistress
Convinced or supplied them, cannot choose
But they must blab –
OTHELLO Hath he said anything?
IAGO He hath, my lord, but be you well assured,
No more than he'll unswear.
OTHELLO What hath he said?
IAGO Faith, that he did – I know not what he did.
OTHELLO What? What?
IAGO Lie.
OTHELLO With her?
IAGO With her, on her – what you will.

9 *venial slip:* pardonable error

12 *bestow't on:* give it to

20 *As doth the raven o'er the infectious house:* A croaking raven was thought to portend death to the plague-stricken inmates of a house

24 *as knaves be such abroad:* as there are villains around

26 *voluntary dotage:* willing infatuation

27 *Convinced or supplied:* overcome or gratified sexually

30 *No more than he'll unswear:* although he won't admit it

OTHELLO	Lie with her? Lie on her? We say 'lie on her' when they belie her. Lie with her? 'Swounds, that's fulsome! Handkerchief – confessions – handkerchief? To confess, and be hanged for his labour? First to be hanged and then to confess! I tremble at it. Nature would not invest herself in such shadowing passion without some instruction. It is not words that shakes me thus. Pish! Noses, ears, and lips! Is't possible? Confess? Handkerchief? O, devil!

He falls down in a trance

IAGO	Work on, my medicine, work! Thus credulous fools are caught,
	And many worthy and chaste dames even thus,
	All guiltless, meet reproach. What ho, my lord!
	My lord, I say! Othello!

Enter Cassio

	How now, Cassio!
CASSIO	What's the matter?
IAGO	My lord is fallen into an epilepsy –
	This is his second fit; he had one yesterday.
CASSIO	Rub him about the temples.
IAGO	No, forbear:
	The lethargy must have his quiet course;
	If not, he foams at mouth, and by and by
	Breaks out to savage madness. Look, he stirs.
	Do you withdraw yourself a little while:
	He will recover straight; when he is gone,
	I would on great occasion speak with you.

Exit Cassio

	How is it, general? Have you not hurt your head?
OTHELLO	Dost thou mock me?
IAGO	I mock you not, by heaven!
	Would you would bear your fortune like a man.
OTHELLO	A horned man's a monster and a beast.
IAGO	There's many a beast then in a populous city,
	And many a civil monster.
OTHELLO	Did he confess it?
IAGO	Good sir, be a man:
	Think every bearded fellow that's but yoked
	May draw with you. There's millions now alive
	That nightly lie in those unproper beds,
	Which they dare swear peculiar. Your case is better.
	O, 'tis the spite of hell, the fiend's arch-mock,
	To lip a wanton in a secure couch,
	And to suppose her chaste. No, let me know;
	And, knowing what I am, I know what she shall be.
OTHELLO	O, thou art wise; 'tis certain.
IAGO	Stand you awhile apart;
	Confine yourself but in a patient list:
	Whilst you were here, o'erwhelmed with your grief –
	A passion most unsuiting such a man –
	Cassio came hither. I shifted him away,
	And laid good 'scuse upon your ecstasy;
	Bade him anon return and here speak with me –
	The which he promised. Do but encave yourself,

34 *fulsome:* lustful; obscene, disgusting

36-37 *First to be hanged and then to confess:* this impossibility indicates Othello's hopeless confusion of mind

38 *shadowing:* darkening

39 *without some instruction:* if there were no basis of fact

45 *Othello:* the first and only time Iago dares to address his general by name, something he can risk only because Othello is unconscious

49 *No, forbear:* No, do not; resist the temptation

50 *lethargy:* unconsciousness, morbid drowsiness

55 *on great occasion:* on an important matter

57 *mock:* make fun

61 *civil:* civilised

63 *bearded fellow:* mature man
63-64 *but yoked May draw with you:* i.e. as an ox is yoked to draw the plough.

65 *unproper:* inappropriate, not theirs

66 *peculiar:* their own private property

68 *lip:* kiss
68 *secure:* safe, free from suspicion

72 *a patient list:* bounds of patience

75 *shifted him away:* got him out of the way

76 *ecstasy:* a fit

77 *anon:* -presently

78 *encave:* hide

	And mark the fleers, the gibes, and notable scorns,		79	*fleers:* sneers
	That dwell in every region of his face.	80		
	For I will make him tell the tale anew:			
	Where, how, how oft, how long ago, and when			
	He hath, and is again to cope your wife.		83	*cope:* meet
	I say, but mark his gesture – marry, patience!			
	Or I shall say you're all in all in spleen,	85	85	*all in all in spleen:* completely overwhelmed by a violent rage
	And nothing of a man.			

OTHELLO   Dost thou hear, Iago?
I will be found most cunning in my patience,
But – dost thou hear? – most bloody.

IAGO   That's not amiss;
But yet keep time in all. Will you withdraw?

Othello withdraws

89   *keep time:* be restrained
89   *withdraw:* leave to hide

	Now will I question Cassio of Bianca,	90		
	A hussy that by selling her desires			
	Buys herself bread and clothes. It is a creature			
	That dotes on Cassio – as 'tis the strumpet's plague		94	*To beguile...by one:* those that deceive another are often deceived themselves
	To beguile many, and be beguiled by one.			
	He, when he hears of her, cannot restrain	95		
	From the excess of laughter. Here he comes.			

Enter Cassio

	As he shall smile, Othello shall go mad;			
	And his unbookish jealousy must construe		98	*unbookish:* ignorant
			98	*construe:* interpret
	Poor Cassio's smiles, gestures and light behavior,		99	*light:* frivolous
	Quite in the wrong. – How do you now, lieutenant?	100		

CASSIO   The worser that you give me the addition
Whose want even kills me.

101   *addition:* title

IAGO   Ply Desdemona well, and you are sure on't:
(Speaking lower) Now, if this suit lay in Bianca's power,
How quickly should you speed!

103   *Ply:* work away at, importune
105   *speed:* attain your desire

CASSIO   Alas, poor caitiff!

106   *caitiff:* wretch

OTHELLO   *(Aside)* Look, how he laughs already.

IAGO   I never knew woman love man so.

CASSIO   Alas, poor rogue! I think i'faith she loves me.

OTHELLO   *(Aside)* Now he denies it faintly, and laughs it out.   110   110   *faintly:* without conviction

IAGO   Do you hear, Cassio?

OTHELLO   *(Aside)*
                     Now he importunes him
To tell it o'er. Go to, well said, well said!

IAGO   She gives it out that you shall marry her
Do you intend it?

CASSIO   Ha, ha, ha!   115

OTHELLO   *(Aside)*
Do you triumph, Roman, do you triumph?

CASSIO   I marry – what, a customer? Prithee, bear some
charity to my wit; do not think it so unwholesome. Ha,
ha, ha!

117   *customer:* harlot, prostitute
117-118   *bear some charity to my wit:* give some credit for my judgement
118   *unwholesome:* morally tainted
123   *scored:* branded

OTHELLO   *(Aside)*
So, so, so, so: they laugh that wins.

IAGO   Faith, the cry goes that you marry her.   120

CASSIO   Prithee say true.

IAGO   I am a very villain else.

OTHELLO   *(Aside)*
Have you scored me? Well.

CASSIO	This is the monkey's own giving out: she is persuaded I will marry her, out of her own love and flattery, not out of my promise.
OTHELLO	(Aside)
	Iago beckons me: now he begins the story.
CASSIO	She was here even now; she haunts me in every place. I was the other day talking on the sea-bank with certain Venetians, and thither comes the bauble: by this hand, she falls thus about my neck –
	Cassio embraces Iago
OTHELLO	(Aside) Crying 'O dear Cassio!' as it were: his gesture imports it.
CASSIO	So hangs, and lolls, and weeps upon me; so shakes, and pulls me– ha, ha, ha!
OTHELLO	(Aside) Now he tells how she plucked him to my chamber. O, I see that nose of yours, but not that dog I shall throw it to.
CASSIO	Well, I must leave her company.
IAGO	Before me, look where she comes!
Enter Bianca	
CASSIO	'Tis such another fitchew – marry, a perfumed one! What do you mean by this haunting of me?
BIANCA	Let the devil and his dam haunt you! What did you mean by that same handkerchief you gave me even now? I was a fine fool to take it! I must take out the work? –A likely piece of work, that you should find it in your chamber, and know not who left it there! This is some minx's token– and I must take out the work? There, give it your hobby-horse.
	She throws down the hankerchief
	Wheresoever you had it, I'll take out no work on't.
CASSIO	How now, my sweet Bianca? How now? How now?
OTHELLO	(Aside) By heaven, that should be my handkerchief.
BIANCA	If you'll come to supper tonight, you may; if you will not, come when you are next prepared for.
Exit	
IAGO	After her, after her.
CASSIO	Faith, I must; she'll rail in the street else.
IAGO	Will you sup there?
CASSIO	Faith, I intend so.
IAGO	Well, I may chance to see you, for I would very fain speak with you.
CASSIO	Prithee come – will you?
IAGO	Go to, say no more.
Exit Cassio	
OTHELLO	[Coming forward] How shall I murder him, Iago?
IAGO	Did you perceive how he laughed at his vice?
OTHELLO	O, Iago!
IAGO	And did you see the handkerchief?
OTHELLO	Was that mine?
IAGO	Yours, by this hand! And to see how he prizes the foolish woman your wife: she gave it him, and he hath given it his whore.

125

130

135

140

145

150

155

160

165

170

130 *bauble:* play-thing

132 *imports:* betokens

135 *plucked:* brought
136-137 *but not that dog I shall throw it to:* when he has cut it off

140 *such another:* 'like all the rest of them' a mocking phrase, often used playfully and affectionately
140 *fitchew:* polecat (animals notorious for lechery)
142 *devil and his dam:* devil and his mother

148 *hobby-horse:* harlot

154 *when you are next prepared for:* i.e never

159 *I would very fain:* I would very much like to

162 *Go to, say no more:* Leave now, say no more

OTHELLO	I would have him nine years a-killing. A fine woman, a fair woman, a sweet woman!
IAGO	Nay, you must forget that.
OTHELLO	Ay, let her rot and perish, and be damned tonight for she shall not live! No, my heart is turned to stone: *(He beats his breast)* I strike it, and it hurts my hand. O, the world hath not a sweeter creature: she might lie by an emperor's side, and command him tasks.
IAGO	Nay, that's not your way.
OTHELLO	Hang her, I do but say what she is: so delicate with her needle, an admirable musician – O, she will sing the savageness out of a bear – of so high and plenteous wit and invention!
IAGO	She's the worse for all this.
OTHELLO	O, a thousand thousand times! And then of so gentle a condition –
IAGO	Ay, too gentle.
OTHELLO	Nay, that's certain – but yet the pity of it, Iago; O Iago, the pity of it, Iago!
IAGO	If you are so fond over her iniquity, give her patent to offend; for if it touch not you, it comes near nobody.
OTHELLO	I will chop her into messes – cuckold me?
IAGO	O, 'tis foul in her.
OTHELLO	With mine officer!
IAGO	That's fouler.
OTHELLO	Get me some poison, Iago; this night. I'll not expostulate with her, lest her body and beauty unprovide my mind again. This night, Iago.
IAGO	Do it not with poison; strangle her in her bed, even the bed she hath contaminated.
OTHELLO	Good, good, the justice of it pleases, very good.
IAGO	And for Cassio, let me be his undertaker: you shall hear more by midnight.
OTHELLO	Excellent good. *Trumpet sounds within* What trumpet is that same?
IAGO	I warrant something from Venice.

Enter Lodovico, Gratiano, Desdemona, and attendants

	'Tis Lodovico, this, comes from the Duke. See, your wife's with him.
LODOVICO	God save you, worthy general!
OTHELLO	With all my heart, sir.
LODOVICO	*(Giving Othello a letter)* The Duke and senators of Venice greet you.
OTHELLO	*(Putting the letter to his lips)* I kiss the instrument of their pleasures. *(Othello opens the letter, and reads.)*
DESDEMONA	And what's the news, good cousin Lodovico?
IAGO	I am very glad to see you, signor – Welcome to Cyprus.
LODOVICO	I thank you – how does Lieutenant Cassio?
IAGO	Lives, sir.
DESDEMONA	Cousin, there's fallen between him and my lord

171 *I would have him nine years a killing:* no punishment would be too severe

179 *not your way:* that's not the way you think or should think

182 *high:* lofty

192 *messes:* pieces of meat

197 *expostulate:* complain, remonstrate; debate
197 *unprovide:* make reluctant

202 *be his undertaker:* deal with him, take care of him

	An unkind breach; but you shall make all well.	220
OTHELLO	Are you sure of that?	
DESDEMONA	My lord?	
OTHELLO	*(Reads)*	
	'This fail you not to do, as you will' –	
LODOVICO	He did not call; he's busy in the paper.	
	Is there division 'twixt my lord and Cassio?	
DESDEMONA	A most unhappy one: I would do much	225
	T'atone them, for the love I bear to Cassio.	
OTHELLO	Fire and brimstone!	
DESDEMONA	My lord?	
OTHELLO	Are you wise?	
DESDEMONA	What, is he angry?	
LODOVICO	Maybe the letter moved him;	
	For, as I think, they do command him home,	
	Deputing Cassio in his government.	
DESDEMONA	Be my troth, I am glad on't.	
OTHELLO	Indeed?	
DESDEMONA	My lord?	230
OTHELLO	I am glad to see you mad.	
DESDEMONA	Why, sweet Othello!	
OTHELLO	*(Striking her)* Devil!	
DESDEMONA	I have not deserved this.	
LODOVICO	My lord, this would not be believed in Venice,	
	Though I should swear I saw't. 'Tis very much –	
	Make her amends: she weeps.	
OTHELLO	O devil, devil!	235
	If that the earth could teem with woman's tears,	
	Each drop she falls would prove a crocodile –	
	Out of my sight!	
DESDEMONA	I will not stay to offend you.	
LODOVICO	Truly, an obedient lady.	
	I do beseech your lordship call her back.	
OTHELLO	Mistress!	
DESDEMONA	My lord?	240
OTHELLO	What would you with her, sir?	
LODOVICO	Who, I, my lord?	
OTHELLO	Ay, you did wish that I would make her turn:	
	Sir, she can turn, and turn, and yet go on	
	And turn again; and she can weep, sir, weep;	245
	And she's obedient, as you say, obedient,	
	Very obedient. – Proceed you in your tears? –	
	Concerning this, sir – O well-painted passion! –	
	I am commanded home. – Get you away;	
	I'll send for you anon. – Sir, I obey the mandate,	250
	And will return to Venice. – Hence, avaunt! –	

Exit Desdemona

	Cassio shall have my place. And, sir, tonight	
	I do entreat that we may sup together.	
	You are welcome, sir, to Cyprus. – Goats and monkeys!	

Exit

LODOVICO	Is this the noble Moor whom our full Senate	255
	Call all in all sufficient? Is this the nature	
	Whom passion could not shake? Whose solid virtue	

---

226 *atone:* reconcile

231 *I am glad to see you mad:* Othello's sarcastic response to Desdemona's delight at Cassio's new title

234 *'Tis very much:* it's an extremely grave matter

236 *teem with:* swarm with

237 *falls:* let fall

241-252 *What would...And turn again:* Here Othello pretends that Desdemona is a harlot and Lodovico a potential client

251 *avaunt:* be gone

256 *sufficient:* competent

257 *passion:* grief
257 *virtue:* courage

The shot of accident nor dart of chance

Could neither graze nor pierce?

IAGO   He is much changed.

LODOVICO   Are his wits safe? Is he not light of brain?

IAGO   He's that he is: I may not breathe my censure

What he might be; if what he might, he is not,

I would to heaven he were.

LODOVICO   What? Strike his wife?

IAGO   'Faith, that was not so well; yet would I knew

That stroke would prove the worst!

LODOVICO   Is it his use?

Or did the letters work upon his blood

And new – create his fault?

IAGO   Alas, alas!

It is not honesty in me to speak

What I have seen and known. You shall observe him,

And his own courses will denote him so

That I may save my speech: do but go after

And mark how he continues.

LODOVICO   I am sorry that I am deceived in him.

Exeunt

258 *accident:* fate

260

261 *censure:* criticism, negative opinion

265 *use:* customary way of behaving

266 *blood:* passion

270 *courses:* conduct
270 *denote:* reveal the truth about

BIANCA AND CASSIO

Iago torments Othello with mental images of Cassio and Desdemona together until the Moor is struck by some kind of seizure. When Othello recovers Iago has him conceal himself nearby. Iago engages Cassio in some disrespectful banter about Desdemona.

The watching Othello assumes Cassio is describing his seduction of Desdemona. Othello also sees Bianca throw his precious handkerchief on the ground. He emerges from his hiding place committed to killing Cassio. After a little persuasion he commits to killing Desdemona as well.

Lodovico arrives with news from Venice. An enraged Othello strikes Desdemona. Lodovico is shocked by the great change that has come over the Moor and wonders if he has gone mad.

ACTION

LINE BY LINE

▶ LINES 1-41:
IAGO CONTINUES TO MANIPULATE OTHELLO

Othello and Iago enter the scene in mid-conversation. Iago torments Othello with various scenarios, filling his mind with images of Cassio and Desdemona together. He suggests that maybe Desdemona did no more than kiss Cassio in an innocent fashion. He also suggests that she lay naked in bed with him: 'An hour or more, not meaning any harm?' (4). Othello has built himself up into a rage, and ridicules such innocent possibilities: 'Naked in bed, Iago, and not mean harm?/ It is hypocrisy against the devil' (5-6).

Iago steers the conversation toward the handkerchief once more, telling Othello that when he gives his wife such a gift she can do what she wants with it. The thought of Cassio possessing the handkerchief hangs over Othello's mind like a raven over an infected household: 'O, it comes o'er my memory/ As doth the raven o'er the infectious house:/ Boding to all – he had my handkerchief' (19-21).

Othello continues to push Iago for information about the 'affair': 'Hath he said anything?' (28). Eventually Iago declares that Cassio his willing infatuation with Desdemona and how he has lain in bed with her: 'With her, on her – what

113

you will' (32). However, he also warns that Cassio will deny it if questioned (30). Othello is already worked up and this latest 'revelation' sends him into an absolute frenzy. His ability to communicate deserts him and he begins to babble almost incoherently: 'Is't possible? Confess? Handkerchief? O' Devil!' (40-1).

▶ LINES 42-100: OTHELLO FALLS INTO A TRANCE-LIKE STATE

Finally, completely overwhelmed, he falls down into a trance. Iago stands over him, congratulating himself on his triumph: 'Work on, my medicine, work! Thus credulous fools are caught'(42). Cassio arrives asking Iago what has happened. Iago lies, declaring that the Moor has had an epileptic fit (47-8). Iago says that Othello will be fine but needs quiet and requests that Cassio leave for a while (53). Yet he also asks Cassio to return a little later (55).

Othello comes out of his trance but is still clearly shaken. Talk quickly turns to Cassio. Iago says that Cassio came by during Othello's black out and will shortly return. He invites Othello to hide or 'encave' (78) himself and watch while Cassio admits his affair with Desdemona: 'I will make him tell the tale anew:/ Where, how, how oft, and when/ He hath, and is again to cope your wife' (81-3).

While Othello hides, Iago informs the audience of his intentions. He will engage Cassio in conversation about Bianca, the courtesan he's been sleeping with (90-2). Cassio, he says, will make fun of Bianca as he describes how this 'strumpet' has pursued him, how this pathetic 'creature' has doted on him (93-6). Jealousy will cause Othello to believe that Desdemona, not Bianca, is under discussion (98-100). Cassio's mocking smiles and gestures will drive the Moor even more insane with jealousy: 'As he shall smile, Othello shall go mad' (97).

▶ LINES 101-144: OTHELLO SPIES ON CASSIO

Cassio returns and Iago begins to put this plan into action. He is quick to mention Bianca, saying that if she had influence Cassio would by now have his old job back: 'Now, if this suit lay in Bianca's power,/ How quickly you should speed!' (104-5).

Cassio is amused by the very mention of Bianca's name. He laughs and calls her a 'poor rogue' and a poor 'caitiff' or creature (106). He has been sleeping with her but clearly bears little respect for her. He

IAGO

MASTER PLOTTER

In this scene Iago once again improvises brilliantly, taking advantage of every opportunity that comes his way:

Cassio shows up during Othello's seizure. Iago tells him to come back a little later.

He persuades Othello to hide and watch, promising that he will get Cassio to describe the sordid details of his 'affair' with Desdemona.

When Cassio returns he concocts a story about Bianca wanting to marry Cassio and manages to elicit from him precisely the sort of reaction he needs to further aggravate Othello.

He also seizes on the opportunity presented by the arrival of Bianca, who angrily throws Othello's handkerchief. It is a disgrace, he says, that Cassio gave the handkerchief to such a 'whore'.

He uses Bianca's angry departure to get rid of Cassio, telling him to go after her. He wants to be alone with Othello so he can complete his poisoning of the Moor's mind.

He also turns Lodovico's arrival to his advantage, speaking cryptically about Othello's madness in order to sow further doubt about the Moor's state of mind.

Iago could not have predicted these occurrences. Yet he seizes on each one as it occurs, improvising fluently and using them to further his objectives.

Iago provoked Othello's jealousy so much in Act 3 Scene 3 that little is needed to send the Moor completely over the edge. Iago knows that Othello is by now completely paranoid.

He guesses that Othello will take Cassio's cruel but light-hearted banter about Bianca as bragging about Desdemona: 'And his unbookish jealousy must construe/ Poor Cassio's smiles, gestures, and light behaviours/ Quite in the wrong' (98-100).

The scene unfolds exactly as Iago predicts. When Cassio mimics Bianca's embrace, Othello believes his greatest fears have been confirmed (132-138). When he emerges from his hiding place Othello is committed to seeking bloody revenge for a fictional affair (163). Iago could not have hoped for anything better.

IAGO

MANIPULATIVE AND PERSUASIVE

In this scene Iago reveals himself once more as a master of leading people on through reverse psychology. We see this at the beginning of the scene. He dangles terrible images like bait before Othello's mind, hinting at the couplings between Cassio and Desdemona. Yet he speaks directly about Cassio's 'confession' to the affair only when Othello is practically begging him to do so.

A similar use of reverse psychology is evident at the scene's conclusion. Lodovico asks about Othello's mental state and Iago answers in what can only be described as a riddling and cryptic fashion. He leads Lodovico on just as he did Othello in Act 3 Scene 1. By refusing to give a straight answer he arouses Lodovico's curiosity and sows seeds of doubt in his mind about Othello's fitness to govern.

Iago, it's important to note, wants to avoid seeming too obvious in his manipulations. Again and again throughout the play he raises spectres in Othello's mind, dismisses their importance, and returns to them a little later once the doubts he's sown have taken root.

By proposing unforgiveable wrongs and then attempting to lessen their significance, Iago manages to drown Othello in his own anger and jealousy, while preserving his own innocent reputation.

Iago uses a more blunt form of persuasion when Othello emerges from his hiding place. The Moor is now committed to killing Cassio and Iago reinforces this decision: 'Did you perceive how he laughed at his vice?...And did you see the handkerchief?' (164-6).

Yet Othello still has doubts about murdering Desdemona. Iago overpowers his objections: he declares that Othello must forget his wife's fair qualities because they make her betrayal all the worse (173-84). He must not be ruled by her beauty: 'Nay, that's not your way' (179).

Iago not only persuades Othello to kill Desdemona, but also successfully advises him on how and where he should do it (199-200). He then helpfully offers to kill Cassio for Othello. The latter accepts this proposal with business-like satisfaction: 'Excellent good' (204).

A BRILLIANT ACTOR

In this scene Iago juggles two performances, a feat that proves his impressive acting skills. He hates Cassio but acts in a friendly fashion toward him throughout the scene, bantering with him about Bianca and even agreeing to dine with him that evening.

At the same time, of course, Iago continues a very different performance with Othello, playing the role of faithful servant who has nothing but his commander's best interests at heart. When he plays this role he acts as Cassio's sworn enemy, committed to exposing and destroying him on his master's behalf.

His acting skills are also evident when he chats to Cassio about Bianca. We imagine this as a loud and vulgar conversation that the watching Othello can almost hear, and perhaps one with many crude gestures. Iago executes these theatrics with aplomb. For every fragment of conversation that passes between Iago and Cassio, Othello's outrage grows.

LACK OF RESPECT FOR CONVENTIONAL VALUES

Iago's lack of respect for sexual morality is evident when he and Othello converse about 'cuckolds' – men whose wives have been unfaithful to them. Othello regards such men as less than human, as beasts or monsters: 'A horned man's a monster and a beast' (59). (Cuckolds were traditionally depicted in a mocking way as having horns growing behind their ears).

Iago, however, takes a different view. Many or most women, he suggests, are unfaithful and have turned their husbands into cuckolded beasts: 'There's many a beast then in a populous city' (60). The women of Cyprus may be refined and civilised but they are also 'monsters' who betray their menfolk: 'And many a civil monster' (61). Iago, then, doesn't expect morality or good behaviour in the sexual arena, especially not from women.

OTHELLO

DIGNITY AND SELF-POSSESSION

The arrival of Lodovico towards the end of the scene serves to remind us how dramatically Othello has changed since arriving in Cyprus. We might recall, how, at the start of the play the Moor had stood before the Venetian senate speaking eloquently and displaying considerable restraint and dignity when addressing Brabantio's accusations. Now, before a dignitary of the state and his wife's cousin, Othello loses control of his speech and of his self-control, striking Desdemona and prompting Lodovico to ask whether he has not gone insane: 'Are his wits safe? Is he not light of brain?' (260).

Much of Othello's anger and frustration stems from the fact that he now sees himself as a 'cuckold', a man whose wife is being unfaithful. When Iago tells him to bear his 'fortune like a man', Othello responds that he is no longer a man with dignity and pride but a 'horned' man, a 'monster and a beast' (59). For someone who has worked as hard as he has to establish a reputation in Venetian society, the notion that his wife might be humiliating him in this manner is too much to bear.

Iago is aware of how sensitive Othello is about this. When Othello's attitude towards Desdemona seems to be softening Iago goads him with the suggestion that he might be happy to be the husband of a cheating wife: 'If you are so fond over her iniquity, give her patent to offend' (190-1). It is this comment that causes Othello to gruesomely declare that he will 'chop [Desdemona] into messes – cuckold me?' (192).

OTHELLO'S LOVE FOR DESDEMONA

When Othello sees the handkerchief he had given Desdemona being passed between Cassio and Bianca, he does not immediately rage against his wife, who he now supposes gave the handkerchief to Cassio as a token of her love. His immediate rage is directed at Cassio, who appears not to value Desdemona if he is willing to give this important love token to Bianca, a prostitute: 'I would have him nine-years a-killing' (171). Desdemona is a 'fine woman, a fair woman, a sweet woman' and the Moor is enraged that Cassio should treat her as nothing more than a casual lover or conquest (171-2).

Love and hate, therefore, wage a wearisome battle inside Othello's mind. On one hand he feels protective and empathetic towards Desdemona; on the other hand, he is deeply wounded and aggrieved by the thought of her disloyalty: 'Ay, let her rot and perish and be damned tonight, for she shall not live... O, the world hath not a sweeter creature' (174-7). In many ways, Othello's love for Desdemona is almost his weakness and it determines the magnitude of his anger.

TRUSTING NATURE

Once again, we see Othello come undone by the unquestioning trust he places in his ensign. Despite the fact that he cannot hear much of the conversation that takes place between Cassio and Iago, he never once challenges the second-hand information he receives – a serious flaw, perhaps, in a decorated military leader.

As we have mentioned before, Othello seems to lack confidence when it comes to the customs and behaviour of people in Venetian society and he places great trust in his ensign's ability to interpret and explain their actions. Iago tells him that 'knowing what I am, I know what she shall be' (70) and the Moor openly applauds his reading of the situation: 'O, thou art wise; 'tis certain' (71).

OTHELLO AS SOLIDER

It is worth remembering that Othello is a highly trained soldier and has spent much of his life on the battlefield. Though he is able to conduct himself with great dignity and self-possession, when his temper gets the better of him, as it does on many occasions in this scene, he seems to revert to his soldierly instincts. Fighting is in his nature and he succumbs easily to feelings of murderous revenge: 'I will be found most cunning in my patience, / But – dost thou hear? – most bloody' (87-8). Following Cassio and Iago's conversation, he has only one form of retribution on his mind: 'How shall I murder him, Iago?' (163).

It is not simply his urge for revenge, but the manner in which he seeks to exact it that highlights Othello's ingrained military mannerisms. Iago's goading reveals Othello's appetite for an all-consuming violence, the kind of destruction more suited to a battlefield than a bedroom: 'I will chop her into messes' (192). With a little prompting from Iago, he discards his original intention to poison her and agrees instead to strangle her in their bed (201). Othello also indulges this violence for the first time later in the scene when he confronts Desdemona and hits her (231).

OTHELLO

seems to find the 'puppy dog' and devoted nature of her love both pathetic and amusing.

Bianca, it seems, has been spreading rumours that she and Cassio are to be married. He finds the notion of actually marrying her hilarious (113-5). She is, after all, little more than a prostitute or 'customer' (117). Cassio laughs again, telling Iago that he would never marry such a woman and asks that he be given some credit for his judgement (117-8).

Iago's plan works. Othello, in his hiding place, completely misunderstands the nature of Cassio's amusement. He thinks Cassio is laughing scornfully about how he managed to win Desdemona's affection: 'Look how he laughs already' (107). To Othello it seems that Cassio briefly denies sleeping with Desdemona before going on to laugh triumphantly as he tells how he seduced her: 'Do you triumph, Roman? Do you triumph?... They laugh that win' (116-9).

Cassio describes how Bianca follows him around: 'She haunts me in every place' (128-9). He mimics how she throws her arms around him. Othello thinks he is mimicking the act of making love to Desdemona (132). Cassio then mimics how Bianca embraces him in a rather pathetic fashion, literally hanging off him: 'She hangs and lolls and weeps upon me' (133-4). Othello once again misunderstands, imagining that Cassio's describing how Desdemona dragged him to their chamber: 'Now he tells how she plucked him to my chamber' (135-6).

Othello is clearly distressed by what he's seen or thinks he's seen. He admits that Cassio has 'scored' or wounded him by sleeping with his wife (123). Yet he is determined to be avenged. He contemplates killing Cassio and feeding his nose to the dogs: 'O, I see that nose of yours, but not that dog I shall throw it to.' (136-7).

▶ LINES 145-161: BIANCA HERSELF TURNS UP

At that very moment Bianca herself shows up. Cassio, as we have gathered, has been treating her with little respect, merely using her for her body. She has grown tired of this poor treatment. She has with her the handkerchief received from Cassio in Act 3 Scene 4.

She assumes he received it from another lover and passed it one to her: 'A likely piece of work, that you should find it in your chamber and know not who left it there! This is some minx's token' (145-8). She flings the handkerchief on the ground in jealousy and disgust.

💬 THINK ABOUT IT

How far away is Othello's hiding place from Cassio? It seems that he can see Cassio's gestures and facial expressions. But what can he actually hear?

We get the impression he can hear at least some of what Iago and Cassio say. Yet their conversation must be muffled for him or he'd realise they're talking about Bianca, not Desdemona.

It is strange, then, that Othello jumps to such strong conclusions when he can seemingly hear so little. Perhaps by now he is in such an agitated state that can't see past his fears and suspicions. His jealousy has taken over and he sees nothing but confirmation of betrayal.

117

She storms off, telling Cassio that if he does not come to supper that evening, he will never be invited again (153-4). Iago urges Cassio to follow her: 'After her, after her!' (155). Cassio reveals his intention to have supper with Bianca that evening and Iago invites himself to join them (156-161). He leaves to go after Bianca.

HANDKERCHIEF FLASHBACK

- Some time ago Othello gave his precious handkerchief to Desdemona as a love token
- In Act 3 Scene 1 a distracted and agitated Othello leaves the handkerchief on the ground having used it to wipe his brow.
- Emilia picks up the handkerchief and gives it to Iago, who had asked about it many times.
- Iago, in an attempt to cause suspicion, leaves it in Cassio's chamber.
- Cassio finds it but had no idea where it came from or to whom it belongs.
- In Act 3 Scene 4 he gave it to Bianca, asking her to copy its exquisite design for him.
- Bianca angrily returns it to him, convinced it is some other woman's love token. She flings it on the ground while Othello watches from his hiding place.

▶ LINES 162-203: OTHELLO IS BENT ON MURDER

Othello emerges from his hiding place. Spying on the conversation has convinced him that the 'affair' is real. It has also greatly amplified his rage. He now seems committed to killing Cassio, asking straight away: 'How shall I murder him, Iago?'

CHARACTER DEVELOPMENT

(163). No torture, he feels, would be severe enough or long enough for this officer who has betrayed him so cruelly: 'I would have him nine years a-killing' (171).

Othello also seems bent on killing Desdemona: 'Ay, let her rot and perish and be damned tonight,/ for she shall not live! No, my heart is turned to stone' (174-5). However he is still filled with doubt. He reminds himself how she is: 'A fine/ woman, a fair woman, a sweet woman!' (172-3). He still sees her delicacy, beauty intelligence and talents (180-3). She is a woman, after all, of so 'gentle a condition' (185-6). Finally, however, he decides that she too must die to avenge his honour: 'I will chop her into messes – cuckold me?' (192).

Iago brilliantly encourages this vengeful mood and the two begin to plot the deaths of the 'adulterers'. Initially Othello considers poisoning his wife: 'Get me some poison, Iago, this night' (196). Iago, however, suggests that Othello kill her in bed, the very place she has allegedly committed her crimes (199-200). Othello agrees to this proposal, seeing it as a form of poetic justice. Iago, meanwhile, declares that he will take care of Cassio 'And for Cassio, let me be his undertaker' (202).

▶ LINES 204-270: LODOVICO ARRIVES WITH A MESSAGE FROM VENICE

Trumpets sound, signalling the arrival of Ludovico, a nobleman who has come from Venice with a letter from the Duke. Desdemona is with him. While Othello absorbs the Duke's message the others converse.

DESDEMONA

STRONG-WILLED AND ASSERTIVE?

Desdemona's submissive behaviour in this scene contrasts strongly with the smart, diplomatic woman who defies her father's wishes in Act 1 Scene 3. When Othello greets her with a series of snide remarks, Desdemona is totally confused. She is just as bewildered when he hits her and claims that she has done no wrong (232). Although she does not understand what she could have done wrong, she accepts that she must be responsible somehow for upsetting him and meekly offers to leave: 'I will not stay to offend you' (238).

Every time that Othello passes a cynical remark at her or challenges her to address his slurs, Desdemona merely responds with passive utterances of 'My lord?' This highlights how submissive she has become. She seems to attempt to pacify his anger with ever-increasing obedience and conformity, but this has only the opposite effect. The more personal power she gives to Othello, the more he abuses it, and this shifting dynamic represents a crucial turning point in their relationship. After further disparaging comments, he dismisses Desdemona and she obeys without a word (249-51).

Desdemona explains that Othello and Cassio have fallen out, but is pleased that Lodovico is now here to make things right again: 'An unkind breach; but you shall make all well' (220). She describes her fondness for Cassio and her hope that the dispute between him and her husband will soon be ended: 'I would do much / T'atone them, for the love I bear to Cassio' (225-6).

Othello finishes reading the letter, which contains instructions for him to return to Venice and to nominate Cassio to succeed him as Governor of Cyprus. Desdemona is delighted by the news. Presumably she feels that returning to Venice will allow her to renew her relationship with her husband. Othello, however, assumes her joy stems from the fact that her 'lover' Cassio has been promoted.

He responds angrily by striking her and calling her a devil (231). Desdemona is utterly shocked, seeing no reason for this harsh treatment from her husband: 'I have not deserved this' (232). She bursts into tears. Othello is unmoved. He continues to call her devil, brands her a 'Mistress' or prostitute and orders her out of his sight (238, 240).

Lodovico is shocked by the Moor's actions, which seem to him completely oiut of character: 'this would not be believed in Venice, / Though I should swear I saw't' (233-4). He asks Othello to apologise, make amends and call her back (234, 239). Othello, however, responds somewhat sarcastically asking Lodovico what he wants with her, as if it's obvious Othello himself could have nothing to say to her.

Othello begins to speak in an agitated, repetitive and disjointed fashion, similar to that which preceded his earlier collapse: 'And she can weep, sir, weep. / And she's obedient; as you say, obedient' (245-6). He gathers himself enough to assure Lodovico that he will obey the letter and return to Venice (250-1). He invites Lodovico to dine with him that evening and departs cursing: 'Goats and monkeys!' (254).

Lodovico is stunned by what he's seen. He finds it hard to believe that this is the same noble, competent and courageous Othello he knew back in Venice: 'Is this the noble Moor, whom our full senate / Call all in all sufficient?' (255-6). He wonders if Othello has gone mad: 'Are his wits safe? Is he not light of brain?' (260). He also wonders if Othello's strange

CHARACTER DEVELOPMENT

CASSIO

LADIES' MAN

Previous scenes have depicted Cassio as a smooth and charming ladies' man, a cultivated and sophisticated type who is popular with women wherever he goes. Yet here he is depicted in a darker light. He comes across as a heartless womaniser who has little respect for those he sleeps with.

Cassio finds Bianca's devotion to him amusingly pathetic: 'Alas, poor rogue! I think i'faith she loves me' (109). He mockingly describes how she follows him around, draping her arms around his neck as she weeps and shakes with emotion (133-4).

To Cassio, then, Bianca is little more than a 'bauble' (130), a pretty but ultimately worthless distraction.

He believes he is above Bianca and finds the idea of marrrying such a woman laughable and an insult to his intelligence: 'I marry – what, a customer? Prithee bear some / Charity to my wit (117-8). His lack of regard for her is evident in his use of numerous unpleasant and insulting names, such as 'caitiff', 'customer', 'monkey', and 'fitchew'. He coldly speaks of ending their relationship: 'I must leave her company' (138).

He greets her arrogantly when she arrives with the handkerchief. Yet when he realises the extent of her anger he acts the 'nice guy' once again: 'How now my sweet Bianca? How now? How now?' (150-1). He jokes with Iago that he will go after her to calm her down, otherwise she will rant and 'rail', complaining about him loudly on the street (156). Cassio, then, may have little respect for Bianca but he is clearly not finished using her.

> **THINK ABOUT IT**
>
> Consider the phrases 'Are you sure of that?' and 'Fire and brimstone!' (221, 227). Are they a response to the contents of the letter, as Lodovico assumes? Or is he reacting to Desdemona's comments? Or could it be a mixture of both?

behaviour is a regular occurrence or a one-off event caused by the news from Venice (265-7).

Iago, manipulative as ever, sows seeds of doubt in Lodovico's mind by refusing to give a straight answer. Othello, he says, is 'much changed' (259). Asked about Othello's possible madness he responds in what can only be described as a riddle (262). He advises Lodovico to study Othello's behaviour and draw his own conclusions: 'You shall observe him, / And his own courses will denote him so' (269-70). Both exit the scene. ◆

ACT 4 SCENE 2

A room in the castle

Enter Othello and Emilia

OTHELLO You have seen nothing then?

EMILIA Nor ever heard, nor ever did suspect.

OTHELLO Yes, you have seen Cassio and she together.

EMILIA But then I saw no harm; and then I heard
Each syllable that breath made up between them.

OTHELLO What? Did they never whisper?

EMILIA Never, my lord.

OTHELLO Nor send you out o' the way?

EMILIA Never.

OTHELLO To fetch her fan, her gloves, her mask, nor nothing?

EMILIA Never, my lord.

OTHELLO That's strange.

EMILIA I durst, my lord, to wager she is honest,
Lay down my soul at stake: if you think other,
Remove your thought; it doth abuse your bosom.
If any wretch have put this in your head,
Let heaven requite it with the serpent's curse;
For if she be not honest, chaste, and true,
There's no man happy: the purest of their wives
Is foul as slander.

OTHELLO Bid her come hither– go.

Exit Emilia

She says enough; yet she's a simple bawd
That cannot say as much. This is a subtle whore,
A closet, lock, and key of villanous secrets;
And yet she'll kneel and pray – I have seen her do't.

Enter Desdemona with Emilia

DESDEMONA My lord, what is your will?

OTHELLO Pray you, chuck, come hither.

DESDEMONA What is your pleasure?

OTHELLO Let me see your eyes –
Look in my face.

DESDEMONA What horrible fancy's this?

OTHELLO *(To Emilia)*
Some of your function, mistress:
Leave procreants alone and shut the door,
Cough, or cry 'Hem!' if any body come.
Your mystery, your mystery – nay, dispatch!

Exit Emilia

DESDEMONA *(Kneeling)*
Upon my knee, what doth your speech import?
I understand a fury in your words,
But not the words.

OTHELLO Why, what art thou?

10 *mask:* worn as a disguise during the Venetian carnival, but also to protect ladies' complexions from the sun

13 *Lay down my soul at stake:* stake my soul as a wager

20 *bawd:* prostitute, or perhaps a brothel-keeper

21 *whore:* Desdemona

22 *A closet, lock and key:* a container

26 *What horrible fancy's this?:* what horrible notion or fantasy is this?

27 *Some of your function:* refers to the idea that Emilia is a brothel keeper and Desdemona a prostitute

28 *procreants:* people engaging in sexual intercourse

30 *mystery:* trade, referring again to Othello's notion of Emilia as Desdemona's brothel-keeper

31 *import:* mean

DESDEMONA	Your wife, my lord; your true and loyal wife.	
OTHELLO	Come, swear it: damn thyself,	35
	Lest, being like one of heaven, the devils themselves	
	Should fear to seize thee. Therefore be double-damned:	
	Swear thou art honest.	
DESDEMONA	Heaven doth truly know it.	
OTHELLO	Heaven truly knows that thou art false as hell.	
DESDEMONA	*(Rising)*	
	To whom, my lord? With whom? How am I false?	40
OTHELLO	Ah Desdemon, away, away, away!	
DESDEMONA	Alas the heavy day, why do you weep?	
	Am I the motive of these tears, my lord?	
	If haply you my father do suspect	
	An instrument of this your calling back,	45
	Lay not your blame on me: if you have lost him,	
	I have lost him too.	
OTHELLO	Had it pleased heavens	
	To try me with affliction, had they rained	
	All kinds of sores and shames on my bare head.	
	Steeped me in poverty to the very lips,	50
	Given to captivity me and my utmost hopes,	
	I should have found in some place of my soul	
	A drop of patience; but, alas, to make me	
	A fixed figure for the scorn of time,	
	To point his slow and moving finger at!	55
	(He groans)	
	Yet could I bear that too, well, very well:	
	But there, where I have garnered up my heart,	
	Where either I must live or bear no life,	
	The fountain from the which my current runs	
	Or else dries up – to be discarded thence,	60
	Or keep it as a cistern for foul toads	
	To knot and gender in! Turn thy complexion there,	
	Patience, thou young and rose-lipped cherubin,	
	Ay there, look grim as hell.	
DESDEMONA	I hope my noble lord esteems me honest.	65
OTHELLO	O ay, as summer flies are in the shambles,	
	That quicken even with blowing. O thou black weed,	
	Who art so lovely fair, and smell'st so sweet	
	That the sense aches at thee, would thou hadst ne'er	
	been born!	
DESDEMONA	Alas, what ignorant sin have I committed?	70
OTHELLO	Was this fair paper, this most goodly book	
	Made to write 'whore' upon? – What committed?	
	'Committed'! O thou public commoner,	
	I should make very forges of my cheeks	
	That would to cinders burn up modesty	75
	Did I but speak thy deeds. What committed?	
	Heaven stops the nose at it, and the moon wink;	
	The bawdy wind that kisses all it meets	
	Is hushed within the hollow mine of earth	
	And will not hear't. – What committed?	80
	Impudent strumpet!	
DESDEMONA	By heaven you do me wrong.	

38 *doth truly know it:* knows it to be true

41 *Ah Desdemon, away, away, away:* Othello can hardly bear to be around Desdemona and weakly attempts to send her away

43 *motive:* cause

54 *A fixed figure for the scorn... moving finger at:* Othello thinks of himself as an object of mockery, pointed at by the hand, which moves so slowly tat it seems not to move at all

57 *garnered:* stored

59 *fountain:* spring

61 *cistern:* water-tank, reservoir

62 *knot:* couple
62 *gender:* procreate
62 *Turn thy complexion:* change colour

66 *shambles:* butcher's slaughter house

67 *quicken:* become alive, receive life

73 *public commoner:* prostitute

77 *moon:* symbolised chastity
77 *winks:* shuts her eyes

81 *Impudent:* insolent, shameless

OTHELLO	Are you not a strumpet?
DESDEMONA	No, as I am a Christian.

If to preserve this vessel for my lord
From any other foul unlawful touch
Be not to be a strumpet, I am none.

OTHELLO	What, not a whore?
DESDEMONA	No, as I shall be saved.
OTHELLO	Is't possible?
DESDEMONA	O heaven forgive us!
OTHELLO	I cry you mercy then.

Enter Emilia

I took you for that cunning whore of Venice
That married with Othello. *(To Emilia)* You, mistress,
That have the office opposite to Saint Peter,
And keeps the gate of hell, you, you! – Ay, you:
We've done our course; there's money for your pains;
I pray you turn the key, and keep our counsel.

Exit

EMILIA	Alas, what does this gentleman conceive?

How do you, madam? How do you, my good lady?

DESDEMONA	Faith, half asleep.
EMILIA	Good madam, what's the matter with my lord?
DESDEMONA	With who?
EMILIA	Why, with my lord, madam.
DESDEMONA	Who is thy lord?
EMILIA	He that is yours, sweet lady.
DESDEMONA	I have none: do not talk to me, Emilia –

I cannot weep, nor answer have I none
But what should go by water. Prithee, tonight
Lay on my bed my wedding sheets, remember,
And call thy husband hither.

EMILIA	Here's a change indeed

Exit

DESDEMONA	'Tis meet I should be used so, very meet.

How have I been behaved, that he might stick
The small'st opinion on my least misuse?

Enter Emilia and Iago

IAGO	What is your pleasure, madam? How is't with you?
DESDEMONA	I cannot tell – those that do teach young babes

Do it with gentle means and easy tasks:
He might have chid me so, for, in good faith
I am a child to chiding.

IAGO	What's the matter, lady?
EMILIA	Alas, Iago, my lord hath so bewhored her,

Thrown such despite and heavy terms upon her
That true hearts cannot bear.

DESDEMONA	Am I that name, Iago?
IAGO	What name, fair lady?
DESDEMONA	Such as she says my lord did say I was.
EMILIA	He called her 'whore': a beggar in his drink

Could not have laid such terms upon his callat.

IAGO	Why did he so?
DESDEMONA	I do not know: I am sure I am none such.
IAGO	Do not weep, do not weep – alas the day!

Glossary:
84 *other:* from the touch of another man
90 *I cry you mercy:* I beg your pardon
95 *We've done our course:* finished our sexual bout
96 *counsel:* secret
97 *conceive:* imagine
99 *Faith, half-asleep:* half-dead, stunned
105 *go by water:* travel by water, i.e. be conveyed by tears
108 *meet:* fit, suitable
110 *The small'st opinion on my least misuse:* the smallest suspicion on my least ill conduct
115 *I am a child to chiding:* I have had little experience of reproof
116 *bewhored:* called her a whore
122 *callat:* slut, whore

EMILIA	Hath she forsook so many noble matches,
	Her father, and her country, and her friends,
	To be called whore? Would it not make one weep?
DESDEMONA	It is my wretched fortune.
IAGO	Beshrew him for't!
	How comes this trick upon him?
DESDEMONA	Nay, heaven doth know.
EMILIA	I will be hanged if some eternal villain,
	Some busy and insinuating rogue,
	Some cogging, cozening slave, to get some office,
	Have not devised this slander; I'll be hanged else.
IAGO	Fie, there is no such man! It is impossible.
DESDEMONA	If any such there be, heaven pardon him.
EMILIA	A halter pardon him, and hell gnaw his bones!
	Why should he call her whore? Who keeps her
	company?
	What place? What time? What form? What likelihood?
	The Moor's abused by some most villanous knave,
	Some base notorious knave, some scurvy fellow.
	O heaven, that such companions thou'dst unfold,
	And put in every honest hand a whip
	To lash the rascals naked through the world,
	Even from the east to th' west!
IAGO	Speak within door.
EMILIA	O, fie upon them! Some such squire he was
	That turned your wit the seamy side without
	And made you to suspect me with the Moor.
IAGO	You are a fool – go to!
DESDEMONA	O God, Iago,
	What shall I do to win my lord again?
	Good friend, go to him; for, by this light of heaven,
	I know not how I lost him.
She kneels	Here I kneel:
	If e'er my will did trespass 'gainst his love,
	Either in discourse, or thought, or actual deed,
	Or that mine eyes, mine ears, or any sense
	Delighted them in any other form,
	Or that I do not yet – and ever did,
	And ever will, though he do shake me off
	To beggarly divorcement – love him dearly,
	Comfort forswear me! Unkindness may do much,
	And his unkindness may defeat my life,
	But never taint my love. I cannot say 'whore':
	It does abhor me now I speak the word,
	To do the act that might th'addition earn
	Not the world's mass of vanity could make me.
IAGO	
(Helping her rise)	I pray you be content: 'tis but his humour;
	The business of the state does him offence,
	And he does chide with you.
DESDEMONA	If 'twere no other –
IAGO	It is but so, I warrant.
	(Trumpets sound within)

130 *How comes this trick upon him:* how has this delusion overcome him

133 *cogging:* deceiving
133 *cozening:* cheating

137 *halter:* hangman's noose

139 *form:* manner

142 *companions:* refers to the dishonest friends that according to Emilia must have deceived Othello

144 *To lash...world:* lashing through the streets was a normal punishment

145 *speak within door:* speak quietly, speak not so loud

146 *squire:* contemptuous, equivalent to fellow

147 *turned your wit the seamy side without:* manipulated your mind so that the worst aspects of your character were prevalent

149 *go to:* an expression with a variety of meanings, in this case meaning 'be quiet'

156 *Delighted them:* took delight

160 *Comfort forswear me:* may I lose all hope of comfort rather than betray him
161 *defeat:* destroy

165 *the world's mass of vanity:* all the empty pride and worthless treasures of the world

130
135
140
145
150
155
160
165
170

123

Hark, how these instruments summon to supper:
The messengers of Venice stay the meat.
Go in, and weep not: all things shall be well.

Exeunt Desdemona and Emilia
Enter Roderigo

	How now, Roderigo?	
RODERIGO	I do not find that thou deal'st justly with me.	175
IAGO	What in the contrary?	
RODERIGO	Every day thou doffest me with some device, Iago, and rather, as it seems to me now, keepest from me all conveniency than suppliest me with the least advantage of hope. I will indeed no longer endure it, nor am I yet persuaded to put up in peace what already I have foolishly suffered.	180
IAGO	Will you hear me, Roderigo?	
RODERIGO	Faith, I have heard too much, for your words and performances are no kin together.	185
IAGO	You charge me most unjustly.	
RODERIGO	With naught but truth: I have wasted myself out of my means; the jewels you have had from me to deliver Desdemona would half have corrupted a votarist; you have told me she hath received them, and returned me expectations and comforts of sudden respect and acquaintance, but I find none.	190
IAGO	Well, go to, very well!	
RODERIGO	'Very well', 'go to'? I cannot 'go to', man, nor 'tis not 'very well'; by this hand, I say 'tis very scurvy, and begin to find myself fobbed in it.	195
IAGO	Very well.	
RODERIGO	I tell you, 'tis not very well! I will make myself known to Desdemona: if she will return me my jewels, I will give over my suit and repent my unlawful solicitation; if not, assure yourself I will seek satisfaction of you.	200
IAGO	You have said now.	
RODERIGO	Ay, and said nothing but what I protest intendment of doing.	
IAGO	Why, now I see there's mettle in thee, and even from this instant to build on thee a better opinion than ever before. Give me thy hand, Roderigo: thou hast taken against me a most just exception; but yet I protest I have dealt most directly in thy affair.	205
RODERIGO	It hath not appeared.	210
IAGO	I grant indeed it hath not appeared; and your suspicion is not without wit and judgment. But, Roderigo, if thou hast that in thee indeed which I have greater reason to believe now than ever – I mean purpose, courage and valour – this night show it. If thou the next night following enjoy not Desdemona, take me from this world with treachery, and devise engines for my life.	215
RODERIGO	Well, what is it? Is it within reason and compass?	
IAGO	Sir, there is especial commission come from Venice to depute Cassio in Othello's place.	220
RODERIGO	Is that true? Why, then Othello and Desdemona	

Glossary (right margin):

172 *stay the meat:* await their meal

177 *doffest:* dost put me off

179 *conveniency:* opportunity

190 *votarist:* a nun, vowed to chastity
191 *comforts:* encouragement
192 *sudden respect:* immediate favour

195 *scurvy:* disagreeable, despicable
196 *fobbed:* duped

202 *You have said now:* you have had your say now
203 *intendment:* intention

205 *mettle:* courage, spirit

208 *taken against...just exception:* taken understandable offence

217-218
devise engines for: devise a plot for

	return again to Venice.
IAGO	O no, he goes into Mauretania and takes away with him the fair Desdemona, unless his abode be lingered here by some accident – wherein none can be so determinate as the removing of Cassio.
RODERIGO	How do you mean 'removing' him?
IAGO	Why, by making him uncapable of Othello's place – knocking out his brains.
RODERIGO	And that you would have me to do?
IAGO	Ay, if you dare do yourself a profit and a right. He sups tonight with a harlotry, and thither will I go to him. He knows not yet of his honourable fortune: if you will watch his going thence – which I will fashion to fall out between twelve and one – you may take him at your pleasure; I will be near to second your attempt, and he shall fall between us. Come, stand not amazed at it, but go along with me: I will show you such a necessity in his death that you shall think yourself bound to put it on him. It is now high supper time, and the night grows to waste: about it!
RODERIGO	I will hear further reason for this.
IAGO	And you shall be satisfied.
Exeunt	

225

227

230

233

235

236

240

241

242

242-243

245

224 *Mauretania:* a country in North Africa

227 *determinate:* conclusive, definite

233 *harlotry:* harlot

236 *fall out:* occur

241 *put:* inflict

242 *high:* fully

242-243

    the night grows to waste: the night is wasting away

EMILIA AND OTHELLO

Othello questions Emilia about Desdemona's behaviour, desperately seeking evidence that his wife is having an affair with Cassio. He also challenges Desdemona, pushing her to admit that she is being unfaithful. Desdemona tries to persuade the Moor of her innocence but he remains deaf to her protestations. Emilia suggests that some evil person must be manipulating Othello with false stories but she fails to see that it is her own husband who is doing this.

Later in the scene Roderigo confronts Iago, accusing him of squandering his money. He threatens to go to Desdemona to retrieve the jewels that Iago claims to have delivered on Roderigo's behalf. Iago manages to calm him down and convince him that the only way he can now be assured of winning Desdemona by murdering Cassio.

ACTION

LINE BY LINE

▶ LINES 1- 19: OTHELLO INTERROGATES EMILIA

Othello interrogates Emilia, asking her if she has ever seen Cassio and Desdemona behave in a suspicious manner. Emilia insists that she has never seen, heard or suspected anything and that she has been privy to their every meeting and their every word: 'I heard / Each syllable that breath made up between them' (4-5).

Othello is unconvinced by what she tells him. He cannot believe that Desdemona never sent Emilia away on some errand so that she and Cassio could be alone together: 'To fetch her fan, her gloves, her mask, nor nothing?' (10). Emilia protests Desdemona's innocence and she pleads with Othello to stop doubting his wife: 'If you think other / Remove your thought' (13-4). If someone is responsible for planting doubts in

the Moor's mind, Emilia says, then such a person should be cursed: 'If any wretch have put this in your head, / Let heaven requite it with the serpent's curse!' (15-6).

Othello asks Emilia to fetch Desdemona and when she leaves he considers what she has told him. Though Emilia has said much, he does not place any trust or significance in her words. He likens her to a 'simple bawd' or brothel keeper and says that his wife is no better than a 'whore' that Emilia strives to protect: 'she's a simple bawd / That cannot say as much' (20-1). Though Desdemona might act like a virtuous and honest woman, praying and kneeling on occasion, Othello is certain that she is concealing wicked deeds from him: 'A closet lock and key of villainous secrets; / And yet she'll kneel and pray' (22-3).

▶ LINES 20-106: OTHELLO SPEAKS TO DESDEMONA

When Desdemona arrives Othello asks to look into her eyes, as though he might see into her heart: 'Let me see your eyes/ Look in my face' (25-6). He instructs Emilia to go and stand guard outside the door while he interrogates his wife: 'Cough or cry 'hem' if anybody come' (29). He suggests that Emilia's guarding of the door is in keeping with her being a brothel keeper: 'Some of your function, mistress' (27).

Desdemona kneels before Othello and pleads to be told what is on her husband's mind. She realises he is furious but cannot comprehend why: 'I understand a fury in your words,/ But not the words' (32-3). He asks her to swear that she is honest but accuses her of being false when she does: 'Heaven truly knows that thou art false as hell' (39). When Desdemona asks in what manner she is being false ('To whom, my lord? With whom? How am I false?') Othello dismisses her: 'Ah, Desdemona! Away, away, away!' (40-1).

The strain of the situation takes its toll on the Moor and he begins to weep. He says that he could tolerate and endure any number of trials and afflictions: having his body covered in sores; poverty; being held in captivity; being an object of mockery for all time (47-56). But to have the body that might ultimately bear his children besmirched and tainted, this he cannot endure. He makes a number of unfavourable comparisons:

- Othello likens Desdemona's body to a fountain that has become infested with toads that breed in its waters: 'a cistern for foul toads/ To knot and gender in' (61-2).

`CHARACTER DEVELOPMENT`

- He tells her that she is as quick to mate as 'summer flies' in a slaughter-house.
- She is like a sweet-smelling weed. 'O thou black weed' (67).
- He likens her to a 'goodly book' upon which the word 'whore' has been written: 'Was this fair paper, this most godly book/ Made to write 'whore' upon?' (71-2).

The Moor tells his wife that to even speak her deeds would be a violent assault on modesty: 'would to cinders burn up modesty,/ Did I but speak thy deeds' (75-6). Her protestations are a farce, an insult to Heaven, and ignored by the moon and the wind: 'Heaven stops the nose at it, and the moon winks;/ The bawdy wind...will not hear it' (77-80). He challenges her cruelly, asking her if she is not a 'strumpet' and a 'whore'. When she says that she is neither of these and that her body is preserved for him alone, he sarcastically tells her he mistakenly took her for the 'cunning whore of Venice/ That married with Othello' (91-2).

Othello calls Emilia back into the room and pays her for standing guard at the door. Again his actions imply that she is nothing but Desdemona's bawd. He tells Emilia to keep quiet about what he has spoken.

💬 TALK ABOUT IT

In this scene Othello challenges and abuses his wife with accusations that she is dishonest. She pleads her innocence but her protestations seem to fall on deaf ears and the Moor never seems open to the possibility that his wife is telling the truth. However, at one point he asks her 'Is't possible?' (88). Some directors interpret this line as a moment when Othello glimpses the possibility that he has been terribly mistaken. Re-read lines 82 to 90 and consider the different ways that these lines might be spoken by an actor playing the role of Othello.

RODERIGO

In this scene it seems for a moment that Roderigo will redeem himself. He comes across almost as a respectable human being, finally standing up to Iago and calling him on his deceitful ways: 'your words and performances are no kin together' (184-5). He has had enough of being manipulated and even threatens to expose some of Iago's lies by asking that Desdemona return his jewels: 'I will make myself known to Desdemona' (197-8). When the jewels are not forthcoming he will 'seek satisfaction' from the man who's made a fool of him (201).

Yet this show of backbone is all too brief. As we've seen, Roderigo is easily manipulated by Iago's lies, falling for his cock-and-bull story about Othello being reassigned to North Africa and taking Desdemona with him. He even believes Iago's outlandish claim that the only way to stop this move is by killing Cassio, Othello's intended replacement as commander of Cyprus. Roderigo, we're inclined to believe, is nothing less than criminally self-deluded: he believes Iago's flattering comments about courage and valour and still – despite all evidence to the contrary – thinks he has a chance of being Desdemona's lover.

When Othello departs Emilia asks Desdemona how she is feeling and what is going on with Othello. Desdemona seems to be exhausted. She tells Emilia that she is 'half asleep' and struggles to comprehend what Emilia is saying to her. Eventually she asks that Emilia to leave her for the moment and to go and put the wedding sheets on her bed and fetch Iago.

▶ **LINES 107 – 172:**
OTHELLO'S BEHAVIOUR IS DISCUSSED

Desdemona cannot understand why Othello has treated her in this manner. She can think of nothing she has done to warrant such abusive treatment: 'How have I been behaved that he might stick/ The small'st opinion on my least misuse' (109-10). Emilia returns with Iago and he asks her how she's feeling. She continues to wonder at Othello's manner of dealing with her – she is not accustomed to being so violently reprimanded: 'I am child to chiding' (115). She asks Iago why her husband chose to call her such terrible names.

Emilia tells Iago that Othello called Desdemona a 'whore'. She says that even a wretched drunk wouldn't use such a term (121-2). She also says that Desdemona sacrificed much when she married the Moor: the prospect of marrying certain wealthy men; here relationship with her father; her home and her friends. Did she give all this up just to be called 'whore'? Emilia wonders if some wicked person has not spread false rumours about Desdemona: 'I will be hanged if some eternal villain… Have not devised this slander' (131-4). She becomes convinced that the Moor's mind has been poisoned by some villainous rogue: 'The Moor's abused by some villainous knave' (140). She reminds Iago how some such person once suggested to him that she had slept with Othello: 'Some such squire he was/ That turned your wit the seamy side without/ And made you to suspect me with the Moor' (146-8). Iago dismisses the possibility that anyone has been poisoning the Moor's mind with such tales: 'Fie, there is no such man! It is impossible' (135).

Desdemona asks Iago what she ought to do to win Othello back. She falls to her knees and says should she ever wrong her husband she would deserve to lose all comfort: 'If e'er my will did trespass 'gainst his love,/ Either in discourse, or thought, or actual deed…Comfort forswear me' (153-60). His foul treatment of her may destroy

OTHELLO

DIGNITY AND SELF-POSSESSION

It is worth remembering that Othello is a military commander, tasked with leading the Venetian army and protecting the state. Though the threat posed by the Turks has abated, he remains in command of an army that has travelled to Cyprus and is responsible for order on the island. That he should be in Desdemona's chamber interrogating her maid, desperately seeking evidence that will confirm what he already believes about his wife is not befitting someone of his rank and a clear indication that Othello has lost sight of his priorities and responsibilities.

Though he might display a little more self-possession in this scene, never flying completely off the handle or resorting to violence, his behaviour is far removed from the dignified and self-possessed general we encountered at the start of the play. He is unpleasant and insulting in his manner to both Emilia and Desdemona, characterising the first as a 'bawd' or brothel keeper and the second as a 'whore'. He quickly loses his patience and makes his displeasure known when he does not receive the answer he desires or demands: 'Ah Desdemon, away, away, away!' (41).

There is a 'fury' in Othello's words and he fails to make his thoughts clear to his wife. She knows he is angry but cannot comprehend why: 'I understand a fury in your words,/ But not the words' (32-3). If he were calm and composed he might be able to entertain the thought that he has been mistaken in his suspicions and doubts. But Othello has gone too far and the notion that his wife has been unfaithful is now so deeply embedded in his mind that he cannot see things differently.

OTHELLO'S LOVE FOR DESDEMONA

There very little evidence now left of the love that Othello once felt for his wife. Though he uses a term of endearment (chuck) when she arrives, he does nothing further to display any form of affection or care. His speech is angry and bitter and he is swift to lose his patience with Desdemona. When she describes herself as his 'true and loyal wife' he demands her to swear that she is honest: 'Come, swear it: damn thyself' (35).

Othello's view of love now seems to be very limited. He is consumed with jealousy at the thought that his wife has slept with Cassio and this notion overrides all other considerations. In his tormented and fevered condition his wife now appears tarnished and tainted by her associations with another man. He tells her that he could tolerate and endure any number of afflictions and trials, but the notion that his wife's body has been given to another man is too much for him to bear. Othello has no reason to believe that Desdemona has slept with anyone other than Cassio, but it matters not – one man might as well be one hundred men, his wife is no better than a common prostitute.

Desdemona is still considered a beautiful and desirable woman but to Othello his wife's beauty now seems to skilfully mask an inner ugliness or corruption. She is 'so lovely fair, and smell'st so sweet', but she is more like a weed than a flower. She is a perfect, virginal page upon which the word 'whore' has now been etched. To him she is damaged goods, contaminated by the touch of another man.

ELOQUENCE

It is hard to imagine when we read this scene to recall how Othello once spoke with such eloquence and restraint. Here again his speech is angry, bitter and sometimes crazed. What is perhaps most shocking is the manner in which he now addresses his wife. She is an 'impudent strumpet', a 'public commoner' and a 'whore'. It is the last term that is most brutal and Desdemona cannot even bring herself to repeat it when she later speaks to Iago about her husband's behaviour: 'Am I that name, Iago?' (119).

Perhaps Othello's speech, in which he outlines the various forms of suffering he could endure, recalls some of the eloquence of the earlier scenes, but the speech quickly descends into bitterness and an ugly vision of his wife as a reservoir in which toads come to procreate: 'a cistern for foul toads/ To knot and gender in' (61-2). The way he responds to and treats Emilia is equally foul and unpleasant, characterising her as a 'simple bawd' and barking orders at her to stand guard at the door and to keep quiet about anything she might have heard him say: 'You, mistress,/ That...keeps the gates of hell, you, you! – Ay, you...keep our counsel' (92-6). Emilia later says that a drunken beggar would never speak as foully as Othello did to his wife: 'a beggar in his drink/ Could not have laid such terms upon his callet' (121-2).

DESDEMONA AND OTHELLO

TRUSTING NATURE

Othello no longer trusts Desdemona and he is suspicious of her every word and act. To him she is now 'false as hell' (39). Even when she is protesting her innocence he is looking for signs of her betrayal, ready to pounce on any term that might be considered ambiguous. When Desdemona tells him that she is 'committed' he chooses to interpret the word to mean that his wife has committed adultery: "Committed'! O thou public commoner' (73).

In Othello's fevered state he seems to think that his wife is toying with him, using language in an artful manner to conceal her unfaithfulness. When Desdemona says that she hopes her husband 'esteems [her] honest' he likens her to a fly in a slaughterhouse, implying that she is as quick and ready to mate as these creatures: 'O ay, as summer flies are in the shambles,/ That quicken even with blowing' (66-7).

It is not just Desdemona that Othello will not trust, but Emilia also. He interrogates her at the start of the scene, demanding to know if she has seen anything that could be construed as suspicious about his wife's relationship with Cassio. Though Emila answers his questions and pleads with him to not doubt his wife, Othello does not place any faith in her words. When she has left he evaluates what she has told him and quickly dismisses it as the words of 'a simple bawd/ That cannot say as much' (20-1). To Othello, his wife's maid is not only aware of Desdemona but is playing an active role in her affairs.

129

IAGO

A MASTER PLOTTER

Iago is a master of his craft. In his conversation with Roderigo Iago comes across yet again as a smooth and confident improviser. Roderigo has finally had enough of being manipulated by Iago and threatens to expose him by going directly to Desdemona and demanding the return of his jewels. (Iago was supposed to pass Roderigo's jewels on to Desdemona but instead sold them and spent the money on himself).

Iago escapes from this jam brilliantly, concocting on the spot a story about Othello leaving with Desdemona for faraway Mauritania. If this were to happen, of course, Roderigo would lose whatever slim chance he has of ever becoming Desdemona's lover. Only murdering Cassio, he says, will have the effect of keeping Othello and his wife on Cyprus.

Throughout this encounter, then, Iago improvises with astonishing fluency. It seems that nothing whatsoever could faze him in his lies. Roderigo begins by threatening to ruin him but concludes by agreeing to murder Cassio instead. Such an assault suits Iago perfectly: if Roderigo dies the threat of exposure is removed, if Cassio dies an old enemy is gone, if both die so much the better. We see Iago spy an opportunity and seize it, quickly turning a potentially disastrous situation into an advantageous one.

A BRILLIANT ACTOR

This scene once again showcases Iago's skills as an actor. He knows exactly why Desdemona is distraught and upset. Yet he pretends to be ignorant of her plight, greeting her cheerfully, 'What is your pleasure, madam? How is't with you?' (111). He feigns confusion at her distressed state asking her, 'What's the matter, lady?' (115). He pretends to be shocked when told about Othello's devastating verbal assault and immediately begins to play the role of gentle comforter: 'Do not weep, do not weep – alas the day!' (125). He claims to be mystified about why Othello would act in such a manner: 'Why did he so?... How comes this trick upon him?' (123, 130). His pretence is at its most audacious when Emilia suggests some 'insinuating rogue/ Some cogging, cozening slave' has been twisting Othello's mind

(132-3). Iago exclaims that such an evil man could not possibly exist, 'Fie, there is no such man! It is impossible' (135). The audience, of course, knows that he himself is the 'villain', the person responsible for poisoning Othello's attitude toward Desdemona.

He comes across as loyal and caring, telling Desdemona that Othello's anger stems only from 'The business of the state' (167). He consoles her, assuring her that everything will be all right: 'Go in, and weep not; all things shall be well'(173). In reality, however, he is scheming to ensure that events turn out anything but well for Desdemona.

MANIPULATIVE AND PERSUASIVE

Iago's powers of persuasion are evident in his confrontation with Roderigo. An angry Roderigo has had enough of being made a fool of by Iago, of being fobbed off with some new 'device' each day (177). He's threatens to demand that Desdemona return jewels she never received, jewels that Iago kept for himself. This, of course, would ruin Iago's reputation for honesty and potentially his expose other darker plots.

Yet by the end of the conversation Roderigo is back on side. Iago manipulates him brilliantly, not only regaining his trust but also persuading him to murder Cassio. He pulls off this feat of persuasion through fear and flattery. He plays on the ego of this snivelling buffoon, saying how he now has a higher opinion of him: 'Why, now I see there's mettle in thee, and even from this instant do build on thee a better opinion than ever before' (205-7). He claims to see in Roderigo the qualities of 'purpose, courage, and valour' – valour that must be proved by the murder of Cassio that very night (215).

Iago also employs fear in this feat of persuasion, specifically Roderigo's fear that he will never be with Desdemona. (The audience, of course, knows that Desdemona has no interest in this idiot but he himself believes he has a chance with her). Iago lies fluently and brilliantly, saying that Othello is about to take Desdemona to North Africa with him, placing her beyond Roderigo's reach forever. He pretends that the surest way of ensuring she stays in Cyprus is through the 'removing of Cassio', who is due to replace Othello as commander of the island (227).

DESDEMONA AND IAGO

Iago, conveniently, will be able to arrange it so that Roderigo has the perfect opportunity to kill Cassio that very night and will even assist in the assault if necessary (232-9). By scene's end, Roderigo is convinced once more that Iago is his ally and prepares yet again to his bidding. Iago has manipulated him brilliantly, playing upon his emotions like a master musician.

MALICIOUS
Iago's malice is evident in the way he probes Desdemona, urging her to repeat the names Othello called her, despite the obvious discomfort it causes: 'What name, fair lady?' (119). This is someone who relishes the discord he has sown and the hurt he's brought to those around him.

He also reveals a disturbing lack of respect for human life. He refers to murder in a disconcertingly casual way as 'the removing of Cassio', talking about it as if he were asking Roderigo to carry out some simple everyday task rather than the taking of human life.

her life but it will never destroy the love she holds for him: 'his unkindness may defeat my life / But never taint my love' (161-2). She says that she can hardly utter the word 'whore' let alone behave in a way that would warrant such a title (162-4).

Iago helps Desdemona to her feet and tries to reassure her about Othello. He says that it is most likely state business that is troubling the Moor and causing him to behave in this manner. Trumpets are sounded, signalling that supper is ready, and so Desdemona leaves with Emilia.

▶ LINES 173 – 244:
RODERIGO CHALLENGES IAGO
Roderigo enters in an angry mood and immediately challenges Iago:
• He says that Iago has been sending him off each day to do pointless things that are in no way beneficial to his quest to win Desdemona.
• Iago has bankrupted him, using his money to purportedly buy jewels and expensive gifts for Desdemona: 'I have wasted myself out of my means' (187-8).

131

• Iago has been leading him to believe that these gifts were working, but Roderigo has seen no proof of this (188-92).

Roderigo tells Iago that he intends to go to Desdemona, apologise for his behaviour and ask for his jewels to be returned. If she does not wish to return the gifts Roderigo says that he will come to Iago for compensation.

Iago is quick to calm the heated Roderigo. He begins by complimenting him, saying that he is impressed with the boldness and courage that Roderigo is displaying: 'Why, now I see there's mettle in thee' (205).

He says that Roderigo is right to challenge him in this manner, but the idea that Iago has not being working honestly on his behalf is unfair: 'I protest I have dealt most directly in thy affair' (208-9).

Iago calls on Roderigo to put his newfound mettle to good use this evening. He promises that if he does as he is instructed he will have Desdemona by his side tomorrow evening: 'If thou the next night following enjoy not Desdemona, take me from this world with treachery' (215-7). Iago concocts a false story, telling Roderigo that a special commission is coming from Venice to install Cassio in Othello's place. Othello and Desdemona, Iago says, are planning a move to faraway Mauritania. Only some drastic event or accident will now keep the Moor and his wife on the island. The murder of Cassio will achieve this and Roderigo is the man to do this.

Iago tells Roderigo that Cassio will dine later with a prostitute. When he leaves to go home, this will be the perfect time to kill him: 'If you will watch his going thence – which I fashion will fall out between twelve and one – you may take him at your pleasure' (235-7). Iago promises to be nearby to lend assistance if necessary. He tells Roderigo that he will further convince him of the need to kill Cassio but that it is now supper-time and the time has come to act. ◆

CHARACTER DEVELOPMENT

DESDEMONA & OTHELLO

DESDEMONA

BEAUTIFUL AND VIRTUOUS

Desdemona's beauty is again alluded to in this scene. Othello tells her that she is 'lovely fair' but his words are now edged with bitterness and doubt and his wife's beauty is no longer considered a virtue but a trap that ensnares and corrupts. With regards her virtuous character, Othello no longer believes in this. Her protestations and pleas of innocence fall on deaf ears. She swears she is a devoted and loyal wife, but he does not believe a word of it.

However, the scene reinforces our sense of Desdemona's good nature:
• Though the most hateful terms are hurled at her, she tries to understand her husband and get to the root of what is bothering him: 'Alas, what ignorant sin have I committed?' (70)
• No matter how unkindly Othello treats her she insists that his behaviour will not spoil the love she feels for him: 'his unkindness may defeat my life, / But never taint my love' (161-2).

🗨 **TALK ABOUT IT**

This scene again demonstrates just how skilful Iago is at manipulating others. Take a close look at how he manages to calm the enraged Roderigo and convince him that it is in his interest to murder Cassio. How does Iago manage to achieve this? What tactics does he deploy?

- When Emilia suggests that some evil person might be feeding Othello false stories, Desdemona says that if this is the case she can forgive her husband all: 'If any such there be, heaven pardon him' (136).
- Though she is suffering intensely and is feeling exhausted, when Othello weeps she looks to comfort him: 'Alas, the heavy day! Why do you weep? / Am I the motive for these tears my lord?' (42-3).

INNOCENT

We might, however, characterise Desdemona's tolerance of her husband's foul and abusive behaviour as naive and innocent. She is not accustomed to being treated in this manner and her response to the abuse she receives is one of bewilderment and shock. As she says herself she is a 'child to chiding' (115). She comes from a privileged background and has enjoyed a soft childhood. Unlike Emilia who seems to be hardened against and accustomed to the ills of the world, Desdemona's innocence means that she is not equipped to deal with the sort of behaviour Othello is now demonstrating.

The events of the past few days are now starting to take their toll. Desdemona is exhausted and unable to defend herself. She even begins to doubt that she is innocent and questions whether she has not, in fact, acted in some manner that justifies the label a whore: 'Am I that name, Iago' (119).

DESDEMONA, IAGO & EMILIA

ACT 4

SCENE 3

Another room in the castle

Enter Othello, Lodovico, Desdemona, Emilia and Attendants

LODOVICO	I do beseech you, sir, trouble yourself no further.
OTHELLO	O, pardon me, 'twill do me good to walk.
LODOVICO	Madam, good night; I humbly thank your ladyship.
DESDEMONA	Your honour is most welcome.
OTHELLO	Will you walk, sir? –
	O Desdemona!
DESDEMONA	My lord?
OTHELLO	Get you to bed
	On th'instant; I will be returned forthwith:
	Dismiss your attendant there – look't be done.

Exit

DESDEMONA	I will, my lord.
EMILIA	How goes it now? He looks gentler than he did.
DESDEMONA	He says he will return incontinent,
	And hath commanded me to go to bed,
	And bid me to dismiss you.
EMILIA	Dismiss me?
DESDEMONA	It was his bidding; therefore, good Emilia,
	Give me my nightly wearing, and adieu:
	We must not now displease him.
EMILIA	I would you had never seen him.
DESDEMONA	So would not I: my love doth so approve him
	That even his stubbornness, his checks, his frowns –
	Prithee unpin me – have grace and favour in them.
EMILIA	I have laid those sheets you bade me on the bed.
DESDEMONA	All's one, good faith, how foolish are our minds!
	If I do die before thee, prithee, shroud me
	In one of those same sheets.
EMILIA	Come, come, you talk!
DESDEMONA	My mother had a maid called Barbary;
	She was in love, and he she loved proved mad,
	And did forsake her. She had a 'Song of Willow'–
	An old thing 'twas, but it expressed her fortune,
	And she died singing it. That song tonight
	Will not go from my mind. I have much to do
	But to go hang my head all at one side
	And sing it like poor Barbary: prithee dispatch.
EMILIA	Shall I go fetch your nightgown?
DESDEMONA	No, unpin me here.
	This Lodovico is a proper man.
EMILIA	A very handsome man.
DESDEMONA	He speaks well.
EMILIA	I know a lady in Venice would have walked
	barefoot to Palestine for a touch of his nether lip.

5

10

15

20

25

30

35

10 *incontinent:* immediately

14 *nightly wearing:* nightclothes

16 *I would you:* I wish you
17 *approve:* commend
18 *checks:* rebukes, reproofs

20 *bade me:* bid me to
21 *All's one:* alright

23 *you talk:* how you prattle!

25 *mad:* faithless

29-30 *I have much to do But to go hang my head:* I find it difficult not to hang my head

33 *proper:* handsome

35-36 *walked barefoot to Palestine:* a most arduous journey, suggests that the woman in question would have done anything to kiss Lodivico
36 *for a touch of his nether lip:* for a kiss

DESDEMONA	*(Sings)*
	The poor soul sat sighing by a sycamore tree,
	Sing all a green willow.
	Her hand on her bosom, her head on her knee;
	Sing willow, willow, willow.
	The fresh streams ran by her and murmured her moans;
	Sing willow, willow, willow.
	Her salt tears fell from her, and softened the stones.
	Sing willow –
	(Speaks) Lay by these –
	(Sings) willow, willow
	(Speaks) Prithee, hie thee: he'll come anon
	(Sings) Sing all a green willow must be my garland.
	Let nobody blame him, his scorn I approve –
	(Speaks) Nay, that's not next. – Hark, who is't that knocks?
EMILIA	It's the wind.
DESDEMONA	*(Sings)*
	I called my love 'false love'; but what said he then?
	Sing willow, willow, willow.
	If I court more women, you'll couch with more men.
	(Speaks) So get thee gone, good night. Mine eyes do itch:
	Doth that bode weeping?
EMILIA	'Tis neither here nor there.
DESDEMONA	I have heard it said so. O, these men, these men!
	Dost thou in conscience think, – tell me, Emilia, –
	That there be women do abuse their husbands
	In such gross kind?
EMILIA	There be some such, no question.
DESDEMONA	Wouldst thou do such a deed for all the world?
EMILIA	Why, would not you?
DESDEMONA	No, by this heavenly light!
EMILIA	Nor I neither, by this heavenly light:
	I might do't as well i'th' dark.
DESDEMONA	Wouldst thou do such a thing for all the world?
EMILIA	The world's a huge thing: it is a great price
	For a small vice.
DESDEMONA	God troth, I think thou wouldst not.
EMILIA	By my troth, I think I should, and undo't when I had done. Marry, I would not do such a thing for a joint-ring, nor for measures of lawn, nor for gowns, petticoats, nor caps, nor any petty exhibition. But for all the whole world? Ud's pity, who would not make her husband a cuckold to make him a monarch? I should venture purgatory for't.
DESDEMONA	Beshrew me, if I would do such a wrong
	For the whole world!
EMILIA	Why, the wrong is but a wrong i'th' world; and having the world for your labour, 'tis a wrong in your own world, and you might quickly make it right.
DESDEMONA	I do not think there is any such woman.
EMILIA	Yes, a dozen – and as many to th'vantage
	As would store the world they played for.
	But I do think it is their husbands' faults
	If wives do fall: say that they slack their duties,

Marginal notes:

37-52 *The poor...more men:* The Willow Song

38 *willow:* an emblem for the grief of lost or unrequited love

40

44 *Lay by these:* put these away

45
45 *hie thee:* hurry up
45 *anon:* any minute

50

52 *couch with:* lie with, sleep with

55

57 *That there... abuse their husbands:* that there are women out there who are unfaithful to their husbands

60

62 *heavenly light:* probably refers to the light of the moon

65

70
71 *joint-ring:* a ring that is made in two separate parts, often decorated with two clasped hands holding a small heart, used to symbolise the union of lovers
71 *lawn:* a fine and costly linen, white in colour
72 *petty exhibition:* trivial gift or allowance
73 *Ud's:* God's

75 *venture purgatory:* risk being condemned to the punishments of purgatory

80

82 *to th'vantage:* in addition
83 *store:* populate
83 *played for:* copulated or gambled for

85 *If wives do fall:* If wives succumb to the temptation to be unfaithful
85 *duties:* marital (including sexual) obligations. It is likely that Emilia is referring to sexual duties here and to her husband Iago

135

And pour our treasures into foreign laps,
Or else break out in peevish jealousies,
Throwing restraint upon us; or say they strike us,
Or scant our former having in despite –
Why, we have galls, and though we have some grace,   90
Yet have we some revenge. Let husbands know,
Their wives have sense like them; they see and smell,
And have their palates both for sweet and sour
As husbands have. What is it that they do,
When they change us for others? Is it sport?   95
I think it is. And doth affection breed it?
I think it doth. Is't frailty that thus errs?
It is so too. And have not we affections,
Desires for sport, and frailty, as men have?
Then let them use us well: else let them know,   100
The ills we do, their ills instruct us so.

DESDEMONA

Good night, good night. God me such uses send,
Not to pick bad from bad, but by bad mend.

Exeunt

86   **And pour our treasures into foreign laps:**
sleep with women other than us their wives

89   *Or scant our former having in despite:* **when out of
spite they reduce they amount they've been giving us**

90   *we have galls:* **we experience resentment**

96   *affection:* **passion, lust**

97   *frailty:* **moral or physical weakness**

101   *The ills:* **the wrongs**

102   *uses:* **habits**

103   *Not to pick bad from bad, but by bad mend:* **not to
imitate the bad behaviour of others, but to learn
from such behaviour how to mend my own vices.**

EMILIA & DESDEMONA

🗨TALK
ABOUT IT

Why do you think Othello asks Emilia to leave? Does he fear her influence over Desdemona? Do you think does he think of her as an obstacle to exacting his revenge? In your opinion, is he committed at this stage to restoring his honour by hurting Desdemona?

This scene focuses exclusively on interactions between the two prominent female leads in the play. It provides them with a platform for intense philosophical debate on core aspects of human behaviour and the potential merits of what is deemed to be a fundementally immoral and unpardonable act: adultery.

ACTION

LINE BY LINE

▶ LINES 1-53: DESDEMONA PREPARES FOR BED

This scene takes place in a room in the castle. Othello appears to have regained his composure after the earlier outburst in Act 4 Scene 2, and his changed temperament is remarked upon by Emilia ('He looks gentler than he did'). Before leaving to go for a walk with Lodovico, Othello orders Desdemona to prepare for bed – their first, uninterrupted night as a married couple.

He also orders that she dismiss Emilia. Emilia seems sceptical and concerned by Othello's command that she leave: 'Dismiss me?' (12). She appears exasperated, worried, and angry and wishes that Desdemona had never met the Moor: 'I would you had never seen him'. (16).

Ever-yielding, Desdemona attempts to pacify Emilia. Her love for Othella enables her to overlook – or perhaps just blinds her to – Othello's more worrying flaws: 'My love doth so approve him[...] his checks, his frowns', (17-8).

An important hallmark of this scene is the number of times that Desdemona unknowingly foretells her own grim destiny. This heightens the tension for the audience who are aware of the arc of Iago's devious ploys. The first of these ominous portents occurs when Desdemona reflects lovingly on their wedding sheets and unintentionally predicts the manner of her own death: 'If I do die before thee, prithee, shroud me / in one of these same sheets' (22-3).

DESDEMONA

DESDEMONA:

INNOCENCE

Desdemona's innocence is given more prominence
in this scene than any of her other qualities
and there is a tactical reason for this. This scene
precedes the fifth and final act of the play,
where the climax of the plot will be revealed,
and Desdemona's guileless disposition is key to
building up the sense of the calm before the storm.

She has had her first glimpse of Othello's rage,
yet continues to believe unconditionally in his
goodness and feels she has sufficiently addressed
all of his concerns. She is in love and blind to the
very real dangers posed by the jealousy of this man
who is, in part, a savage warrior.

Where Emilia remains distinctly ill-at-ease
about Othello following his jealous outburst,
Desdemona's innonence dupes her into believing
that nothing is awry. In his flaws she sees only
more things to love:

My love doth so approve him
That even his stubbornness, his checks, his
frowns—
Prithee unpin me—have grace and
favour in them (17-9).

Reflecting on the cause of Othello's jealousy, she
expresses utter disbelief that women could ever
be adulterous and asks Emilia if such women
really exist. 'Dost thou in conscience think – tell
me Emilia –/ That there be women do abuse their
husbands/ In such gross kind?' (56-58).

She is scandalised (as only an innocent can be) and
finds it difficult to accept Emilia's pronouncement
that yes, women cheat, and – moreover – that
Emilia herself would do it in certain circumstances
(65-76).

BEAUTIFUL AND VIRTUOUS

Desdemona's faith in the inherent goodness of
the people around her in and humanity at large
shapes her interactions, her relationships, and has a
profound impact – whether for better or worse – on
her decision-making. Note that, even though she is
shocked by Emilia's revelation, Desdemona does
not seriously judge her for it, merely accepts it.

However, she makes it clear that she does not
agree with this kind of sentiment. She consciously
decides not to fall in line with the sexual cynicism
described by Emilia: 'God me such uses send/Not
to pick bad from bad, But by bad mend' (102-3).
It is a personal pledge not to perpetuate the

cycle of mistakes and betrayals that poison so many romantic relationships. We get the impression that she wants to heal the damage caused by the flaws of those around her.

STRONG-WILLED AND ASSERTIVE?

In earlier sections of the play, Desdemona displays a steely resolve and independent streak beyond her years and social standing. However, we begin to see this wane in Act 4 Scene 2. Where once she defied her father to pursue a controversial marriage, she is now meek and obedient in the face of Othello's temper. It's not clear whether this change results from a sense of wifely obligation or from fear – or both – but either way, she is anxious not to provoke or disobey him.

In the opening lines, we see Othello lean on his military upbringing in the way that he interacts with Desdemona. The terrain between them has been changed by Iago's insinuations and Othello reverts to his soldierly ways, issuing firm orders to maintain the illusion of control in a relationship that, deep down, he believes is drifting away from him. What is noticeable is that, in this very brief conversation, Desdemonda is surprisingly compliant. Her new submissiveness is encapsulated in a few short lines:

DESDEMONA: He...hath commanded me to go
              to bed,
              And bid me dismiss you.
EMILIA: Dismiss me?
DESDEMONA: It was his bidding; therefore,
              good Emilia,
              Give me my nightly wearing,
              and adieu:
              We must not now displease him.
              (10-5)

💬THINK ABOUT IT
Think about the verbs used by Desdemona here.
'Command', 'bid', 'dismiss'.
What do these tell us about the dynamic of the relationship?
Do you think it has changed?

This foreshadowing continues when she reveals some of the family history. Her mother's maid, a woman called Barbery (an alternative form of Barbara, but also an allusion to Othello's Berber ethnicity), fell in love and 'he she loved proved mad, / and he did forsake her' (25-6).

As Emilia helps her prepare for bed, Desdemona's makes a wistful reference to Lodovico in line 32, describing him as an educated and 'proper' (or handsome) gentleman. This reminds us of the fine noblemen from her own class that she spurned in her desire to marry Othello.

She begins to sing the Willow Song, a now-famous Shakespearean lament, wherein a woman mourns the loss of her absconding husband. Strangely, Desdemona mixes up a verse, prematurely singing the section where the woman in the song selflessly defends her husband's betrayal. Here, too, Desdemona inadvertently anticpates her violent end: 'The fresh streams ran by her and murmured her moans; / Sing willow, willow, willow. / Her salt tears fell from her, and softened the stones. / Sing willow, willow, willow... Let nobody blame him his scorn I approve – / (speaks) Nay, that's not next' (41-8).

▶ LINES 54-97:
EMILIA AND DESDEMONA DISCUSS ADULTERY

The song's reference to blame also foreshadows some of the circumstances of Desdemona's death. She interrupts the song on several occasions by urging Emilia to leave, in line with Othello's earlier command: 'Prithee, hie thee: he'll come anon... So get thee gone, goodnight' (45, 53).

Following Othello's earlier accusation, innocent Desdemona questions the existence of women who cheat on their husbands. Emilia assures her that these woman do, in fact, exist. When pushed, Emilia admits that she herself would commit adultery, and not for any trivial affair but for the sake of her husband's benefit:

Desdemona: Wouldst thou do such a thing
             for all the world?
Emilia: The world's a huge thing: it is a
             great price for a small vice.
Desdemona: God's troth, I think thou
             wouldst not.

139

Emilia: By my troth, I think I should... I would not do such a thing for a joint-ring, nor for measures of lawn, nor for gowns, petticoats, nor caps, nor any petty exhibition. But for all the whole world?... I should venture purgatory for't (65-75).

Shakespeare's wording here alludes quite strongly to well-known Biblical tales of Satan tempting Christ with all of the kingdoms in the world in exchange for his worship.

The confession – albeit hypothetical – appalls Desdemona, but tough and worldly Emilia is quick to counter. Women are judged differently to men and Emilia criticises this double-standard:

- She points out that women are punished cruelly by men for minor shortcomings and failings (82-6).

- She says that women, like men, have sexual appetites: 'Their wives have sense like them; they see, and smell / And have their palates both for sweet and sour / As husbands have' (92-4).

- Men cheat on their wives due to a combination of passion, excitement, and human weakness ('affections, / Desires for sport, and frailty') (98-9). Yet women also experience these things, so why are they expected to behave any differently?

- She claims that when women stray, they merely follow the example of the men around them: 'Then let them use us well: else let them know / The ills we do, their ills instruct us so' (100-1).

- The scene concludes with Desdemona going to bed. As she does, she prays that she herself will not fall victim to the sexual cynicism referred to by Emilia. ◆

EMILIA:

Up to this point, Emilia did not seem like a major character. At times, she seemed somewhat dim-witted and blissfully unaware of Iago's suspicious behaviour and bizarre requests. Act 4 Scene 3 reveals a facet of her personality that was shrouded until now. With little plot progression in this scene, Shakespeare's objective must have been to delve more deeply into these characters and contrast them.

JADED AND WORLDLY

Where the Moor's wife is inexperienced, generous of spirit and trusting in her outlook, Emilia can be said to be the opposite: worldly, cynical (particularly in her view of men), and wary of the intent of others.

World-weary Emilia tries not to engage in Desdemona's wistful conversation and attempts to keep her feet on the ground when she sings the Willow Song. The lament is an important lens that reveals key differences in these two women. Desdemona romanticises the grief that the song explores, luxuriates in the melancholy of it. Emilia retreats from it, often giving clipped responses. She is far more practical and experience has taught her better than to indulge sentimentality where life and death are concerned.

Emilia's speech about adultery is a key moment that accentuates just how different these women are. She takes a pragmatic view of this kind of betrayal. She would sleep with another man if she thought it would bring her husband material or professional gain. She later remarks that it would be a worthy sacrifice and that she would risk the safety of her soul for it were the benefits substantial enough:

DESDEMONA: Wouldst thou do such a thing for all the world?
EMILIA: The world's a huge thing: it is a great price /
For a small vice (65-6).

This raises the questions of whether or not Emilia has already betrayed Iago. He is driven to hurt Othello partly out of a rumour that he slept with Emilia. This may be simply paranoia, but this scene suggests to us that she at least has the capacity for it: 'Uds pity, who would / make her husband a cuckold to make him a / monarch? I should venture purgatory for't' (73-5).

EMILIA

Emilia has a philosophical side. Having pondered the behaviour of men and women she concludes that adultery begets adultery. She proposes what, for the time, is a radical interpretation of the reasons why women cheat. Her conclusion is that men have cheated and betrayed their wives for long enough, and that it spurred wives to abandon the loftier moral standards applied to them.

She examines the sort of gender-based hypocrisy that has blighted women for centuries, rationalising that women are often punished heavily for minor oversights while men lived more liberal lifestyles. She says that women are not blind to this double standard and as a result will be more inclined to give into the same carnal lapses (82-101).

PROTECTIVE AND LOYAL

In this scene, Emilia comes across as extremely protective of and loyal to Desdemona. She openly expresses her resentment of Othello – both for the effect he is having on Desdemona and for depriving her of a life with a more refined suitor.

She cherishes Desdemona's assertiveness and determination and is bitterly disappointed when she sees these qualities perish under the fog of love. Her rancor is evident in line 15 when she says: 'I would you had never seen him'. These are strong – even brazen – words for a waiting-woman to a general's wife.

We also see her protective instincts at play when Desdemona comments on Lodovico's good looks. Emilia is quick to latch on to this sentiment.

Perhaps she wishes for Desdemona to leave Othello and marry a man who shares the same social background and upbringing as her.

DESDEMONA: This Lodovico is a proper man.
EMILIA: A very handsome man.
DESDEMONA: He speaks well.
EMILIA: I know a lady in Venice would have walked / barefoot to Palestine for a touch of his nether lip (33-6).

Emilia has also shown herself to be extremely loyal to Iago. We saw this earlier when she procured the handkerchief for him. She is blindly dutiful to him throughout the play. Though her apparent willingness to stray in marriage could seem like an act of disloyalty, it is important to remember that she would do so only for his gain (69-73). In this context, it seems more like a warped sense of devotion than of promiscuity.

SPIRITED AND INDEPENDENT

While Emilia is devoted, she is no lap dog. She has a fiery streak and we see this when she openly criticises Othello to his own wife (16). We also see it in her bold and insightful speech about sexual morality. She stresses that women are also sexual beings and are subject to the same impulses and desires that affect men. She defies the conventions of the time, particularly the double standard to which women are held, and the harsh treatment meted out to them by their husbands.

ACT 5

SCENE 1

Cyprus. A street

Enter Iago and Roderigo

IAGO		Here, stand behind this balk; straight will he come.
		Wear thy good rapier bare, and put it home –
		Quick, quick, fear nothing, I'll be at thy elbow.
		It makes us or it mars us: think on that,
		And fix most firm thy resolution.
RODERIGO		Be near at hand, I may miscarry in't.
IAGO		Here, at thy hand: be bold and take thy stand.

He Retires

RODERIGO	*(Aside)*	I have no great devotion to the deed,
		And yet he hath given me satisfying reasons –
	(Aloud)	'Tis but a man gone: forth my sword, he dies!
IAGO	*(Aside)*	I have rubbed this young quat almost to the sense,
		And he grows angry. Now, whether he kill Cassio,
		Or Cassio him, or each do kill the other,
		Every way makes my gain. Live Roderigo,
		He calls me to a restitution large
		Of gold, and jewels, that I bobbed from him,
		As gifts to Desdemona –
		It must not be. If Cassio do remain,
		He hath a daily beauty in his life
		That makes me ugly; and besides, the Moor
		May unfold me to him: there stand I in much peril –
		No, he must die. But so: I hear him coming.

Enter Cassio

RODERIGO		I know his gait, 'tis he. *(Attacking Cassio)* Villain, thou diest!
CASSIO		That thrust had been mine enemy indeed,
		But that my coat is better than thou know'st –
		I will make proof of thine.

He wounds Roderigo

RODERIGO		O, I am slain!

Iago wounds Cassio in the leg from behind, and exit

CASSIO		I am maimed for ever. Help, ho! Murder, murder!

Enter Othello

OTHELLO	*(Aside)*	
		The voice of Cassio: Iago keeps his word.
RODERIGO		O, villain that I am!
OTHELLO	*(Aside)*	It is even so.
CASSIO		O, help, ho! Light! A surgeon!
OTHELLO	*(Aside)*	'Tis he: O brave Iago, honest and just,
		That hast such noble sense of thy friend's wrong,
		Thou teachest me! – Minion, your dear lies dead,
		And your unblest fate hies: strumpet, I come!
		Forth of my heart those charms, thine eyes, are blotted;
		Thy bed, lust– stained, shall with lust's blood be spotted.

Exit

He is going to kill Desdemona. *(handwritten note)*

Line numbers and glosses:

Line	Gloss
1	*balk:* timber beam
2	*rapier:* sword
2	*bare:* unsheathed
2	*put:* thrust
3	*I'll be at thy elbow:* I'll be close-by to help
6	*I may miscarry in't:* I may not be successful in my attempt
7	*bold:* brave
10	*forth my sword, he dies!:* Roderigo rehearses the murder in his mind
11	*quat:* pimple; small boil
11	*to the sense:* to the quick
14	*makes my gain:* will profit me
14	*Live Roderigo:* if Roderigo lives
15	*restitution:* compensation, repayment
16	*bobbed:* swindled
19-20	*He hath a daily beauty in his life / That makes me ugly:* Iago refers to Cassio's good manners and charm, something that makes Iago jealous
21	*unfold:* expose
22	*But so:* but so be it
23	*gait:* the way a person or an animal moves, his walk
25	*coat:* protective coat of mail, or leather jerkin
26	*make proof of thine:* test you
30	*Is it even so:* Othello may have mistaken Roderigo's voice for Cassio's and agrees that he is a villain
32	*brave:* worthy
34	*Minion:* mistress
35	*unblest fate hies:* damned fate hurries to meet you
36	*charms:* not just 'charming things' but also 'magical tokens'
36	*blotted:* effaced

Enter Lodovico and Gratiano

CASSIO	What ho! No watch? No passage? Murder, murder!
GRATIANO	'Tis some mischance; the voice is very direful.
CASSIO	O, help!
LODOVICO	Hark!
RODERIGO	O wretched villain!
LODOVICO	Two or three groan. It is a heavy night;
	These may be counterfeits: let's think't unsafe
	To come in to the cry without more help.
RODERIGO	Nobody come? Then shall I bleed to death.

Enter Iago with a light and his sword drawn

LODOVICO	Hark!
GRATIANO	Here's one comes in his shirt, with light and weapons.
IAGO	Who's there? Whose noise is this that cries on murder?
LODOVICO	We do not know.
IAGO	Do not you hear a cry?
CASSIO	Here, here! For heaven sake help me!
IAGO	What's the matter?
GRATIANO	This is Othello's ensign, as I take it.
LODOVICO	The same indeed, a very valiant fellow.
IAGO	What are you here that cry so grievously?
CASSIO	Iago? O, I am spoiled, undone by villains –
	Give me some help!
IAGO	O me, lieutenant! What villains have done this?
CASSIO	I think that one of them is hereabout
	And cannot make away.
IAGO	O treacherous villains!
	(To Lodovico and Gratiano)
	What are you there? Come in and give some help.
RODERIGO	O, help me here!
CASSIO	That's one of them.
IAGO	O murd'rous slave!
	O villain!
	He Stabs Roderigo
RODERIGO	O damned Iago! O inhuman dog!
	(Roderigo groans)
IAGO	Kill men i'th' dark? Where be these bloody thieves?
	How silent is this town! Ho, murder, murder!
	(To Lodovico and Gratiano)
	What may you be? Are you of good or evil?
LODOVICO	As you shall prove us, praise us.
IAGO	Signor Lodovico?
LODOVICO	He, sir.
IAGO	I cry you mercy – here's Cassio hurt by villains.
GRATIANO	Cassio?
IAGO	How is't, brother?
CASSIO	My leg is cut in two.
IAGO	Marry, heaven forbid!
	Light, gentlemen: I'll bind it with my shirt.

Enter Bianca

BIANCA	What is the matter, ho? Who is't that cried?
IAGO	Who is't that cried?
BIANCA	O my dear Cassio,
	My sweet Cassio, O Cassio, Cassio, Cassio.

---

38   *passage:* passers-by

39   *mischance:* unpredictable outcome

40

43   *heavy:* dark and gloomy

44   *conterfeits:* fake, pretended

45   *To come in to:* to approach

48   *in his shirt:* i.e. night wear

50

55   *spoiled:* badly injured, destroyed

59   *make away:* escape

60

65

69   *I cry you mercy:* pardon me

70

75

IAGO
O notable strumpet! Cassio, may you suspect
Who they should be, that have thus mangled you?

CASSIO
No.   80

GRATIANO
I am sorry to find you thus; I have been to seek you.

IAGO
Lend me a garter. So.

He binds Cassio's leg

O for a chair to bear him easily hence!

BIANCA
Alas, he faints! O Cassio, Cassio, Cassio!

IAGO
Gentlemen all, I do suspect this trash   85
To be a party in this injury.
Patience a while, good Cassio!
(to Lodovico and Gratiano)   Come, come,
Lend me a light: *(Going to Roderigo)* know we this
    face, or no?
Alas, my friend and my dear countryman,
Roderigo! no? – Yes, sure! – O heaven, Roderigo!   90

GRATIANO
What, of Venice?

IAGO
Even he, sir – did you know him?

GRATIANO
Know him? Ay.

IAGO
Signor Gratiano? I cry your gentle pardon;
These bloody accidents must excuse my manners   95
That so neglected you.

GRATIANO
                    I am glad to see you.

IAGO
How do you, Cassio? *(Calling)* O, a chair, a chair!

GRATIANO
                            Roderigo?

IAGO
He, he 'tis he.

Enter attendants with a chair   O, that's well said – the chair!
Some good man bear him carefully from hence,
I'll fetch the general's surgeon.   100
(To Bianca) For you, mistress,
Save you your labour. – He that lies slain here, Cassio,
Was my dear friend. What malice was between you?

CASSIO
None in the world; nor do I know the man.

IAGO
(To Bianca) What? Look you pale? *(To Attendants)* O, bear him out   105
    o'th' air!
(To Lodovico and Gratiano) Stay you, good gentlemen.

Exeunt attendants with Cassio in the chair (and the body of Roderigo)

(To Bianca) Look you pale, mistress?
(To Lodovico and Gratiano) Do you perceive the gastness of her eye?
(To Bianca) Nay, if you stare, we shall hear more anon.
(To Lodovico and Gratiano) Behold her well, I pray you, look upon her: 110
Do you see, gentlemen? Nay, guiltiness
Will speak though tongues were out of use.

Enter Emilia

EMILIA
'Las, what's the matter? What's the matter, husband?

IAGO
Cassio hath here been set on in the dark
By Roderigo and fellows that are scaped: 115
He's almost slain, and Roderigo quite dead.

EMILIA
Alas, good gentleman! Alas, good Cassio!

IAGO
This is the fruits of whoring. Prithee, Emilia,
Go know of Cassio where he supped tonight.
(To Bianca) What, do you shake at that?   120

79   *mangled:* mutilated

85   *trash:* Iago is referring to Bianca

95   *accidents:* disasters, unfortunate events

98   *that's well said:* well done!

102   *Save you your labour:* don't trouble yourself

105   *O, bear him out o'th' air:* fresh air was thought to be dangerous for the sick and wounded

106   *Stay you:* Do not leave

108   *gastness:* a frightened look

112   *though tongues were out of use:* even if human beings were to lose the power of speech

119   *know of:* learn from, ask

BIANCA	He supped at my house, but I therefore shake not.
IAGO	O did he so? I charge you go with me.
EMILIA	O, fie upon thee, strumpet!
BIANCA	I am no strumpet,
	But of life as honest as you that thus
	Abuse me.
EMILIA	As I! Foh! Fie upon thee!
IAGO	Kind gentlemen, let's go see poor Cassio dressed.
(To Bianca)	Come, mistress, you must tell's another tale. –
	Emilia, run you to the citadel
	And tell my lord and lady what hath happed.

Exit Emilia

(Lodovico and Gratiano) Will you go on afore? *(Aside)* This is the night
That either makes me, or fordoes me quite.

Exeunt Lodovico and Gratiano, followed by Iago

122 *charge:* command
125 *Abuse:* mistreat
126 *Let's go see poor Cassio dressed:* Lets go see poor Cassio's wounds
127 *tell's another tale:* make the truth known to us
131 *fordoes:* undoes
131 *quite:* utterly

IAGO AND RODERIGO

Iago and Roderigo wait in the street to ambush Cassio. When Cassio appears Roderigo attacks him, but is himself badly wounded. Lodovico and Gratiano are alerted to the scene. Iago arrives shortly after and discreetly stabs Roderigo in order to finish him off. He also looks to blame Bianca for the brawl.

ACTION

LINE BY LINE

▶ LINES 1-74: RODERIGO ATTACKS CASSIO

It is late at night. Iago and Roderigo are waiting in the street to ambush Cassio. Iago has persuaded Roderigo to kill Cassio as a means for him to win Desdemona. As they wait for Cassio to arrive, he primes Roderigo for the gruesome task at hand: 'Wear thy good rapier bare...and fix most firm thy resolution' (2-5). He assures Roderigo that he will be at his side throughout the confrontation: 'fear nothing, I'll be at thy elbow' (3).

In an aside, Iago acknowledges how he has goaded Roderigo into a murderous rage. He feels he will benefit no matter what the outcome of the impending fight: 'Every way makes my gain' (14). Both men are proving vexatious for Iago, and he has reasons for wanting them both out of the picture.

As we know, Iago has a long-standing resentment of Cassio and would gladly see him dead: 'If Cassio do remain / He hath a daily beauty in his life / That makes me ugly' (18-20). On the other hand, he has conned Roderigo out of a great deal of money. If Cassio prevails in the fight and kills Roderigo, Iago can never be called to account for this: 'Live Roderigo, / He calls me to a restitution large / Of gold, and jewels, that I bobbed from him' (14-16).

Cassio arrives. While Iago watches from the shadows, Roderigo attacks him. However, Cassio is wearing protective armour and is unharmed by Roderigo's assault (25). He fatally wounds Roderigo, who lies dying on the ground: 'O, I am slain!' (26). When Cassio retreats from the scene of the fight to call for help, Iago stabs him from behind, injuring him badly in the leg: 'O, I am maimed forever!' (27).

Othello is nearby and hears Cassio's cries for help. However, he does nothing. Seeing and hearing Cassio only reinforces his sense of betrayal at the non-existent affair between him and Desdemona. He reaffirms his continued faith in Iago's honesty, brands Desdemona a witch, and envisions her murder on their marriage bed (32-7).

Lodovico and Gratiano come upon the scene moments later, and Iago too makes his presence known, pretending to be an innocent passery-by. In the darkness and confusion, the men struggle to establish what's going on, and more importantly who is friend or foe (43-60).

Some distance away, and dying from his wounds, Roderigo calls for help. Cassio hears his cries and identifies him as his assailant (61). Iago knows that Roderigo, if found alive and questioned, is a liability and could potentially expose him. Without hesistating, he slips away from the others and stabs Roderigo to death before he can be incriminated (62-63).

▶ LINES 75-132: IAGO BLAMES BIANCA

Cassio's lover, Bianca arrives. She is clearly distressed by the sight of Cassio's injuries: 'O Cassio, Cassio, Cassio!' (77). Iago accuses her of involvment in the assault on Cassio: 'Gentlemen all, I do suspect this trash / To be party in this injury' (85-6). He tells her to leave the wounded Cassio alone and make no attempt to help or nurse him: 'For you, mistress, / save you your labour' (101-2). He asks her why she looks so pale, suggesting to the others that guilt and fear might be responsible for her pallor (105-12).

Iago's blaming of Bianca, of course, is designed to deflect suspicion and attention away from himself: Bianca's morally ambiguous lifestyle as a courtesan makes her an easy target and engages the suspicions of Lodovico, Gratiano, and (eventually) Emilia. A secondary result of this tactic is that it means that, by the end of this scene, all three female characters in the play have suffered the insult of 'whore'.

Throughout all of this, the bleeding Cassio drifts in and out of consciousness, making it impossible for him to defend Bianca against Iago's accusations. Iago binds his wounds and calls frantically for a 'chair' or stretcher (97). Eventually attendants arrive and carry him off, with Iago urging them to 'bear him out o'th'air' to a place where he can rest and recuperate (105).

Emilia is the final character to arrive at the scene of this night-time commotion. She, too, is disturbed by the violence that has occured: 'Alas, good Cassio' (117). She seems to accept Iago's suggestion that Bianca was involved in the assualt, and curses her for doing so: 'O, fie upon thee, strumpet!' (123). She has little time for Bianca's denials (125).

Iago suggests that Cassio was attacked because of his involvement with a 'loose woman' like Bianca 'This is the fruits of whoring' (118). He asks Emilia to find out where Cassio ate that night and when Bianca says it was at her house, he suggests that this is further evidence of her guilt (118-20). At the scene's conclusion he all but takes Bianca into custody, 'charging' her to accompany him as he leaves with the others to check on Cassio (122-9). ◆

OTHELLO

SOLDIER

There is a sharp constrast between the Othello of this scene and that of Othello in Act 2 Scene 3. In the earlier scene, Othello came across as a military commander. His greatest concern was for order and civility in the town under his command. His response to the earlier fight between Cassio and Roderigo was stern and immediate. Now, however, he seems uninterested in maintaining law and order in the city. He gives no response at all to the chaos unfolding nearby and is instead focused on the alleged affair. His own jealously has overshadowed his sense of public duty as a soldier.

OTHELLO

💬 THINK ABOUT IT

Why is it easy for Iago to convince the others that Bianca is involved in the attack? She is a courtesan. These were cultured, high-end, prostitutes who formed semi-permanent relationships with their clients. As such she is considered morally suspect by the others and they are quick to believe Iago's accusations.

IAGO

In this frenetic scene, we catch a glimpse of the complete spectrum of Iago's nefarious qualities in full swing. His persuasive arguments set Roderigo along a trajectory of murder and though this plan miscarries, he still manages to skillfully control an unstable situation.

MASTER PLOTTER

According to many critics this is the scene where we see Iago's abilities as a plotter at their most refined. He wants Cassio dead, but rather than dirty his own hands with the task, he convinces Roderigo to do it for him. We must emphasise once again that Iago is more of a brilliant improviser than a meticulous plotter.

In this scene, he sets in motion a wave of chaos and surfs it masterfully. He gives a masterful display of his ability to steer a fluid and highly changeable situation to his own advantage:

- He is uncertain how the fight he has instigated will turn out, but is confident that it will be to his advantage.
- He takes advantage of the fact that Cassio has retreated, attempting to stab him in the back without revealing his identity.
- When help arrives, he deliberately adds to the confusion as the characters attempt to identify one another in the dark and work out what's going on.
- He exploits this chaos to slip away and murder Roderigo.
- He also exploits Bianca's arrival, deflecting attention away from himself by blaming her for the attack.
- Most gallingly of, he feigns grave, brotherly concern for Cassio, binding his wound and calling frantically for help.

Throughout the scene, we see Iago reacting to events he could not have predicted and turning them to his advantage.

MANIPULATIVE AND PERSUASIVE

In the early exchanges of the scene, Roderigo acknowledges the strength of Iago's persuasion. Though Roderigo is not the most discerning of characters, his admission still reveals the powerful influence Iago holds over others: 'I have no great

CASSIO & IAGO

devotion to the deed, / And yet he hath given me satisfying reasons' (8-9). Iago himself exults his own manipulative ability: I have rubbed this young quat almost to the sense, / And he grows angry (11-2).

Later in the scene, he convinces Lodovico and Gratiano that Bianca is somehow involved in co-ordinating the attack. This illustrates Iago's incredible persuasive abilities. He had not anticipated her arrival, but almost instantly finds a use for her in his web of lies. He blames her for the attack, sewing seeds of suspicion in the other characters' minds (85-6, 105-12).

Othello's brief appearance in this scene further reinforces Iago's almost supernatural sway over others. He has fallen so hard for Iago's lies that he is convinced the affair is real. He ignores Cassio's plight. He now seems committed to killing Desdemona in order to avenge what he sees as his wounded honour: 'Thy bed, lust-stained, shall with lust's blood be spotted' (37).

A BRILLIANT ACTOR

Iago makes use of his extensive theatrical capabilities, shifting effortlessly between the role of general with Roderigo, innocent but wary bystander with Lodovico and Gratiano, protector with Cassio, and prosecutor with Bianca. With Roderigo, Iago is demanding but encouraging, doling out orders as well as moral support (1-7).

When Lodovico and Gratiano are drawn close by the commotion, Iago slips into another persona. Despite being the villain, he feigns a believable façade of fearfulness, courage, and even confusion at the chaos that he himself created (49-51).

All of this accentuates his apparent innocence in Cassio's assault and feeds into his larger swamp of propaganda. Lodovico and Gratiano buy into this act too, confirming Iago's self-sustaining cult of personality.

GRATIANO: This is Othello's ensign, as I take it.
LODOVICO: The same indeed, a very valiant
                fellow (52-3).

Iago brilliantly plays the role of Cassio's protector, despite having plotted his murder, stabbing him, cursing and conspiring against him for the duration of the play. He feigns concern for Cassio's wellbeing: 'O me, Lieutenant! What villains have done this?' (57). He calls for help and binds the wound that he himself inflicted. The mock kinship with which he addresses Cassio is almost intolerable for the audience:

IAGO: How is't, brother?
CASSIO: My leg is cut in two.
IAGO: Marry, heaven forbid!
          Light gentlemen: I'll bind it with
          my shirt (71-74).

MALICIOUS, CALLOUS, AND DESTRUCTIVE

Iago's destructive nature has never been more obvious than in this scene. Roderigo is neither an explicit nor an immediate threat, and murdering him is one of Iago's more depraved acts. His decision to not only kill Roderigo but also to slander him is instant and unwavering, exemplifying Iago's destructive and cold-blooded instincts.

OTHELLO

ACT 5

SCENE 2

Enter Othello with a light, and Desdemona in her bed asleep

OTHELLO It is the cause, it is the cause, my soul –
Let me not name it to you, you chaste stars:
It is the cause. Yet I'll not shed her blood,
Nor scar that whiter skin of hers than snow
And smooth as monumental alabaster –   5
Yet she must die, else she'll betray more men.
Put out the light, and then put out the light –
If I quench thee, thou flaming minister,
I can again thy former light restore,
Should I repent me; but once put out thine,   10
Thou cunning'st pattern of excelling nature,
I know not where is that Promethean heat
That can thy light relume. When I have plucked thy rose,
I cannot give it vital growth again,
It needs must wither: I'll smell thee on the tree –   15

(He kisses her) O balmy breath, that dost almost persuade
Justice to break her sword – one more, one more!

(He kisses her) Be thus when thou art dead, and I will kill thee
And love thee after – one more, and that's the last.

(He kisses her) So sweet was ne'er so fatal. I must weep,   20
But they are cruel tears: this sorrow's heavenly,
It strikes where it doth love. She wakes.

DESDEMONA Who's there? Othello?
OTHELLO   Ay. Desdemona.
DESDEMONA Will you come to bed, my lord?
OTHELLO Have you prayed tonight, Desdemona?
DESDEMONA   Ay, my lord.   25
OTHELLO If you bethink yourself of any crime
Unreconciled as yet to heaven and grace,
Solicit for it straight.
DESDEMONA Alack, my lord, what may you mean by that?
OTHELLO Well, do it, and be brief; I will walk by: 30
I would not kill thy unprepared spirit,
No – heavens forfend! – I would not kill thy soul.
DESDEMONA Talk you of killing?
OTHELLO   Ay, I do.
DESDEMONA   Then heaven
Have mercy on me.
OTHELLO   Amen, with all my heart.
DESDEMONA If you say so, I hope you will not kill me.   35
OTHELLO Humh!
DESDEMONA And yet I fear you, for you're fatal then
When your eyes roll so. Why I should fear I know not,

1 *cause:* reason, motive

4 *whiter skin of hers than snow:* her skin, whiter than snow
5 *monumental alabaster:* alabaster was the preferred stone for tomb sculpting

7 *Put out the light...and...light:* first put out the candle, and then snuff out Desdemona's life
8 *minister:* servant; magistrate, minister of justice

11 *cunning'st...nature:* most exquisitely formed example of nature's craftsmanship when she excels herself
12 *Promethean:* Prometheus brought fire to men
13 *relume:* relight

16 *balmy:* deliciously sweet

20 *fatal:* ominous, deadly, doomed

28 *Solicit:* plead (for absolution)

32 *forfend:* forbid

37-38 *Why I should fear...yet I feel fear:* I am scared, though I do not know why, as I am not guilty of any crime

150

	Since guiltiness I know not; but yet I feel I fear.	
OTHELLO	Think on thy sins.	40
DESDEMONA	They are loves I bear to you.	
OTHELLO	Ay, and for that thou diest.	
DESDEMONA	That death's unnatural that kills for loving.	
	Alas, why gnaw you so your nether lip?	
	Some bloody passion shakes your very frame:	45
	These are portents; but yet I hope, I hope,	
	They do not point on me.	
OTHELLO	Peace, and be still.	
DESDEMONA	I will so. What's the matter?	
OTHELLO	That handkerchief which I so loved and gave thee,	50
	Thou gav'st to Cassio.	
DESDEMONA	No, by my life and soul –	
	Send for the man, and ask him.	
OTHELLO	Sweet soul, take heed,	
	Take heed of perjury: thou art on thy death-bed.	
DESDEMONA	Ay, but not yet to die.	
OTHELLO	Yes, presently.	
	Therefore confess thee freely of thy sin;	55
	For to deny each article with oath	
	Cannot remove nor choke the strong conception	
	That I do groan withal: thou art to die.	
DESDEMONA	Then Lord have mercy on me.	
OTHELLO	I say, Amen.	
DESDEMONA	And have you mercy too. I never did	60
	Offend you in my life; never loved Cassio,	
	But with such general warranty of heaven	
	As I might love. I never gave him token.	
OTHELLO	By heaven, I saw my handkerchief in's hand.	
	O perjured woman, thou dost stone my heart,	65
	And makes me call what I intend to do	
	A murder, which I thought a sacrifice.	
	I saw the handkerchief.	
DESDEMONA	He found it then;	
	I never gave it him – send for him hither;	
	Let him confess a truth.	
OTHELLO	He hath confessed.	70
DESDEMONA	What, my lord?	
OTHELLO	That he hath – 'ud's death! – used thee.	
DESDEMONA	How? Unlawfully?	
OTHELLO	Ay.	
DESDEMONA	He will not say so.	
OTHELLO	No, his mouth is stopped –	
	Honest Iago hath ta'en order for't.	
DESDEMONA	O, my fear interprets – what, is he dead?	75
OTHELLO	Had all his hairs been lives, my great revenge	
	Had stomach for them all.	
DESDEMONA	Alas, he is betrayed, and I undone.	
OTHELLO	Out, strumpet! – Weep'st thou for him to my face?	
DESDEMONA	(grasping him in supplication)	
	O, banish me, my lord, but kill me not!	80

41 *They are loves I bear to you:* her only sin is that she loves Othello too much

46 *portents:* indications
47 *point on me:* indicate my fate

52-53 *Sweet soul...perjury:* committing such a sin so close to death would ensure her damnation

54 *presently:* at once

56 *article:* item or count in a criminal indictment
57 *conception:* belief

61 *Offend:* wrong

65 *stone:* turn to stone

71 *used:* i.e. sexually

73 *his mouth is stopped:* i.e. he is dead
74 *ta'en order for't:* taken steps for it

77 *stomach:* appetite, capacity

OTHELLO	Down, strumpet!	
DESDEMONA	Kill me tomorrow, let me live tonight!	
	(She struggles with him)	
OTHELLO	Nay, if you strive –	
DESDEMONA	But half an hour! But while I say one prayer?	
OTHELLO	It is too late.	
(He smothers her)	Being done, there is no pause.	85
DESDEMONA	O Lord, Lord, Lord!	
EMILIA *(Within)*	My lord, my lord! What ho! My lord, my lord!	
OTHELLO	What noise is this? Not dead? Not yet quite dead?	
	I that am cruel am yet merciful:	
	I would not have thee linger in thy pain –	90
	So, so.	
	(He smothers her again)	
EMILIA *(Within)*	What, ho, my lord, my lord!	
OTHELLO	Who's there?	
EMILIA *(Within)*	O, good my lord, I'd speak a word with you.	
OTHELLO	Yes – 'tis Emilia – *(calling)* by and by! – She's dead.	
	'Tis like she comes to speak of Cassio's death:	95
	The noise was high. Ha! No more moving?	
	Still as the grave. Shall she come in? Were't good?	
	I think she stirs again – no. What's best to do?	
	If she come in, she'll sure speak to my wife –	
	My wife, my wife! What wife? I have no wife.	100
	O insupportable! O heavy hour!	
	Methinks it should be now a huge eclipse	
	Of sun and moon, and that th' affrighted globe	
	Should yawn at alteration.	
EMILIA	*(Within)* I do beseech you	
	That I may speak with you – O good my lord.	105
OTHELLO	I had forgot thee – *(Calling)* O come in, Emilia! –	
	Soft – *(Calling)* by and by! – let me the curtains draw.	
	He closes the bed curtains	
(To Emilia)	Where art thou?	
	Unlocks the door	
Enter Emilia		
	What's the matter with thee now?	
EMILIA	O, my good lord, yonder's foul murders done.	
OTHELLO	What? Now?	
EMILIA	But now, my lord.	110
OTHELLO	It is the very error of the moon;	
	She comes more nearer earth than she was wont,	
	And makes men mad.	
EMILIA	Cassio, my lord, hath killed	
	A young Venetian called Roderigo.	
OTHELLO	Roderigo killed?	
	And Cassio killed?	115
EMILIA	No, Cassio is not killed.	
OTHELLO	Not Cassio killed?	
	Then murder's out of tune, and sweet revenge	
	Grows harsh.	
DESDEMONA	O, falsely, falsely murdered.	120
EMILIA	O Lord! What cry is that?	

85   *Being done, there is no pause:* now the deed has begun, I cannot stop

94   *by and by:* soon, in a minute

96   *high:* loud

101   *O insupportable! O heavy hour:* Oh, unbearable, oh sorrowful hour. Othello already repents his actions

104   *yawn:* gape; split open
104   *alteration:* the unnatural change brought about by Desdemona's death

111   *error:* straying off course

113   *mad:* the supposed power of the moon to induce madness is imbedded in the term 'lunatic'

OTHELLO	That? What?	
EMILIA	Out, and alas! That was my lady's voice.	
	She opens the curtains	
	Help, help, ho help! O lady, speak again!	
	Sweet Desdemona, O sweet mistress, speak!	
DESDEMONA	A guiltless death I die.	
EMILIA	O, who hath done this deed?	125
DESDEMONA	Nobody – I myself. Farewell –	
	Commend me to my kind lord – O, farewell!	
	She Dies	
OTHELLO	Why, how should she be murdered?	
EMILIA	Alas, who knows?	
OTHELLO	You heard her say herself it was not I.	
EMILIA	She said so: I must needs report the truth.	130
OTHELLO	She's, like a liar gone to burning hell:	
	'Twas I that killed her.	
EMILIA	O, the more angel she, and you the blacker devil!	
OTHELLO	She turned to folly, and she was a whore.	
EMILIA	Thou dost belie her, and thou art a devil.	135
OTHELLO	She was false as water.	
EMILIA	Thou art rash as fire	
	To say that she was false. O, she was heavenly true!	
OTHELLO	Cassio did tup her: ask thy husband else.	
	O, I were damned beneath all depth in hell	
	But that I did proceed upon just grounds	140
	To this extremity. Thy husband knew it all.	
EMILIA	My husband?	
OTHELLO	Thy husband.	
EMILIA	That she was false to wedlock?	
OTHELLO	Ay, with Cassio. Nay, had she been true,	
	If heaven would make me such another world	
	Of one entire and perfect chrysolite,	145
	I'd not have sold her for it.	
EMILIA	My husband?	
OTHELLO	Ay,'twas he that told me on her first;	
	An honest man he is, and hates the slime	
	That sticks on filthy deeds.	
EMILIA	My husband?	
OTHELLO	What needs this iteration, woman? I say, thy husband.	150
EMILIA	O mistress, villany hath made mocks with love:	
	My husband say that she was false?	
OTHELLO	He, woman;	
	I say thy husband – dost understand the word? –	
	My friend, thy husband, honest, honest Iago.	
EMILIA	If he say so, may his pernicious soul	155
	Rot half a grain a day! He lies to th'heart:	
	She was too fond of her most filthy bargain.	
OTHELLO	Ha?	
EMILIA	Do thy worst:	
	This deed of thine is no more worthy heaven,	160
	Than thou wast worthy her.	
OTHELLO	Peace, you were best.	
EMILIA	Thou hast not half that power to do me harm	
	As I have to be hurt. O gull, O dolt	

Glossary notes (right margin):

134   *folly:* wickedness; un-chastity

138   *else:* if you don't believe me

141   *extremity:* extreme violence

145   *chrysolite:* semi-precious stone

148   *slime:* moral pollution

150   *iteration:* repetition

151   *made mocks with love:* used love as a plaything

155   *pernicious:* dangerous, destructive

162   *Peace, you were best:* be quiet, if you know what's good for you

164   *As I have the capacity to be hurt:* as I have the capacity to endure pain

As ignorant as dirt, thou hast done a deed –   165

Othello threatens her with his sword

I care not for thy sword, I'll make thee known,
Though I lost twenty lives: help, help, ho, help!
The Moor hath killed my mistress! Murder, murder!

Enter Montano, Gratiano, Iago, and others

MONTANO	What is the matter? How now, general?
EMILIA	O, are you come, Iago? you have done well, 170
	That men must lay their murders on your neck!
GRATIANO	What is the matter?
EMILIA	Disprove this villain, if thou be'st a man:
	He says thou told'st him that his wife was false;
	I know thou didst not – thou'rt not such a villain. 175
	Speak, for my heart is full.
IAGO	I told him what I thought, and told no more
	Than what he found himself was apt and true.
EMILIA	But did you ever tell him she was false?
IAGO	I did. 180
EMILIA	You told a lie, an odious damned lie,
	Upon my soul, a lie, a wicked lie:
	She false with Cassio? Did you say with Cassio?
IAGO	With Cassio, mistress – go to, charm your tongue!
EMILIA	I will not charm my tongue; I am bound to speak: 185
	My mistress here lies murdered in her bed.
MONTANO, GRATIANO and IAGO	O heavens forfend!
EMILIA	And your reports have set the murder on.
OTHELLO	Nay, stare not, masters, it is true indeed.
GRATIANO	'Tis a strange truth.
MONTANO	O monstrous act! 190
EMILIA	Villainy, villainy, villainy! Now
	I think upon't, I think I smelled a villainy –
	I thought so then.I'll kill myself for grief.
	O villainy, villainy!
IAGO	What, are you mad? I charge you get you home. 195
EMILIA	Good gentlemen, let me have leave to speak:
	'Tis proper I obey him, but not now.
	Perchance, Iago, I will ne'er go home.
OTHELLO	O, O, O!

He falls on the bed

EMILIA	Nay, lay thee down and roar; 200
	For thou hast killed the sweetest innocent
	That e'er did lift up eye.
OTHELLO	*(Rising)* O, she was foul!
	I scarce did know you, uncle: there lies your niece,
	Whose breath, indeed, these hands have newly stopped: 205
	I know this act shows horrible and grim.
GRATIANO	Poor Desdemona, I am glad thy father's dead:
	Thy match was mortal to him, and pure grief
	Shore his old thread in twain; did he live now,
	This sight would make him do a desperate turn, 210
	Yea, curse his better angel from his side
	And fall to reprobance.

176 *My heart is full:* her heart is about to break i.e. bursting with emotion

184 *charm your tongue:* be silent

193 *I thought so then:* Emilia is referring to her taking the handkerchief for Iago

210 *turn:* deed

212 *reprobance:* state of damnation

OTHELLO	'Tis pitiful; but yet Iago knows
	That she with Cassio hath the act of shame
	A thousand times committed – Cassio confessed it,
	And she did gratify his amorous works
	With that recognizance and pledge of love
	Which I first gave her: I saw it in his hand,
	It was a handkerchief, an antique token
	My father gave my mother.
EMILIA	O God, O heavenly God!
IAGO	'Swounds, hold your peace.
EMILIA	'Twill out, 'twill out! I peace?
	No, I will speak as liberal as the north;
	Let heaven and men and devils, let them all,
	All, all, cry shame against me, yet I'll speak.
IAGO	Be wise, and get you home.
EMILIA	I will not.

Iago threatens Emilia with his sword

GRATIANO	Fie, your sword upon a woman?
EMILIA	O thou dull Moor, that handkerchief thou speak'st of
	I found by fortune, and did give my husband:
	For often, with a solemn earnestness –
	More than indeed belonged to such a trifle –
	He begged of me to steal't.
IAGO	Villanous whore!
EMILIA	She give it Cassio? No, alas, I found it,
	And I did give't my husband.
IAGO	Filth, thou liest!
EMILIA	By heaven I do not; I do not, gentlemen:
	O murderous coxcomb, what should such a fool
	Do with so good a woman?

Othello runs at Iago, but is disarmed by Montano; Iago kills his wife

OTHELLO	Are there no stones in heaven
	But what serve for the thunder? Precious villain!
GRATIANO	The woman falls: sure he hath killed his wife.
EMILIA	Ay, ay. O, lay me by my mistress' side.

Exit Iago

GRATIANO	He's gone, but his wife's killed.
MONTANO	'Tis a notorious villain. Take you this weapon
	Which I have here recovered from the Moor;
	Come, guard the door without; let him not pass,
	But kill him rather. I'll after that same villain,
	For 'tis a damned slave.

Exeunt Montano and Gratiano

OTHELLO	I am not valiant neither:
	But ever puny whipster gets my sword.
	But why should Honour outlive Honesty?
	Let it go all.
EMILIA	What did thy song bode, lady?
	Hark, canst thou hear me? I will play the swan,
	And die in music: *(Sings)* 'willow, willow, willow'
	Moor, she was chaste; she loved thee, cruel Moor –
	So come my soul to bliss, as I speak true!
	So speaking as I think, alas, I die.

She dies (and falls on the bed)

216   *gratify:* reward

217   *recognizance:* token

224   *liberal as the north:* unrestrainedly as the north wind

238   *coxcomb:* fool
238-239   *what should such a fool Do:* what did he do to deserve
239-240   *Are there no stones in heaven / But what serve for the thunder:* to punish such wickedness

244   *notorious:* obvious, conspicuous

249   *puny:* inferior, subordinate
249   *whipster:* one who whips out his sword

250   *But why should Honour outlive Honesty:* why should reputation outlive desert

215
220
225
230
235
240
245
250
255

OTHELLO	I have another weapon in this chamber,	
	It is a sword of Spain, the ice-brook's temper –	
	O, here it is: uncle, I must come forth.	
GRATIANO	*(Within)* If thou attempt it, it will cost thee dear:	260
	Thou hast no weapon, and perforce must suffer.	
OTHELLO	Look in upon me then, and speak with me,	
	Or, naked as I am, I will assault thee.	

Enter Gratiano

GRATIANO	What is the matter?	
OTHELLO	Behold, I have a weapon –	
	A better never did itself sustain	265
	Upon a soldier's thigh: I have seen the day	
	That, with this little arm and this good sword,	
	I have made my way through more impediments	
	Than twenty times your stop: But O vain boast!	
	Who can control his fate? 'Tis not so now.	270
	Be not afraid, though you do see me weaponed:	
	Here is my journey's end, here is my butt	
	And very sea-mark of my utmost sail.	
	Do you go back dismayed? 'Tis a lost fear;	
	Man but a rush against Othello's breast,	275
	And he retires. Where should Othello go?	

He goes to the bed

	Now: how dost thou look now? O ill-starred wench,	
	Pale as thy smock, when we shall meet at count,	
	This look of thine will hurl my soul from heaven,	
	And fiends will snatch at it. Cold, cold, my girl?	280
	Even like thy chastity. O cursed, cursed slave!	
	Whip me, ye devils,	
	From the possession of this heavenly sight,	
	Blow me about in winds, roast me in sulphur,	
	Wash me in steep-down gulfs of liquid fire –	285
	O Desdemon! Dead Desdemona! Dead! O, O!	

Enter Lodovico, Montano, Iago with officers guarding him, and Cassio in a chair

LODOVICO	Where is this rash and most unfortunate man?	
OTHELLO	That's he that was Othello: here I am.	
LODOVICO	Where is that viper? Bring the villain forth.	
OTHELLO	I look down towards his feet – but that's a fable:	290
	If that thou be'st a devil, I cannot kill thee.	

He wounds Iago

LODOVICO	Wrench his sword from him.	
IAGO	I bleed, sir, but not killed.	
OTHELLO	I am not sorry neither: I'd have thee live;	
	For in my sense 'tis happiness to die.	295
LODOVICO	O thou, Othello, thou was once so good,	
	Fallen in the practice of a damned slave,	
	What shall be said to thee?	
OTHELLO	Why, any thing –	
	An honourable murderer, if you will,	
	For naught I did in hate, but all in honour.	300
LODOVICO	This wretch hath part confessed his villainy:	
	Did you and he consent in Cassio's death?	
OTHELLO	Ay.	
CASSIO	Dear general, I never gave you cause.	

258 *sword of Spain:* the quality of Spanish blades was legendary
258 *ice-brook's:* the sword was tempered by plunging it into icy water

263 *naked:* unarmed

269 *your stop:* your efforts to stop or impede me

272 *butt:* goal
273 *sea-mark:* object that served to guide sailors at sea, a beacon
273 *utmost sail:* furthest point of my voyage
275 *Man:* wield

277 *ill-starred:* ill-fated
278 *count:* judgement day
279-280 *This look of thine will hurl my soul from heaven, And fiends will snatch at it:* Othello recognises that he is damned
281 *slave:* Othello is speaking of himself, not of Iago

283 *possession of this heavenly sight:* Othello feels that he no longer deserves to possess the heavenly Desdemona

290 *fable:* that a devil supposedly had cloven feet

297 *fallen in the practise of a damned slave:* victim to the treacherous plotting of a damned slave

302 *consent:* agree

304 *Dear:* this epithet shows Cassio's noble forgiveness as well as his love for Othello

OTHELLO	I do believe it, and I ask your pardon:	305
	Will you, I pray, demand that demi-devil	
	Why he hath thus ensnared my soul and body?	
IAGO	Demand me nothing: what you know, you know;	
	From this time forth I never will speak word.	
LODOVICO	What, not to pray?	310
GRATIANO	Torments will ope your lips.	
OTHELLO	Well, thou dost best.	
LODOVICO	Sir, you shall understand what hath befallen,	
	Which, as I think, you know not: here is a letter	
	Found in the pocket of the slain Roderigo,	315
	And here another – the one of them imports	
	The death of Cassio to be undertook	
	By Roderigo.	
OTHELLO	O villain!	
CASSIO	Most heathenish and most gross!	
LODOVICO	Now here's another discontented paper,	320
	Found in his pocket too; and this, it seems	
	Roderigo meant t'have sent this damned villain,	
	But that, belike, Iago in the nick	
	Came in and satisfied him.	
OTHELLO	O the pernicious caitiff!	
	How came you, Cassio, by that handkerchief	325
	That was my wife's?	
CASSIO	I found it in my chamber;	
	And he himself confessed it but e'en now	
	That there he dropped it for a special purpose	
	Which wrought to his desire.	
OTHELLO	O fool, fool, fool!	
CASSIO	There is besides in Roderigo's letter	330
	How he upbraids Iago, that he made him	
	Brave me upon the watch, whereon it came	
	That I was cast; and even but now he spake –	
	After long seeming dead – Iago hurt him,	
	Iago set him on.	335
LODOVICO	*(To Othello)* You must forsake this room, and go with us:	
	Your power and your command is taken off,	
	And Cassio rules in Cyprus. For this slave,	
	If there be any cunning cruelty	
	That can torment him much and hold him long,	340
	It shall be his. You shall close prisoner rest	
	Till that the nature of your fault be known	
	To the Venetian state. Come, bring away!	
OTHELLO	Soft you, a word or two before you go:	
	I have done the state some service, and they know't –	345
	No more of that. I pray you in your letters,	
	When you shall these unlucky deeds relate,	
	Speak of me as I am; nothing extenuate,	
	Nor set down aught in malice: then must you speak	
	Of one that loved not wisely, but too well;	350
	Of one not easily jealous, but being wrought,	
	Perplexed in the extreme; of one whose hand,	
	Like the base Indian, threw a pearl away	
	Richer than all his tribe; of one whose subdued eyes,	

311 *Torments will ope your lips:* torture will ensure you speak

319 *heathenish:* barbarous, abominable

323 *in the nick:* at the critical moment

324 *satisfied him:* gave him a satisfactory explanation

327 *confessed:* Iago is willing to confess his deeds, but not his motives

333 *cast:* dismissed

340 *hold him long:* keep him alive for a long time

344 *Soft you:* one moment

351 *wrought:* agitated, worked up

352 *Perplexed:* bewildered

354 *subdued eyes:* overcome by grief, weeping

157

Albeit unused to the melting mood,
Drop tears as fast as the Arabian trees
Their medicinal gum. Set you down this;
And say besides that in Aleppo once,
Where a malignant and a turbaned Turk
Beat a Venetian and traduced the state,   360
I took by th' throat the circumcised dog
And smote him – thus.

He stabs himself

LODOVICO   O bloody period!

GRATIANO   All that's spoke is marred.
OTHELLO   I kissed thee ere I killed thee – no way but this:
Killing myself, to die upon a kiss.   365

He kisses Desdemona, falls on the bed and dies

CASSIO   This did I fear, but thought he had no weapon,
For he was great of heart.

LODOVICO   O Spartan dog,
More fell than anguish, hunger, or the sea,
Look on the tragic loading of this bed;   370
This is thy work. The object poisons sight –
Let it be hid.

(They close the bed curtains)

               Gratiano, keep the house
And seize upon the fortunes of the Moor,
For they succeed on you; (*To Cassio*) to you, lord governor,
Remains the censure of this hellish villain –   375
The time, the place, the torture, O enforce it;
Myself will straight aboard, and to the state
This heavy act with heavy heart relate.

Exeunt

---

355 *melting:* being overwhelmed with grief, dissolving into tears

357 *medicinal gum:* myrrh

358 *Aleppo:* a city in Turkey

359-361 *turbaned...dog:* ritual signs of Islamic allegiance

362 *smote him:* stabbed him

363 *period:* ending

368 *Spartan dog:* notorious for their fierceness
368 *great of heart:* proud, magnanimous, high-spirited
369 *fell:* deadly

373 *seize upon:* take legal possession of

374 *they succeed on you:* you inherit them

375 *censure:* trial

DESDEMONA & OTHELLO

Othello enters the room where Desdemona sleeps, determined to kill her. He behaves in a calm and composed fashion, convinced that her death is just and warranted. When Desdemona wakes he tells her to pray, that she is about to die and there is nothing she can do to prevent this from happening. When Desdemona hears that Cassio has been killed and realises that her protestations of innocence are futile she begs to be allowed to live. But Othello is incapable of believing her and, enraged again at the thought of her sleeping with Cassio, smothers her with a pillow.

Just as he is doing this Emilia approaches the room, crying out that a murder has taken place. When Othello eventually permits her to enter the room she tells him that Cassio has killed Roderigo. Desdemona manages to speak one last time before she dies and when Othello admits that he is responsible for her death Emilia starts to scream 'murder'.

Emilia's cries bring Iago, Gratiano and Montano running. Emilia confronts her husband about his deception, branding him a liar and a villain. She reveals the truth about how the handkerchief ended up in Cassio's passion. Iago stabs her and runs off. Emilia dies beside her mistress.

Othello realises, too late, that Desdemona was never unfaithful to him. He is overcome with guilt and despair. Lodovico arrives with Cassio and a team of officers. Iago has been captured and has partly confesses his crimes but refuses to say any more. However, letters found on Roderigo's person reveal much about his varous schemes.

Lodovico curses Iago for his crimes and decrees that he will be imprisoned and tortured. Cassio will be the new governor of Cyprus. Othello will be stripped of his command and taken into custody. However, after a final moving speech, Othello stabs himself and dies while kissing Desdemona's lips.

LINE BY LINE

▶ LINES 1-86: OTHELLO GOES TO KILL HIS WIFE

Othello enters the bedroom where Desdemona is sleeping. He carries a candle. As he approaches the bed he seems to be reminding himself why Desdemona must die: 'It is the cause, it is the cause, my soul'. The 'cause' is Desdemona's infidelity but he does not wish to speak it aloud, as though to do so would offend the heaven's: 'Let me not name it to you, you chaste stars' (2).

Though he has spoken in the past of wanting to enact bloody revenge, now that he is has come to kill her he wishes to do it as cleanly and as mercifully as possible. He does not wish to 'shed her blood' nor does he want to scar her perfectly white and smooth skin. But he is convinced that Desdemona must die. Were she to live she would only continue in her wanton ways, betraying other men: 'Yet she must die, else she'll betray more men' (6).

Before he kills her Othello will extinguish the candle that he carries. Once he has put out this light he will extinguish the light that is Desdemona's life: 'Put out the light, and then put out the light' (7). He knows that the candle can be relit but his wife's life, once extinguished, cannot be restored: 'I know not where is that Promethean heat/ That can thy light relume' (12-3). Othello also likens murdering her to the plucking of a rose and again thinks how such an act can never be undone – the plucked rose must wither and there is nothing that he can do to restore its vitality: 'When I have plucked thy rose,/ I cannot give it vital growth again' (13-4).

Othello kisses Desdemona several times and her sweet-smelling breath almost causes him to reconsider killing her: 'O balmy breath, that dost almost persuade/ Justice to break her sword' (16-7). The thought of her death is painful but in the Othello's mind it is an unavoidable act of justice. He wishes, however, that Desdemona will remain as lovely in death as she is now so that he can kill her and then love her again: 'Be thus when thou art dead, and I will kill thee/ And love thee after' (18-9).

Othello begins to weep over Desdemona's sleeping body and she wakes. When she asks him to come to bed he responds by asking her if she has prayed. He tells her that, if there are any sins that she has

not confessed, now is the time to repent so that her soul might reach heaven when she dies. Desdemona is baffled by her husband's advice but he makes his intentions somewhat clearer when he says that he does not wish to murder her soul: 'I would not kill thy soul' (32).

His words alarm Desdemona and she asks him to be merciful. Although he seems to agree with her plea, she can see violence in his eyes: 'you're fatal then/ When your eyes roll so' (37-8). Othello scares her but she cannot comprehend why, claiming he has no motivation: 'Since guiltiness I know not; but yet I feel fear' (39). Her only sins, she claims, have been to love Othello too much: 'They are loves I bear to you' (41). She hopes that his murderous whims are not directed at her (45-7).

When Othello accuses Desdemona of giving the hankerchief to Cassio, she denies it fervently. She asks for him to verify her argument with Cassio, but the Moor has lost all trust in his wife and can no longer be pursuaded to believe a word she says. He advises her not to lie on her deathbed, because doing so could compromise her soul when she dies. (52-3).

Desdemona asks Othello to be merciful. She tells him that she 'never loved Cassio' the way Othello is suggesting, only as a friend, and she never gave him any love token. Othello insists that he saw the handkerchief in Cassio's hand. If this is the case, Desdemona counters, then Cassio must have found it somewhere, because she never gave it to him. Othello says that Cassio has already confessed to having an affair with Desdemona: 'He hath confessed… That he hath…used thee' (70-1). He tells her that Iago has killed Cassio and he cannot therefore speak in her defence (73).

Desdemona understands this to mean that Cassio is dead and she now sees that her life is very much in danger. She takes hold of Othello and begs him to send her away, to banish her but not kill her: 'O, banish me, my lord, but kill me not!' (80). If he is not willing to do this she begs that he let her live another day, or at the very least a half hour more so that she can pray: 'But half an hour! But while I say one prayer?' (84).

EMILIA

PROTECTIVE AND LOYAL

Emilia's loyalty toward her mistress is strongly in evidence throughout this scene. When she sees Desdemona's dead body she expresses genuine grief and fondness for her: 'Help, help, ho, help! O lady, speak again! / Sweet Desdemona, O sweet mistress, speak!' (123-4).

In her grief and anger she defies Othello himself. She likens Desdemona to an angel and bravely – perhaps recklessly – brands Othello a demon: 'O, the more angel she, and you the blacker devil!' (133). Othello's threats are meaningless to her. Her repeated insults ("filthy bargain", "O gull, o dolt, as ignorant as dirt") provoke him, but fear does not seem to be able to penetrate her veil of sadness and anger. She is determined to reveal what Othello has done: 'I care not for thy sword, I'll make thee known' (166).

EMILIA

She is fiercely protective of Desdemona's memory. When Othello sets out her alleged crimes and faults, Emilia jumps without hesitation to her defence (136-7). She is convinced that Desdemona was not unfaithful to him. She clears Desdemona's name by showing her husband to be liar and revealing the truth about the handkerchief. She does this despite her husband's threats and even though it reflects badly on herself.

Emilia's loyalty towards Desdemona is evident even after she's fatally stabbed by her husband. In a final poignant gesture of respect toward her mistress, she asks to be laid next to Desdemona and dies singing the Willow Song.

STRONG-WILLED AND ASSERTIVE

Emilia's strong-willed and assertive nature is evident throughout the scene, especially when she repeatedly criticises Othello for the terrible act he has committed. It is hugely risky of Emilia to do this – not only does she ignore social etiquette by speaking out of turn and disrespectfully to an honoured man, but she ignores her own safety by doing so with an experienced soldier who has just murdered his wife.

This assertiveness is also evident when she realises that it is her husband who planted doubts about Desdemona's integrity in Othello's mind. It comes to the fore when she realises how the handkerchief was used to advance this deception. She is determined to expose Iago as a villain and perseveres bravely, defying societal norms again and again by speaking out against her husband's wishes: "Tis proper I obey him, but not now' (197).

Emilia pays with her life for this crusade. Iago loses his patience and stabs her, but by then she has succeeded in getting justice for her friend. Othello has been exposed as her killer and Iago as a master puppeteer who has deceived them all.

TALK ABOUT IT

Many readers feel that in this scene Emilia exhibits signs of a guilty conscience, that she feels guilty for her part in the disaster that's unfolding. After all, it could be argued that by passing the handkerchief on to Iago she contributed greatly to this tragic outcome. What line or phrases could be read as suggestions of the guilt Emilia feels?

IAGO & EMILIA

IAGO

MALICIOUS, CALLOUS AND DESTRUCTIVE

Iago's callous and malicious nature is evident in this scene. He is unrepentant about what he has done, utterly lacking in remorse and empathy. We see this when he argues that he told Othello only what the Moor already believed or was ready to believe: 'I told him what I thought; and told no more / Than what he found himself was apt and true' (177-8).

His malicious streak is also evident when Emilia starts to expose him. He threatens her and insults her again and again, urging her to shut up and commanding her to leave. He fatally wounds her with his sword. Whereas Iago killed Roderigo out of strategy, he kills Emilia entirely out of spite. By the time he stabs her with his sword, she has already revealed his deception. Murdering her cannot benefit him. In fact, it only invites

greater punishment from those present. Yet he does it anyway.

Iago's callousness is also evident toward the conclusion of the scene. Othello demands to know what compelled him to do what he did. He is desperate to know Iago's motivation for 'ensnaring' him in this way. Iago, however, will say no more: 'From this time forth I never will speak word' (309). He has destroyed Othello's life but will not give him the satisfaction of telling him why.

The strength of Iago's scheming is evidenced by Othello's refusal to believe what Emilia is saying. The Moor still holds on to the delusion that Cassio effectively confessed to the affair when he saw him holding Desdemona's handkerchief – a moment that was engineered by Iago much earlier and which, even now, is protecting him from the looming storm (213-20).

▶ LINES 85-105: OTHELLO SMOTHERS DESDEMONA

Othello says that it is too late. He takes a pillow and uses it to smother her. At this very moment Emilia approaches the room, calling out to Othello: 'My lord, my lord!' (87). The Moor seems to think that Emilia's cries are coming from Desdemona and a sign that she is 'not yet quite dead' (88). Not wanting her to suffer a slow, drawn-out death, he attempts to smother her again. Emilia continues to approach the room calling out to Othello. The Moor soon recognises the voice and thinks that Emilia must be crying out to him because Cassio has been killed: 'Tis like she comes to speak of Cassio's death: / The noise was high' (95-6).

Now that he has gone through with the act of killing his wife, Othello's calm composure begins to crack. His mind races as he thinks about whether he should let Emilia enter the room and whether or not his wife is yet dead: 'Shall she come in? Were't good? / I think she stirs again – no. What best to do?' (97-8). He knows that if he allows Emilia into the room she will wish to speak with his wife. However, the moment he utters the word 'wife', Othello reaslises that he no longer has one: 'My wife, my wife! What wife? I have no wife' (100). The awful truth of what he has done suddenly hits him: 'O insupportable! O heavy hour!' (101). He has committed a monstrous act and he thinks that such a deed ought to upset the natural order of things. The Moor imagines a 'huge eclipse / Of sun and moon' and a massive earthquake tearing the planet apart: 'that th' affrighted globe / Should yawn at alteration' (102-4).

▶ LINES 106-168: EMILIA DISCOVERS THE TRUTH

Emilia calls out to Othello once again, asking to be let into the room. Othello tells her to wait and while she does he adjusts the curtains around the bed to conceal Desdemona's body. When she is finally allowed to enter the room she tells him that murder has been committed: 'yonder's foul murder done' (109). Othello swiftly offers a reason why such a deed might have been committed this evening, saying that the moon has come closer to the earth and it is making men behave madly: 'It is the very error of the moon; / She comes nearer earth than she was wont, / And makes men mad' (111-3). However, when he hears that Cassio has killed Roderigo but has not himself been killed, Othello reflects on how things have not gone according to plan: 'Then murder's out of tune, and sweet revenge / Grows harsh' (118-9).

Desdemona's weak voice is suddenly heard, alerting Emilia to her presence in the room. She draws back the curtains around the bed and is startled to see her mistress close to death. Desdemona again proclaims her innocence, saying that it is a 'guiltless death' she dies: 'O falsely, falsely murdered' (120). However, when Emilia asks her who is responsible for her condition, Desdemona lies to protect her husband, saying, 'Nobody – I myself' (126). She bids them farewell and dies.

At first Othello denies that Desdemona has been murdered and that he had any role to play in her death: 'You heard her say herself it was not I' (129). However, he quickly changes tack, admitting to the murder and condemning Desdemona for lying: 'She's, like a liar gone to burning hell! / 'Twas I that killed her' (131-2). Her death was justified because Desdemona was leading a wicked and unchaste life: 'She turned to folly, and she was a whore' (134). The Moor tells Emilia that Desdemona was having an affair with Cassio and that she need only ask Iago to confirm this: 'Cassio did tup her: ask thy husband else' (138).

Emilia is startled to hear that her husband had any role to play in this tragic event and she asks Othello again and again to confirm that it was Iago who told him Desdemona was being unfaithful. Othello can't comprehend why

Emilia should be bewildered by the notion that her husband, an 'honest man' who despises 'filthy deeds', should have told him of Cassio and Desdemona's affair: 'What needs this iteration, woman? I say, thy husband… dost understand the word' (150-3). When Emilia realizes that it is Iago who has been pouring poison into the Moor's ear, she does not hesitate to condemn him and to label Othello a fool for believing what he was told: 'may his pernicious soul / Rot half a grain a day… O dolt / As ignorant as dirt, thou hast done a deed' (155-65). Though Othello threatens her with his sword, Emilia will not be intimidated and bravely pledges to make the Moor's crime known: 'I care not for thy sword, I'll make thee known' (166). She calls aloud, 'The Moor hath killed my mistress! Murder, murder', attracting the attention of Montano, Gratiano and Iago, who come to the room.

▶ LINES 169-239: EMILIA CONFRONTS IAGO

Emilia's cries cause Montano, Gratiano, and Iago to come running. Emilia seems desperate to believe that Iago did not manipulate Othello, that he could not have convinced the Moor that Desdemona was unfaithful: 'he says thou told'st him that his wife was false; / I know thou didst not' (174-5). She pleads with her husband to deny this charge: 'Speak, for my heart is full' (176).

Iago, however, refuses to do so. He freely admits to telling Othello that Desdemona was unfaithful (180, 184). He claims that he told Othello only what the Moor already believed or (in some sense) wanted to believe: 'I told him what I thought, and told no more / Than what he found himself was apt and true' (177-8). He tells his silences his wife: 'go to, charm you tongue!' (184).

> **💬 THINK ABOUT IT**
> There is an interesting contrast between Desdemona and Emilia in this scene. Desdemona is meekly obedient to her husband even when he's in the process of murdering her. Emilia, on the other hand, defies her husband openly and brings the circumstances of this terrible murder to light. We must remember, then, that the play is set at a time when women were expected to honour and obey their husbands in all things.

This admission enrages Emilia who brands her husband a villain: 'Villainy, villainy, villainy!' (191). She condemns him for telling 'an odious damnèd lie' (181).

She accuses Iago of misleading Othello so much that he murdered Desdemona: 'My mistress here lies murdered in her bed…And your reports have set the murder on' (186, 188). She ignores her husband's command that she go home and asks the assembled gentlemen for permission to speak, to reveal what she now suspects are her husband's evil deeds (195-6).

Othello seems shocked at what he's done but also unrepentant. His anguished cry of 'O, O, O!' reveals his sorrow at the 'pitiful' sight of Desdemona's corpse (199, 213). He knows the situation looks bad: 'I know this act shows horrible and grim' (206). Yet he remains convinced that Desdemona was 'foul', that she was unfaithful to him with Cassio many times (203, 214-5). As evidence he cites the handkerchief he gave Desdemona, describing how he saw this precious gift in Cassio's hand (218). Iago, he says, will be able to confirm this story because Cassio confessed it to him (213-5).

Emilia is determined to reveal her husband's treachery, even if it means speaking out of turn (223-6). Iago repeatedly urges her to keep quiet, calling her 'filth', a liar, a 'Villainous whore' and even threatening her with his sword (222, 227, 234). Yet she is determined to speak the truth. The handkerchief, she says, wasn't given to Cassio by Desdemona as a token of their affair. Instead she herself found it by chance and passed it on to her husband who had often asked her to steal it: 'She give it Cassio? No, alas, I found it,/And I did give't my husband' (234-5).

▶ LINES 240-256: EMILIA DIES

No sooner has Emilia told her sorry tale than Iago vengefully stabs her and runs off. Montano pursues him while Gratiano guards the door to the bedroom. Othello is warned that if he tries to leave he will be killed: 'Come guard the door without, let him not pass, but kill him rather' (246-7).

Emilia knows her wounds are fatal. Her last wish is to die beside Desdemona: 'O, lay me by my mistress' side' (242). As she dies next to her friend she sings a few lines of the Wiillow Song, which Desdemona had sung that very evening as she prepared for bed (253). Among her last words she chides Othello for the terrible act he has committed: 'Moor, she was chaste; she loved thee, cruel Moor' (254).

▶ LINES 257-286: OTHELLO IS OVERCOME WITH GUILT

Othello now realises the terrible mistake he's made. He knows that Iago manipulated him. He realises that Desdemona was never unfaithful, and that there was no need to kill her to avenge his honour. He is overcome with guilt.

He locates another sword and makes to leave the chamber but is warned to remain by Gratiano, who is on guard duty at the door (257-60). He then asks Gratiano to come and speak to him, as if he feels to compelled to confess his crimes to this man who is, after all, Desdemona's relative.

Othello reminisces in a distressed and distracted manner about his former glories. He remembers cutting through enemies with the same blade: 'I have seen the day/ That, with this little arm and this good sword,/ I have made my way through more impediments/ Than twenty times your stop' (266-9).

Yet he knows such days are behind him: ''Tis not so now' (270). Although he's armed, he tells Gratiano that he has no reason to fear him or fall back 'dismayed' from this once fearsome warrior: 'Be not afraid…'Tis a lost fear' (271, 274). Now he is broken man whose journey as a soldier is at an end (272). He is incapable of withstanding even a single charge (275).

Wracked with grief he goes to bed and observes Desdemona's corpse, remarking on its coldness and its paleness. These qualities remind him of how chaste and faithful she was to him, despite his suspicions to the contrary (280-1). He curses himself and decrees that his terrible crime will deny his soul access to paradise: 'This look of thine will hurl my soul from heaven' (279). He is almost eager to welcome the torments that he is convinced await him in hell. He seems to believe that he deserves no better, or that the torture meted out by the fiends of hell will somehow cleanse his terrible sin (281-5).

▶ LINES 287-344: LODOVICO ARRIVES WITH A TEAM OF OFFICERS

Lodovico and Montano arrive with a team of officers. Iago is with them. He has been captured and has partly confessed his crimes. Cassio, still wounded from the assault earlier that evening, is carried in on a chair or stretcher. Othello thinks that Iago could be some kind of demon.

OTHELLO

OTHELLO

DIGNITY AND SELF-POSSESSION

Othello is very calm as he enters the room where Desdemona sleeps. He does not seem agitated nor is he in anyway unsure about what he is about to do. He has decided that she deserves to die and sees the act that he is about commit as one of justice rather than revenge: 'she must die, else she'll betray more men' (6). Even when Desdemona wakes and Othello keeps his cool and does not allow either feelings of love or hate to influence his actions. He calmly tells Desdemona to prepare herself for death, to pray and seek forgiveness for her sins. Although the act that he is about to commit is a cruel one, it will be merciful: 'I that am cruel am yet merciful' (89).

However, the moment that the Moor thinks of Cassio and Desdemona making love he immediately loses his temper. When Desdemona presses him to tell her what Cassio has confessed to, Othello can barely speak the deed: 'That he hath – 'ud's death! – used thee' (71). Once he has mentioned this all his rage and frustration resurfaces. He calls Desdemona a 'strumpet' and begins to smother her.

LOVE FOR DESDEMONA

Othello now firmly believes that Desdemona has been sleeping with Cassio and that her wicked deeds have tarnished her. He thinks that her actions have made her a 'whore' and that she deserves to die for what he believes she has done: 'she must die, else she'll betray more men' (6). In his twisted mind he imagines that she has shamefully slept with Cassio a thousand times: 'That she with Cassio hath the act of shame / A thousand times committed' (214-5). He thinks that killing her is an act of mercy and justice, telling Emilia that Desdemona's murder was a righteous act: 'I did proceed upon just grounds to this extremity' (140-1).

However, the Moor still recognises Desdemona's beauty and when he is in her presence he struggles with his feelings for her. He kisses her as she sleeps and says that the scent of her sweet breath is almost powerful enough to make him change his mind: 'O balmy breath, that dost almost persuade / Justice to break her sword' (16-7). The moment she is dead he realises what a heinous act he has committed: 'O insupportable! O heavy hour!' (101). But his true remorse only comes when it is made clear to him that Iago has been deceiving him and that his wife was always faithful. There is no way he can live with the monstrous deed he has committed and so ends his life, saying that he loved 'not wisely, but too well' (350).

He stabs him to test this theory, knowing that if he is indeed a devil he cannot be killed: 'If that thou be'st a devil, I cannot kill thee' (291). Iago's wound, however, is not a fatal one (293).

Lodovico expresses sympathy for Othello, describing him as 'rash' or impulsive but also as 'unfortunate' (286). Crucially he remembers the Moor's noble qualities: 'O thou, Othello, that was once so good' (291). He has no doubt that Iago is the real villain here. He calls Iago a 'villain' and a 'viper' and laments that Othello has fallen victim to his treachery, that he has 'fallen in the practice of a damnèd slave' (296-8).

Othello claims he is an 'honourable murderer', a man who acted not out of hatred for Desdemona but out of a desire to restore his honour: 'For naught I did in hate, but all in honour' (300). Othello confesses that he plotted with Iago to kill Cassio and asks for his forgiveness. He now knows that Cassio did nothing to offend him (305).

Othello wants to know why Iago manipulated him so cruelly, why he 'ensnared my soul and body' (307). He simply wants to understand why Iago did what he did, but Iago refuses to elaborate. (308-9). Despite his silence much of the truth behind his various schemes is revealed:

- Iago has already confessed, offstage, to planting the handkerchief. Cassio now confirms how he found it in his chamber (326-9).
- Letters have been found on Roderigo's person. They reveal how Iago persuaded him to provoke Cassio during watch duty in Act 2 Scene 3 and get him fired from his position as lieutenant (330-4).
- These letters show how in Act 4 Scene 2 Roderigo was ready to expose Iago to Desdemona, until Iago persuaded him not to (321-4).
- These letters also reveal how Iago persuaded Roderigo to make the attempt on Cassio's life (335-8).
- Furthermore it is revealed that Roderigo has lived at least long enough to corroborate what he wrote in his letters. (333-5).

Lodovico, as the senior officer present, sets about restoring order. Othello is relieved of his command: 'Your power and your command is taken off' (337). He will be taken into custody to await the judgment of the Venetian state

(341-3). Cassio, as his lieutenant, will take his place as commander of the island: 'And Cassio rules in Cyprus' (338). Iago, meanwhile, will be imprisoned and tortured terribly for his crimes: 'If there be any cunning cruelty / That can torment him much and hold him long, / It shall be his' (339-41).

▶ LINES 344-378: OTHELLO KILLS HIMSELF

Othello asks for the opportunity to explain himself: 'Soft you, a word or two before you go' (344). He knows that Lodovico will soon be telling the Venetian authorities about the 'unlucky deeds' that have taken place (347). He wants his actions to be described honestly: 'Speak of me as I am' (348). He doesn't want his sins exaggerated out of malice, but neither does he want them downplayed or extenuated (348-9).

He describes himself as man whose actions stemmed from a love that was too great, too intense or impulsive, saying he is 'one that loved not wisely, but too well' (350). The murder of Desdemona, he now realises, was an incredibly wasteful act, one by which he threw away the thing most precious to him. He compares himself to an ignorant or 'base' Indian who tossed aside a pearl more valuable than all the riches of his tribe put together (353-4).

He claims that by nature he is 'not easily jealous' but was 'wrought' or manipulated into behaving so (351). Iago's machinations left him 'Perplexed in the extreme' and bamboozled him into acting wildly out of character (352).

Othello also makes reference to the service he has give the Venetian state as a soldier and a general: 'I have done the state some service, and the know't' (345). He recalls how once, in Aleppo, he killed a 'malignant and a turbaned Turk' who was beating a Venetian citizen and cursing the Venetian state (358-62). Just as he killed stabbed the Turk on that long ago day he now stabs himself. He falls beside his beloved Desdemona and kisses her as he expires: 'Killing myself, to die upon a kiss' (365).

Lodovico orders the bed-curtains be drawn to conceal this grim scene with its three bodies: 'The object poisons sight – Let it be hid' (371-2). He nominates Gratiano, related to Desdemona by blood and to Othello by marriage, to inherit

DESDEMONA

the Moor's wealth (372-4). He reaffirms Cassio's position as governor of Cyprus and urges him to ensure that Iago is tortured for his crimes (374-5). Lodovico, heavy-hearted, assumes the responsibility of returning to Venice and relating the bleak events that have occurred (377-8). ◆

TALK ABOUT IT

It is easy to assume that Othello and Desdemona have consummated their marriage but there are suggestions throughout the play that this has not happened. When Othello speaks of plucking Desdemona's 'rose' in line 13, some interpret this to be an allusion to taking his wife's virginity (the plucked rose being a symbol of lost virginity) and that the way the line is phrased suggests that this has yet to happen: 'When I have plucked thy rose...' Also, once Othello realises that his wife was faithful and that she never slept with Cassio he speaks of her 'chastity', saying that it grows cold with her body: 'cold my girl?/ Even like thy chastity' (280-1).

CHARACTER DEVELOPMENT

DESDEMONA

As we observed in recent scenes, Desdemona is meekly tolerant of her husband's unnatural and, at times, brutish behaviour. When she realises that he has come to kill her she makes some effort to defend herself and convince him that he has no reason to doubt her, but her efforts are meek and achieve nothing. It is almost as if she has accepted her fate, even though she can see no reason for having to die. When Othello tells her that she is must die her response is one of resignation: 'Then Lord have mercy on me' (59). Perhaps there was little or nothing that she could have done to save her life, but she does not even make the effort to scream or fight. It is interesting to contrast her behaviour with that of Emilia who is not shy about challenging Othello and screaming 'murder' when she realises what he has done.

167

CHARACTERS

IAGO

BACKGROUND AND SOCIAL CLASS

Iago is a veteran soldier in the army of Venice. When we first meet him he occupies the rank of 'ensign' or standard-bearer. Though he is only twenty-eight years old (I.3.311-2) he has fought in numerous battles and seems to be an experienced and distinguished soldier.

An important aspect of Iago's background is the fact that he seems to come from a lower social class than the other characters. Othello, Desdemona, Barbantio and Roderigo are lords and ladies of noble birth. Iago and his wife Emilia, on the other hand, are commoners. She is a maidservant and he is a common soldier.

Iago is presented as a somewhat rough and ready type who lacks the airs, graces and scholarly education of the other characters. We see this when Cassio suggests that 'you may relish him more in the soldier than in the scholar' (2.1.166-7). According to Cassio, he 'speaks home', suggesting that his manner of speech is plain or common, and lacks a gentleman's finesse (2.1.166). Iago takes delight in simple, vulgar rhymes that would be deemed inappropriate for a lord or lady, in jokes and riddles designed 'to make fools laugh i'th' alehouse' (2.1.141-2).

It has often been suggested that Iago is motivated by his resentment of this class difference. On this reading Iago resents the fact that the other characters occupy powerful positions in society simply because they were born to noble families, while he is forced to remain a simple soldier. It is also possible that he suspects Cassio was promoted ahead of him more because of his noble birth than because of his military abilities. Many critics have suggested that Iago's anger about this inequality feeds his destructive urges.

MALICIOUS, CALLOUS AND DESTRUCTIVE

According to the scholar A.C. Bradley, 'Evil has nowhere else been portrayed with such mastery as in the character of Iago'. This notion of Iago as a kind of 'devilish' personality is reinforced when he explicitly aligns himself with the forces of darkness at the end of Act 1: 'Hell and night / Must bring this monstrous birth to the world's light'. (1.3,401-2). His 'monstrous' plots will be 'born' or brought to fruition with the aid of hell itself. He also associates himself with the devil act the end of Act 2 (2.3.337-9).

As the great poet Coleridge remarked, Iago is 'haunted by the love of exerting power, on those especially who are his superiors in practical and moral excellence'. Iago controls people through lies and psychological manipulation, manoeuvring the other characters as one would the pieces in a game of chess. He takes a perverse delight in ensnaring those around him in a complex web of lies. We see this when he watches Cassio kiss Desdemona's hand: 'With as little a web as this will I ensnare as great a fly as Cassio' (2.1.169-70).

From the play's very beginning Iago comes across as an extremely callous and malicious individual. In the play's opening scene he maliciously encourages Roderigo to wake Desdemona's father with the news of her marriage, knowing that the senator will be incensed by the news: 'Call up her father, / Rouse him, make after him, poison his delight' (1.1.66-7).

Our sense of his almost bottomless malice is reinforced in Act 1 Scene 3 when he describes how he uses Roderigo for 'sport and profit' (1.3.384) and conceives a callous scheme to destroy both Cassio and Othello (1.3.390-401).

In Act 3 Scene 3 he takes great pleasure in how Othello is consumed by jealousy, gloating that the Moor's poisoned mind will soon be beyond all help and will never know 'sweet sleep' again, irrespective of whatever 'drowsy syrups' he might take to aid his rest (3.3.333-4).

His callous nature is similarly obvious in the way he probes Desdemona, urging her to repeat the names Othello called her, despite the obvious discomfort it causes her: 'What name, fair lady?' (4.2.119). This is someone who relishes the discord he has sown and the hurt he's brought to those around him.

Iago is also something of a 'con-man' motivated by greed for material possessions. We see this in his treatment of Roderigo. Iago urges Roderigo to sell all his land (1.3.379-80). Roderigo uses the money from the sale to buy precious jewels, which he gives to Iago to pass on to Desdemona as tokens of his love (4.2.188-90). Iago, however, keeps these precious stones for his own purposes. Iago give us the impression that this type of thievery is by no means unusual for him: 'Thus do I ever make my fool my purse' (1.3.381).

As if all this wasn't enough Iago also reveals a disturbing lack of respect for human life. In Act 4, he refers in a disconcertingly casual way to 'the removing of Cassio', talking about murder as if he were asking Roderigo to carry out some simple everyday task (4.2.227). He coldly murders Roderigo in order to ensure his treachery remains unexposed.

Yet, where Iago killed Roderigo out of strategy, he kills Emilia entirely out of spite. By the time he stabs her she has already revealed his deception. Murdering her cannot benefit him. In fact, it only invites greater punishment from those present. Yet he does it anyway.

Finally it is important to note that Iago seems to have little or no conscience, demonstrating no guilt for ruining the lives of those around him. He remains unrepentant about the misery he's caused, as he shows at the play's conclusion when he argues that he told Othello only what the Moor already believed or was ready to believe: 'I told him what I thought, and told no more/ Than what he found himself was apt and true' (5.2.177-8).

IAGO'S SENSE OF SUPERIORITY

Iago comes from a lower social class than the play's other characters, but he has a great sense of superiority to those around him. There can be little doubting his self-confidence and self-belief.

He seems to consider his position as ensign or standard-bearer to be beneath him and is outraged at having been passed over for lieutenant: 'I know my price, I am worth no worse a place' (1.1.10). He will not accept this slight. He is not like 'Many a duteous and knee-crooking knave' who humbly accept their lot and serve another all their lives (1.1.44-7). Iago will continue to serve Othello as long as it suits his interests to do so but seems sure that it is only a matter of time before he achieves greater things.

Iago thinks of Roderigo as a 'snipe' and of Othello as an 'ass' (1.3.383, 400). To the audience he boldly declares that he will 'ensnare' Cassio and detune the instruments that make the music of Othello's newfound joy: 'O, you are well tuned now!/ But I'll set down the pegs that make this music' (2.1.169, 198-9).

He is convinced that he can use his powers of deception to bamboozle the moor: 'making him egregiously an ass' (2.1.308). Othello, he feels, will be easily led by a master of manipulation like himself. He, 'will as tenderly be led by the nose/ As asses are' (1.3.399-400). He is certain that he will be able to poison Othello's mental state, destroying his 'peace and quiet' by filling his mind with jealousy. He will 'put the Moor/ At least into a jealousy so strong/ That judgement cannot cure' (2.1.299-301) and drive him 'Even to madness' (2.1.310).

A MASTER PLOTTER

Iago's approach to plotting is perhaps best summarised when he declares that 'Knavery's plain face is never seen till used' (2.1.311). He is more an improviser than a meticulous planner. He is content to draw the broad strokes of a plan then work around events as they arise, using accident and circumstance to his advantage.

Throughout the play Iago proves superb at adjusting his schemes to fit the shifting conditions of the world around him and able to take advantage of almost every opportunity that comes his way. He resembles more a clever boxer, quickly and skilfully responding to his opponent's movements than a genius chess master seeing twenty moves move ahead.

This is evident in Act 1 Scene 3 when Iago conceives a plan that will effectively kill two birds with one stone: he will destroy both Cassio and Othello by convincing Othello that Cassio is sleeping with Desdemona (1.3.390-400). However, it is important to note that Iago's plan is not detailed or complete. His scheme has been conceived, fertilised or 'engender'd' (1.3.401) but it has not yet fully developed or emerged: 'Hell and night/ Must bring this monstrous birth to the world's light' (1.3.401-2).

Act 2 Scene 1 reinforces our sense that Iago's schemes work more through brilliant improvisation than meticulous planning. By the scene's end his plan to destroy Othello has found a sharper focus though its outline is still somewhat blurred: 'Tis here, but yet confused' (2.1.310). It is only when he actually puts his plan into practise that its finer details will emerge (2.1.311). Indeed at this stage Iago seems to be juggling several plots or potential plots at the same time.

Iago's improvisational skills are especially evident in Act 2 Scene 3, where he aims to get Cassio drunk and ultimately fired from his position as lieutenant. He acknowledges that his plan remains somewhat loose and requires a certain amount of good fortune, calling upon 'consequence' to 'approve [his] dream' (2.3.57). Yet he also knows that if he gets everyone drunk, the chances are he will find a way to get Cassio in trouble.

We can see that he is quick to respond to events as they unfold, for example when he directs Roderigo to provoke Cassio as soon as the opportunity arises and then waking Othello with shouts that a riot is taking place on the island. Furthermore, once Cassio has been fired, Iago immediately convinces him to seek Desdemona's help: 'Confess yourself freely to her; importune her help to put you in your place again' (2.3.307-8).

He knows that Desdemona will do her best to convince Othello to forgive Cassio and that he will find a way to make the Moor suspicious of the relationship between his wife and his lieutenant. His fiendish plans to destroy the people that he despises now seem to be coming to fruition and it won't be long before the 'net' he is weaving 'shall enmesh them all' (2.3.347-8).

Again and again we see Iago function as a ruthless opportunist, taking advantage of every stroke of luck that comes his way. There are many twists and turns that Iago could not have predicted but he seizes on each one as it occurs, improvising fluently and using them to further his objectives.

He must be delighted, for instance, when Cassio follows his advice and pleads with Desdemona for his job back. He promises Cassio that he will keep Othello distracted while this meeting takes place: 'I'll devise a mean to draw the Moor / Out of the way' (3.1.36-7). We can be certain, however, that he arranges things so that he and Othello arrive while Cassio and Desdemona are talking. He then uses the fact that a shame-filled Cassio slips quietly and guiltily away to begin filling Othello's mind with doubts: 'Ha? I like not that', 'I Cannot think it / That he would steal away so guilty-like, / Seeing you coming' (3.3.33, 37-9).

Iago enjoys another stroke of good fortune when Cassio shows up during Othello's seizure. Iago tells him to come back and talk a little later. Meanwhile he persuades Othello to hide and observe their conversation, promising that he will get Cassio to describe the sordid details of his 'affair' with Desdemona: 'I will make him tell the tale anew: / Where, how, how oft, how long ago, and when / He hath, and is again to cope your wife.' (4.1.81-3).

He guesses that Othello will misinterpret Cassio's cruel but light-hearted banter about Bianca as bragging about Desdemona: 'And his unbookish jealousy must construe / Poor Cassio's smiles, gestures, and light behaviours / Quite in the wrong' (4.1.98-100). When Cassio returns he concocts a story about Bianca wanting to marry him and manages to elicit from him precisely the sort of reaction he needs to further aggravate the watching Othello: 'She gives it out that you shall marry her', 'I marry – what, a customer? Prithee, bear some / charity to my wit; do not think it so unwholesome. Ha, / ha, ha!' (4.1.113, 117-8).

He also seizes on the opportunity presented by the arrival of Bianca herself, who angrily throws Othello's handkerchief on the ground. It is a disgrace, he says, that Cassio gave the handkerchief to such a 'whore': 'did you see the handkerchief?', 'And to see how he prizes the / foolish woman your wife: she gave it him, and he hath / given it his whore' (4.1.166, 168-70). Furthermore, he turns Lodovico's arrival to his advantage, speaking cryptically about Othello's madness in order to sow further doubt about the Moor's state of mind: 'He's that he is: I may not breathe my censure / What he might be; if what he might, he is not' (4.1.261-2).

Opportunism, too, marks his encounter with Roderigo in Act 4 Scene 2. Roderigo has finally had enough of being manipulated and he threatens to expose Iago by going directly to Desdemona and demanding the return of his jewels: 'I will make myself known / to Desdemona' (4.2.198-9). Iago escapes from this jam brilliantly, concocting on the spot a story about Othello leaving with Desdemona for faraway Mauritania, 'he goes to Mauretania, and takes away with him the fair Desdemona, unless his abode be lingered here by some accident' (4.2.224-6).

Throughout this encounter Iago improvises with astonishing fluency. It seems that nothing whatsoever could faze him in his lies. Roderigo begins by threatening to ruin him but concludes by agreeing to murder Cassio instead. Such an assault suits Iago perfectly: if Roderigo dies the threat of exposure is removed, if Cassio dies an old enemy is gone, if both die so much the better. We see Iago spy an opportunity and seize it, quickly turning a potentially disastrous situation into an advantageous one.

However, Iago's greatest act of opportunism occurs when Emilia presents him with Desdemona's discarded handkerchief. He has urged his wife 'a hundred times' to steal this love token, knowing he can use it for his own ends (3.3.295). He now further stokes Othello's jealousy by planing it in Cassio's chamber. He knows that a jealous mind will find such a flimsy piece of evidence convincing: 'Trifles light as air / Are to the jealous confirmations strong / As proofs of holy writ' (3.3.324-6).

According to many critics, Act 5 Scene 1 shows Iago's improvisational abilities at their most refined. He sets in motion a wave of chaos and surfs it masterfully. He gives a masterful display of his ability to steer a fluid and highly changeable situation to his own advantage: he is uncertain how the fight which he has instigated will turn out, but is confident that it will be to his advantage.

He takes advantage of Cassio's retreat, attempting to stab him in the back without revealing his identity. When help arrives, he deliberately adds to the confusion as the characters attempt to identify one another in the dark and work out what's going on. He then exploits this chaos to slip away and murder Roderigo shouting, 'That's one of them / O murd'rous slave! / O villain!' before striking him with his sword(5.1.61-2). He also exploits Bianca's arrival, deflecting attention away from himself by blaming her for the attack: 'Gentlemen all, I do suspect this trash / To be a party in this injury' (5.1.85-6). Throughout the scene, we see Iago yet again reacting to events he could not have entirely predicted and turning them to his advantage.

A BRILLIANT ACTOR

Perhaps Iago's most impressive skill is to convince the other characters that he is an honest, good-natured and well-meaning person. Nothing, of course, could be further from the truth. Every character in the play is convinced of Iago's sincerity and they repeatedly refer to him as 'honest Iago'.

Othello begins this trend when he refers to Iago as a man of 'honesty and trust' and entrusts him with the care of Desdemona (1.3.284-6). Cassio, too, is convinced of Iago's goodness and follows his advice to the letter: 'I never knew a Florentine more kind and honest' (3.1.39). Desdemona is also taken in by Iago's act, declaring 'O, that's an honest fellow' (3.3.5) Roderigo is convinced that Iago is on his side and will assist him in the winning of Desdemona. He sells his land to raise money that Iago (rather than Roderigo himself) will ultimately make use of: 'I am changed: I'll go sell all my land' (1.3.378-9).

There is a sense in which the other characters regard Iago as being 'honest' in the old sense of simple or unsophisticated. To them he is little more than an amusing character with his simple rhymes and bad jokes from the alehouse. Little do they suspect that this apparently unsophisticated soldier will bring ruin to them all: 'But I'll set down the pegs that make this music, / As honest as I am' (2.1.199-200). Indeed it is Othello's implicit trust in Iago that allows him to be so easily convinced of Desdemona's 'unfaithfulness'.

The play is littered with Iago's superb performances. In Act 1, for instance, he claims to have been so angered by Roderigo's slurs against Othello that he wanted to kill the young nobleman: 'I had thought to have yerk'd him here under the ribs' (1.2.5). He acts as if he has Othello's best interests at heart when he tells him that Brabantio is looking for him and that the senator is a powerful man, capable of making Othello's life a misery (1.2.11-17). Little does Othello know that it was Iago who set these people against him in the first place.

He expertly fakes distress at the fight between Cassio and Montano and acts as if he wishes to stop the brawl (2.3.149). He pretends to find the commotion that he himself instigated shocking and upsetting. When Othello arrives, he continues to act as though he is appalled at the men's behaviour: 'Have you forgot all sense of place and duty?' (2.3.158). He manages to look so upset that according to Othello he appears 'dead with grieving' (2.3.168).

In Act 4 Scene 1 Iago brilliantly juggles two performances, a feat that proves his impressive acting skills. He hates Cassio but acts in a friendly fashion toward him throughout the scene, bantering with him about Bianca and even agreeing to dine with him that evening. At the same time, of course, Iago continues a very different performance with Othello, playing the role of faithful servant who has nothing but his commander's best interests at heart. When he plays this role he acts as Cassio's sworn enemy, committed to exposing and destroying him on his master's behalf.

Act 4 Scene 2 provides yet another showcase of Iago's acting ability. He knows exactly why Desdemona is distraught and upset. Yet he feigns confusion at her distressed state (115). He pretends to be shocked when told about Othello's devastating verbal assault and immediately begins to play the role of gentle comforter: 'Do not weep, do not weep – alas the day!' (125). He comes across as loyal and caring, telling Desdemona that Othello's anger stems only from 'The business of the state' (167). He consoles her, assuring her that everything will be all right (173). In reality, however, he is scheming to ensure that events worsen for Desdemona.

Act 5 Scene 1 also sees Iago shift effortlessly between a variety of different performances. In the chaos of the midnight assault and its aftermath he plays the role of encouraging commander with Roderigo, innocent but wary bystander with Lodovico, concerned protector with Cassio and accuser with Bianca.

Yet is it is surely the 'temptation' scene that provides the greatest display of Iago's acting prowess. Iago convinces Othello that he's on his side, that the accusation he levels against Desdemona comes only from the love he bears Othello: 'I hope you will consider what is spoke/ Comes from my love' (3.3.219-20). Again and again he mentions how he acts only out of loyalty and respect: 'My lord, you know I love you…I humbly do beseech you of your pardon/ For too much loving you' (3.3.120, 215-6).

In a final false display of loyalty and brotherhood, Iago kneels beside Othello in what can almost be described as an act of prayer, the two of them swearing by the heavens or the seas. Othello vows to be avenged, Iago vows to assist him in this 'bloody business', offering his whole self to Othello's service (3.3.464-70).

Throughout this scene we are reminded again and again how completely Othello has been fooled by Iago. He welcomes Iago's devotion and declares that he will be loyal to him in return: 'I greet thy love', 'I am bound to thee for ever' (3.3.471, 216). Othello, we're reminded, considers Iago to be an exceptionally honest person: 'This fellow's of exceeding honesty' (3.3.122, 261).

Indeed, the fact that the text of the play is so littered with references to 'honest Iago' serves as the ultimate tribute to his acting ability. He cares only about himself: 'I follow but myself' (1.1.57) but he has somehow convinced everyone that he is a loyal and trustworthy friend. (It has, however, been suggested that Iago's wife Emilia may harbour some suspicion as to the true nature of his personality).

MANIPULATIVE AND PERSUASIVE

Perhaps the most insidious aspect of Iago's evil is the manner in which he preys upon the weaknesses of the other characters. He is an expert at identifying something each character fears or desires and using it to manipulate him or her. Roderigo's yearning for Desdemona allows Iago make him his puppet, embezzling his money and using him as a pawn in his various schemes. Each time Roderigo objects to this treatment Iago reassures him that Desdemona's love, the thing he wants most in life, will soon be his if only he does what Iago tells him.

Iago also brilliantly exploits Barbantio's fear and suspicion of black people. Iago expertly plays upon Barbantio's prejudices in the play's opening scene, especially his horror at the prospect of his daughter entering an interracial marriage. Iago uses language calculated to evoke his racial hatred and motivate him to take action against Othello: 'an old black ram is tupping your white ewe…the devil will make a grandsire out of you' (1.1.88-91).

We also see Iago function as a kind of 'tempter' in Act 2 Scene 3. He has identified Cassio's weakness with regard to alcohol and uses peer pressure to encourage him to drink more than he should: 'Tis a night of revels; the gallants desire it' (2.3.38-9), although Cassio is initially reluctant to join the party he is ultimately persuaded by Iago to do so: 'I'll do't, but it dislikes me' (2.3.42).

Iago also plays upon an aspect of Desdemona's personality to further his evil ends. He realises that Desdemona is unable to refuse any request for her help: 'For 'tis most easy/ Th'inclining Desdemona to subdue/ In any honest suit' (2.3.325-7). Iago makes use of this 'weakness' when he sends Cassio to seek her help, knowing that she will plead with Othello on Cassio's behalf. Iago hopes that her efforts to get Cassio his job back will only serve to stoke the fires of Othello's jealousy.

Another excellent example of Iago's manipulation occurs in Act 3 Scene 3, where he gradually fills Othello's mind with suspicion about Desdemona's unfaithfulness. At the scene's beginning Othello has no suspicions whatsoever that an affair might be taking place between Cassio and Desdemona. By its conclusion, however, he is convinced that the affair is real and threatens to kill them both. It is fascinating to watch how Iago gently leads Othello on this journey into suspicion, doubt and jealous rage.

In general, he does this by dropping hints and letting Othello's own imagination do most of the work. Iago is much too clever to simply blurt out his false accusation. Instead he begins by sowing tiny seeds of doubt regarding Cassio's relationship with Desdemona.

These simple statements naturally arouse Othello's curiosity, but Iago refuses to expand on them for as long as possible. At first he pretends not to know what Othello's getting at: 'Honest, my lord?', 'Think, my lord?' (3.3.105, 108). Then, when challenged more directly to reveal his suspicions, he comes up with a number of reasons not to do so, citing his over-active imagination, the possibility his suspicions might be false, the dangers of jealousy and his desire to avoid blackening anybody's name (3.3. 138-73).

This reticence proves a brilliant tactic. It allows time for the seeds of doubt to sprout and flourish in Othello's mind. It also causes the Moor's curiosity to reach fever pitch – after all we are never more curious than when someone is keeping a secret from us. Eventually, Othello is practically begging Iago to reveal what's on his mind. Furthermore, Iago's apparent caution and concern for others' reputations make his accusation sound much more plausible when he finally reveals it.

In revealing his 'suspicion', Iago plays expertly on Othello's insecurities. He suggests that, as an outsider, Othello doesn't know how promiscuous and untrustworthy the women of Venice actually are: 'In Venice they do let God see the pranks/ They dare not show their husbands' (3.3.205-6). He mentions the possibility that eventually

Desdemona will find herself attracted to someone from her own race and background: 'I may fear/ Her will, recoiling to her better judgement,/ May fall to match you with her country forms,/ And happily repent' (3.3.239-42).

He also brings up Desdemona's history of betrayal: the fact that she betrayed her father in marrying Othello means it's more likely she's betraying the Moor now: 'She did deceive her father, marrying you', 'She that, so young, could give out such a seeming/ To seal her father's eyes up close as oak -/ He thought 'twas witchcraft' (3.3.209, 212-4).

It is important to note how long Iago delays in telling concrete and definite lies about other people. He waits until the end of the scene when, as he puts it: 'The Moor already changes with my poison' (3.3.327). It is only at this point he tells Othello how he see's Cassio wipe his beard with Desdemona's handkerchief and how he's heard him talk about their affair in his sleep (3.3.432-4, 411-426).

He has waited until precisely the right moment, when Othello's passions are so inflamed that he is no longer thinking clearly. These final barefaced lies are enough to overcome Othello's remaining doubts and tip him into a homicidal rage.

It's important to note that Iago wants to avoid seeming too obvious in his manipulations. Again and again throughout the play he raises spectres in Othello's mind, dismisses their importance, and returns to them a little later once the doubts have taken root. By proposing unforgiveable wrongs and then attempting to lessen their significance, Iago manages to drown Othello in his own anger and jealousy, while preserving his own innocent reputation.

We see this reverse psychology at work at the beginning of Act 4 Scene 1. He dangles terrible images like bait before Othello's mind, hinting at the illicit couplings between Cassio and Desdemona. Yet he speaks directly about Cassio's 'confession' to the affair only when Othello is practically begging him to do so: '"What hath he said?' (4.1.30). Iago replies that the two lay together: 'With her, on her – what you will' (4.1.32). Iago uses a blunter form of persuasion when Othello emerges from his hiding place. The Moor is now committed to killing Cassio and Iago reinforces this decision: 'Did you perceive how he laughed at his vice? And did you see the handkerchief?' (4.1.164-6) Othello still has doubts about murdering Desdemona but Iago overpowers his objections by telling Othello that he must forget his wife's qualities because they make her betrayal all the worse (4.1.173-84). He warns him not be ruled by her beauty: 'Nay, that's not your way' (4.1.179). Ultimately, Iago not only persuades Othello to kill Desdemona, but also successfully advises him on how and where this terrible deed should be accomplished (199-200).

IAGO'S SHIFTING MOTIVATIONS

Why does Iago behave in such a terrible fashion? This is a question readers and audience members have asked themselves since the play was first performed over 400 years ago.

The answer is that he is driven by a thirst for revenge. This desire for vengeance has two sources: firstly, Othello has decided not to promote him to the rank of lieutenant; secondly, he suspects that Othello has slept with his wife.

Iago feels he should have been promoted to the rank of lieutenant: 'I know my price, I am worth no worse a place' (1.1.10). After all, he has served Venice with distinction in many battles: 'At Rhodes, at Cyprus, and on other grounds/ Christian and heathen' (1.1.28-9). Furthermore, he has been recommended for promotion by three of Venice's leading senators: 'three great ones of the city,/ In personal suit to make me his lieutenant'. (1.1.7-8).

Othello, however, has decided not to give Iago the lieutenantcy he desires so much. Instead he declares that Iago will be given the much lesser rank of 'ensign' or standard-bearer (1.1.32). Iago, it seems, feels incredibly bitter about being passed over for promotion. He has become filled with hatred for Othello: 'I do hate him as I do hell's pains' (1.1.155). He vows to bring down not only Othello but also Michael Cassio, who was awarded the lieutenantcy he feels should have been rightfully his.

Iago also bears a second grudge against Othello. He suspects the Moor has slept with his wife: 'it is thought abroad that 'twixt my sheets/ He has done my office' (1.3.385-6). Iago will not rest until he has avenged himself. He will destroy not only Othello but also Desdemona: 'nothing can or shall content my soul/ Till I am evened with him, wife for wife'

(2.1, 297-8). Ideally, then , Iago would like to seek revenge by sleeping with Desdemona. Failing this, however, he would be happy to ruin their marriage by filling Othello's head with thoughts of jealousy (2.1.299-301).

Since the play was first performed, however, many critics have rejected this rational understanding of Iago's motivations, agreeing with the great poet Coleridge that his malice is ultimately 'motiveless' in nature. Iago's precise motivations, they argue, remain blurred, shifting and confused, perhaps even to himself. They present him as an almost satanic character who relishes evil deeds more for their own sake than for any particular gain they can bring him.

According to this view, then, Iago does evil simply because he is evil, and his destructive plotting is fuelled more by his love of wickedness than by the grudges he bears Othello. After all, we have seen how Iago acts like a remorseless sadist, taking a perverse pleasure in the misery he inflicts on those around him. Furthermore, even though Iago is promoted to the rank of lieutenant at the end of Act 2 he continues to plot the destruction of the other main characters.

CONCLUSION

It's been suggested that Shakespeare's inspiration for Iago came from the character known as 'Vice' who appeared in many medieval dramas. Vice was a supernatural, devilish figure who would attempt to lure the play's heroes into the path of evil and wickedness. Iago certainly shares certain characteristics with Vice. Like Vice he is a 'tempter', playing upon the desires and weaknesses of each character in order to bring them to destruction.

However, critics with a more modern bent have identified in Iago certain characteristics associated with the condition known as 'psychopathy'. Contemporary psychology defines a psychopath as an individual who has no sense of guilt or conscience. One study described psychopaths as manipulative, charming, glib, deceptive, parasitic, irresponsible, selfish, callous, impulsive, and aggressive individuals who have no concern for the welfare of others and experience little remorse or guilt as a result of their injurious and antisocial behaviour'.

Many commentators have suggested that there could be no better description than this of Iago's personality. It is a tribute to Shakespeare's skill that Iago has inspired so much fascination and debate in readers over the centuries, with everything from medieval theology to modern psychology used to explain his behaviour.

In the end, however, Iago remains a mystery. In the play's final scene, as Iago prepares to be tortured and executed, Othello demands to know what compelled him to do what he did. He is desperate to know Iago's motivation for 'ensnaring' him in this way. Iago, however, will say no more: 'From this time forth I never will speak word' (5.2.309). He has destroyed Othello's life but will give neither him nor the audience the satisfaction of knowing why.

OTHELLO

OTHELLO'S MERITS

Othello is not a young man. As he remarks himself in Act 3 Scene 3 he has 'declined / into the vale of years' (267-8). But he has lived an eventful life and experienced many dangers and hardships. Along the way he has earned the respect of those that he serves and those who serve under him. It is not hard to see why so many people have such admiration for this man. Even Iago must acknowledge that Othello is fundamentally a decent guy: 'The Moor… Is of a constant, loving, noble nature' (2.1.279-80).

Othello is an honest person, someone who seems to have nothing to hide. When Brabantio comes looking for him, enraged at learning that his daughter has secretly wed the Moor, Othello refuses to run and hide: 'Not I – I must be found: / My parts, my title, and my perfect soul / Shall manifest me rightly' (1.2.30-3). In turn Othello expects that others will be honest and forthright with him. Iago, of course, is well aware of this and takes advantage of his General's trusting nature: 'The Moor is of a free and open nature / That thinks men honest that but seem to be so, / And will as tenderly be led by th' nose / As asses are' (1.3.387-9).

But it is not easy to make the Moor suspicious. He finds nothing immediately suspect about Cassio speaking to his wife, nor the fact that the former lieutenant slips away when he arrives (3.3.45-50). Even when Iago characterises Cassio's behaviour as 'guilty-like' the Moor barely takes notice. He has faith in people and says that he thinks 'Cassio's

an honest man' (3.3.130). Othello is also happy to have a wife who is 'fair, loves company, / Is free of speech' and claims that he is not someone prone to jealousy (3.3.185-94). His faith in those he loves is not fickle and he tells Iago that he will only doubt someone's good character when it has been clearly demonstrated that they have acted inappropriately: 'I'll see before I doubt; when I doubt, prove' (3.3.192).

Othello is someone who does not easily lose his cool. When Iago tries to incense him with tales of Roderigo saying terrible things about him, the Moor refuses to get wound up (1.2.6). When Brabantio confronts him and accuses him of being a 'thief' and using witchcraft to seduce his daughter – a most insulting and degrading accusation – Othello remains dignified and composed, never once losing his temper: 'Good signor, you shall more command with years / Than with your weapons' (1.2.60-1). Perhaps this self-control stems from the fact that he is as outsider, a black man in white Venetian society who must work harder than others to prove himself.

Othello's bravery is also much admired. Even Iago must acknowledge the Moor's steely composure in the face of great danger: 'I have seen the cannon / When it hath blown his ranks into the air / And, like the devil, from his very arm / Puffed his own brother' (3.4.130-3). All of Cyprus, it seems, holds Othello in very high esteem and feel safer the minute he sets foot on the island. Cassio describes how Cyprus 'does approve the Moor' and how his arrival will lift the spirits of the entire island: 'That he may bless this bay with his tall ship…And bring all Cyprus comfort' (2.1.45, 79-82).

However, though he is held in high esteem and has been praised and rewarded for his achievements, Othello remains a humble man. When he stands before the court in Act 1 he presents himself as a warrior rather than an orator and, though he speaks with great eloquence, claims that his warlike life has left his mode of speaking fairly rough and ready: 'Rude am I in my speech, / And little bless'd with the soft phrase of peace' (82-3). But he is proud or what he has achieved and knows his worth: 'my demerits / May speak unbonneted to as proud a fortune / As this that I have reached' (1.2.22-4). In his final speech he makes a somewhat modest allusion to the military work he has done for Venice: 'I have done the state some service, and they know't' (5.2.338).

BACKGROUND AND LIFE IN VENICE

Othello's origins lie far from the prosperous European city of Venice in a land beyond the Mediterranean. He describes his country of origin as a bleak place, a country of enormous caves ('antres vast') and endless deserts (1.3.140). It is a rugged, mountainous land full of 'Rough quarries, rocks and hills whose heads touch heaven' (141). According to Othello this wilderness is peopled by bizarre and fantastic races. He mentions cannibals, headless men whose features appear on their torsos and the 'Anthropophagi' who were a cannibalistic race from Greek legend (143-5).

From an early age Othello was involved in 'battles, sieges, fortunes' (1.3.130). There were times when he escaped death by only a hair's breadth: 'hair-breadth scapes i' the imminent deadly breach' (136). He suffered 'disastrous chances' and many a 'distressful stroke' of bad fortune, enduring 'accidents' caused by war and by natural disaster (134, 135, 157). He was captured by his enemies and sold into slavery only to eventually win or be granted his freedom (137-8). As A.C. Bradley says, 'There is something mysterious in his descent from men of royal siege; in his wanderings in vast deserts and among marvellous peoples; in his tales of magic handkerchiefs and prophetic Sibyls' and the citizens of Venice find him fascinating.

On the one hand Othello is very much a part of the Venetian society that he protects and serves. He has become its experienced military leader, commanding the respect and admiration of the Duke, the Senate, and many Venetian citizens. He is also, like them, a Christian. But despite all this he remains a foreigner, an outsider, set apart from white Venetian society by his colour and origins.

It is interesting to note how Othello is very rarely referred to by name. He is more often than not referred to simply as 'the Moor'. The very society that celebrates him and turns to him in its hour of need is quick to subject him to overt racism. Roderigo refers to him as 'thick-lips' and Iago seeks to enflame Brabantio's prejudices and fears by telling him that it is 'an old black ram' and 'Barbary horse' that his daughter has run away with (1.1.88, 110). Though the city is happy for him to act as their guardian, protecting them from the threat of their enemies, when it comes to him marrying one of their own they are less happy.

Brabantio perhaps embodies this two-faced attitude to Othello better than any other character. He was once happy to invite Othello to his house and hear the fantastic tales he had to tell. As Othello tells the Senate, 'Her father loved me; oft invited me;/ Still question'd me the story of my life,/ From year to year, the battles, sieges, fortunes,/ That I have passed./ I ran it through, even from my boyish days,/ To the very moment that he bade me tell it' (1.3.128-32). But when Brabantio hears that his daughter has married the Moor his attitude is suddenly very different. He believes Desdemona's interracial marriage can only be the result of Othello's trickery: 'O thou foul thief, where hast thou stowed my daughter?/ Damned as thou art, thou hast enchanted her' (1.2.62-3).

OTHELLO AS SOLDIER

In order to properly understand Othello and the way he behaves we must appreciate that he has spent much of his life on the battlefield: 'The tyrant custom, most grave senators,/ Hath made the flinty and steel couch of war/ My thrice-driven bed of down' (1.3.226-8). Othello is someone who has experienced war and bloodshed his whole life. Since he was seven years old he has known little but the 'tented field' of battle (1.3.84-6). Warfare is his only area of expertise: 'And little of this great world can I speak,/ More than pertains to feats of broil and battle' (187-8). He is referred to as 'the warlike Moor Othello' (2.1. 28) and is said to possess all the qualities of a true soldier: 'the man commands/ Like a full soldier' (2.1. 36-7). Being a soldier means so much to him. Though it is a hard and dangerous life, it has brought him much glory and prestige and he relishes the pomp and ceremony of battle: 'the neighing steed and the shrill trump,/ The spirit-stirring drum… The royal banner, and all quality,/ Pride, pomp, and circumstance of glorious war' (3.3.352-5).

Othello is a stern military commander, someone who places great value on discipline. When his men act in rowdy manner the first night in Cyprus, he is quick to restore order. He takes swift and decisive action when roused by the sound of the brawl and puts an immediate stop to this fracas, threatening the next person to raise a hand with execution (2.3.154-5). He fairly quickly gets to the bottom of what caused the disturbance and fires Cassio on the spot for his indiscretion (230).

Othello is also an accomplished strategist and general. No sooner has he reached the counsel chamber than the Duke asks him to lead the expedition against the Turks (1.3.49-50). Though Cyprus already has a commander in place – 'a substitute/ of most allowed sufficiency' (222-3) – the Duke believes Othello should replace him and lead the island's defense: 'opinion, a sovereign mistress of effects, throws a more safer voice on you' (243-4). Othello, we're told, knows Cyprus's fortifications better than anyone, an indication of his vast military experience (221).

RELATIONSHIP WITH DESDEMONA

Othello's marriage to Desdemona seems to crown a life of great military achievement and success. Not only this, but it introduces a much-needed calm into his life of turmoil and battle. The Moor can barely believe that such joy and love is possible: 'I cannot speak enough of this content;/ It stops me here, it is too much of joy' (2.1.191-2). It is almost as if he fears that such contentment cannot possibly last: 'my soul's joy… If I were now to die,/ 'Twere now to be most happy; for I fear/ My soul hath her content so absolute/ That not another comfort like to this/ Succeeds in unknown fate' (2.1.179-88). He attaches great significance to his love for Desdemona, believing that it offers him a relief or reprieve from the chaos of life and that should it ever vanish his life will once again be thrown into turmoil: 'perdition catch my soul/ But I do love thee! and when I love thee not,/ Chaos is come again' (3.3.91-3).

It is possible that Othello has his doubts about Desdemona before Iago begins his scheming. His new bride is a very beautiful woman and is much younger than him. He thinks that she loves him because of the fascinating life he has lived, but cannot think why else Desdemona would choose him for a husband: 'She lov'd me for the dangers I had pass'd' (1.3.167). Desdemona, it seems, was simply blown away by Othello's tale. She found his story both fascinating nad moving: 'She swore, in faith, twas strange, 'twas passing strange,/ 'Twas pitiful, 'twas wondrous pitiful' (160-1). It is hardly surprising that Desdemona fell for this exotic foreigner with his incredible tale. To her he must have seemed different and attractive, sexy and exciting. The Duke suggests that Othello and his story might well prove irresistible to any woman. As he puts it: 'I think this tale would win my daughter too' (171).

The Moor is also surely aware of the widespread prejudice in Venice and must wonder why Desdemona would defy her culture and fellow white Venetians by marrying a black man. Both Roderigo and Cassio remark at the fact that the Moor has wooed such a fine woman. Roderigo, bitter and envious, wonders how Othello could be so lucky: 'what full fortune does the thick-lips owe/ If he can carry't thus?' (1.1.66-7). Cassio believes that Othello has married the finest woman in Venice: 'he hath achieved a maid/ That paragons description and wild fame' (2.1.61-2).

OTHELLO'S INSECURITIES AND DEPENDENCY ON IAGO

Othello places a lot of trust in Iago: 'This honest creature doubtless/ Sees and knows more, much more than he unfolds' (3.3.246-7). He believes that his ensign has a much better understanding of Venetian society and the ways of its people than he: 'This fellow's of exceeding honesty,/ And knows all qualities, with a learned spirit/ Of human dealings' (3.3.261-3). Iago in turn knows that the Moor places a lot of faith in him and his opinions and uses this to his advantage: 'He holds me well:/ The better shall my purpose work on him' (1.3. 379-80). He tells Othello that Venetian women are known to be unfaithful and that it is not something of which they are ashamed. As long as their husbands are unaware of their behaviour they feel no remorse: 'In Venice they do let God see the pranks/ They dare not show their husbands; their best conscience/ Is not to leave't undone, but keep't unknown' (3.3.205-7).

Iago also cleverly touches upon the fact that Desdemona could have married any number of men from her native city: 'Not to affect many proposed matches/ Of her own clime, complexion, and degree,/ Whereto we see in all things nature tends' (3.3.232-5). He contends that Desdemona chose to marry Othello because of his exotic looks and origins and that this was an unnatural choice for her to make: 'One may smell in such a will most rank,/ Foul disproportions, thoughts unnatural' (236-7). It is, Iago suggests, only a matter of time before Desdemona comes to her senses and gives Othello up for someone from her native land: 'I may fear/ Her will, recoiling to her better judgment,/ May fall to match you with her country forms' (239-42).

Such suggestions expose or bring to the surface certain insecurities and doubts in the Moor's mind. He suddenly begins to question how someone as fair and lovely as Desdemona could desire him. He is older than her and is not as refined as some of the Venetian gentlemen who have attempted to woo her: 'I am black/ And have not those soft parts of conversation/ That chamberers have, or for I am declined/ Into the vale of years' (3.3.266-9).

OTHELLO'S LOSS OF COMPOSURE

It is only when he allows his mind to be poisoned with jealous thoughts and suspicions that Othello's composure and self-discipline begin to crack. Lodovico is startled to see the normally composed Moor lose his temper and strike Desdemona: 'Is this the noble Moor, whom our full Senate/ Call all in all sufficient? Is this the nature/ Whom passion could not shake? Whose solid virtue/ The shot of accident nor dart of chance/ Could neither graze nor pierce?' (4.1.256-60). He is suddenly consumed with jealousy at the thought that his wife has slept with Cassio and this notion overrides all other considerations. In his tormented and fevered condition his wife now appears tarnished and tainted by her associations with another man. Although Othello has no reason to believe that Desdemona has slept with anyone but Cassio, it matters not – one man might as well be a hundred men. His wife is now no better than a common prostitute.

In the end Othello applies the resolve and ruthless determination that served him so well on the battlefield to his own personal affairs with tragic consequences. He suppresses any feelings of love that he has for Desdemona and encourages his more violent passions to surface and take control: 'Arise, black Vengeance from thy hollow hell,/ Yield up, O Love, thy crown and hearted throne/ To tyrannous Hate' (3.3.447-9). Once he has made up his mind that his wife has been unfaithful he sets upon a course of revenge from which there is no turning back: 'Like to the Pontic Sea,/ Whose icy current and compulsive course,/ Ne'er feels retiring ebb…Even so my bloody thoughts, with violent pace,/ Shall ne'er look back, ne'er ebb to humble love' (3.3.453-8).

It is interesting to note how the eloquence of Othello's speech fades as his suspicions grow. His language at times is brutal, violent and dark. The transformation in his manner of speech is shocking and tells of how disturbed Othello is by the thought that his wife is not who he thought she was. He calls Desdemona a 'whore' and an 'impudent strumpet' (4.2.80, 84). As Iago turns the screw and introduces ever stronger doubts into Othello's mind, the Moor can only respond with short exclamations of outrage and despair: 'O monstrous! Monstrous!' (3.3.428), 'O, blood, blood, blood!' (451). It is a terrible and sad transformation to behold, a far cry from the composed and dignified man we meet at the start of the play.

CONCLUSION

That Othello does place so much trust in Iago is not a sign of any foolishness on the Moor's behalf. His confidence is certainly misplaced but it is understandable that he places such faith in his ensign – after all, practically everyone who knows Iago thinks him an honest fellow. Nor do Othello's doubts and suspicions about Desdemona necessarily make him a jealous man. Desdemona is not being completely naïve when she tells Emilia that the Moor is not the jealous sort. It is not until the latter stages of the play that Othello begins to act in a manner that might be considered jealous – and at this stage it seems somewhat natural given what Iago has led him to believe.

If we want to find fault with Othello we might say that when he does decide to act on his suspicions he does so with unreasonable impulsiveness and violence. Perhaps, as one critic has suggested, 'Othello's mind, for all its poetry, is very simple'. He is not as astute as he ought to be and does not seem naturally prone to reflection. He is not given to long and careful deliberation, preferring to act without hesitation once he has established what needs to be done. When he trusts, he does so completely and when he experiences emotions of love and jealousy they are powerful and absolute. Before he dies he acknowledges that he loved 'not wisely, but too well' (5.2.340).

Desdemona is ultimately the tragic victim of the Moor's misguided resolve and over-powering passions. As he admits himself, he is not prone to jealousy but when jealous thoughts enter his mind they take a violent and powerful hold: 'Then must you speak…Of one not easily jealous but, being wrought,/ Perplexed in the extreme' (5.2.341-2).

CASSIO

BACKGROUND

Cassio is the handsome young officer Othello has chosen to be his lieutenant. Like Othello, he serves in the Venetian army but is not from Venice originally. Cassio is a citizen of the nearby Florentine Republic, which sometimes served as Venice's ally, sometimes as its rival (1.1.19). Perhaps the fact that both Othello and Cassio are outsiders or foreigners contributes to the bond that obviously exists between them.

Cassio is an educated and refined member of the upper classes. As he declares in Act 2 Scene 1 he is a man of 'breeding' (102). If Iago speaks 'home', in a crude and common fashion, Cassio, by contrast, speaks in the flamboyant language of the nobility. He perhaps has his own first-class education in mind when he refers to Iago as a soldier rather than a scholar (163-4).

Cassio may be an educated man but according to Iago he has little or no experience of combat. Iago suggest that he has 'never set a squadron in the field, / Not the division of battle knows' (1.1.21-2). He is a 'great arithmetician', more akin to an accountant than a soldier, a man whose knowledge of warfare comes from books rather than experience: 'Mere prattle without practice / Is all his soldiership' (1.1.25-30). We might question however, if Iago's bitterness makes him unfairly harsh on Cassio here. After all, Desdemona later suggests that Cassio and Othello have faced many 'dangers' together (3.4.92).

Cassio has been brought up to treat women in an extremely chivalrous and courteous manner. We see this in Act 2 Scene 1 when Iago bitterly remarks how Cassio exhibits great 'courtship' or courtesy and 'plays the sir' (165-73). It is evident when he kisses Emilia when she arrives at the quayside (97-9). His chivalry also comes across in his treatment of Desdemona as they wait nervously on the quayside for Othello to arrive.

Cassio's noble background is also evident in the self-disgust he displays at the conclusion of Act 2 Scene 3. As a member of the noble classes he places great stock in manners, chivalry and breeding. He feels he has let himself down greatly by drunkenly fighting in the street.

To nobles like Cassio reputation is all-important. He displays great concern, therefore, for the damage this late night brawl has done his standing in the community. Reputation, he declares, is the soul or immortal part of each person. Everything else is 'bestial', is animalistic and unimportant: 'I have lost the immortal part of myself, and what remains is bestial' (254-5).

CASSIO'S DEVOTION TO OTHELLO

When the play opens Cassio and Othello have been friends for some time. As Desdemona declares: 'you [Cassio] do love my lord, / You have known him long' (3.3.10-11). According to Desdemona the two have 'Shared dangers' together as they fought side by side in the army of Venice (3.4.93-95). It was Cassio who helped his friend win the hand of Desdemona, serving as a go-between for the lovers in the early stages of their relationship. Cassio, Othello declares, 'went between us very oft' (3.3.99).

Cassio, therefore, seems to enjoy a close relationship with Othello and it is obvious that he holds him extremely high esteem. He is often portrayed as a young and somewhat naïve officer who hero-worships his vastly more experienced commander.

He is extremely concerned when Othello's s ship is missing at sea: 'O, let the heavens / Give him defence against the elements' (2.1.44-5). He calls on the god Jove to protect 'our great captain' and bring him safely ashore. According to Cassio, Othello is such a great leader that his mere presence on the island will lift the spirits of its population and 'bring all Cyprus comfort' (2.1.82). When he drinks during the party scene he toasts Othello's health: 'To the health of our general!' (2.3.78).

His high regard for Othello is also evident after he loses his post as lieutenant. Cassio is disgusted with himself for letting Othello down: 'to make me frankly despise myself' (2.3.271-2). He shows no bitterness towards Othello for firing him, instead blaming himself for what has happened. He no longer considers himself worthy of serving such a great man: 'I would rather sue to be despised rather than to deceive so good a commander with so light, so drunken and so indiscreet an officer' (2.3.254-6).

He is so upset at letting Othello down that he doesn't sleep at all that night. First thing the following morning he attempts to arrange a meeting with Desdemona, in order that she might use her influence with Othello to get him his job back (2.3.307). He hears from Emilia that Othello has spoken well of him and will look to reinstate him as lieutenant when the time is right (3.1.42-49). Yet Cassio still pushes for this meeting with Desdemona (3.1.49-52). It seems that he is so desperate to have Othello think well of him again that he will do all he can to restore their relationship.

He restates his devotion in Act 3 Scene 4, describing how he honours Othello with 'all the office of my heart' and longs to be restored to his affections, that something might 'ransom me into his love again' (3.4.114). His mind, he says, has been filled with 'leaden thoughts' since he let Othello down (3.4.172). If he fails to mend the breach between himself and the Moor he will only sadly and reluctantly get on with his life: 'So shall I clothe me in a forced content/ And shut myself up in some other course' (3.4.116-7).

CASSIO AS LADIES' MAN

Cassio, throughout the play, is something of a ladies' man. According to Iago, he is a 'proper man', a handsome individual who is most attractive to the opposite sex (1.3.374). He stresses that Cassio has all the qualities young ladies look for: 'Besides, the knave is handsome, young, and hath all those requisites in him that folly and green minds look after' (1.3.238-40).

Cassio is something of a smooth-talking charmer. His noble upbringing has left him educated, well spoken and courteous, no doubt contributing to his polished manner. As he himself declares: 'Tis my breeding/ That gives me this bold show of courtesy' (2.1.98-99). We see evidence of Cassio the charmer when he kisses Emilia on her arrival in Cyprus (2.1.98-102).

He has used this charm to help Othello win the hand of Desdemona, smoothing over certain difficulties that emerged during their courtship. Whenever Desdemona experienced doubts or negative feelings toward Othello it was Cassio who would dispel them: 'Michael Cassio/ That came a-wooing with you, and so many a time,/ When I have spoken of you dispraisingly/ Hath ta'en your part' (3.3.70-73).

Act 3 Scene 1 reinforces our sense that women generally find Cassio an attractive and sympathetic figure. He seems confident that Emilia will arrange the meeting he desires with Desdemona, who will in turn speak to her husband on his behalf. Emilia is very willing to assist him and we learn that Desdemona has already spoken 'stoutly' in his defense. We might question if these women would show such support were Cassio was not so charming and pleasing on the eye.

Bianca's behaviour provides further evidence of Cassio's attractiveness to women. Bianca loves Cassio almost to the point of obsession. She is extremely disappointed that he hasn't visited her for a full week (3.4.165-9). Iago tells us that Bianca 'dotes on Cassio' and her behaviour toward him seems to border on that of an obsessive stalker: 'She haunts me in every place' (3.4.128). We're told how she follows him around, throwing herself at him, crying and making a general show of herself (3.4.128-136).

Cassio's relationship with Bianca is often said to reveal the darker side of his ladies' man persona because it shows him as a cruel womaniser more than a smooth-talking charmer.

We get the distinct impression that he is using Bianca, that he sees her only when it suits him. After all we learn in Act 3 Scene 4 he has stayed away for the past seven nights and makes only the vaguest commitment to visit her soon (3.4.173-4).

Their encounter here reflects poorly on him. He lies that he just on his way to visit her when he was doing nothing of the sort (3.4.166). His reassurance of love for her is also far from convincing: 'Not that I love you not' (3.4.191). Indeed, he seems ashamed to be seen with her in public and and urges her to depart before Othello sees them together: 'I think it no addition, nor my wish,/ To have him see me womaned' (3.4.188-9).

He also speaks to her very severely throughout the scene. He criticises her harshly when she suggests that the handkerchief is a token from some other lover: 'Go to woman!/ Throw your vile guesses in the devil's teeth' (3.4.179-80). He roughly orders her to leave him alone and to make a copy of the handkerchief: 'Take it and do't, and leave me for this time' (3.4.196).

He treats Bianca even more harshly in the following scene, bitterly making fun of her behind her back. He finds her devotion to him amusingly pathetic: 'Alas, poor rogue! I think i'faith she loves me' (4.1.109). He mockingly describes how she follows him around, draping her arms around his neck as she weeps and shakes with emotion (4.1.133-4).

He believes he is above Bianca and finds the idea of marrying such a woman laughable and an insult to his intelligence: 'I marry – what, a customer? Prithee bear some/ Charity to my wit (117-8). His lack of regard for her is evident in his use of numerous unpleasant and insulting names, such as 'caitiff', 'customer', 'monkey', and 'fitchew'. He coldly speaks of ending their relationship: 'I must leave her company' (138).

Cassio, then, may have little respect for Bianca but he is clearly not finished using her. He greets her arrogantly when she arrives with the handkerchief. Yet when he realises the extent of her anger he acts the 'nice guy' once again: 'How now my sweet Bianca? How now? How now?' (150-1). To Cassio, then, Bianca is little more than a 'bauble', a pretty but ultimately worthless distraction to be toyed with for a while then cast aside (4.1.130). In his dealings with her he comes across as a heartless womaniser who has little respect for those he sleeps with.

WHAT ARE CASSIO'S FEELINGS TOWARD DESDEMONA?

Cassio obviously holds Desdemona in extremely high esteem. Her beauty, he declares, is almost beyond description: 'a maid/ That paragons description and wild fame' (2.1.61-2). He also refers to her as an 'exquisite lady' as 'perfection' as a 'fresh and delicate creature' (2.1.16-24). He claims that she is so perfect even the stormy ocean will calm itself to allow her safe passage to Cyprus (2.1.67-73). On her arrival at Cyprus he refers to her as 'the riches of the ship' and urges the assembled Cypriots to kneel before her (2.1.82-87).

Does Cassio, then, secretly harbour sexual or romantic longings towards Desdemona? Iago seems to think so: 'That Cassio loves her, I do well believe't' (2.1.285). As they wait nervously on the quayside for news of Othello's vessel, Cassio holds Desdemona's hand in an attempt to comfort her (2.1.163). Iago convinces Roderigo that this display of courtesy suggests the sexual tension that exists between the two (2.1.256-70).

However, there is also evidence to suggest that his feelings towards Desdemona are strictly honourable or platonic. After all it was Cassio who helped Othello win Desdemona's affections, something he would presumably not have done if he desired her himself. He also seems delighted that the two of them are married and hopes that Othello will soon be in Cyprus so he can make love to Desdemona: 'That he may bless this bay with his tall ship/ And make love's quick pants in Desdemona's arms' (2.1.79-80).

This is also evident in Act 2 Scene 3. Iago makes several suggestions about how Desdemona is not only sexually desirable but also filled with desire herself, describing how she must be 'full of game' (2.3.14-19). Cassio, however, refuses to rise to this bait. He praises Desdemona's beauty, describing her as a 'most exquisite lady' and a 'most fresh and delicate creature' (2.3.18, 20). Yet he also praises her modesty or sexual restraint (2.3.23).

CASSIO'S WEAKNESS

Cassio is often considered to be a somewhat weak character. We are given a hint of Cassio's weakness at the very beginning of the play when Iago declares him to be an inexperienced commander who has 'never set a squadron in the field' and who has gained his knowledge of warfare from textbooks rather than the heat of combat (1.2.23-27). The suggestion, then, is that Cassio is a weak officer, unfit for the command that has been given him. (It is important to note, however, that Iago's view of Cassio may well be coloured by jealousy of his new promotion).

Cassio's weakness is particularly evident in the 'drinking scene' in Act 2, where he lets Othello down very badly. Othello asks him to make sure that the party to celebrate the destruction of the Turkish fleet doesn't get out of hand: 'Good Michael, look you to the guard tonight./ Let's teach ourselves that honourable stop,/ Not to outsport discretion' (2.3.1-3). Cassio promises to make sure that the celebrations remain decent and civilised: 'with my personal eye/ Will I look to't'. (2.3.5-6).

Cassio, however, does not make good on this committment. His weakness is evident in the appalling lack of will power he demonstrates in this scene. Though he knows that he has 'poor and unhappy brains for drinking' he is easily cajoled into having too much wine. Iago uses peer pressure to get him drunk, pressure that Cassio proves all too incapable of resisting.

Iago refers to another weakness in Cassio's character: he has a quick temper and often exhibits rashness and poor decision making when angry: 'Sir he's rash and very sudden in choler' (2.1.263). On the night of the victory celebration an inebriated Cassio is easily provoked into assaulting Montano (2.3.133-140).

By becoming drunk and quarrelsome, then, Cassio lets Othello down in several different ways. He brings chaos and disorder to Cyprus when it was his job to make sure that the celebrations passed off peacefully. His behaviour is particularly inappropriate because the town is still on a war footing. Cassio and Montano are officers of the peace and should be keeping an eye out for any renewed Turkish threat not fighting among themselves. Their concern, as Othello puts it, should be the 'court and guard of safety; not their own private quarrels (2.3.196-7).

Though the immediate Turkish threat has passed, the people of Cyprus are still nervous and uneasy: 'What, in a town of war, / Yet wild, the people's hearts brimful or fear'. By beginning a street fight, therefore, Cassio is responsible for frightening and disturbing the whole town, which could have easily led to a riot. It is unsurprising, then, that Othello condemns his behaviour as 'monstrous' (2.3.198).

Cassio is also presented as a somewhat self-obsessed and self-pitying individual. His first reaction to the brawl in Act 2, Scene 3 is concern for his own reputation: 'reputation, reputation, reputation! O, I have lost my reputation!' (2.3.242-3). His immediate response, then, is to worry about himself, not about Montano, who he has wounded, or the townsfolk he has disturbed.

Cassio's weakness is also glimpsed in Act 3 Scene 3 where he avoids confronting Othello about the possibility of getting his job back. Cassio flees as soon as he notices Othello approaching, leaving Desdemona to do the 'dirty work' of attempting to persuade Othello to take him back (3.3.29-33). In this scene, then, Cassio reveals a distinct lack of 'moral fibre'. There is something almost cowardly about the manner in which he slinks away instead of facing Othello himself. This moment of cowardice will have tragic consequences, for it allows Iago to begin manipulating Othello, planting in his mind the seeds of the suspicion that will ultimately lead him to murder his wife.

CONCLUSION

What *can* be said for Cassio, however, is that he remains steadfast in his devotion to his general. Othello has conspired with Iago to have Cassio killed. Yet after Othello's death Cassio speaks of him generously, describing him as great of heart' (5.2.359). He claims to have suspected that Othello's great sense of honour might lead him to kill himself (5.2.358). Despite being bequeathed with Othello's position as ruler of Cyprus – a seat of power that represents professional and military success – his thoughts remain with his dead commander.

EMILIA

BACKGROUND

Emilia is Iago's wife and Desdemona's maidservant. Whereas most of the play's charcters come from the nobility, Emilia and Iago belong to the lower classes.

EMILIA AS A 'WOMAN OF THE WORLD'

Emilia comes across as someone who has much experience of life's ups and downs and has a realistic and sometimes cynical view of relationships. Her negative view of the relations between men and women is perhaps most evident when she declares that: 'They are all stomachs, and we are all but food; / They eat us hungerly, and when they are full, / They belch us' (4,3.98-100). According to Emilia, men treat women like tasty snacks that are to be quickly consumed and just as quickly forgotten.

Whereas a sheltered noblewoman like Desdemona has difficulty even saying the word 'whore', Emilia has no such qualms (4.2119-20). Desdemona innocently wonders if unfaithful wives actually exist: 'I do not think there is any such woman' (81). Emilia cynically suggests that the world is full of such adulterous wives (4.3.82-3) Desdemona could never imagine being unfaithful to her husband: 'Beshrew me, if I would do such a wrong / For the whole world' (4.3.76). Emilia, on the other hand, would sleep with another man in order to secure her husband power and prestige: 'who would not make her husband a cuckold to make him a monarch?' (4.3.72-3).

Emilia declares that women are only unfaithful because men have shown them the way: 'The ills we do, their ills instruct us so' (4.3.100-1). She criticises the double standard according to which women must remain pure and faithful while men are allowed to fool around. Women, after all, are subject to the same desires that effect their men folk: 'Their wives have sense like them; they see and smell,/ And have their palates both for sweet and sour' (4.3.92-3). Women, like men, experience frailty, love and the desire for pleasure. Is it any wonder, therefore, that if men stray women will too?

Emilia has a profound understanding of the nature of jealousy. She realises that jealousy can appear without cause in a person's mind and remain there, festering dangerously: 'Tis a monster / Begot upon itself, born on itself' (3.4.153-6). She appreciates that, all too often, jealous thoughts cannot be dislodged by means of rational explanation: 'But jealous souls will not be answered so;/ They are not ever jealous for the cause,/ But jealous for they're jealous' (3.4.154-6). She urges Desdemona to pray Othello hasn't fallen prey to this dangerous emotion (3.4.159).

Emilia is also intelligent and quick-witted. She is quick to realise that Othello's changed attitude toward Desdemona stems from jealousy: 'Is not this man jealous?' (3.4.93). She is the only character who suspects that 'some busy and insinuating rogue' has planted these notions in Othello's head. (4.2.128-32). She rightly suspects that this 'base notorious knave' is attempting to corrupt Othello's mind in order to gain power for himself.

Several critics have suggested that Emilia may have some inkling that her own husband Iago is in reality the 'knave' who has poisoned Othello's mind. Other readers dispute this, however, pointing to the fact that she seems reluctant to believe Iago's guilt in the final scene and seems shocked to discover that he is, after all, the villain of the piece: 'He says that thou tolds't him his wife was false./ I know thou dids't not, thou'rt not such a villain' (5.2.171-4).

An interesting question relates to whether Emilia actually slept with Othello. According to Iago it's rumoured that she did so: 'And it is thought abroad,/ that 'twixt my sheets He has done my office' (1.3.385-6). Emilia has dismissed his suspicions, claiming they are the result of jealousy and malicious rumour-mongering: 'Some such squire he was/ That turned your wit the seamy side without/ And made you to suspect me with the Moor' (4.2.146-8). Yet her attitude towards

infidelity suggests that she might indeed have slept with Othello, perhaps to gain her husband advancement in the army.

EMILIA'S KINDNESS

Throughout the play Emilia comes across as an essentially decent person. She comforts Cassio when he comes to visit Desdemona after losing his post as lieutenant: 'Good morrow, good lieutenant; I am sorry/ For your displeasure; but all will sure be well' (3.1.39-40). She also arranges for Cassio to spend some time alone with Desdemona so he can plead his case to her: 'I will bestow you where you shall have time/ To speak your bosom freely' (3.1.53-54). Her concern for him is also evident after his wounding by Iago: 'Alas, good gentleman! Alas, good Cassio!' (5.1.115).

PROTECTIVE AND LOYAL

Throughout the play Emilia is extremely loyal toward and protective of her mistress. She defends Desdemona when Othello asks her if she has seen anything untoward taking place. Emilia stresses that the friendship between Desdemona and Cassio is entirely innocent: 'But then I saw no harm, and then I heard/ each syllable that breath made up between them' (4.2.4-5).

She attempts to convince Othello that his suspicions are groundless, declaring that if any woman is faithful Desdemona: 'if she be not honest, chaste, and true,/ There's no man happy: the purest of their wives/ Is foul as slander' (4.2.16-18).

She is highly critical of the cruel manner in which Othello treats Desdemona: 'He called her 'whore': a beggar in his drink/ Could not have laid such terms upon his callat./ Why did he so?' (4.2.120-1). She is distraught that Desdemona has given up so much to be with Othello only to be treated by him in such a terrible fashion: 'Would it not make one weep?' (4.2.124-6).

She adopts a similar tone in Act 4 Scene 3. She seems uneasy that Othello has asked for her to be dismissed as if she doesn't feel safe leaving her mistress with her enraged husband: 'Dismiss me?' (4.3.12). She laments once again that Othello has treated Desdemona so cruelly: 'I would you had never seen him'(4.3.16). She joins Desdemona in wistfully thinking about Lodovico, who she no doubt feels would have made a better match for her mistress (4.3.35-6).

Emilia's loyalty is strongly in evidence after Desdemona's death in the final scene. When she sees Desdemona's dead body she expresses genuine grief and fondness for her: 'Help, help, ho, help! O lady, speak again! / Sweet Desdemona, O sweet mistress, speak!' (5.2.123-4).

In her grief and anger she defies Othello himself. She likens Desdemona to an angel and bravely – perhaps recklessly – brands Othello a demon: 'O, the more angel she, and you the blacker devil!' (5.2.133). Othello's threats are meaningless to her. Her repeated insults ("filthy bargain", "O gull, o dolt, as ignorant as dirt") provoke him, but fear does not seem to be able to penetrate her veil of sadness and anger. She is determined to reveal what Othello has done: 'I care not for thy sword, I'll make thee known' (5.2.166).

She is fiercely protective of Desdemona's memory. When Othello sets out her alleged crimes and faults, Emilia jumps without any hesitation to her defence (136-7). She repeatedly condemns Othello for the murder and continues to protest that Desdemona was the 'the sweetest innocent / That e'er did lift up eye' (5.2.199-200).

Emilia's loyalty towards Desdemona is evident even after she's fatally stabbed by her husband. In a final poignant gesture of respect toward her mistress, she asks to be laid next to Desdemona and dies singing the Willow Song.

EMILIA AND THE HANDKERCHIEF

While Emilia is generally considered to be one of the play's more likeable characters, she too commits an act of betrayal when she gives Desdemona's handkerchief to Iago (3.3). Emilia is fully aware that the loss of the handkerchief will cause Desdemona great distress: 'Poor lady, she'll run mad / When she shall lack it' (3.3.318-19). Yet she still steals this most precious love token and later denies all knowledge of its whereabouts (3.4.20).

In Emilia's defence, however, she seems to have no inkling of the terrible mischief Iago intends to cause with the handkerchief: 'What will he do with it, heaven knows, not I' (3.3.300). She betrays her mistress simply to please her husband, who has continually pleaded with her to steal it (3.3.294-295). It is Emilia's tragedy that this fairly minor act of betrayal will lead, indirectly, to the deaths of both herself and Desdemona.

An interesting feature of the play is the shift in Emilia's loyalties. In the early part of the play her loyalty is divided between her mistress and her husband: we see this when she gives Iago the handkerchief. As the play proceeds toward its grim conclusion, however, she begins to side exclusively with her mistress. Indeed, it has often been suggested that her reckless determination to expose Othello as Desdemona's killer and Iago as his puppeteer stems from her guilt at having taken the handkerchief in the first place.

SPIRITED AND INDEPENDENT

While Emilia is devoted, she is no lap dog. She has a fiery streak and we see this when she openly criticises Othello to his own wife (4.3.16). This fiery temperament in also in evidence when she criticises the 'eternal villain' who has been poisoning Othello's mind: 'Some busy and insinuating rogue, / Some cogging, cozening slave, / To get some office, Have not devised this slander' (4.2). Little does she suspect, of course, that her own husband is the 'rogue' in question.

She repeatedly defies the conventions of the time, particularly the double standard by which women were expected to be 'seen and not heard' and to obey their husbands in all things. We see this in her bold and insightful speech about sexual morality, where she stresses that women, too, are sexual beings and are subject to the same impulses and desires that affect men.

Emilia's strong-willed and assertive nature is nowhere more evident than in the play's final scene, especially when she repeatedly criticises Othello for the terrible act he has committed. It is hugely risky of Emilia to do this – not only does she ignore social etiquette by speaking out of turn and disrespectfully to an honoured man, she also ignores her own safety by doing so with an armed and experienced soldier who has just murdered his own wife.

Her assertiveness is also evident when she realises that it was her husband who planted doubts about Desdemona's integrity in Othello's mind. It comes to the fore when she realises how the handkerchief was used to advance this deception. She is determined to expose Iago as a villain and perseveres bravely, defying societal norms again and again by speaking out against her husband's wishes: "Tis proper I obey him, but not now' (5.2.197).

Emilia pays with her life for this crusade. Iago loses his patience and stabs her, but by then she has succeeded in getting justice for her friend. Othello has been exposed as Desdemona's killer and Iago as a master puppeteer who has deceived them all.

There is an interesting contrast between Desdemona and Emilia in this final scene, where each is murdered by her husband. Desdemona is meekly obedient to her husband even when he's in the process of killing her. Emilia, on the other hand, is stabbed to death because she defies her husband openly and brings his plotting to light. Desdemona, it could be argued, dies because she is too obedient to her husband, Emilia because she is too spirited and disobedient.

DESDEMONA

BACKGROUND

Desdemona is a picture of Elizabethan perfection. Beautiful and fundamentally pure of heart, she embodies many of the lofty female virtues that were championed by the moral and political figures of Shakespeare's era.

BEAUTY AND PURITY

Desdemona, it seems, has had a sheltered and privileged upbringing, so much so that she had never seen a black person and was frightened by Othello's appearance the first time she met him (1.3.96-100). Iago speaks of how she would 'shake and fear' Othello's appearance when he first began to visit her father's house (3.3.210). Her father describes her as a quiet, gentle and timid girl: 'A maiden never bold' (1.3.96). Perhaps Desdemona's sheltered background made her more likely to be won over by Othello's exotic background and colourful tales of faraway lands.

Desdemona's beauty is often mentioned in the play. Cassio lavishes praise on her comely appearance: 'a maid/ That paragons description and wild fame' (2.1.63-4). He considers her an 'exquisite lady', 'a most fresh and delicate creature' and 'perfection' (2.3.18, 20, 24). She is the object of Roderigo's obsession. Iago, too, admits that he lusts for her 'Now I do love her too'(2.1.290). There is also the possibility that Cassio has feelings for her as well. He believes that she is 'indeed perfection' (2.3.24) and talks of how the seas calmed and parted for 'The divine Desdemona' (2.1.75).

Othello speaks of her beauty, both inner and outer. However, as the play progresses the Moor becomes convinced that his wife's inner purity is a sham and that her physical beauty is a trap that attracts, ensnares and destroys the men who feast upon it. At first he finds it hard to imagine that someone so innocent could ever be dishonest: 'If she be false, O then heaven mocks itself' (3.3.281). However, he soon starts to believe Iago when he says that Desdemona is deceitful: 'She that, so young, could give out such a seeming/ To seal her father's eyes up' (3.3.212-3). He says that he believes his wife to be 'honest', but quickly changes his opinion (3.3.386). It is not long before his mind is filled with coarse images of Desdemona sleeping with other men and her name which once represented all that was pure and good in the world, has become tarnished: 'Her name, that was as fresh/ As Dian's visage, is now begrimed and black/ As mine own face' (3.3.388-90).

INNOCENT AND NAIVE

Desdemona seems at times to be naïve, especially when it comes to marital relationships. She is besotted with her new husband and believes passionately in the worth of their marital vows. She places huge faith in fidelity, holding absolute and uncompromising beliefs about romantic relationships as well as what's right and wrong. She proclaims idealistic viewpoints with the kind of fire that only inexperience can breed. At one point she asks Emilia if it is possible that a woman would cheat on her husband: 'dost thou in conscience think – tell me, Emilia, –/ That there be women do abuse their husbands/ In such gross kind?' (4.3.56-8).

We can contrast Desdemona's outlook with that of her maid Emilia. Emilia takes a more practical view of marriage. Life has taught her to accept adultery as a normal and unavoidable function of marriage. Rather than rage against it, she tries to rationalise it and understand it, suggesting that adultery is a worthy sacrifice where it has the capacity to bring a couple more power or material security (4.3.69-75). This blasé attitude horrifies innocent Desdemona (4.3.62-76). Her wholesome outlook is as much her strength as it is her weakness. She lacks the street-smart guile that we find in Emilia. Ultimately, the goodness that sets her apart from her peers is also what contributes to her death.

Desdemona's behaviour also sometimes reveals an immaturity on her part. She does not think for a moment that she might be interfering in military matters by lobbying for Cassio's reinstatement nor does she seem to show consideration for Othello's demanding role as general. Though he tells her that he is busy and cannot see Cassio immediately, she persists in her demand that he set a date: 'Not now, sweet Desdemona – some other time. / But shall't be shortly? / ... Shall't be tonight at supper?... Tomorrow dinner, then?' (3.3.56-9). Her unfortunate reference to Cassio as a 'suitor' (3.3.42) also adds to Othello's suspicions that she is unfaithful to him.

We might also characterise Desdemona's tolerance of her husband's foul and abusive behaviour as naive and innocent. She is not accustomed to being treated in this manner and her response to the abuse she receives is one of bewilderment and shock. As she says herself, she is a 'child to chiding' (4.2.115). She comes from a privileged background and has enjoyed a soft childhood. Unlike Emilia, who seems to be hardened against and accustomed to the ills of the world, Desdemona's innocence means that she is not equipped to deal with the sort of behaviour Othello demonstrates in the latter stages of the play.

HUMANE AND PEACEABLE

Desdemona is fundamentally a kind and decent person. Cassio refers to her as the 'virtuous Desdemona' and Iago reminds him that she's inclined to respond to any honest request that's made of her: 'She is of so free, so kind, so apt, so blessed a disposition, she holds it a vice in her goodness not to do more than she is requested' (2.3.318, 308-11). In his final soliloquy, Othello describes how Desdemona is as generous and giving as nature itself: 'She's framed as fruitful / As the free elements' (2.3.327-8). She seems to genuinely want to do her best for Cassio, promising the former lieutenant that she will do everything in her power to convince Othello to reinstate him: 'I will do / All my abilities in thy behalf' (3.3.1-2). She tells him that when she makes a promise to a friend she does everything she can to keep it: 'If I do vow a friendship, I'll perform it / To the last article' (3.3.21-2).

Even when she is struggling to cope with her husband's erratic and violent behaviour, Desdemona remains tolerant, understanding and forgiving. Though the most hateful terms are hurled at her, she tries to understand her husband and get to the root of what is bothering him: 'Alas, what ignorant sin have I committed?' (4.2.70). No matter how unkindly Othello treats her she insists that his behaviour will not spoil the love she feels for him: 'his unkindness may defeat my life, / But never taint my love' (4.2.161-2). When Emilia suggests that some evil person might be feeding Othello false stories, Desdemona says that if this is the case she can forgive her husband all: 'If any such there be, heaven pardon him' (4.2.136). Though she is suffering intensely and is feeling exhausted, when Othello weeps she looks to comfort him: 'Alas, the heavy day! Why do you weep? / Am I the motive for these tears my lord?' (4.2.42-3).

When in the final scene of the play, Desdemona understands that Othello intends to kill her, she makes some effort to defend herself and convince him that he has no reason to doubt her, but her efforts are weak and achieve nothing. It is almost as if she has accepted her fate, even though she can see no reason for having to die. When Othello tells her that she must die her response is one of resignation: 'Then Lord have mercy on me' (5.2.59). Perhaps there was little or nothing that she could have done to save her life, but she does not even make the effort to scream or fight. It is interesting to contrast her behaviour with that of Emilia who is not shy about challenging Othello and screaming 'murder' when she realises what he has done.

Desdemona also functions as something of a solitary but persistent peacekeeper at various points in the play. The world the characters inhabit is awash with pockets of conflict and – whether by accident or design – Desdemona is often caught in the middle of it and spurred on to broker the peace. She is portrayed as a soothing influence whose presence alone can quell storms and settle battles: 'Tempests themselves, high seas, and howling winds / The guttered rocks and congregated sands...As having sense of beauty, do omit / Their mortal natures, letting go safely by / The divine Desdemona' (2.1.70-5).

She skilfully pacifies her father by calmly explaining her decision to marry Othello avoids situations that could cause further angst – for example by leaving her father's house so as not to aggravate him: 'Nor I; I would not there reside' (1.3.243). Desdemona is very sympathetic to Cassio after Othello demotes him for his drink-fuelled behaviour. She recognises that he is genuinely remorseful and immediately volunteers to intercede on his behalf: 'Do not doubt, Cassio,/ But I will have my lord and you again/ As friendly as you were' (3.3.5-7).

On any of the occasions where Othello confronts her about the handkerchief or Cassio, Desdemona always attempts to assuage his anger. She is a pacifist and chooses not to engage or fight back in fraught situations because she does not think it will resolve anything. It is simply not part of her belief system. This is also highlighted in her conversation with Emilia about adultery: 'God me such uses send,/ Not to pick bad from bad, but by bad mend' (4.3.102-3).

DESDEMONA'S JOURNEY - SPIRITED TO SUBMISSIVE

In the early stages of the play Desdemona comes across as strong-willed and assertive. Although she comes from a privileged background, she is no mere gentle princess. Here is a young girl, the daughter of respected Venetian nobility, admitting to having secretly entered into a controversial marriage with a foreign soldier of the state. She is radical but also demonstrates immense poise. When her marriage is unceremoniously pushed into the public spotlight, she appears completely unruffled. Her father's malcontent does not surprise her – or even seriously upset her. She acknowledges all that her father has done for her but asserts that her loyalty now rests with her husband: 'To you I am bound for life and education;/ My life and education both do learn me/ How to respect you; you are the lord of duty;/ I am hitherto your daughter: but here's my husband' (1.3.181-5). She is also forthright in her desire to accompany Othello to Cyprus and even though she asks for permission to do this, we get the impression that she is merely extending Brabantio a courtesy rather than waiting for his approval: 'Let me go with him' (1.3.260).

Desdemona also proves a worthy verbal sparring partner for Iago when they initially arrive in Cyprus, simultaneously encouraging and playfully criticising his bawdy rhymes (2.1.104-65). She also seems unfazed and unembarrassed by this somewhat crude banter of the men sitting around in the 'alehouse' (2.1.142). She is something of a playful and fun-loving spirit. She tells Cassio that she will 'tame' her powerful husband and turn their bedroom into a schoolroom and their

lodgings into a confessional until Othello agrees to her demands: 'His bed shall seem a school, his board a shrift' (3.3.24). When Othello appears she seems to tease him by telling him she has just been talking to a 'suitor' (3.3.42). She then playfully harasses him to meet with Cassio as soon as possible: 'Why then tomorrow night, or Tuesday morn,/ On Tuesday noon, or night, or Wednesday morn' (3.3.61-2).

Unfortunately Desdemona undergoes a significant transformation over the course of the play. When Othello begins to act strangely and starts to make snide and unpleasant comments, Desdemona is totally confused: 'Fire and brimstone!/ My lord?/ Are you wise?/ What, is he angry?' (4.1.227-8) She is just as bewildered when he hits her and claims that she has done no wrong: 'Why, sweet Othello!/ ...I have not deserved this' (4.1.231-2). Although she does not understand what she could have done wrong, she accepts that she must be responsible somehow for upsetting him and meekly offers to leave: 'I will not stay to offend you' (4.1.238).

Ultimately Desdemona seems to attempt to pacify Othello's anger with ever-increasing obedience and conformity, but this has only the opposite effect. The more personal power she gives to Othello, the more he abuses it, and this shifting dynamic represents a crucial turning point in their relationship. Things eventually begin to take their toll and Desdemona, exhausted and unable to defend herself, also begins to doubt her and questions whether she has not, in fact, acted in some manner that justifies being labeled a whore: 'Am I that name, Iago?' (4.2.119). In the final act, when Othello openly acknowledges his intent to kill her, Desdemona is nothing more than doleful and acquiescent: 'Talk you of killing?', 'Ay/ I do', 'Then heaven/ Have mercy on me.' (5.2.33-4). Gone is the scrappy and defiant young woman we witnessed in the early parts of the play.

THEMES

RACE

OTHELLO: A STRANGER FROM A SAVAGE LAND

Othello's racial background is obviously different to that of the Venetians he lives among. Yet skin colour is not the only difference between the Moor and those whose armies he leads into battle.

Then as now, Venice was a beautiful modern city, a place of wealth, elegance and sophistication. Othello's homeland, by contrast, is bleak and desolate, a country of enormous caves ('antres vast') and endless deserts (1.3.140) 'Rough quarries, rocks and hills whose heads touch heaven' (1.3.141).

Venice is a civilised place, a republic governed by the rule of law. Othello, on the other hand, comes from a barbaric and violent land, one peopled by cannibals and by monsters such as the dreaded 'Anthropophagi' (1.3.143-5). Warfare is all he knows: 'And little of this great world can I speak, / More than pertains to feats of broil and battle' (1.3.88-9). From an early age, it seems, he was involved in 'battles, sieges, fortunes' and was at one point even sold into slavery (1.3.130).

To many of the Venetians he lives among, then, Othello must seem a savage stranger from a savage land. We can imagine them viewing him as a primitive creature, a beast whose ferocity could be employed against their enemies but who was ultimately to be treated with contempt and mistrust.

Perhaps the great elegance with which Othello speaks is an attempt to disprove this viewpoint. He makes a great show of describing himself as a simple and uneducated man whose speech is 'Rude' (1.3.83). This, however, is only the false modesty often associated with good public speaking. For even when Othello talks business he does so in complex and elaborate poetry.

We see this especially in his early speeches, such as those made before the council in Act 1 Scene 3, where he spins out long and winding sentences that are beautiful but also very convoluted. Perhaps he intends his intricate speechifying to compensate – or overcompensate – for his savage past. Perhaps it is meant to show the Venetian nobles that despite his origins he can match them for elegance and refinement.

BIGOTRY AND RACISM

There can be little denying that there is a strong undercurrent of racism in play. Othello, as a black man and a foreigner, encounters what can only be described as vile bigotry and the most gruesome racist attitudes.

This is evident at the very beginning of the play when Iago suggests that Othello's Moorish background makes him not only a 'devil' but also a kind of animal. Iago describes him as an 'old black ram': 'Even now, now, very now, an old black ram / Is tupping your white ewe' (1.1.88-9). He also refers to Othello as a horse: 'you'll have your daughter covered with a Barbary horse' (1.1.102). Iago, then, paints Othello as a crude and animalistic being and insinuates that he is sexually corrupting the innocent Desdemona.

Here we see Iago play on the old racist fear of miscegenation (or the intermingling of different races): 'Awake the snorting citizens with the bell, / Or else the devil will make a grandsire of you' (1.1.90-1). According to Iago if Othello and Desdemona were to have children they will be subhuman creatures: 'you'll have your nephews neigh to you; you'll have coursers for cousins and gennets for germans' (1.1.113-4).

As the play goes on Iago continues to harp on about the unnatural nature of the relationship between Othello and Desdemona. This abnormal affair, he tells Roderigo, cannot last long: 'It cannot be that Desdemona should long continue her love to the Moor…nor he his to her' (1.3.342-5).

He later suggests to Othello himself how 'rank' and 'foul' it is that Desdemona didn't do as nature intended and marry a man from 'Of her own clime, complexion, and degree' (3.3.233-5). He also suggests that Desdemona may regret or 'repent' having married the Moor and leave him for someone more like herself: 'May fall to match you with her country forms / And happily repent' (3.3.241-2). Iago, of course, is attempting to manipulate Othello here. But the fact he succeeds so easily indicates just how pervasive such attitudes were in Venice at the time.

Brabantio echoes these attitudes. He claims that the relationship between Othello and Desdemona is not a natural one. Desdemona, he says, has erred 'preposterously' and has gone against 'all rules of nature' by falling in love with a black man

(1.3.103). Desdemona, he says, should have feared Othello for his skin-colour, not fallen in love with him: 'To fall in love with what she fear'd to look on!' (1.3.100). According to Brabantio only someone with 'maim'd and most imperfect judgment' could believe this occurred naturally (1.3.101).

Brabantio's bigotry is all too evident when he refers to Othello stealing Desdemona away to his 'sooty bosom' (1.2.71-3). He plays to a negative racial stereotype when he associates Othello, as a black man, with potions, voodoo and dark magic, with 'spells and medicines' and 'mixtures powerful o'er the blood' (1.3.61-2, 106).

Even the Duke's suggestion that Othello's virtues make him 'fair' rather than black, that he is somehow white on the inside, is a reminder of the casual racism that pervades Venetian society: 'And, noble signior, If virtue no delighted beauty lack, / Your son-in-law is far more fair than black' (1.3.290-1). It could be argued that Emilia expresses a similar attitude when she describes Othello as a 'blacker devil' for murdering Desdemona (5.2.133).

Strangely enough, as the play goes on even Othello himself begins to express the connection between blackness and wickedness. When he begins to think of Desdemona as impure or treacherous he describes how she has been 'blackened' in his eyes: 'Her name, that was as fresh / As Dian's visage, is now begrimed and black / As mine own face' (3.3.388-390). In Act 5 Scene 1 he describes how her charms have been 'blotted', as if smeared with black ink: 'Forth of my heart those charms, thine eyes, are blotted' (5.1.36).

He associates the negative and destructive concept of vengeance with the colour black: 'Arise, black vengeance, from thy hollow cell' (3.3.447). At the play's conclusion, meanwhile, he seems to associate Desdemona's pale skin with the fairness or goodness of her personality. He is reluctant to stain her snow-white skin with blood: 'Yet I'll not shed her blood, / Nor scar that whiter skin of hers than snow / And smooth as monumental alabaster' (5.2.3-5).

THE ATTRACTIONS OF THE EXOTIC

If the play features racist attitudes it also highlights how people from different backgrounds can often strike us as fascinating and exotic, their very difference making them attractive. As Brabantio's guest, Othello told his life-story, which was full

of battles and crazy adventures, of daring escapes and terrible misfortunes (1.3.129-45). Desdemona was very taken with this exotic and romantic tale: 'This to hear / Would Desdemona seriously incline' (1.3.145-6).

She would rush to complete her household chores in order to hear more of Othello's story: 'She'd come again, and with a greedy ear / Devour up my discourse' (149-50). She asked Othello to stretch the story out so it lasted as long as possible, often weeping at some misfortune or 'distressful stroke' Othello had suffered during his youth (1.3.151-7). Eventually Desdemona hinted to Othello that she had fallen in love with him due to his exotic life of bravery, misfortune and resilience: 'She loved me for the dangers I had pass'd' (1.3.167). This, rather than through witchcraft, was how he won Desdemona's love (1.3.169).

THE TURKS

It could be argued that racial hatred also raises its head in the attitude of the Venetians toward their Turkish enemies. While the Turks never physically appear in the play, the threat they pose casts a long shadow over its action. The people of Venice regard the 'general enemy Ottoman' with fear and hatred.

The hatred and fear with which the Venetians regard the Turks is evident Act 1 Scene 3. An atmosphere of panic and confusion fills the council chamber as the Duke and his senators debate the size and intentions of the Turkish fleet (1.3.1-31). We get a sense that the Turks are no everyday adversary, that the incursion of their fleet fills the assembled lords with dread.

We also see this in the elation that greets the destruction of the Turkish fleet. A gentleman on the quayside joyfully describes how a 'desperate tempest hath so banged the Turks' and Othello himself echoes this happy sentiment: 'News, friends: our wars are done, the Turks are drowned' (2.1.11, 200-2). Othello orders the fleet's demise to be celebrated with a massive party, where there will be dancing, bonfires and the indulging of every vice or pleasure (2.2.1-8).

For the Venetians, to be a Turk is to be a sinner or a criminal, to be something less than human. Iago makes a similar point in Act 2 Scene 1: 'Nay, it is true, or else I am a Turk: / You rise to play, and go to bed to work' (2.1.117-9). To swear on one's status as a non-Turk is like swearing on one's reputation, or even on one's life.

We also see this in Act 2 Scene 3 when Othello upbraids those involved in the night-time brawl. Their brawling goes against the Christian values they've been brought up with: 'For Christian shame, put by this barbarous brawl!' (1.3.163). Such violent indiscipline would disgrace even their barbaric Turkish enemies: 'Are we turned Turks, and to ourselves do that / Which Heaven hath forbid the Ottomites?' (1.3.162-3).

Othello may be the victim of racism but he himself exhibits a racist attitude toward the hated Turks. At the play's conclusion he describes killing a particular Turk in Aleppo, referring to him as 'a malignant and a turbaned Turk' and as a 'circumcised dog' (5.2.359-61).

IS OTHELLO A RACIST PLAY?

Othello confronts the stereotypical view that black people are not only gullible and easily manipulated but also rash, impulsive and prone to violence. As Iago puts it: 'These Moors are changeable in their wills' (1.3.357-8). Initially the play seems to rebut these stereotypes. Though Othello comes from a foreign land he occupies a powerful and influential place in Venetian society.

He is a respected general who has won many victories and is chosen to lead the all-important defence of Cyprus. His keen intelligence is evident in the poetic and sophisticated speeches he gives before the council. He is calm, composed and assured, confidently disproving Brabantio's charges of witchcraft. As if all this wasn't enough he has managed to marry a beautiful and much-desired beauty of the city.

Yet as the play goes on the stereotype seems to be confirmed. Othello does indeed show himself to gullible and pliable, proving all too susceptible to Iago's temptations and manipulations. He also exhibits rashness and poor judgement, deciding that Desdemona is unfaithful based on only the flimsiest evidence and failing to properly investigate the matter. The murder of Desdemona, of course, suggests that he has a stereotypically violent Moorish disposition.

Indeed, Othello's final speech suggests that he views himself in this light, depicting himself almost as a primitive barbarian: 'Like the base

Indian, threw a pearl away / Richer than all his tribe' (5.2.353-4). He presents himself almost as an impulsive fool who allowed himself to be governed by passion and emotion rather than reason, describing how he was 'Perplex'd' and 'loved not wisely but too well' (5.2.350-2).

Many modern critics have described *Othello* as a racist play, one that reinforces a negative racist stereotype. Others, however, disagree, viewing the world of the play as racist rather than the drama itself. The play, they suggest, is a largely positive depiction of an interracial marriage, albeit one doomed to fail in the racist climate of Venice.

One the play's most bitter ironies comes in the way Iago uses Othello's insecurities to manipulate him. Iago, as we've seen, plays upon Othello's status as an outsider in Venice and on the racial differences between him and Desdemona. He sows the seeds of doubt that the relationship cannot last, that Othello doesn't understand Venetian women, that Desdemona must eventually leave him and marry someone from her own background. To a large extent, then, it is through Othello's insecurity regarding his racial status that he fulfills the negative racial stereotype described above.

IDENTITY

OTHELLO

To a large extent Othello's sense of self is related to his life as a soldier. He is keenly aware that he's an experienced and hardened warrior whose origins lie in a hard land far from the prosperous, European city of Venice. He describes his country of origin as a bleak and dangerous place, a country of enormous caves ('antres vast') and endless deserts (1.3.140). It is a rugged, mountainous land peopled by bizarre and fantastic races like the cannibalistic 'Anthropophagi' (1.3.141-5).

He seems proud that warfare is all he knows: 'And little of this great world can I speak, / More than pertains to feats of broil and battle' (1.3.187-8). He tells the assembled councilors that since he was seven years old he's known little but the 'tented field' of various warzones (1.3.84-6). He's experienced 'battles' and 'sieges', disasters and 'hair-breadth' escapes, and at one stage was even captured by his enemies and sold into slavery (1.3.130-9). There is surely both pride and resignation when he describes how warfare for him has become a matter of routine, indeed almost of comfort: 'The tyrant custom, most grave senators, / Hath made the flinty and steel couch of war / My thrice-driven bed of down' (1.3.229-31).

Yet Othello thinks of himself as more than a savage swordsman from a barbaric land. He is keenly aware of himself as an accomplished strategist and general, as a commander whose leadership has been most valued by the Venetian state: 'My services which I have done the signiory' (1.2.18). We see this when the Duke declares that Othello should lead the defense of Cyprus: 'opinion, a sovereign mistress of effects, throws a more safer voice on you' (1.3.234-6). Othello, we're told, knows the island's fortifications better than anyone – an indication of his vast military experience (1.3.222-3).

As a commander he is keenly aware of discipline, order and duty. Having survived a storm at sea, he disembarks at Cyprus and proceeds immediately to the castle, presumably to begin taking care of government and military business (1.3.300). He is adamant that the order be maintained on the island even during the party to celebrate the loss of the Turkish fleet: 'let's teach ourselves that honourable stop / Not to out-sport discretion' (2.3.2-3).

Othello reveals himself to be a stern and fearsome general when the brawl breaks out between Cassio and Montano. He arrives and immediately imposes his authority upon the situation, threatening to kill the next man who dares to move: 'He that stirs next to carve for his own rage / Holds his soul light: he dies upon his motion' (2.3.164-5). He is horrified at the breakdown of discipline this brawl represents and doesn't hesitate to punish the man responsible, stripping his good friend Cassio of his position as lieutenant (2.3.240).

However, Othello is not only a fighter – he is a lover too. His love for Desdemona is especially evident when he safely docks at Cyprus and declares he could die happy having seen her face once more: 'If it were now to die, / 'Twere now to be most happy; for I fear / My soul hath her content so absolute' (2.1.188-90). It is only for Desdemona that he would give up the freewheeling ways of the bachelor soldier: 'But that I love the gentle Desdemona, / I would not my unhoused free condition / Put into circumscription and confine / For the sea's worth' (1.2.26-8).

There is perhaps a sense in which Othello's love for Desdemona 'softens' him, compomising or undermining his identity as a warrior. He finds himself doting on her in public rather than speaking in his usual fashion of a hardened general: 'O my sweet, I prattle out of fashion, and I dote / In mine own comforts! (2.1.204-6). Othello is a self-reliant man who's survived countless battles and who from the age of seven had to fend completely for himself. Yet falling in love with this beautiful young woman has left him psychologically vulnerable in a way he's never been before. For if their love somehow fails he will be left in a terrible emotional state: 'But I do love thee! And when I love thee not, / Chaos is come again' (3.3.92-3).

As Othello falls under Iago's spell his identity, both as a soldier and as lover, begins to rapidly collapse. Desdemona hauntingly captures this loss of identity, memorably describing the change in personality that has suddenly struck her husband: 'My lord is not my lord' (3.4.120). Iago himself makes a similar point: 'The Moor already changes with my poison' (3.3.327).

Act 4 Scene 1 finds Othello's behaving in a most unsoldierly fashion. He agrees to Iago's suggestion that he spy on Cassio's conversation: Do but encave yourself, / And mark the fleers, the gibes, and notable scorns, / That dwell in every region of his face' (4.1.78-80). Such skulking and underhanded behavior is unbecoming of this fearsome warrior. Furthermore, given that Othello has lived his whole life as a soldier we might expect him to confront Cassio directly about his alleged misdeeds, or at the very last challenge him to some kind of duel, rather than sneakily conspiring to have him assassinated.

His identity as a soldier decays further during his conversation with Lodivico. This is Othello's superior officer, a senior representative of the state he serves so proudly. Yet Othello greets him in a most inappropriate fashion. He curses, hits Desdemona and makes several statements that must strike the recently arrived Lodivico as bizarre (4.1. 227, 231). This general, who values discipline so highly, sees his own discipline collapse, welcoming and cursing at his commanding officer in the very same breath: 'You are welcome, sir, to Cyprus. – Goats and monkeys!' (4.1.254).

A similar point can be made about the attempt on

Cassio's life in Act 5 Scene 1. When the previous brawl broke out Othello was quick to intervene, rising from bed to impose his authority, put paid to the 'monstrous' in-fighting and restore order to the town. In Act 5 Scene 1, however, Othello does nothing to quell this fresh disturbance of the peace. He wanders through the scene in a distracted fashion, his mind focused completely on Desdemona's death (5.1.32-37). He is still the island's commander but is in complete dereliction of his duties.

After Desdemona's murder Othello's identity as a soldier disappears completely. It's as if committing this terrible act robs him of his will to fight. He attempts to kill Iago but Montano disarms him, seemingly without too much trouble. He tells Gratiano that he was once capable of cutting through swathes of his enemies but now feels incapable of resisting a single assault: 'Man but a rush against Othello's breast, / And he retires' (5.2.275-6).

His identity as a lover, too, is no more, for he has turned against and killed the very woman he loves. He captures the unbearable hollowness this brings: 'of one whose hand, / Like the base Indian, threw a pearl away / Richer than all his tribe' (5.2.352-4). By this point Othello feels like a person completely without identity. He is in a real sense no longer himself: 'That's he that was Othello: here I am' (5.2.298).

His final speech is an attempt to restore or salvage something of his identity. He focuses on his reputation, asking those present to depict what happened fairly and honestly, to describe him as someone 'not easily jealous' and who 'loved not wisely, but too well' (5.2.350-1). This echoes Cassio's earlier comments about reputation, which he presents as being at the very centre of his identity and sense of self: 'Reputation, reputation, reputation! O, I have lost my reputation. I have lost all the immortal part of myself, and what remains is bestial' (2.3.253-6).

As he prepares to take his own life Othello's identity rests on the one thing that no one can take from him; the battles he has fought and won on behalf of the Venetian state: 'I have done the state some service, and they know't' (5.2.345). Fittingly his last words describe how he once killed a Turk who beat a Venetian and 'traduced' or shamed the state of Venice (5.2.359-62). In the end this record of service is all Othello can cling to.

IAGO

If Othello's sense of identity decays throughout the action of the play, Iago, it seems, never had one to begin with. The shifting chameleon-like nature of his identity is summed up in the haunting phrase: 'I am not what I am' (1.1.64).

Iago seems convinced that human beings can reshape their interior lives, that through the force of our own wills we can reshape the nature of our emotions, thoughts and perhaps even our personalities. Iago views all emotions, including even love, as mere bodily functions that can be controlled by the exercise of will: 'Virtue! a fig! 'tis in ourselves that we are thus or thus. Our bodies are our gardens, to the which our wills are gardeners' (1.3.319-21). A strong-willed person, then, can reshape the garden of emotions as he wishes, cultivating for himself a whole new personality.

Othello, as we've seen, defines himself to a great extent by service and by duty. Iago has no truck with such notions. He may serve as Othello's ensign but does so only to further his own ends: 'following him, I follow but myself. / Heaven is my judge, not I for love and duty, / But seeming so for my particular end' (1.1.58-9).

Reputation, too, means nothing to him. Both Othello and Cassio, as we've seen, define themselves largely through how others see them, through the stock in which they're held by fellow soldiers. According to Iago, however, the only estimation that should matter to a man is his own: 'You have lost no reputation at all, unless you repute yourself such a loser' (2.3.261-2).

Indeed, Iago is determined that his shifting inner self remains hidden, secret and unknowable. His goal is that his 'outward action' will never reveal 'native act and figure of my heart' (1.1.60-1). We see this determination, too, when he refuses to let Othello know what's on his mind: 'You cannot, if my heart were in your hand; / Nor shall not, whilst 'tis in my custody' (3.3.166-7).

By the end of the play, Othello attempts to reassert his sense of self through a moving speech. Iago, by contrast, asserts his through silence. Though the game is very much up, he refuses to reveal the motivations behind his destructive gamesmanship: 'Demand me nothing: what you know, you know; / From this time forth I never will speak word'

(5.2.309). This is the paradoxical essence of Iago's identity; he is most himself when refusing to let us know what that self really is: 'I am not what I am'.

CLASS DIFFERENCE

Class distinction plays a significant role in *Othello* and is one of many powerful drivers of Iago's behaviour. The play is littered with characters from opposing ends of the class spectrum and when they commingle, the results can be unpredictable. We will see that there are distinct character hierarchies in the play and these tend to remain in place regardless of how personal a relationship seems to be:

DESDEMONA AND EMILIA
Lower/middle class Emilia maintains a caring friendship with Desdemona, but she is also Desdemona's attendant – a position that is explicitly made known to the audience by Othello in Act 1 Scene 3 (:'Honest Iago,/ My Desdemona I must leave to thee;/ I prithee let thy wife attend on her') (1.3.295-7). When Desdemona is getting ready for bed in Act 4 Scene 3, Desdemona is not shy about issuing instructions to Emilia ('give me my nightly wearing and adieu', 'prithee unpin me', etc.) Similarly, we see Emilia sometimes 'report' to Desdemona: 'I have laid those sheets you bade me on the bed' (4.3.20).

Although they are close, even sisterly, it is not always a relationship of equals and, at times, the conversation takes on the sort of business-like tone that is shown above. However, this tends not to cause any strain however, because Emilia is of a lower class than Desdemona, and so the hierarchy is expected. Emilia despairs at Desdemona's choice of husband. She knows that a senator's daughter could have any number of socially-appropriate suitors – including Lodovico, who is mentioned in Act 4 Scene – and she frequently reminds us of this: 'Hath she forsook so many noble matches,/ Her father, and her country, and her friends,/ To be called a whore? Would it not make one weep?' (4.2.126-8).

CASSIO AND IAGO: LIEUTENANT VS ENSIGN
The play opens with Iago expressing dissatisfaction at Cassio's promotion to lieutenant ahead of him. Iago imagines himself to be a victim of class discrimination, raging that Cassio, 'the bookish theoric', does not deserve to rise to the office of lieutenant when he himself has been labouring on the battlefied for years as Othello's ensign (a low-grade officer).

In his opening speech, he challenges Cassio's masculinity, his ability as a soldier and his patriotism. He ridicules all of the things that make Cassio a member of the upper classes including his education, the quality of his experience (more theoretical than practical) and his background. As far as Iago is concerned, Cassio is a pampered book-worm who simply does not have the mettle to truly serve and protect Venice. Cassio, the Florentine, 'a great arithmetician' who knows as much about the ferocity and demands of battle as a spinster does, a man who is all brain and no brawn (1.1.18-26).

For Iago, Othello's decision to promote Cassio ahead of him is an unforgiveable slur. He considers it a personal rather than a professional selection and so it represents a dishonorable betrayal – one working-class soldier snubbing another. What Iago, in his anger, cannot see is that Cassio is a perfect foil for Othello. His academic ability and cerebral skills complement the grit and grizzle that make Othello an inspirational soldier. They can form an excellent military partnership. Cassio's upperclass background does indeed see him promoted ahead of Iago, but it is primarily because of the tactical and diplomatic competence he gained from his high-brow education. Cassio occupies an unusual position. He is of a lower military rank than Othello, but shares the same bourgeois upbringing as Brabantio and Desdemona. He shows unwavering allegiance and deference to Othello, despite their class differences. Similarly, he is the only character in the play who does not hold disprove, question or judge the socially-skewed pairing of Othello and Desdemona.

OTHELLO: FROM SOLDIER TO COMMANDER
Othello's working-class background is a key ingredient in his status as the tragic hero of this play.

Historically, high-ranking military offices were the preserve of the upper classes, which makes his unlikely rise to become a general in the Venetian army hugely impressive. Through merit and work ethic alone, Othello manages to defy the social conventions of the time.

By marrying Desdemona, the daughter of a senator, he is seen to win a mate who is more socially attractive and worthy than he. It is a contentious marriage, derided by many of those from Desdemona's class (Brabantia, Roderigo, assorted politicians, etc.) and met with bitter jealousy by those from Othello's class (Iago). Othello's romantic and military accomplishments no doubt spur others of his pedigree to dream of similar successes – and when they do not achieve the same, it can perhaps inspire the kind of resentment and begrudgery we see in Iago.

Despite his uncultivated origins, his years waging war and his lack of education, Othello carries himself with finesse and speaks eloquently. He is respected by men from all quarters of life and this makes his fall from grace all the more tragic. As Lodovico ruefully says in Act 5 Scene 2, when Desdemona's murder is revealed: 'Oh, thou Othello, that was once so good' (296).

Othello's tragedy lies in the heartbreak of him rising above his lot and tasting greatness, only to lose it all in a moment of madness and blind jealousy.

JEALOUSY AND ENVY

Envy is an emotion related to wanting or coveting something that someone else has. Jealousy is the emotion related to the fear that something you have will be taken by someone else.

Iago, for example, envies Cassio because Cassio has been appointed lieutenant, a position that Iago coveted and expected would be his. He is especially bitter about the fact that Othello choose someone who has no experience of battle: 'And what was he?/ Forsooth, a great arithmetician... a Florentine... That never set a squadron in the field' (1.1.17-21). Iago also envies Othello because the Moor has achieved the kind of success and glory that the ensign longs for.

Roderigo envies the Moor because he has won Desdemona's hand. This is particularly grating for Roderigo because he expected that Desdemona would surely have favoured marrying a white, aristocratic Venetian and not the foreign Othello: 'What a full fortune does the thick-lips owe/ If he can carry't thus!' (1.1.65-6).

It seems that Iago might also be jealous of Othello,

suspecting that the Moor has slept with his wife: 'I hate the Moor,/ And it is thought abroad, that 'twixt my sheets/ He has done my office' (1.3.384-6). The only way that he can think to address the situation is to sleep with Desdemona or at least make the Moor experience an even stronger form of jealousy: 'nothing can or shall content my soul/ Till I am evened with him, wife for wife;/ Or, failing so, yet that I put the Moor/ At least into a jealousy so strong/ That judgement cannot cure' (2.1.297-301). We get a sense of Iago's jealousy later in the play when Emilia suggests that some villain might be influencing Othello and reminds Iago that some such person once made him suspect that she was sleeping with the Moor: 'Some such squire he was/ That turned your wit the seamy side without,/ And made you to suspect me with the Moor' (4.2.146-8).

Bianca also suffers from jealousy. When she finds Desdemona's handkerchief in his room she becomes enraged and suggests to Cassio that the handkerchief 'is some token from a newer friend/ To the felt absence now I feel a cause' (3.4.176-7). Cassio tells her to 'Go to, woman!/ Throw your vile guesses in the devil's teeth,/ From whence you have them. You are jealous now/ That this is from some mistress, some remembrance' (3.4.179-82). His words are eventually enough to soothe her and fortunately Bianca does not let her jealousy get the better of her.

OTHELLO'S JEALOUSY

Is Othello jealous by nature? Prior to Iago making him suspicious of Desdemona, the Moor was happy to see her in the company of Cassio: 'Tis not to make me jealous/ To say my wife is fair, feeds well, loves company,/ Is free of speech, sings, plays and dances well;/ Where virtue is, these are more virtuous' (3.3.186-9). Just because his wife is outgoing doesn't mean that she is flirting or having affairs with other men. Also, when Iago does begin to suggest that Desdemona is being unfaithful, Othello says that he will not doubt her until he has seen proof of her infidelity: "Nor from mine own weak merits will I draw/ The smallest fear or doubt of her revolt;/ For she had eyes, and chose me' (3.3.190-2). Certainly Desdemona does not think the Moor is the jealous sort: 'I think the sun where he was born/ Drew all such humours from him' (3.4.25-6).

However, it is only when Iago starts to plant seeds of doubt in Othello's mind that we clearly see evidence of jealousy. Iago is very clever in the way he goes about this. He tells Othello to be careful of jealousy, but the warning is designed to make Othello think jealous thoughts: 'Beware, my lord, of jealousy' (3.3.168). He plants the word in the Moor's mind, knowing that it will take root and grow.

Iago gives a fine definition of what jealousy entails:

It is the green-eyed monster which doth mock
The meat it feeds on; that cuckold lives in bliss
Who, certain of his fate, loves not his wronger;
But, O, what damned minutes tells he o'er
Who dotes, yet doubts, suspects, yet strongly loves!
(3.3.168-173)

It was believed that jealousy was a bilious condition that was supposed to impart a greenish hue to the complexion. The way Iago describes it, jealousy is a brutal emotion that eats away at a person's heart. And while the heart is being consumed the person is riddled with feelings of shame: 'doth mock/ The meat it feeds on' (169-70). The 'monster' is also insatiable and the person who suffers from jealousy can know no peace. He says that if you have reason to be suspicious of the one you love, every minute of your life will become torture: 'what damned minutes tells he o'er/ Who dotes, yet doubts' (172-3). Later on Emilia speaks of the nature of jealousy, saying that it is an emotion that can arise without cause : 'But jealous souls will not be answered so;/ They are not ever jealous for the cause,/ But jealous for they're jealous. It is a monster/ Begot upon itself, born on itself' (3.4.154-7).

What causes Othello is suffer most is suspecting but not knowing. He claims to be free from jealousy and tells Iago that he will only begin to doubt when he has concrete visual proof of his wife's infidelity: "No, Iago;/ I'll see before I doubt; when I doubt, prove;/ And on the proof, there is no more but this, –/ Away at once with love or jealousy!" (3.3.192-5). But Iago is aware of the fact that the Moor will doubt and suspect in advance of receiving the 'ocular proof' he desperately wants. Othello believes he is not the jealous type but he also believes that Iago is his honest friend.

Iago tells Othello just enough to get him thinking in a jealous manner. He tells him to watch Desdemona closely, not with a jealous or suspicious eye nor with a completely trusting eye: 'Look to your wife: observe her well with Cassio,/ Wear your eye thus: not jealous, nor secure' (3.3.200-1). It is clever piece of reverse psychology

– telling someone not to be jealous whilst giving them cause to be. He later gives the Moor greater cause to be jealous when he brings the handkerchief into play. Though the handkerchief might initially seem a rather innocuous item and its misplacement hardly a cause for distress, Iago knows that the jealous mind is capable of making something significant out of nothing much: 'Trifles light as air/ Are to the jealous confirmations strong/ As proofs of holy writ' (3.3.324-6).

It is not long before Othello is overwhelmed by his jealousy. He tells Iago that his life has become hellish and that there is no respite from his jealous thoughts: 'Thou hast set me on the rack:/ I swear 'tis better to be much abused/ Than but to know't a little' (3.3.337-9). Iago does not allow the Moor a moment's peace, continuing to make insinuations about what Cassio and Desdemona might be doing in bed: 'How 'satisfied', my lord?/ Would you the supervisor grossly gape on?/ Behold her tupped?' (3.3.396-8). Eventually Othello is so overcome by imagined 'Noses, ears, and lips' that he collapses: (4.1.40).

Tragically Othello never learns how to cope with or overcome the jealousy that has taken hold of his mind. He eventually convinces himself that killing his wife is the righteous thing to do: 'She turned to folly, and she was a whore' (5.2.134). When he discovers too late that she was innocent of all that he had suspected he does not hesitate to kill himself. In his final speech he describes himself as one not easily made jealous but once agitated by the emotion, capable of becoming extremely tormented: 'Of one not easily jealous, but being wrought,/ Perplexed in the extreme' (5.2.351-2).

LOVE AND HATE

As in so many Shakespearean works, the opposing emotions of love and hate feature strongly in Othello. The ebb and flow of these powerful and conflicting feelings wreak havoc on the lives of the characters and exert huge control over how they behave.

LOVE
Love is far more manifest in the 16th century Venetian world of the play than in today's more socially reserved climate. The characters in the play are quite demonstrative. Men and women alike are effusive in the love and loyalty they bear one another, all the more so when war is waging in the background.

There are three distinct kinds of love on display in Othello:

- Romantic love (e.g. between a husband and wife);
- Platonic love (between friends); and
- Fraternal love (brotherly affection).

ROMANTIC LOVE

Most of the major characters are already married or intimately involved and though they exhibit an ardent affection to each other, romantic love remains the most fickle kind of love in the play. The newlyweds, Othello and Desdemona, are very much in love and the intensity of it drives them to face serious threats and make incredible sacrifices. Othello puts his career on the line by eloping with the daughter of an esteemed senator. Similarly, by marrying the Moor and disobeying her father's wishes, Desdemona sacrifices the only immediate family she has. Her refusal to side with Brabantio results in him severing all ties.

When Othello is sent to Cyprus to stave off a hostile Turkish fleet, Desdemona chooses to travel with him. Logic would dictate that she remain in the safe haven of Venice until the Ottomite threat has been dealt with but she insists on accompanying Othello across the seas with an armada of military vessels and personnel. Desdemona faces an anxious wait while Othello battles against stormy seas and their Turkish antagonists. They are reunited in Act 2 Scene 1 in a show of immense and emphatic joy: 'O, my fair warrior!', 'My dear Othello!' (181).

Othello, especially, is overjoyed to see her: 'It gives me wonder great as my content / To see you here before me...I cannot speak enough of this content: / It stops me here, it is too much of joy' (182-96). However, the potency of their love does not reflect its longevity. Despite all their fervour, when Othello begins to suspect his wife of being unfaithful, the relationship crashes spectacularly. Love, affection, loyalty – these sentiments disappear swiftly, leaving bitterness and fury in their wake.

Iago and Emilia are another such couple, but their marriage is waning significantly under Iago's morose and uncaring disposition. The relationship is characterised by rivalry, bickering and one-upmanship – the complete opposite of Othello and Desdemona's fanciful infatuation. Iago and Emilia's arrival in Cyprus is laced with contempt: 'Sir, would she give you so much of her lips / As of her tongue she oft bestows on me, / You'd have enough' (2.1.104-6).

This relationship transitions from bad to worse towards the end of the play. When Emilia confronts Iago about the stories he fed to Othello, she begs him to prove her wrong. Although the love in their marriage has faded to nothing more than a tiny flicker, it is enough for Emilia to feel betrayed by Iago's actions. She does not want to think that someone she loves – no matter how much or how little – could deliberately wreak this chaos and hurt on others: 'He says thou told'st him that his wife was false; / I know thou didst not – thou art not such a villain. Speak for my heart is full' (5.2.174-6).

Cassio and Bianca are the third couple in the play. Theirs is another flighty relationship. As a courtesan, Bianca fulfils all of the emotional and sexual duties of a wife in exchange for money and without a legal or religious committment. This is part of her job description and makes her far more socially significant than a mere prostitute. However, Bianca has fallen for Cassio and demonstrates a wish for it to become more than a romantic business engagement.

Although Cassio indicates that he cannot reciprocate, Bianca stands by him. While she is upset, Cassio's rebuff does not sway her love for him. When Cassio is injured, Bianca's true feelings shine through again. She is awash with concern and devotion: 'O my dear Cassio, / My sweet Cassio, O Cassio, Cassio, Cassio...Alas, he faints! O Cassio, Cassio, Cassio!' (5.1.76-84). Iago notes that she is shaking and has become pale. It is both tragic and comic that the most socially illegitimate pairing in the play is possibly the most genuine and loving.

PLATONIC AND FRATERNAL LOVE

What is noticeable in this play is that the love between friends and comrades noticeably outweighs the love between spouses. Despite all of the love he claims to have for Desdemona, Othello ultimately places his trust in his ensign – not his wife. When Othello is trying to determine the cause of Cassio's drunken brawl in Act 2 Scene 2, he looks to Iago for answers: 'Honest Iago, that looks dead with grieving, / Speak: who began this?– on thy love I charge thee!' (2.3.168-9). Similarly, in Act 3, Scene 3, Desdemona recognises the brotherly love that Cassio has for Othello: 'You do love my lord' (10). Cassio worries that Othello with forget the loyalty and devotion that he has shown him: 'My lord will forget my love and service' (3.3.18).

When Iago begins to poison Othello against his wife and lieutenant, he tries to varnish his lies with words of fraternal love: 'My lord, you know I love you' (3.3120). It seems that the characters have greater trust in their friends and comrades than in their partners. This may be because these kinds of relationships have been tested more sternly by time and circumstance. Othello would have relied on Iago and Cassio to provide him with practical and strategic support on the field of battle and these experiences would engender a strong trust. On the other hand, while Othello loves Desdemona, his time with her has been short and unproven.

Emilia and Desdemona also share a strong platonic love. As Desdemona's waiting-woman, Emilia provides support for a number of domestic and cosmetic chores. However, she is also Desdemona's confidante. Since Desdemona has been forced to abandoned her family and friends in favour of marrying Othello, Emilia also provides a source of much-needed female friendship.

Emilia offers high praise of Desdemona and is distraught when she finds that Othello has murdered her: 'O she was heavenly true!', 'For thou hast killed the sweetest innocent / That e'er did lift up eye' (5.2.137 and 201-2). Incredibly, she launches a vicious verbal assault on Othello, telling him that his supposed honour-killing is a serious sin and that he was never worthy of his wife: 'This deed of thine is no more worthy of heaven, / Than thou was worthy of her' (5.2.160-1). Her decision not to cover up her own husband's crimes in favour of getting justice for Desdemona is the ultimate sign that romantic love is not valued in the way that platonic and fraternal love is.

HATE

While the play concludes with a great number of the characters seething at one another, it can be argued that very few of them truly hate. Brabantio, to a degree, demonstrates a hateful nature in his treatment of his own daughter. When he learns that Desdemona has willingly married Othello, he claims that she has turned him off children: 'I am glad at soul I have no other child: / For thy escape would teach me tyranny, / To hang clogs on them' (1.3.196-7). Not only does Brabantio turn against her, but he actively tries to turn Othello against her too – an act of incredible spite: 'Look to her, Moor, if thou hast eyes to see: / She has deceived her father, and may thee' (1.3.293-4).

However, the only one who holds an unprovoked hate in his heart is Iago. He has a propensity for it and he feeds that propensity willingly. Where other characters are provoked to hate by external forces, Iago is the only character who welcomes it into his mind and deliberately infects others with it. And he enjoys it. He relishes the chaos he is capable of instilling in others.

He hates Cassio for being promoted ahead of him and he hates Othello for giving it to him. He embarks on a quest of disproportionate retribution and is determined to destroy the lives of those who have gone against him. This is all we know of Iago. The play begins with Roderigo remarking on the deep disdain that Iago has for Cassio: 'Thou told'st me thou didst hold him in thy hate' (1.1.6).

His narrow-minded opinion of women (2.2.113-7) indicates a mysogynistic outlook and this is compounded by the callous way in which he speaks to both Desdemona and Emilia throughout the play.

Every single thing that Iago does is done out of malice. He does not speak one true word of kindness or compassion. There is not one act or gesture that does not further his despicable objectives.

While Othello turns very quickly to hate in the latter part of the play, it is a baseless hate, one born from the immense jealousy that Iago stirs in him. He struggles with it visibly as he watches Desdemona sleep and once he realises the truth he is deeply remorseful. He is overcome with guilt and takes his own life.

Iago is quite different in this respect. When all of his scheming has been revealed, he is unrepentant – even arrogant. He stabs his wife and refuses to explain his actions. He offers no apology to Othello or Cassio.

He has been thwarted. Three bystanders (Desdemona, Emilia and Roderigo) have died in his relentless desire for revenge and he faces torture and death for his crimes. And still, he is indifferent. This is true hatred.

CHAOS AND DISORDER

STORM AND SEA

The storm described so brilliantly in Act 2 Scene 1 is an example of chaos in the natural world. Montano mentions that the tempest may well be the worst Cyprus has ever seen: 'Methinks the wind hath spoke aloud at land –/ A fuller blast ne'er shook our battlements' (2.1.5-6). One of the Gentlemen agrees with this assessment: 'I never did like molestation view/ On the enchafed flood' (2.1.16-7). He describes the storm-tossed sea as a raging beast that threatens to quench the stars themselves: 'The wind-shaked surge with high and monstrous mane/ Seems to cast water on the burning Bear/ And quench the guards of th' ever-fixed Pole' (2.1.13-15).

Montano speculates that the Turkish fleet must have been 'drowned' in the stormy conditions (2.1.17-9). Another gentleman confirms this. He has spoken to Cassio, whose ship has survived the storm and reached Cyprus safely. Cassio witnessed how the 'desperate tempest' brought 'wrack and sufferance' to the Turkish ships, forcing them to halt their invasion plans (2.1.21-4). The elements, therefore, seem to have saved Cyprus from the Turkish hordes: 'News, lads! Our wars are done' (2.1.20).

The raging chaos of the waters seems to have brought the Venetians victory over their would-be Turkish invaders. Yet the storm eerily foretells the disorder that will grip the island's commander and his circle in the subsequent days. Othello and Cassio are separated by the stormy ocean, just as they will be separated by the 'foul and violent tempest' of Iago's schemes (2.1.33-4). As Cassio puts it: 'The great contention of the sea and skies/ Parted our fellowship' (2.1.94-5). Just as Cassio lost Othello on the physical ocean, soon he will lose him to the treacherous currents of Iago's temptations: 'For I have lost him on a dangerous sea.' (2.1.47).

There is a terrible irony in this scene when Othello declares he would willingly face such terrible storms again and again if Desdemona was waiting for him at the end of each one: 'If after every tempest come such calms,/ May the winds blow till they have wakened death' (2.1.184-5). Little does he know he will soon have to face the psychological storms provoked by Iago's manipulations. Desdemona will indeed be waiting

for him at the end of this internal tempest, only for him to misguidedly take her life.

There is irony, too, in the way that Cassio describes how Desdemona's beauty is enough to calm the very waves themselves: 'Tempests themselves, high seas, and howling winds…As having sense of beauty, do omit/ Their mortal natures, letting go safely by/ The divine Desdemona.' (2.1.70-5). The tragedy, of course, is that Desdemona's good looks and admirable nature will not be enough to calm the psychological storms that will rage in Othello's mind.

There are several other instances where sea-imagery indicates rage, sorrow and inner turmoil. Brabantio compares his dismay at Desdemona's marriage to being overpowered by a devastating flood 'for my particular grief/ Is of so flood-gate and o'er bearing nature/ That it engluts and swallows other sorrows' (1.3.56-8).

Othello, meanwhile, refers to several different seas when describing the relentless nature of his desire for vengeance: 'Never, Iago. Like to the Pontic Sea,/ Whose icy current and compulsive course,/ Ne'er feels the retiring ebb, but keeps due on/ To the Propontic and the Hellespont,/ Even so my bloody thoughts, with violent pace,/ Shall ne'er look back' (3.3.454-9).

These bodies of water existed between the western powers that were allied with Venice and her sworn enemy, Turkey. The seas can therefore be viewed as murky and stormy boundaries that separate good from evil – a metaphorical battleground upon which the characters' collective and individual moral strength is tested.

Othello, indeed, seems to tell his whole sorry tale through the medium of sea-imagery. He won Desdemona's affection partly with tales of 'flood and field' (1.3.135). He loves only her and would marry no other woman 'For the seas' worth' (1.2.28). Desdemona, he then declares, was 'false as water', suggesting the tendency of liquid to shift and take on different shapes (5.2.136). Finally, as he prepares to end his life, he declares: 'Here is my journey's end, here is my butt/ And very sea-mark of my utmost sail' (5.2.272-3).

SOCIAL OR EXTERNAL CHAOS

There are also several examples of social or external chaos in the play's early scenes. In the opening scene Iago urges Roderigo to wake Brabantio in a manner designed to cause as much chaos as possible: 'Do, with like timorous accent and dire yell/ As when, by night and negligence, the fire/ Is spied in populous cities' (1.1.74-6). This has the desired effect of disturbing the city's night-time peace as Brabantio prepares to wreak vengeance on Othello for stealing his daughter away: 'Get weapons, ho!/ And raise some special officers of night' (1.1.182-3).

The brawl between Montano and a drunken Cassio in Act 2 Scene 3 provides another example. Their fight represents a serious and unacceptable breakdown of discipline by leading soldiers. Furthermore the men involved were supposed to be on guard duty at the time. To make matters worse the fight occurs in a town that is on a war-footing and facing possible invasion. The sound of swordplay and of the alarm bell ringing in the middle of the night is likely to bring terror, confusion and chaos to the town, especially if its populace think the invading Turks have arrived.

It is Iago, of course, who instigates these bouts of social unrest. There is a sense in which he relishes chaos for its own sake. Yet chaos is also the environment in which he thrives. A fluid improviser, he works best in shifting, out-of-control circumstances. His method is not to plan his misdeeds in detail, but set in motion a wave of chaos and ride it brilliantly, adjusting his goals and tactics to suit the changing conditions. This is nowhere more evident than in Act 5 Scene 1, where Iago manipulates everyone who comes on the scene of Cassio's attempted murder.

If Iago is a master of chaos then Othello is a guardian of order. He rushes from bed to break up the brawl, immediately imposes himself upon the situation and threatens the next man to move with instant death: 'He that stirs next to carve for his own rage/ Holds his soul light: he dies upon his motion' (2.3.164-5). He is horrified at the 'monstrous' breakdown of order this brawl represents and doesn't hesitate to punish the man responsible, even when that person is his good friend and right-hand man (Cassio). (2.3.208, 239-40).

Yet as Othello comes under Iago's influence he too becomes an agent of chaos. The public

disturbance in Act 5 Scene 1 is caused by the attempt on Cassio's life, an attempt that Othello himself conspired in. He brought an immediate end to the previous brawl but does nothing about this one. Instead he wanders through the scene in a distracted fashion, his mind focused completely on Desdemona's death (5.1.32-37). He is still the island's commander but does nothing to maintain its order.

It is often said that the three night-time public disturbances (Act 1 Scene 1, Act 2 Scene 3 and Act 5 Scene 1) all serve as metaphors for the chaos that engulfs Othello's mind as he becomes 'convinced' of Desdemona's infidelity. The scene in the council chamber might be added to this list, the turmoil of rumour and counter-rumour prefiguring the chaos in Othello's mind as he succumbs to the half-truths woven by Iago.

PSYCHOLOGICAL CHAOS

Othello describes how Desdemona's love is all that stands between him and a state of complete inner turmoil: 'Excellent wretch, perdition catch my soul/ But I do love thee! And when I love thee not,/ Chaos is come again' (3.3.91-3). This sentiment proves grimly prophetic. No sooner does he begin to doubt the integrity of their relationship than all tranquillity leaves him: 'Farewell the tranquil mind; farewell content' (3.3.350).

Confusion fills his mind: 'I think my wife be honest, and think she is not/ I think that thou art just, and think thou are not' (3.3.386-7). His mind is gripped by an irrational fury as he vows to tear Desdemona 'to pieces' and demands to see Cassio dead within 'three days' (3.3.432, 474-5). So chaotic does his mental state become that in Act 3 Scene 4 he begins to lose his power of speech, uttering 'The handkerchief' over and over again (3.4.87-94).

Othello, once such a fine and poetic public speaker, sees his powers of speech decay further in Act 4 Scene 1. He begins to jabber in a repetitive, chaotic and incoherent fashion: 'Pish! Noses, ears, and lips! Is't possible? Confess? Handkerchief? O, devil!' (4.1.40-1). Finally, his mind completely overcome, he lapses into some kind of trance or fit.

The increasingly chaotic state of Othello's mind does not go unnoticed by others. An anguished Desdemona is desperate for her husband to be once more the man he was (4.2.98-170). Lodovico, too, notices Othello is changed: 'Are his wits safe, is he not light of brain?' (4.1.260). When Desdemona sees him in her chamber she describes how he seems to boil with anger, jealousy and a misguided lust for vengeance: 'Alas, why gnaw you so your nether lip? / Some bloody passion shakes your very frame: / These are portents' (5.2.44-6). Indeed Othello seems to realise his own deranged state in the aftermath of Desdemona's murder: 'It is the very error of the moon; / She comes more nearer earth than she was wont / And makes men mad' (5.2.111-3).

So confused is he that he sees Desdemona's murder as some kind of religious ceremony or sacrifice: 'Thou dost stone my heart, / And makes me call what I intend to do / A murder, which I thought a sacrifice' (5.2.65-7). It is only when the terrible deed is done that his mind regains some semblance of order. He quickly realises the terrible mistake he's made: 'O fool, fool, fool!' (5.2.329). He realises all too late how Iago has poisoned and manipulated him, disordering his mind: 'Demand that demi-devil / Why he hath thus ensnared my soul and body' (5.2.306-7).

Ironically, it is Iago – the master of human psychology – who compares the human mind to a weighing scales, balanced precariously between reason and passion: 'If the balance of our lives had not one scale of reason to poise another of sensuality' (1.3.327-8). It is only reason, he declares, that controls 'our raging motions, our carnal stings, our unbitted lusts' (1.3.331-2). The play's tragedy, then, is that in Othello's case the scales of reason become defective allowing his 'raging motions' to run riot and plunge his mind, and indeed his life, into absolute turmoil.

GENDER

A PATRIARCHAL SOCIETY
The play is awash with powerful male characters – men who are socially respected and hold huge political and military clout:

- Othello is a Venetian general and an inspiring leader
- Brabantio is a well-known and revered senator
- Cassio is a lieutenant
- Montano is the Governor of Cyprus
- The Duke of Venice.

When we look at the female characters, we see that there are fewer of them and they play much more passive roles:

- Desdemona is Brabantio's daughter and Othello's wife
- Emilia is Iago's wife and Desdemona's companion
- Bianca is a courtesan.

This is a strong reflection on the relative value of men and women in Shakespeare's time. The men wield the power and the women are expected to follow and meekly obey. Men also seem to value the opinion of other men more than they do women, even their wives. Othello is far more willing to believe whatever lies Iago feeds him about Desdemona than he is to believe Desdemona – a woman he has just married and supposedly loves. This says much about Othello's view of women and his fickle sense of loyalty to his new wife.

Even Cassio, who seems to be one of the more gentlemanly characters in the play, is dismissive of Bianca. When he gives her the handkerchief to copy the design, she worries that it is a token from another lover. He finds her concerns irritating and unseemly. He dismisses them immediately, re-iterates his firm instructions to have the pattern duplicated and tells her to leave, stressing that he does not want Othello to see him 'womaned': ''Go to, woman!... Take it and do't, and leave me for this time...I do attend here on the general, / And think it no addition nor my wish / To have him see me womaned' (3.4.179-91).

WOMEN AS PROMISCUOUS AND FALSE
The women of *Othello* face an impossible situation. They are burdened with unattainable standards but receive the most severe punishments – even when ethically outperforming their male counterparts. Just about every male character in the play assumes that women are promiscuous and disloyal.

Iago offers a cutting appraisal of women as lascivious creatures who shirk their domestic duties: 'You are pictures out of doors; / Bells in your parlours; wild-cats in your kitchens...Players in your housewifery; and housewives / In your beds' (2.1.109-13). Although it is delivered in a tongue-in-cheek way, it is laced with derision. For Iago – and, no doubt, for many others – there is a kernel of truth in his description. In Act 3 Scene 3, Iago tells Othello that Venetian women are notoriously promiscuous: 'Look to't. I know our country disposition well:/ In Venice they do let God see the pranks/ They dare not show their husbands./ Their best conscience/ Is not to leave't undone, but keep't unknown' (201-4).

Brabantio perpetuates this stereotype of women as deceivers. He suggests to Othello that since Desdemona deceived her father when she eloped, she is likely to deceive her husband: 'Look to her, Moor, if thou hast eyes to see:/ She has deceived her father, and may thee' (1.3.10). Iago picks this up later in the play, again suggesting to Othello that Desdemona's deceiving her father makes her more likely to cheat on him: 'She did deceive her father, marrying you' (3.3.18). Rather than see his wife's decision to elope without her father's approval as a sign of her love for him, Othello sees it as a prelude to her infidelity.

This notion is also extended to Bianca, whose job as a high-brow escort merely substantiates the social view of women as untrustworthy and lecherous characters. According to Iago such women 'beguile' the men that they sleep with: 'tis the strumpet's plague/ To beguile many' (4.1.92-3). Ironically, such women are thought to desire the love of one man whereas women such as Desdemona are thought to be promiscuous. Iago states that women like Bianca invariably end up being deceived by the one man they fall in love with. Bianca is in fact in love with Cassio and thinks that he will marry her, but Cassio has no intention of doing this: 'This is the monkey's own giving out: she is persuaded I will marry her' (4.1.124-5). Cassio jokes about such matters when he speaks to Iago: 'when he hears of her, cannot refrain/ From the excess of laughter' (4.1.94-5).

MALE IDENTITY
Men too, are subject to being negatively typecast. In the play, any man who is seen to deviate from the norm is thought to be somehow less masculine. Cassio is a perfect case in point. Although he is Othello's right-hand man, he is perceived by Iago (and possibly by other low-ranking soldiers) as not manly enough to be their lieutenant. Iago and Roderigo look at his lack of combat experience as a sign that he is untested and, therefore, not deserving of his newly-appointed position as Othello's second-in-command. What Cassio has is academic prowess, but it is nothing more than a source of ridicule for Iago, who views it as a sign that he is soft and not cut out to for the hardness of a soldier's life. This is ironic considering Iago

himself does not have the backbone to follow through on his own words and kill Cassio – he solicits Roderigo to do it instead.

Elsewhere, we see clues that the men of the time were often unfairly pilloried and mocked for the actions of their wives. The term 'cuckold' is used several times throughout this play and is a mocking handle for men whose wives cheat. A cuckold is a source of intense social ridicule in this and other Shakespearean plays. Here is a man who is laughed at because his spouse is dishonest. Rather than be given sympathy from the audience or the public for the betrayal he has suffered, he is scorned either for not controlling his wife or for not satisfying her. This seems illogical and unfair considering that a man in this situation has not done anything wrong.

MARRIAGE
Marriage in Othello seems to be looked at as a transactional process – one where a prized possession is traded by one male owner to another. In this case, Desdemona is Brabantio's treasure and Othello is the new 'owner'. Iago, Roderigo and Brabantio all use the term 'robbed' to describe her marriage to Othello: 'You're robbed; for shame, put on your gown!' (1.1.85).

Meanwhile, Desdemona is categorised as holding the same value to Brabantio as his material possessions do: 'What ho, Brabantio! Thieves! Thieves! Thieves! Look to your house, your daughter and your bags!' (1.1.79-80). In this case it is Othello who is branded a 'thief' for taking Desdemona away from her father: 'O thou foul thief, where has thou stow'd my daughter?' (Brabantio, 1.2.64). Othello's own attitude does little or nothing to correct the view of women as possessions: 'I won his daughter' (Othello, 1.3.96). Within marriage, women are expected to be obedient and to do their husbands' bidding. Despite having defied her father to pursue her own wants, Desdemona becomes increasingly passive once she marries. Once Othello's trust in Desdemona starts to slip, he is content to order her around like a lowly foot-soldier. When she drops her handkerchief in Act 3 Scene 3, he tells her to 'let it alone', and she obeys (290-1). He instructs her to dismiss Emilia in Act 4 Scene 3 and here, too, she is keen to obey him.

DECEIT: APPEARANCE AND REALITY

Central to the play is Iago's ability to manipulate and deceive other characters, especially Othello, Cassio and Roderigo. He has every character in the play convinced that he is an honest and trustworthy person and tragically each character puts their faith in him.

IAGO DECEIVES RODERIGO

Roderigo is in love with Desdemona and Iago has convinced him that the best way to win her hand is to ply her with gifts and jewels. Iago has also convinced him that he is the best person to deliver these gifts to Desdemona and if Roderigo allows him access to his funds the ensign will ensure that he will win Desdemona's favour. Of course, Iago has been taking Roderigo's money but he has been spending it on himself and not on the gifts that he promised to buy on Roderigo's behalf.

At times Roderigo seems to almost glimpse the deception. The play opens with him challenging Iago about Desdemona's marriage to Othello. How could Iago continue to take his money to spend on gifts for Desdemona if he knew that she was going to wed the Moor: 'I take it much unkindly / That thou, Iago, who hast had my purse / As if the strings were thine, shouldst know of this' (1.1. 1-3). Later in the play Roderigo grows so frustrated with the lack of results that he again challenges Iago: 'you have told me she hath received them, and returned me expectations and comforst of sudden respect and acquaintance, but I find none' (4.2.188-91). Yet each time Iago is quick to convince him that he is wrong to doubt and that if he just holds his faith the results will be forthcoming. Roderigo is foolish enough to believe Iago again and again and in the end he pays a heavy price.

When it suits his interests to do so, Iago convinces Roderigo that something is happening between Cassio and Desdemona. The ensign tells him that Desdemona's devotion to Othello is a sham and that she is open to promiscuity. Roderigo cannot believe that the seemingly virtuous Desdemona could be like this but again Iago is able to make him believe his version of reality: 'I cannot believe that in her: she's full of most blest condition' (2.1.242). Towards the end of the play Roderigo finds himself standing in the street waiting to attack Cassio. He does not really have the heart to kill but he will go through with the attack because Iago has convinced him that this is the right thing to do: 'I have no great devotion to the deed, / And yet he hath given me satisfying reasons' (5.1.8-9).

What makes Roderigo an especially gullible character is the fact that Iago is open about who he is and what his motivations are. He tells Roderigo that he is not who he appears to be: 'I am not what I am' (1.1.66). He follows Othello because it suits his interests to do so: 'In following him, I follow but myself... not I for love or duty, / But seeming so for my peculiar end' (60-2).

He pretends to be loyal to and to love in order to get what he wants, but the love and loyalty that he displays are not genuine: 'Yet for necessity of present life / I must show out a flag and sign of love, / Which is indeed but a sign' (1.1. 155-6). Despite all this, Roderigo never fully grasps that Iago is not being straight with him.

IAGO DECEIVES OTHELLO

Iago has Othello convinced that he is his faithful friend and devoted and loyal ensign. The Moor places a lot of trust and faith in Iago's words: 'This fellow's of exceeding honesty, / And knows all qualities, with a learned spirit / Of human dealings' (3.3.261-3). Iago has him convinced that he is a moral person, someone who despises dishonesty: 'Men should be what they seem -/ Or those that not be, would they might seem none' (3.3.130-1). The ensign pretends to be appalled and upset when bad things happen. He tells Othello that he is incapable of acting in an evil manner even when the occasion seems to necessitate it: 'I lack iniquity / Sometimes to do me service' (1.2.3-4). When a fight breaks out during the first night on Cyprus, Othello turns to his ensign to find out who was responsible, never once thinking that Iago was the cause: 'Honest Iago, that looks dead with grieving, / Speak: who began this?' (2.3.168-9).

Iago knows that the Moor trusts him and uses this to his advantage: 'He holds me well: / The better shall my purpose work on him' (1.3. 388-9). When Iago tells him something the Moor gives great weight to his every word: 'these stops of thine fright me the more -/ For such things in a false, disloyal knave / Are tricks of custom, but in a man that's just, / They're close dilations, working from the heart / That passion cannot rule' (3.3.125-7).

Iago paints an unflattering picture Venetian women for Othello, in order to make him doubt Desdemona. He tells him that Venetian women are known to be unfaithful and that it is not something of which they are ashamed. As long as their husbands are unaware of their behaviour they feel no remorse: 'In Venice they do let God see the pranks/ They dare not show their husbands; their best conscience/ Is not to leave't undone, but keep't unknown'. (3.3.205-7). He also makes Othello suspicious of his wife's behaviour by suggesting that Cassio is sneaking away when the Moor approaches: 'Ha? I like not that' (3.3.33). In Act 4 he has Othello witness what he thinks is a conversation between the ensign and Cassio about Desdemona, when in actual fact they are discussing Bianca.

In each case, Iago manipulates Othello so that the Moor sees the appearance that Iago wants him to see, rather than the reality of what is actually happening. Othello initially struggles with the version of reality that Iago is presenting. How, he asks, could someone appear so virtuous and yet be dishonest: 'If she be false, O then heaven mocks itself:/ I'll not believe it' (3.3.281-2). For a while he is torn between what he thought was true and what he now must believe is true: 'By the world,/ I think my wife be honest, and think she is not;/ I think thou art just, and think thou art not' (3.3.385-7).

Othello is finally made to see the world the way Iago wishes him to see it. He thinks his wife is a 'whore' even though she is loyal and faithful and he believes his former lieutenant is sleeping with her. The Moor is convinced that both Desdemona and Cassio deserve to die. In the final scene of the play he goes to kill his wife, firm in the belief that Iago has gone to kill Cassio. When Othello hears Cassio's cry he assumes that Iago has kepth to his word and fulfilled his part of the bargain: 'The voice of Cassio: Iago keeps his word' (5.1.28). Little does he know that in reality it is Roderigo who has attempted to kill his former lieutenant and that Cassio still lives.

IAGO DECEIVES CASSIO

Cassio is yet another character who is convinced that Iago is the most honest fellow in the world. Little does he know that it was Iago who orchestrated the brawl that loses him his job and that the ensign is busy filling Othello's mind with notions that Cassio is sleeping with Desdemona. According to Cassio there is no more honest man than Iago in all of Florence: 'I never knew a Florentine more kind and honest' (3.1.40). Iago pretends to love Cassio - 'I had rather have this tongue cut from my mouth/ Than

it should do offence to Michael Cassio' (2.3.212-3) – when in actual fact he despises him, thinking him a mere 'counter-caster' and undeserving of the position of lieutenant: (1.1.30).

DESDEMONA DECEIVES HER FATHER

It is interesting how Desdemona, a symbol of virtue and honesty, begins the play by deceiving her father in marrying Othello. Brabantio is greatly upset at his daughter's behaviour: 'O, she deceives me/ Past thought!' (1.1. 166). He considers it a treasonous act and concludes that women are inherently untrustworthy: 'O treason of the blood!/ Fathers, from hence trust not your daughters' minds' (1.1. 171). He warns Othello to be careful, telling him that if his daughter deceived her father she is very likely to deceive her husband: 'Look to her, Moor, if thou hast eyes to see./ She has deceived her father, and may thee' (1.3.289-90).

Iago later cleverly reminds Othello of Brabantio's warning, suggesting to the Moor that Desdemona is not who she appears to be: 'She did deceive her father, marrying you;/ And when she seemed to shake and fear your looks,/ She loved them most' (3.3.209-11). Iago characterises her as a crafty and manipulative actress, someone who skilfully deceived her father: 'She that so young could give out such a seeming/ To seel her father's eyes up, close as oak' (3.3.212-3). Othello, initially sceptical about the notion that his wife is anything but who she claims to be, eventually begins to doubt that he knows Desdemona at all: 'Heaven truly knows that thou art false as hell' (4.2.39). Towards the end of the play his understanding of who and what is wife is has been utterly corrupted, telling her sarcastically at one point that he took her for 'that cunning whore of Venice/ That married with Othello' (4.2.90-1).

OTHELLO'S HONESTY

In contrast to Iago, Othello is an honest person. And yet, at the start of the play he is accused of deceit. Brabantio claims that he beguiled and deceived Desdemona into marrying him: 'She is abused, stolen from me, and corrupted/ By spells' (1.3.61). But Brabantio's claims are just those of an angry and disappointed father who is heartbroken at having lost his daughter. His accusations are also the result of racial prejudices against the Moor. The Othello that we mencounter at the start of the play is, in fact, transparent and open, refusing to hide when Brabantio comes looking for him: 'Not I: I must be found./ My parts, my title, and my perfect soul/ Shall manifest me rightly' (1.2.30-2).

Ultimately, however, because of Iago's machinations and schemes, Othello finds himself having to pretend to be what he is not. He speaks to Desdemona as if everything is fine whilst inside he is struggling with jealous thoughts. Such acting does not come naturally to him and he struggles to keep his true feelings concealed: 'O, hardness to dissemble' (3.4.32).

Towards the end of the play Othello acts in a manner that makes some doubt they knew him properly. When Lodovico witnesses him hit his wife he is moved to say that Othello is not the person he thought he was: 'I am sorry that I am deceived in him' (4.1.274).

EMILIA
Emilia is oneof the play's more honest and straightforward characters. She is under no illusions about her relationship with Iago. Unlike Desdemona, she does not think that she has found the perfect love, nor does she believe that such love is to be found. Life has taught Emilia that things are complicated and messy and she looks to open Desdemona's eyes to the realities of the world. Whereas Desdemona pretends to be happy when she is in fact feeling miserable - 'I am not merry;/ but I do beguile/ The thing I am by seeming otherwise' (2.1.122-3) - Emilia is open about her feelings and about her views.

But, things may not be exactly how they first appear. We might recall that Emilia is not initially honest with Desdemona about the lost handkerchief, neglecting to mention that she found the item and gave it to her husband, even when she sees how much distress its loss is causing her mistress. There is also the question of whether or not Emilia slept with Othello. Certainly Iago thinks that she did and when Desdemona asks her if she would cheat on her husband 'for all the world', Emilia says that 'The world's a huge thing: it is a great price/ For a small vice' (4.3.63-5).

ANIMALS AND MONSTERS

IAGO'S USE OF ANIMAL IMAGERY
Iago often compares other characters to animals, usually in a rather cruel and coarse manner. When he arrives at Brabantio's house he informs the senator of his daughter's elopement with Othello by describing their sexual union using animal imagery. Othello is likened to a black horse: 'you'll have your/ daughter covered with a Barbary horse' (1.1.110). The Moor is also compared to 'an old black ram' and Desdemona likened to a 'white ewe' (1.1.88-89).

Iago also uses animal imagery to convey the weaknesses that he perceives in others. He thinks that Othello's open and honest nature is a weakness that he can exploit: 'The Moor is of a free and open nature/ That thinks men honest that but seem to be so,/ And will as tenderly be led by th' nose/ As asses are' (1.3. 388-391). Iago also sees Roderigo as a 'snipe' that can be used for his own 'sport and profit' (374). When Roderigo threatens to drown himself, Iago uses animal imagery to convey how pathetic he perceives such action to be: 'Ere I would say I would drown myself for the love of a guinea-hen, I would change my humanity with a baboon' (1.3.310). When taking advantage of Cassio's weakness for alcohol, Iago compares him to his wife's dog: 'If I can fasten but one cup upon him,/ With that which he hath drunk tonight already,/ He'll be full of quarrel and offence/ As my young mistress' dog.' (2.3.44-47).

Such imagery is also used to convey the animalistic tendencies and behaviour of people. Iago paints vivid pictures of Desdemona's supposed infidelity by comparing Cassio and her to animals: 'Were they as prime as goats, as hot as monkeys/ As salt as wolves in pride, and fools as gross/ As ignorance made drunk' (3.3.405-407). At the end of the play Iago himself is likened to an animal. Roderigo terms him an 'inhuman dog' (5.1.620 and Lodovico calls him a 'viper' and a 'Spartan dog' (5.2.283). Othello also compares Iago to a dog when he thinks that his ensign might be deceiving him: 'Thou hadst better have been born a dog/ Than answer my naked wrath' (3.3.364-5).

OTHELLO'S USE OF ANIMAL IMAGERY
It is interesting to note how Othello's language comes to resemble that of his ensign as the play progresses. This is most apparent in his use of animal imagery:

- When he thinks that Desdemona is sleeping with other men he says that he would rather be 'a toad/ And live upon the vapour of a dungeon/ Than keep a corner in the thing I love/ For others' uses' (3.3.273-275).
- A similar image occurs later in the play when Othello thinks that Desdemona's body has been polluted by her lecherous behaviour: 'The fountain from which my current runs/ Or else dries up- to be discarded thence,/ Or keep it as a cistern for foul toads/ To knot and gender in!' (4.2.59-62).
- He says that his wife is as quick to mate as flies in the slaughterhouse: 'O ay, as summer flies are in the shambles,/ That quicken even with the blowing' (4.2.66-7).

- He compares the bitter news of his wife's supposed infidelity to snakes' poisonous venom: 'Swell, bosom, with thy fraught, / For 'tis of aspics' tongues' (3.3 448-9).
- Driven to despair and enraged at Desdemona's actions he uses the expression 'Goats and monkeys!' before storming off in Act 4 Scene 1 (255).
- He likens the tears that Desdemona sheds to crocodile tears: 'O devil, devil! / If that the earth could teem with woman's tears, / Each drop she falls would prove a crocodile- / Out of my sight! 4.1.235-8.

THE 'MONSTROUS'

There are a number of references in the play to monsters and beasts and the behaviour of certain characters is sometimes considered 'monstrous':

- Iago describes the coupling of Othello and Desdemona as a beastly act: 'I am one, sir, that comes to tell you your daughter and / the Moor are now making the beast with two backs' (1.1.115-116).
- The ensign tries to convince Othello that people are not as honest and decent as he might like to believe: 'There's many a beast then in a populous city, / And many a civil monster' (4.1.59-60).
- Iago characterises the despicable plot he is hatching as 'monstrous': 'I have't! It is engendered: Hell and night / Must bring this monstrous birth to the worl'ds light' (1.3.391-2).
- Jealousy is described as a monstrous emotion that feeds upon the heart of those who experience it: 'O beware, my lord, of jealousy! / It is the green-eyed monster, which doth mock / The meat it feeds on' (3.3.169-171).
- Othello fears that Iago knows something too 'monstrous' to mention: 'Think, my lord? By heaven, thou echo'st me, / As if there were some monster in thy thought / Too hideous to be shown' (3.3.109-111).
- Iago calls for pity when Othello loses his cool and threatens to destroy him, characterising the world as a 'monstrous' place if one as honest as he should be punished for being forthright: 'O monstrous world! Take note, take note, O world, / To be direct and honest is not safe!' (3.3.379-380).
- Montano describes the horror that unfolds at the end of the play as a 'monstrous act' (5.2.187).

IAGO'S SCHEMES

The following table illustrates how Iago's focus shifts from scheme to scheme and objective to objective over the course of the play:

PLOT	OBJECTIVE	TIME FRAME	OUTCOME
Iago informs Barbantio that Othello is having an affair with Desdemona.	To discredit Othello	(1.1 - 1.3)	*Failure.* It emerges that Othello and Desdemona are secretly married. Their union is accepted by her father and the elders of Venice.
Gets Cassio drunk and has Roderigo provoke him into brawling.	To discredit Cassio in the eyes of Othello so he loses the job of lieutenant.	(2.1 – 2.3)	*Success.* A drunken Cassio becomes violent, wounds Montano and is demoted by Othello for his poor behaviour.
Tells Montano that Cassio has a drink problem.	To discredit Cassio.	(2.3)	*Success.* Montano declares that Othello must be informed of Cassio's 'weakness'.
Convinces Cassio to visit Desdemona in an effort to get his job back. Arranges for Othello to see them together.	To make Othello suspect that Cassio and Desdemona are having an affair.	(2.3 – 3.3)	*Success.* Othello sees Cassio slip out of Desdemona's chamber. Iago uses this to begin to poison Othello's mind.
Places Desdeomona's handkerchief in Cassio's apartment for him to find.	To make Othello suspect that Cassio and Desdemona are having an affair.	(3.3 – 4.1)	*Success.* Othello eventually sees Bianca throw the handkerchief back in Cassio's face, reinforcing his suspicion that Desdemona is unfaithful.
Has Othello eavesdrop on a conversation between himself and Cassio about Bianca.	To make Othello suspect that Cassio and Desdemona are having an affair.	(4.1)	*Success.* Othello believes Cassio is bragging about his affair with Desdemona when in reality he is talking about Bianca
Convinces Roderigo to attack Cassio.	The death of Cassio. Iago would also be happy if Roderigo died.	(4.2 – 5.1)	*Partial success.* In the chaos of the affray Iago manages to murder Roderigo himself. Cassio, however, survives.

REVISION: **THE HANDKERCHIEF**

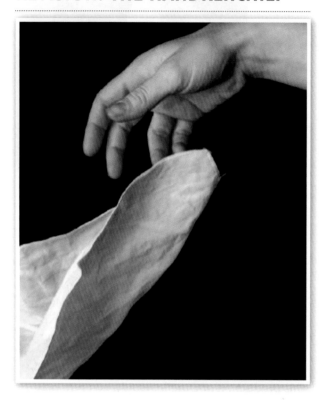

In Act 3 Scene 4 we learn of the handkerchief's exotic and mysterious background. According to Othello it was given to his mother by an Egyptian enchantress or prophetess (53). This enchantress – reported to be 200 years old – sewed it herself with silk from sacred silk-worms, and dyed it in a medicinal liquid (66-72). Othello's mother gave it to him on her deathbed.

Importantly, given the themes of the play, the handkerchief's medicinal dye was thought to protect against jealousy. The enchantress told Othello's mother that the handkerchief would increase her desirability and guarantee the loyalty of her husband (55-56). Losing the handkerchief, on the other hand, would draw her husband's contempt and cause him to pursue other women (57-60). When we consider how the play turns out the enchantress's words do indeed possess a strange and haunting ring of prophecy.

The handkerchief's elaborate stitching and embroidery clearly make it a thing of great beauty and value. When Emilia finds it she decides to have its design copied before passing it on to her husband (3.3.). Cassio, too, wishes to have it copied when he comes upon it in his quarters and gives it to Bianca for this very purpose (3.3.174-5).

HANDKERCHIEF TIMELINE:

▶ We know that some time ago Othello gave this precious handkerchief to Desdemona as a token of his love (3.4.49). In Act 3 Scene 3 Othello is an extremely agitated state. Desdemona uses it in an attempt to soothe the headache that has beset him. But he dismisses her efforts, describing the handkerchief as too small.

▶ The handkerchief ends up on the ground. Othello commands Desdemona to leave it there and they depart (3.3.286-292). At this point the doubts sown by Iago have clearly left Othello in an extremely distracted state of mind. He orders his wife to leave the precious handkerchief lying on the floor. Furthermore, he later seems to have no memory of how it came to be lost.

▶ Emilia finds the handkerchief and gives it to Iago, revealing that he has asked about it many times (3.3.293-316).

▶ Iago lies to Othello, saying how he's seen Cassio use the handkerchief to wipe his beard (3.3.434-440).

▶ Othello confronts Desdemona about the handkerchief, demanding that she show it to him. Of course she is unable to do so (3.4.89-94).

▶ Iago, in an attempt to cause further suspicion, plants the handkerchief in Cassio's chamber (3.3.323-324).

▶ At some unseen point, Cassio finds the handkerchief in his room. He gives it to Bianca, asking her to copy its exquisite design (3.3.174-175).

▶ Later Bianca angrily returns the handkerchief to him, convinced that it is some other woman's love token. She flings it on the ground while Othello watches from his hiding place (4.1.142-151).

SOME **NOTABLE PRODUCTIONS**

Over the past four hundred years Othello has been staged countless times and has been adapted for film, ballet and opera. From Josh Harnett to Anthony Hopkins, Othello has attracted some the biggest names in film and television and has consistently remained one of Shakespeare's most popular works.

FRANK FINLAY (L) & LAURENCE OLIVIER (R)

RICHARD BURBAGE

RICHARD BURBAGE: 1600s

Richard Burbage was lead actor in Shakespeare's drama company, which was known first as the Lord Chamberlain's men and later as the King's Men. Burbage was the first actor to portray not only Othello but also Hamlet, Macbeth and Julius Caesar. Burbage was considered the greatest actor of his day and when he died in 1619 his performance as the Moor was hailed as one his finest.

LAURENCE OLIVIER: 1965

In the 1960s the great actor Sir Laurence Olivier portrayed Othello in 'blackface' (black makeup), even though by this time the practise was considered racist and had fallen out of favour. This riveting stage production was filmed for posterity. Frank Finlay played Iago and a Maggie Smith played Desdemona. The production has something of a Harry Potter connection – Maggie Smith would later appear as Professor McGonagall while Michael Gambon, who had a minor role in this production of Othello, would go on to play Professor Dumbledore.

IAN MCKELLEN: 1990

Directed by the great Trevor Nunn, this staged production ran for more than three hours. Sir Ian McKellen played Iago

IAN MCKELLEN

while singer Willard White took the role of Othello. McKellen's performance was widely acclaimed, being described as electrifying and unforgettable. The production was later filmed preserving McKellen's masterful portrayal for the ages.

ORSON WELLES

ORSON WELLES: 1952

This 90-minute film was directed by – and starred – one of the best directors in film history: Orson Welles. The project was very much a labour of love for Welles, who shot the movie over a three-year period in Morocco and Italy. The project received very little external funding and Welles was forced to dip into his own personal finances to bring it to fruition. He played Othello while Irish actor and director Micheál MacLiammóir took the role of Iago. Today the film is considered a classic.

PATRICK STEWART

PATRICK STEWART: 1997

This brave staging of Othello starred Patrick Stewart of Star Trek and X-Men fame. It was notable for 'reversing' the racial composition of Venetian society. In this production, Stewart – playing Othello – was the only white actor while the rest of cast members were black. ◆

CUT-OUT-AND-KEEP QUOTES

Come on, come on! You are pictures out of doors;
Bells in your parlours; wild-cats in your kitchens;
Saints in your injuries; devils being offended;
Players in your housewifery; and housewives
In your beds

Iago 2.1.112-117

---

a great arithmetician,
One Michael Cassio, a Florentine,
A fellow almost damned in a fair wife;
That never set a squadron in the field,
Nor the division of a battle knows
More than a spinster

Iago 1.1.17-22

O, beware, my lord, of jealousy;
It is the green-eyed monster which doth mock
The meat it feeds on

Iago 3.3168-170

But I will wear my heart upon my sleeve
For daws to peck at: I am not what I am

Iago 1.1.63-64

Reputation, reputation, reputation! O, I have lost
my reputation! I have lost the immortal part of
myself, and what remains is bestial. My reputation,
Iago, my reputation!

Cassio 2.3.253-256

I am hitherto your daughter: but here's my husband,
And so much duty as my mother showed
To you, preferring you before her father,
So much I challenge that I may profess
Due to the Moor my lord.

Desdemona 1.3.184-189

This fellow's of exceeding honesty,
And knows all qualities, with a learned spirit
Of human dealings

Othello 3.3.262-263

That handkerchief
Did an Egyptian to my mother give;

Othello 3.4.262-263

Ay, you did wish that I would make her turn:
Sir, she can turn, and turn, and yet go on
And turn again; and she can weep, sir, weep;
And she's obedient, as you say, obedient,
Very obedient

Othello 4.1.243-247

I hate the Moor:
And it is thought abroad, that 'twixt my sheets
He has done my office: I know not if't be true;
But I, for mere suspicion in that kind,
Will do as if for surety

Iago 1.3.384-388

Ay, let her rot and perish, and be damned tonight
for she shall not live! No, my heart is turned to stone

Othello 4.1.174-175

If I can fasten but one cup upon him,
With that which he hath drunk tonight already,
He'll be as full of quarrel and offence
As my young mistress' dog

Iago. 2.3.43-46

Ay, you did wish that I would make her turn:
Sir, she can turn, and turn, and yet go on
And turn again; and she can weep, sir, weep;
And she's obedient, as you say, obedient,
Very obedient

Othello 4.1.243-247

We cannot all be masters, nor all masters
Cannot be truly followed

Iago 1.1.44

O insupportable! O heavy hour!
Methinks it should be now a huge eclipse
Of sun and moon, and that th' affrighted globe
Should yawn at alteration

Othello 5.2.101-104

I will be hanged if some eternal villain,
Some busy and insinuating rogue,
Some cogging, cozening slave, to get some office,
Have not devised this slander; I'll be hanged else

Emilia 4.2.131-134

Nay, had she been true,
If heaven would make me such another world
Of one entire and perfect chrysolite,
I'd not have sold her for it

Othello 5.2.143-146

---

my love doth so approve him
That even his stubbornness, his checks, his frowns
[...] have grace and favour in them

Desdemona 4.3.17-19

This deed of thine is no more worthy heaven,
Than thou wast worthy her

Emilia 5.2.160-161

---

who would
not make her husband a cuckold to make him a
monarch? I should venture purgatory for't

Emilia 4.3.73-74

in Aleppo once,
Where a malignant and a turbaned Turk
Beat a Venetian and traduced the state,
I took by th' throat the circumcised dog
And smote him – thus

Othello 5.2.358-362

Let husbands know,
Their wives have sense like them; they see and smell,
And have their palates both for sweet and sour
As husbands have.

Emilia 4.3.101-104

I have done the state some service, and they know't –
No more of that.

Othello 5.2.345-346

I have done the state some service, and they know't –
No more of that.

Othello 5.2.345-346

have not we affections,
Desires for sport, and frailty, as men have?
Then let them use us well: else let them know,
The ills we do, their ills instruct us so

Emilia 4.3.98-101

I have rubbed this young quat almost to the sense,
And he grows angry. Now, whether he kill Cassio,
Or Cassio him, or each do kill the other,
Every way makes my gain.

Iago 5.1.11-14

Like the base Indian, threw a pearl away
Richer than all his tribe

Othello 5.2.353-354